CONSERVATIVE ENGLAND
AND THE
CASE AGAINST VOLTAIRE

CONSERVATIVE ENGLAND

AND THE

CASE AGAINST VOLTAIRE

BERNARD N. SCHILLING

OCTAGON BOOKS

A DIVISION OF FARRAR, STRAUS AND GIROUX

New York   1976

Copyright 1950 Columbia University Press

Reprinted 1976
by special arrangement with Columbia University Press

OCTAGON BOOKS
A DIVISION OF FARRAR, STRAUS & GIROUX, INC.
19 Union Square West
New York, N.Y. 10003

Library of Congress Cataloging in Publication Data

Schilling, Bernard Nicholas.
    Conservative England and the case against Voltaire.

    Reprint of the ed. published by Columbia University Press, New
York.

    Bibliography: p.
    Includes index.
    1. Voltaire, François Marie Arouet de, 1694-1778—Philosophy.
    2. France—History—Revolution, 1789-1799—Courses and char-
acter.   I. Title.
PQ2130.S34   1976   194   75-43720
ISBN 0-374-97099-8

Manufactured by Braun-Brumfield, Inc.
Ann Arbor, Michigan
Printed in the United States of America

To Andrew

ACKNOWLEDGMENTS

IN THE YEARS since *Conservative England and the Case against Voltaire* was begun, I have incurred many obligations. Professor Lewis P. Curtis of the Department of History at Yale first suggested the possibilities of this subject, and he has since given me the benefit of his impressive command of English intellectual history. Professor Norman L. Torrey, now of Columbia University, was good enough to confirm my belief in the value and interest of the subject. From his great knowledge of Voltaire's career, Professor Torrey sustained my early enthusiasm. I am greatly obliged also to Professors Stanley T. Williams and Robert D. French of the Department of English at Yale who encouraged me in studying the history of ideas.

Most of my work has been done in the library of Yale University, in the British Museum, and especially in the Henry E. Huntington Library. I am most grateful for the chance to use the fabulous resources of these libraries, to profit from their excellent service and working conditions. My foundations were laid in the superb collection of eighteenth century materials at Yale. Later I received a grant from the committee on funds for research at Northwestern University to continue my work in the British Museum Library. I am much obliged to the committee and especially to Professor Moody E. Prior for his friendly help. I was able greatly to strengthen the French side of my investigation in the British Museum, and would have continued to work there save for the outbreak of war which postponed the entire project for six years. I had received useful help while in England from the Catholic Record Society, and found myself under particular obligation to the generous assistance and hospitality of the Hon. Charles Clifford of Chudleigh who placed his family records at my disposal. These contained a number of letters from the Abbé Barruel of great interest and usefulness.

When the end of the war made continuation of such studies again relevant, I was fortunate to be granted a fellowship at the Henry E. Huntington Library. On finding a great deal of new and valuable material, I was again happy to be granted a renewal of the fellowship so that I might bring my work to a more satisfactory conclusion. To the trustees of the Huntington Library I am under the greatest obligation for their generous support of my project. To the members of the permanent research staff, I owe many thanks for their confidence and encouragement. I must thank in particular Professor Louis B. Wright for his consistent help from beginning to end. The fine example he gave in his own untiring work, his impressive grasp of intellectual problems of various kinds, his many useful suggestions and unselfish willingness to offer any help within his power have left me under obligations which I can only acknowledge but never repay. It would be difficult to single out anyone from the general library staff for thanks or praise at this point. All are so cheerfully willing to do everything possible for the benefit of one enjoying their hospitality, that I can only add my tribute to what has been said by others. Everyone at the Huntington Library contributes to the creation of as nearly perfect a set of working conditions as can be imagined, so that I am not the first, nor the last, to say that he is under lifelong obligations to this institution.

A further attraction of great value at the Huntington Library is the chance to draw on the learning of others who are working there. I am greatly obliged to Mr. Bernard Spivack of Columbia University and to Dr. Clara Marburg Kirk of Rutgers University for bringing new materials to my attention. Professor William Sweet of the University of Chicago was good enough to read a part of the manuscript and to give a number of excellent suggestions for the treatment of eighteenth century theology. My friend Professor Henry Nash Smith of the University of Minnesota gave me the benefit of his wide learning and exceptional judgment, both on specific parts of the manuscript and on the ideas involved as a whole. I received great benefit and stimulus from long discussions with my friend Professor Helen Randall of Smith College, who was good enough to test the validity of my general plan against her great command of eighteenth century English literature and history. These and other readers at the Huntington Library were a source of unfailing encouragement.

My view of conservative anti-intellectualism and the danger of general ideas in any social order owes much to Alfred North Whitehead's *Adventures of Ideas*. I am thankful to my former colleague Professor Stuart Gerry Brown of Syracuse University for bringing this aspect of Whitehead to my attention. My own ideas were later clarified by discussion with another student of Whitehead, my friend Miss Joan McGrane of Columbia University. To her and to my friend Miss Jean Beno of Columbia University I am grateful for valuable help, especially with the manuscript in its later stages.

I have incurred great obligations among my colleagues at the University of Rochester. The administration of the University has been most helpful in supporting the publication of my work. Their aid was willingly given and is here gratefully acknowledged. In the Department of English Professor Emeritus John R. Slater read the entire manuscript and offered a number of useful criticisms. Professor Kathrine Koller has given all possible encouragement throughout.

I am grateful, finally, for the editorial assistance of Miss Matilda Berg of Columbia University Press.

BERNARD N. SCHILLING

Rochester, N.Y.
April 1, 1949

CONTENTS

CONTENTS

PART ONE
CONSERVATIVE ENGLAND

I · INTRODUCTION

THE IMMENSE ACHIEVEMENT of Voltaire contains many admirable things. Among the most agreeable is the generous treatment offered to England and her institutions. Like other advanced Frenchmen of his time, Voltaire was impressed by the features of English life, especially the atmosphere of liberty, which seemed far in advance of anything his own country could offer. On his visit to England, 1726–29, he was graciously received by both George I and George II. He had already known Bolingbroke and now achieved friendly intimacy or acquaintanceship with a great variety of distinguished Englishmen. Lord Hervey, Lord Peterborough, Walpole, Bubb Dodington, Pope, Edward Young, Swift, Chesterfield, Berkeley and others came to know Voltaire and were in varying degrees impressed by his genius. After his return to France, he himself reports that he had received twenty invitations to return to England for another visit. In 1743 he was honored by election to the Royal Society of London. His own attitude remained favorably critical, and except for such deviations as the attack on Shakespeare, Voltaire's view of England is a record of justice and generosity.

This admiration seems to have been mutual, as it was for the most part during Voltaire's personal visit. His works were widely read and appreciated in England, and his great stature as a man of letters acclaimed. Yet during the last two decades of his life, Voltaire's English reputation began to suffer. He would never have been received amiably by George III had he come for a second visit to England after 1760. On a false report of Voltaire's death in 1763, Goldsmith devotes Letter XLIII of *The Citizen of the World* to a generous estimate of his great contemporary. He joins other men of letters in praising the humanity, virtue, and attainments of Voltaire, yet he regrets that the philosopher has endured the calumny of a thousand enemies who have degraded his character and vilified his writings. Voltaire has been scourged by unmerited reproach, pursued by malevolence, characterized as a monster whose genius is in detestable contrast to the baseness of his principles.

This violent reaction grew worse until during the French Revolution the opinion was widespread in England that Voltaire was one of the worst enemies of mankind within memory: his pernicious influence had caused the French upheaval, had indeed given it a character ruinous to all existing institutions in church and state. Long after the French Revolution had passed into history the English continued to distrust Voltaire. Until well into the nineteenth century the great infidel was still the whipping post of pious English conservatives. In 1849 Lord Campbell reported that "indiscriminate abuse" of Voltaire "has been in England the test of orthodoxy and loyalty." [1] One's devotion to the *status quo* could be shown by the degree of one's anger against Voltaire. As late as 1892 it was still to be regretted that "considering the noble justice Voltaire showed to England and her institutions, he should have received such scant justice from England in return. The mocking laugh and the irreverent jest are remembered; but the incessant and noble toil in the cause of others is forgotten." [2]

Why was it that Voltaire suffered so much and so long from the disapproval of England? The question would in itself hardly demand an answer, except that it raises other questions of great importance. Voltaire was condemned because English conservatism was as it was in the eighteenth century. The reason for studying his former English reputation, then, is to get some insight into the nature of English conservatism in the eighteenth century. In the analysis of what went into its make-up we may find out more about English conservatism in general, and best of all, we may better understand similar tendencies among human beings at all times and in all places.

The whole subject is almost inexhaustible and intellectually unlimited if followed out to all of its implications and connections. Some kind of boundaries must be imposed for this inquiry and these will have to be designed arbitrarily to suit the needs of a work which in the end focuses on Voltaire and what was thought of him at a certain period. Phases of conservatism must be chosen with respect to the English case against Voltaire, not for an ideally complete analysis of English conservative thought. It may well be objected that the four main points under emphasis here are not the best ones to choose if one is to inquire into the meaning of eighteenth century conservatism. But the analysis can aim only at a single specialization; it must then choose the best background from which to move into this special problem of Voltaire's reputation. The case against him must follow from and blend in with what is said of conservatism generally, since his bad reputation is not directly connected with all parts of the conservative temper. This explains to some extent why the role of the church is so greatly emphasized here. Since the special form of conservatism to be studied is the case against Voltaire and since the church was so prominent in stating and prosecuting this case, we must take a view of conservatism which allows wide scope for the influence of the church. It must be shown that both in theory and practice the church stood against change of a certain kind, if we are to see why her officers and members fell upon Voltaire as their natural enemy.

There must then be a certain arbitrariness in the choice of limits; there must also be a choice of terms suited to the subject before us. The title itself tries to give the impression of a regular charge which was formally stated, along with "proofs" which are expressly listed, leading to a final condemnation or sentence. Hence the term "case" to suggest an indictment with clearly defined parts leading to a conclusion as in a court of law; Voltaire did undermine the church in France before the revolution; it *is* essential to peaceful maintenance of order that the people cling to their religious belief; the revolution *was* made easier by the weakening of the church for which Voltaire was largely responsible; **this** *can* be proved from his works, especially from his correspondence; therefore he *was* the original mover of the revolution, to be denounced and abhorred by all civilized men.

It is less easy to defend the four main terms or headings under which the most relevant parts of English conservatism are summarized. The words Complacency, Metaphysical Optimism, Realism, and Fear are not satisfactory in that they are not mutually exclusive. They are vague and not always applicable to the various attitudes and feelings which result in conservatism. A certain amount of overlapping occurs and things are discussed under one heading which are as clearly related to others. English devotion to what is traditional, for instance, need not be discussed under realistic anti-intellectualism more than elsewhere; its influence is pervasive in conservatism. Here the lead of Leslie Stephen is followed; he equates the traditional with the empirical—being led by facts, not having any preconceived theories or doctrines by which to be governed, letting things grow and develop as circumstances demand. Thus the love of the traditional goes with the distrust of abstract principles and symmetrical plans. This leads to the typically English series of compromises, dependence on experience, feeling one's way as time goes on, the reference to past practice or ancestral wisdom, observance of the rule of thumb and the logic of facts. Theories like the social contract are thought up afterwards to give philosophical justification for what has already stood the test of time and experience.

In treating this and other phases of so large a subject, one cannot find terms which are so firm and exclusive as to eliminate all overlapping, interconnection, and repetition. The word "realism" as used here seems to be the least satisfactory of the labels. It has so many associations, literary, philosophical, critical, that it is bound to be weak when used to summarize a special complex of ideas arbitrarily grouped under it. Yet the related term "empiricism," for example, has too obvious a philosophical meaning; the very vagueness of the word "realism" is a factor in its present usefulness since it is large enough to embrace almost anything one needs to use it for. Here it is taken to sum up a number of attitudes or feelings toward the realities of human life and human nature, toward the operation of man's affairs in the world—things which are so whether men like them or not, truths which have to be faced because they cannot be eliminated or avoided and must be lived with as part of what is real and not what is only wished for or imagined. A further defense of the term is found in its use by a well-known writer, Anthony M. Ludovici, in his *Defense of Conservatism*.[3] His second chapter deals with the connection between "Conservatism and Realism."

Such arbitrary names call for other reservations. In order to be an eighteenth century conservative, a man did not have to hold all of these special attitudes at once. Any one of them might lead to a conservative temper. Further, an Englishman might even oppose one or more of these views and yet be as conservative as anyone could wish at the other levels. Johnson, for example, is not complacent as the word is used here; he certainly despised metaphysical optimism and opposed the chain of being. He was a sombre realist as to human nature and life, a realistic anti-intellectual as well. He believed strongly in subordination and rank in society, yet he did not share the "fear" of those who refused to educate the poor because of the social danger of informing their minds. As he said in a fine sentence in his review of Soame Jenyns' principal work, "I am always afraid of determining on the side of envy or cruelty." Again, it is possible for a man to be anti-intellectual, as the term is used under "Realism," and still be anything but conservative in the eighteenth century. Priestley, for example, shares Burke's dislike of a priori speculation, yet he was liberal for his time.

Such admissions and reservations become more specific when one sees the various important and fruitful aspects of conservatism in the eighteenth century which have been passed over, and concedes that even the four main headings have not been exhausted. Any one of these will repay much deeper study since they are used here only to contribute to the general picture. Certainly the immense possibilities of anti-intellectualism are sharply limited.

Nothing is said of the romantic distrust of logical reasoning to arrive at truth, nor of the primitivist's belief in the blessings of ignorance. The weakness and danger of ideal concepts of things as analyzed here, the distrust of theoretical plans and abstract constructions with which life as it is cannot possibly conform, seem to be more related to the "Common Sense" or general empirical school of philosophy. Yet since the Scottish common sense doctrine has largely to do with an area of philosophical theory, and since the empirical side of realistic anti-intellectualism is already dealt with, the point to be made from discussing the common sense views seems already well established on other grounds.[4] Other anti-rational views which might have been emphasized are that reason as such is an instrument too weak to achieve absolute truth, as shown by increasing knowledge of other nations and histories; what one people holds sacred is considered evil by another, showing that reason as such is no sure guide to truth. There is also the aristocratic view that most men are incapable of reasoning well and that therefore what they arrive at rationally is likely to be unsound. Mandeville takes a variation of this, and says that the reason of all men is defective because it is influenced by some subrational desire or passion which has nothing to do with what is reasonable. These views of anti-intellectualism are not considered here, unless it be the aristocratic distrust of the reason of most of mankind (which is taken up under "Fear") and the realistic low view of human nature.

Other possible influences on the conservative temper are omitted from the literary and political scene. Little is made of antiquarianism in the eighteenth century, since the excessive love for and study of the facts and details of the past are stressed elsewhere. Various phases of Neoclassicism such as belief in reason or common sense universally diffused—an apparent contradiction to realistic anti-intellectualism—and the adherence to certain established forms are passed over as well. At the political level more might have been made of the steadying influence of a body of common law to which difficulties and objections could be referred.

In general all phases of conservatism whose main development comes later than the eighteenth century are ignored. Such an element as imperialism, for example, which is now associated with conservatism in politics; tariff reform or the effort to regulate trade by authority; nearly all matters of foreign policy or foreign affairs as conservatism sees them—these and similar matters are omitted as not helpful for the present purpose. We are in search rather of certain ideas or attitudes of mind, certain feelings or ways of looking at life whose implications in eighteenth century England seem to be conservative and which, contributing as they did to the dominant temper of the time, made the case against Voltaire inevitable.

It may well be asked why more was not made, however, of the enmity between England and France from time immemorial as a partial explanation for the dislike of a great individual Frenchman like Voltaire. The answer is that this feeling is so well known as hardly to need emphasis, and that it comes out in numerous ways in the course of this discussion as it is. Then, too, it is easy to exaggerate its influence among the educated classes in England. Englishmen of books, travel, learning, and cosmopolitanism did not always share the anti-French prejudices of the lower and middle-classes, of the more chauvinistic Whigs. Actually a great deal of intimate cultural and intellectual association was enjoyed between England and France in the eighteenth century. London and Paris were in close touch with each other at these levels, and advanced Englishmen found themselves as much at home in one as in the other. Many of the people who reflect the conservative English case against Voltaire were the very people of books, travel, and learning who were intimate with and interested in France, and were welcome there before the Revolution. In politics, too, it is at least worth mentioning that Pitt tried to get approval for a commercial treaty with France and to establish the idea that England and France were natural friends and not natural enemies. This plan had no chance against Fox and other Whigs in a century which saw two years out of every five spent in war with France.

Yet at the level of ideas and attitudes of mind, it has seemed best not to make too much of the dislike of France as a factor in the condemnation of Voltaire.

Now to look at the eighteenth century as a long era of conservatism and resistance to change is not to deny that in many ways it was genuinely optimistic, hopeful, forward-looking. It was alive with movements of thought and changing currents going away from the past and marking the transition toward modern views. Rationalism, freedom of thought, enlightenment, deism, romantic individualism, belief in human perfectibility, humanitarianism, liberal or even revolutionary impulses toward change; the more cheerful, comforting, and reassuring Arminianism of the English church leading away from the old Calvinistic gloom; the more hopeful Wesleyan belief in human spiritual and personal improvement with the help of God and its democratic certainty that each individual could be saved and was worth saving—all these things were present in England throughout the eighteenth century at various times and gained more and more strength as the French Revolution drew near. And although England was far behind America in the development of these particular ideas and did not always draw liberal implications from them, yet these movements helped toward the greater liberalism of England after the strongest conservative influences of the eighteenth century were past.

Our view of the eighteenth century then will have to take these changing influences into account. It will be seen that these liberalizing forces become stronger after the middle of the century, but again no effort can be made to deal with or to exhaust them all. Enough will be said, however, to suggest that the process of liberal ferment was clearly present before the French Revolution forced a retreat to extreme conservatism in England once more. Omitting the romantic movement in literature as such and other literary influences toward democracy, passing over nonconformity in itself in favor of Wesleyanism as a fundamentally democratic impulse, and selecting what seems most useful for the present purpose among all the many forces moving against the conservative temper, we choose to suggest the national awakening of liberal or radical tendencies in England by a brief discussion of humanitarianism as seen in the anti-slavery movement, of the religious revival led by Wesley, of economic liberalism and the new opportunities of the industrial revolution, of Bentham and legal reform, and finally of the movement for parliamentary reform.

When these have been reviewed and allowance made for the more liberal and cheerful side of the eighteenth century we shall find that in the French Revolutionary period, along with some hope on the part of many sympathetic Englishmen, the revolution drove England back to her natural temper, which was conservative, and which made the case against Voltaire automatic. A view of human nature and of human life was common which had conservative implications and which did much to resist change throughout the eighteenth century in England. Especially in theology there is a continuation of the seventeenth century gloom of Calvinism and Puritanism. At other levels there is a continuing foundation of traditional English ideas remaining the same and tending to keep things in general the same. All the new and transitional movements and forces making for change from old to new and encouraging the progress to modern views may be thought of as a superstructure. This eventually becomes the main part of the building, but here it is thought of as resting on an old and firm basis, on a continued acceptance and steady belief in the older ideas of man and life, and of England and English life in particular.

The evidence for this view of the eighteenth century—complacent, traditional, gloomy, and realistic all at once—is taken from a variety of persons, groups and parties as well as from all parts of the century. The term "eighteenth century" is meant to cover the generations between 1688 and the end of the French Revolution. No single period or "age" is chosen. An effort is made to suggest that the basic attitudes from which conservatism grew were diffused throughout the English scene. It is hoped that the names and dates given in the notes will show this variety in sources of opinion and chronology. References will be found to Whigs and Tories, to the devout and the skeptical, to stern theologians and cynical freethinkers. While in the discussion of "Realism" there is much reliance on Calvinists and Scotch Presbyterian divines, this is supplemented by Anglican views, both moderate and Evangelical. A number of references are made to foreign works in English translation when these are in keeping with already established English ideas, suggesting too that conservative Englishmen could find their opinions confirmed outside their own national literature in works made available in English; no matter where such Englishmen might read, they could find documentation for their favorite ideas and attitudes.

Looking back over all these carefully imposed limitations, reservations, and painful attempts to make everything clear that is intended, to anticipate all objections and adverse comments by those who would prefer another emphasis or who might distrust all attempts of this kind anyway—reviewing this, one is reminded of R. H. Tawney's admission in a similar predicament. In *Religion and the Rise of Capitalism* he points out that if a writer allows himself too much selection and reservation and cautious exclusion, and then indulges in too much arbitrary terminology of his own, he ends by begging the question. He asks for so much from the reader that the thing to be proved has to be granted almost from the outset before the work can proceed. In the end every plan is bound to have something wrong with it from someone's point of view. If one tries to anticipate all objections and modifies his plan so as to meet every single demand that it conform to, or take into account, all possible objections; if one tries thus to satisfy all shades of opinion one is bound to weaken the original plan so much that it will cease to have the virtues it might have had if left to stand on its merits. Therefore a plan which includes some things, and by its nature has to exclude others, must be adopted and offered for what it is worth.

The present study follows this outline: The eighteenth century in England was strongly conservative; typical attitudes and ideas are suggested under the headings of Complacency, Metaphysical Optimism, Realism, and Fear. Some time after the middle of the century, however, a strong liberal impulse showed itself in a variety of ways, gradually modifying the extreme conservatism of the generations since 1688. Before this new trend could be developed fully, it was halted by the French Revolution. At this period English conservatism reasserted itself more powerfully than ever and dominated the nation completely. One special manifestation of its temper is seen in the condemnation of Voltaire who was blamed for the French Revolution. Because of his critical attitude toward the church and the ferment of ideas to which he gave rise, Voltaire offended English conservatism at the level particularly of realistic anti-intellectualism and fear. The case against him was inevitable in England then, since one of the chief elements of conservative fear was that public peace and stability was impossible in a nation unless the people were held in check by strong religious belief. Voltaire's attack on the church which preceded the French Revolution was held to have been an indispensable preliminary to the outbreak, something which the revolutionists themselves seemed to admit when they exhumed Voltaire's body and carried it in triumph to the Pantheon. Nothing remains to be said finally, when the conservative mind becomes convinced that the revolution was the result of a deliberate plan to tear down all of the basic structures of the existing order in church and state. Since Voltaire was at the outermost point of this progress from irreligion to universal rebellion he was charged with responsibility for the entire disaster and became the natural target of timid and devout English conservatism.

The term "Conservatism" is hardly more than a century old, but it stands for certain qualities that make up one half of human nature. The most obvious of these is the dislike of change. It is easier to rely on the familiar than to accept the unknown; men avoid the search and inquiry needed to make sure that something new is valuable. Change is not only wearisome, but perhaps dangerous as well; experience has shown the mass of mankind that it is wiser, safer, and easier to leave things as they are. The force of custom leans toward what is old and established. Men are more inclined to accept what is inherited from the past than to adopt a new thing which seems more reasonable in the abstract or more useful. Authority, custom, tradition, inheritance, antiquity have more effect than truth and reason or the fitness of things. One who would change or improve society must overcome the mental inertia and blindness to new ideas which make most men satisfied to go on as they are. Those who profit from the existing order are always inclined to hope for its stability, are contented to go on in the use or enjoyment of what they have, and will resist any attack on their prejudices and old certainties. Again, their conservatism is a thing of feeling and not of reason. Those who are less fortunate are deeply involved in the effort to make a living; their situation must become desperate indeed before they initiate radical changes. It has been said that "the history of mankind is a sombre record of the fatalistic patience with which the average man endures the ills he has . . . ," [5] rather than, as Hamlet says, fly to others of which he knows nothing. People also suffer from a desire to seem right in their own eyes, and "have a strong aversion even against publicly acknowledging, that they have ever been in the wrong." [6] Then, too, in times of personal distress or illness, inherent conservatism leads men back to the safety and comfort of the familiar. In the fullness of life and energy, rebellion is easier; there may be questioning, nonconformity, and bold venturing in the days of unthinking health, but in extremity one is inclined to return to the solid common denominators of life. The conservative and accepted ways of things would seem to be the permanent ones; the nonconformist, questioning, and rebellious way becomes in the end only a temporary aberration, a wrong from which men are forced back by experience and the nature of things.

It is said that the English people in particular represent these and other conservative tendencies. Carlyle says that "Bull is a born Conservative," as indeed all great peoples are; Bull is an especially solid character however, "a well-conditioned blockhead," patient of error and slow to believe in novelty. An Englishman is traditionally devoted to peace and quiet; he is loyal to what is established and what has come down from the past, sanctified by long acceptance and custom; he dislikes sudden and sweeping changes and is inclined to compromise rather than to hurry into some theoretical plan for making things better. Horace Walpole's friend, the Reverend William Cole, had imbibed his principles early in life and had never seen any occasion to change them. "All my ambition," he says, "was to see things pass quietly and regularly." [7] Indeed, according to Bolingbroke, when a freeholder is asked what the duties of his station in life are, he must answer, "To endeavour, as far as I am able, to preserve the public tranquillity." [8] The prophet Isaiah says, "Their strength is to sit still," to be stable and fixed. The Bible may be invoked to a similar effect, but with mortification for the modern reader who has seen the danger of believing too much in this passage: "above all things, an Englishman loves *quiet. Give us peace in our time*—is the language of his prayers, and the silent wish of his heart." [9]

Edmund Burke has long been famous for his classical expression of English devotion to the past. His appeal to "prescription" recognizes that most ideas and feelings are inherited. Men themselves, their social and political arrangements are the slow growth of time. There was a good reason in the past for the rules and customs then established. The present must take these things into account, preserve what is useful and good, and be careful to maintain a continuity with the past as a still influential and sound part of the organic social order. Blackstone says too that the present must defer to its ancestors and must not suppose "that they acted wholly without consideration." [10] Yet the heritage of the past has virtue even though its original uses are sometimes obsolete; the English therefore cling to "a network of old customs, associations, and traditions" which prevent hasty action and insure that nothing is lost which might contribute to the solidarity of the political order." [11]

If so much is to be gained by devotion to the past, it follows that "nothing can be more dangerous than the altering, or touching the parts of an old fabric." [12] Aside from the fact that there are always good reasons for things remaining as they are, it is much safer to avoid "all councils or designs of innovation, in ancient and established forms and laws, especially those concerning liberty, property, and religion." [13] An Englishman seems ever afraid lest any change should be for the worse, and he wants to know even the remote consequences of an action before adventuring upon it. He is especially opposed to sudden or violent attempts to improve what already exists, even in the face of glaring evils or weaknesses. He opposes the introduction of a much better government without first observing what steadiness, forbearance, and patience will accomplish. A familiar metaphor is invoked by Soame Jenyns to show that "it is with old establishments as with old houses, their deformities are commonly their supports, and these can never be removed without endangering the whole fabric." [14] This very English sentiment exasperates the liberal Richard Price; he finds that even when "abuses so gross as to make our boasts of liberty ridiculous" are called up for correction in England, "a clamour immediately arises against innovation; and an alarm spreads, lest the attempt to repair should destroy." [15] Lord Chesterfield is hardly the type of radical innovator, yet he was ahead of his government in urging reform of the old Julian calendar in 1751. Its inconveniences were evident, but a sudden alteration was also charged with difficulties. Chesterfield consulted the Duke of Newcastle, who seemed alarmed at so bold an undertaking. "He conjured the earl not to stir matters, that had long been quiet, and added that he did not love new-fangled things." [16] Even the ancient English barons and their cry "Nolumus leges Angliae mutari" are quoted against new projects, for the established order should be slow in acceding to change, receiving "with wholesome jealousy, every proposition which aims at altering the usual course of society in any important branch." [17] Lecky summarizes well therefore, in speaking of

the singular union in the English character of self-reliance, practical good sense, love of compromise, and dislike to theoretical, experimental, or organic change. . . . The patient acquiescence in all kinds of theoretical irregularities and anomalies provided they worked well; the reverence for habit, precedent, and tradition; the dislike to pushing principles to their extreme logical consequences, and the essential moderation which the English people have almost always shown even in the periods of their greatest excitement, have been main causes of the longevity and the reality of their freedom.[18]

Now if these things are true of English conservatism generally, they apply with particular force to the eighteenth century. This in turn has its special forms, one of the most obvious of which we have chosen to call "Complacency."

II · COMPLACENCY

Eighteenth century England has seldom been surpassed in eloquent self-congratulation. Once life had become quiet after the disturbances of the seventeenth century, the English were pleased with their ways. They found in England and in themselves a variety of fine qualities which they constantly praised as superior to anything to be seen in the world. They edified themselves and the world by their possession of virtues which are endlessly admired in their own works. England emerges as the embodiment of Christian charity, manly prudence, true religion, and unfeigned virtue; she is a prodigy of humanity, liberality, justice, and liberty; her people display reverence, loyalty, warm friendship, delicate honor, unbounded benevolence, manly indignation, bashful virtue, courage, sincerity, and independence. Nowhere in the world is there such a wide diffusion of learning and good sense. As a result, poor Gulliver is dumbfounded at the attitude of the King of Brobdingnag: "my colour came and went several times, with indignation to hear our noble country, the mistress of arts and arms, the scourge of France, the arbitress of Europe, the seat of virtue, piety, honour and truth, the pride and envy of the world, so contemptuously treated." [1]

Swift may be thus bitterly ironical, but his countrymen are undisturbed and account for their overwhelming perfections on the score of their friendship with God. Indeed, how is the phenomenon of England to be explained save by the assumption that God has singled out this nation for the special indulgence of His bounty? Warburton is carried away by his enthusiastic conviction that England is the pride and confidence of our friends! The envy of our neighbours! The terror of our enemies, and the admiration of mankind! Happy nation! the nurse of heroes, the school of sages, the seminary of holy martyrs, the distinguished favorite of Heaven! . . . we *Englishmen* . . . are at present most indebted to Providence of the whole race of mankind.[2]

The alliance of God and England is especially observed from the pulpit on occasions of national devotion or pleas for divine help in time of peril. The Fast Day Sermon before the House of Commons in 1778 assures an audience willing to believe it that "no nation under heaven hath greater reason to praise God than we have, for those many and invaluable blessings he hath bestowed upon us." [3] The prayer for a general fast "On account of the Troubles in America" praises the blessed Lord "who hast manifested thy abundant favor to these realms, in thy marvellous protection of our religion, laws, and liberties, from the secret conspiracies, and open attempts of our enemies." [4] No doubt there is much honest piety here, with reverence and fear of God, but there is also great assurance that what is not English can hardly expect to be favored of Heaven. Indeed, "a people by Providence designed, and by valour qualified, to give laws to the globe" [5] must have been able to count on the help of God against their enemies.

> Oft has kind Heaven annulled each dark design
> Of plotting foes to crush, Britannia thine;
> Replyed in thunders to their threatening host,
> In tempests caught 'em, and in whirlwinds tost. . . .[6]

The steady progress of England shows that "divine providence had greater things in view in favour of these kingdoms." [7] The fortunate inhabitants of these blessed realms can only be thankful for "the general excellence, the many natural advantages, and the peculiar privileges and prerogatives, which through the bounty of providence are the portion of Britain." [8]

For the eighteenth century, the favor of God had showed itself already in 1688, permitting the glorious revolution to make ready for great advances under the House of Hanover. Horace Walpole is even sure that "we never were a great and happy country till the

Revolution." [9] This is not to say that the English were not aware
of the difficulties and contradictions caused by the change of rulers
in 1688, nor to ignore the fact that the restoration of the Stuarts
was a distinct possibility for many years. Throughout the seventeenth century political writers with few exceptions had insisted
on the doctrines of divine right, passive obedience, and nonresistance. Convictions of such long standing could not be forgotten
without a struggle, especially by the clergy, who had to admit that
the new government rested on principles which contradicted the
doctrines of the church.[10] Bishop Hoadly is surprised that such a
clamor should have greeted his liberal sermon in favor of the right
of resistance when this very right had been invoked to justify the
late revolution and to set up the present establishment in England.[11] Yet a lingering distrust of the action taken in 1688 is shown
in the revival of such a superstition as the royal touch for the
King's evil. After William's death, Anne seemed once more to be a
regular English sovereign, sanctified by the hand of God, and pos-
sessing a virtue and power unlike any that an irregular political
force could bestow; she might then have the ancient power to cure
the scrofula by her touch.[12] More clearly still, the Sacheverell case
proved that the nation had not quite made up its mind where the
lawful title to power lay. Certainly the Reverend Henry Sacheverell aroused great popular support for his view that action against
the ruling powers was licentious and unjustifiable for Christians.[13]
Fortunately, the Pretender, by a most un-English theoretical consistency, clung to his Catholicism, so that the fear of Popery was in
time strong enough to offset the old devotion to legitimate kingship and Toryism.

But it is the nature of the revolution itself which in the end
renders it a striking "political wonder" and a matter for further
self-praise and congratulation.[14] It is a conservative revolution
which, although it forced a change of rulers, maintained the continuity of English institutions and indeed had for its main reason
the need of overcoming an arbitrary attack on the great English
heritage and restoring the same to its rightful perfection. William

III probably would have been exaggerating had he actually said that the English "seemed as much to forget what they had called me over for, as that they had called me over," this being Lyttleton's opinion.[15] But just as the best way to recommend a novelty to the English "is to make them believe that it is a revival," [16] so the best defense of their revolution was to say that it was a recovery or restoration of the "inherited and immemorial liberties of Englishmen." [17] Roderick Random is obliged to instruct an ignorant French soldier in these refinements, assuring him that "those insurrections of the English, which are branded with the name of rebellion by the slaves of arbitrary power, were no other than glorious efforts to rescue that independence which was their birthright, from the ravenous claws of usurping ambition." [18] This is to say that the Whigs, men active in politics, religion and trade, saw their property and privileges threatened by the crown and church; their revolution was designed to fit their practical needs, which called for limited royal power and the right of resistance.[19] The Whigs therefore said, during the trial of Sacheverell, that the original scheme of government as fixed in King, Lords, and Commons must be returned to; that one of these parts had tried to subvert this plan in its own favor, and that the revolution was justified because it tried to recover and preserve the old government anciently agreed upon.[20] The very language of the Bill of Rights was quoted to show that nothing old had been violated; in fact, James was therein declared to have "abdicated" his throne, not to have been violently deprived of it. This seemingly dishonest and transparent fiction was the means by which the revolution had been made peaceful and the continuity of English institutions had been maintained. The phrase of abdication "was a pledge, that the old laws and customs of the realm should remain, and that no cataclysms should disturb the orderly development of the national life." [21] The 1688 revolution was then most satisfyingly English in that it changed without upsetting too violently what was already old and cherished. The whole affair was unmarred by any speculative nonsense or fanciful theories aimed at upsetting the accepted ideas and gradations of society. Past grievances were redressed, improvements were left to the gradual alterations of time, subordination was preserved, and confusion prevented.[22]

Once the revolution was over, the tumults of the seventeenth century were at an end and England was ready for generations of happy quiescence. Religious and political storms had spent their force; "the social and political storms of the modern era had not yet begun to blow." [23] People wanted now to enjoy the repose which the revolution had gained for them, to stabilize the results of the "abdication" of James II, to quiet all party issues and religious feuds.[24] Nothing was done by the Whigs in the early Hanoverian period to disturb the general slumber, lest a lingering sympathy for the Stuarts should rekindle the violence of parties. Unlike France, England had her revolution behind her and was in no mood for change or reform.[25] Locke wrote simply to justify a revolution that had already occurred, and not to encourage new attempts at change. His view that the function of government was chiefly the negative one of preserving order and defending life and property prevailed. As for the abstract right of the people which Locke had championed, it had already been exercised in 1688 and had laid down once and for all the principles which were sufficient to guide future generations of Englishmen. Blackstone considers the revolution settlement on "the solid footing of authority" and sees no reason to dissent from it; the ancestors of his age had decided the matter and it "is now become our duty . . . to acquiesce in their determination; being born under that establishment which was built on this foundation, and obliged by every tie, religious as well as civil, to maintain it." [26] The favorite Whig toast later in the reign of George III shows the prevailing attitude: "May the example of one revolution prevent the necessity of another!" [27] So effective was this example that for a hundred years afterwards no organic change took place and chartered rights were largely safe from attack. If it seemed that anything serious might be done to "alter and impair that plan of government, under which we and our ancestors have lived free," there were always men like

Chesterfield who would "point out the means of completing the great end of the revolution" and "give the alarm upon any future attacks that may be made . . . upon the constitution." [28] For surely the present scheme of things must excite "the warmest gratitude to Heaven for blessing in so peculiar a manner these happy kingdoms" whose people should unite in everlasting praise for "the steady valour of our patriotic ancestors, whose magnanimity won, guarded and transmitted such glorious rights to their much envied posterity!" [29] To what is it that the English owe "these singular and invaluable happinesses," Bishop Hoadly inquires, and replies: ". . . we owe them all entirely to the late revolution, and those principles upon which it was founded. . . . Could one think it possible for any to be insensible of our present happy estate; or of the unhappiness of the contrary?" [30]

In her very revolution then, England might see the favor of God, whose kindness permitted the redress of what was wrong and the preservation of all that was right and good. In the later years of the eighteenth century, however, thanksgiving was sometimes given to God for what modern times can hardly consider a sign of His bounty: the gift of George III as King of England. Mrs. Carter was of the opinion that the three best monarchs ever to occupy the throne of England were the three members of the house of Hanover.[31] The third of these figures is the subject of extravagant praise, which however hypocritical and conventional it often was, shows a complacent assurance that the King of England must be great in view of the position he holds.

No doubt much of the exaggerated respect and humble submission expressed in the language of such a document as *The Humble Address of the House of Commons* to the King in 1762 is meant for George's office and not for his person. As Adam Smith remarked, the idea that "kings are the servants of the people, to be obeyed, resisted, deposed, or punished, as the public conveniency may require, is the doctrine of reason and philosophy; but it is not the doctrine of nature." The natural thing is to submit to kings, to tremble and bow down before their high station.[32] Further the stated rights and prerogatives of the king demand honor and reverence; he is described with almost divine attributes in English law, and the thirty-third of his thirty-four defined prerogatives calls for love and allegiance to the king "his most excellent majesty being the pillar that supports, the star that guides the ship of the commonwealth." [33] Yet these admissions do not entirely explain the fulsome praise bestowed upon George in spite of his evident limitations. The attempt to assassinate him, which existed more in intention than in act by an insane woman,[34] only solidified his popularity. His ministers had, especially early in his reign when George had developed illusions of his own grandeur, fallen to an almost humiliating abasement in their servility to him. The great Chatham himself behaved as if he were in the presence of divinity when at a levee he would make so low a bow that the tip of his Roman nose was to be seen between his legs.[35] While it was against the law to speak contemptuously of the king or to give out that "he wants wisdom, valour, or steadiness," [36] yet there was nothing in George to warrant the language of the dedication to the poem *Royal Perseverance*. The author addresses himself to that prince whose piety, clemency, moderation, magnanimity, and other Christian and patriotic virtues, are the admiration of all mankind. George is "the most pious, clement, amiable, humane, and benevolent prince now living," one "who is, what other kings would seem." [37] Miss Talbot, writing to Mrs. Carter, is hardly able to express her joy on the accession of George to the throne in 1760. George's character is even superior to her hopes. He possesses "not only a steadiness of judgment, a wisdom and prudence . . . a mildness and benignity, an openness and sincerity . . . but . . . a readiness, a presence of mind, a grace and address, a propriety of ease and dignity that every body is charmed with." [38] And more wonderful still, George is British, a fact which inspires patriotic devotion not only to himself but to the England which is so blest in her royal master. He is "a king who glories in the name of Briton, whose virtues in domestic life are an amiable example . . . whose great and noble sentiments in his public capacity bespeak him to be formed by Providence to reign only over a free and glorious people." [39] Much of this may be the sentiment of a ministerial hireling, but it is true as a general sign of that self-conscious virtue and national pride which George himself symbolized. He had apparently read Blackstone's *Commentaries* in manuscript and Bolingbroke's *Idea of a Patriot King,* both under the auspices of Bute.[40] George no doubt liked to imagine that he was thought of by his subjects, as indeed he largely was, in Bolingbroke's terms: a king, looked upon with admiration and glowing affection, using his great power to spread concord and prosperity throughout a happy land, commanding great fleets which covered the ocean while "bringing home wealth by the returns of industry; carrying assistance or terror abroad by the direction of wisdom; and asserting triumphantly the right and honour of Great Britain." [41] Surely, if such a king be George, England is again blest by Providence and envied by the rest of the world.

> On the white clifts of Albion, see fame where she stands,
> And her shrill swelling notes reach the neighbouring lands:
> Of the natives free born, and their conquests, she sings,
> The happiest of men, with the greatest of Kings.[42]

But a perfect revolution and a perfect king by no means exhaust the signs of the friendship of God for England. The inhabitants of those islands have received "all things essential to the welfare and grandeur of a people" [43] from the hand of Providence. The climate, the fortunate situation of England as a separate island, her natural resources, and her immense progress in trade and manufactures are constant sources of complacent satisfaction. While it is not pretended that the climate is uniformly mild and balmy, it is none the less "peculiarly happy"; it is not too "intemperately cold" yet it confers "vigor and courage" which are "glorious foundations for British liberty to build upon." [44] The insular situation of England gives that perspective which enables the inhabitants to compare themselves with other nations and to prosper commercially as well as imperially. This comparison has given rise to a certain well-known insularity which was especially current in the

eighteenth century. The dislike of foreign influence or interference
may have been due partly to ignorance of what the rest of the world
was capable of, or more probably to a happy realization that England in fact was peculiarly blessed. Being an island helped her to
suppose that there had been something deliberate in the choice of
her situation which was to emphasize her difference from, and
superiority to, other nations by an actual physical separation from
them. A certain amount of unfavorable comment was visited upon
the practice of some upper class youths who would travel abroad
from England "in ignorant wonder and curiosity" at the institutions of other countries before having their tastes and habits formed
by the genius of their own superior nation.[45] Their wiser countrymen who had stayed at home could see that while some foreign
countries might surpass England in certain particulars, "none will
be found on the whole so truly complete."[46] The poet Shenstone
wishes no further qualification of England's proud glory:

> Bid me no more a servile realm compare,
> No more the muse of partial praise arraign;
> Britannia sees no foreign breast so fair,
> And if she glory, glories not in vain.[47]

The island's commercial supremacy might be supposed to result
from the fact that the inhabitants are "an active, industrious, commercial, opulent, and potent people."[48] But England may again
point to the friendship of God to explain this part of her greatness.
Not only does she have all the commodities that neighbouring nations want, but

We are placed at a most convenient distance from them, as if destined,
by a special providence, for their general market. . . . Our seas are the
most navigable, our shipping the finest, our shores the safest, our sailors
the best, and our harbours the most numerous, spacious, and commo-
dious, in the known world . . . while a shilling is exchanged in Europe,
there is not the least doubt but we shall still come in for our share.[49]

Small wonder that David Hume should look with happy satisfaction upon England in the first half of the eighteenth century when
all these virtues and advantages were being enjoyed to the fullest.

He sees that public liberty amid internal peace and order has flourished; trade, manufactures, and agriculture have increased; the arts, sciences, and philosophy have been cultivated; even religious parties have been obliged to lay aside their customary rancor. Then, too, the glory of England has spread throughout Europe, derived "equally from our progress in the arts of peace, and from valour and success in war." Hume cannot find another instance in the entire history of mankind when a nation has enjoyed so glorious a period for so long.[50] The little island has indeed become a mighty nation "which is the astonishment of the present, and will be the wonder of future ages." [51]

And still we have not come to the end of the blessings of God, for it is in her government, her "happy constitution" that England is most gifted of Heaven. The chorus of complacent praise for the English constitution is an unceasing refrain from one end of the eighteenth century to the other. "From Cornwall to Caithness, every one comprehends the nature of the constitution, as by law established, every one vies in admiration of it, and every one admits the reasonableness of submitting to it." [52] The fact that "the glorious structure of our divine constitution" [53] is so ideally perfect shows that it must be in conformity to the will of God. Bishop Hoadly would go so far as to say that if it had pleased "Almighty God to have pointed out any particular form, as of necessity to be submitted to by all nations, I should certainly think that *this* was the best, and happiest that could be devised.[54] The virtuous forefathers who formed the law of England were directed in their efforts by that Providence which has been the "constant protector" of the English nation.[55] Since He had taken such an active role in its formation, it is perhaps appropriate, as Leslie Stephen says, that "God was often justified by showing that his conduct was conformable to the provisions of the British Constitution." [56] Certainly it was a constitution which was the "best that ever was reduced to practice in any part of the world." [57] It was composed of the good of every form and cleansed of the faults and dangers of them all.[58] But "this fine fabrick, this stupendous plan, this masterpiece of sense, this pride of man; This wond'rous work of many a struggling age," [59] was chiefly praised for its gift of liberty to the people, and for its beautiful, symmetrical structure of checks and balances.

De Lolme ends his hymn of praise on English government by exclaiming that in England "liberty has at length disclosed her secret to mankind, and secured an asylum to herself." [60] Indeed, from the Saxon conquest itself, the fortunate island has never degenerated from liberty; now after many shocks to its stability, the constitution has "fixed itself at the highest point of liberty that is compatible with government." [61] No other people are known to enjoy so high a degree of liberty, because England is the "only nation in the world where liberty, in all its latitude, is the sole end of every civil and political institution." [62] Under such a condition of happy freedom, the English have only themselves to blame, as Mandeville says, if they do not enjoy as much happiness as the condition of human beings will allow. Aside from the fact that most of their complaints are "frivolous and unreasonable," there are remedies available for any real grievances, and these of the greatest efficacy.[63] The Bill of Rights has given the people access to the throne, so that they may bring charges against evil ministers. The doors of both houses of Parliament are ever open to the petitions of the people, and "the ears of the members ever attentive to their complaints"; [64] the laws are by no means inflexible and may be changed at any time for the better so that what is injurious may be removed and what is beneficial retained.[65] In his celebration of "Liberty" the poet James Thomson hails the freedom of dispute which has obtained since the Magna Carta; "the wholesome winds of Opposition" sweep away the blight of corruption; the pestilence of evil courts and ministers is purged "And ventilated states renew their bloom." [66]

But in the end the internal arrangements of the constitution call forth the greatest raptures. Here is a plan of government which may be contemplated with an almost aesthetic pleasure. The English are indifferent traditionally to the symmetry of a thing so long as it works well; yet here they vie with one another in praise of the theoretical perfection of their own government. The English constitution is praised as "the most rational system, the most complete and beautiful political fabrick, of which the world can boast." [67] Blackstone finds it "in theory the most beautiful of any, in practice the most approved." [68] But it was a foreigner who captured the imagination and flattered the pride of those fortunate enough to live under so admirable a system. Montesquieu bestowed his praise with special force on the system of mixed government and the three powers which check and balance one another to produce an ideal harmony and stability.[69] While it is true that Montesquieu did not invent the theory of checks and balances, his book enormously swelled the chorus of acclaim for this typically English device.[70] His contemporary Burlamaqui had also pointed to England as proof of the excellence of mixed governments,[71] but Montesquieu's special enthusiasm was taken up by a number of writers who made it their duty to interpret the great French thinker to their countrymen. Aside from the work of De Lolme, there are echoes of Montesquieu in Blackstone, Paley, Burke, Adam Smith, Gibbon, Adam Ferguson, and James Beattie, to mention the most prominent.[72] These are followed and echoed by a crowd of minor enthusiasts who make up in fervor their deficiencies in understanding. The poet Thomson again is moved by the perfect plan

> Of Britain's matchless Constitution, mixt
> Of mutual checking and supporting powers,
> King, Lords, and Commons. . . .[73]

This three-fold combination is found to be the "highest pitch of political happiness." The mixture of three forms is wonderfully composed, "the power of each so naturally adapted to its share in the government, and so nicely balanced as reciprocal checks and helps, that, above the reach of human contrivance, it seems the product of higher wisdom than usually rules the affairs of men." [74] This suggests the help of that perpetual friend of England, God. In this case, divine aid has probably used for its operation the natural English dislike of pushing any part of a plan to extremes. As Burke says, "the whole scheme of our mixed Constitution is to prevent any one of its principles from being carried as far as, taken by itself, and theoretically, it would go." [75] Extremes are in this way avoided; the excess of one branch "is checked by the prudent coolness of the other," [76] and the machine of government operates with a stable efficiency. Such a belief in the ideal state as a permanent deadlock [77] accounts largely for the long period of stagnation when reform was hardly even attempted in the central English government or the representative system. It was feared that such reform might upset the delicate balance which gave the English so much aesthetic, intellectual, and emotional pleasure to contemplate.[78]

With God on her side, with her peculiarly English revolution behind her, with an ideal governmental system of universal popularity to guide the nation in the development of all her gifts, there was evidently no limit to the future possibilities of the happy island. Even John "Estimate" Brown after administering a severe rebuke to his age for its effeminate luxury, is scarce able to find words to express his sense of England's superiority:

Let us do justice to our age and country in every regard. A political constitution, superior to all that history hath recorded, or present times can boast; a religious establishment, which breathes universal charity and toleration: a separation from the continent, that naturally secures us from the calamities of invasion, and the temptations to conquest: a climate, fertile in the substantial comforts of life: a spirit of liberty, yet unconquered: a general humanity and sincerity beyond any nation upon earth: an administration of justice that hath even silenced envy. . . . Search thro' all the most admired countries, the most flourishing aera's of Greece, Italy, or France; and tell me, if in any of these, such an Union can be found? [79]

Clearly England had not yet arrived anywhere near the possible summit of her grandeur. Just as the limits of the British Empire were bounded only by the confines of the globe, so might it be hoped that its duration would extend to the period allotted to this earth.[80] Surely nothing to be seen among other nations could hope to rival England's overwhelming perfections. "Oh! happy *England!* happy, happy *England!* happy its monarch! happy its people!" [81] Well may she hope, "Thro' a mild and watchful providence" to become in the noblest sense of the term, the "QUEEN OF NATIONS." [82] The blooming morn will cover with fresh beauty through the years her exquisite hills and vales. A brighter sun will

> . . . diffuse his cheering ray,
> And shed the glories of celestial day.
> Industrious, op'lent, healthy, brave, benign,
> In justice bright her happiest state will shine,
> In stable peace with watchful wisdom steered,
> At home united, and abroad revered.
> All, in one social sacred pleasure's flood,
> Will reap their private in the public good;
> Unspotted truth with love unbounded reign,
> One endless bliss: King, Lords, and Commons gain.[83]

The need for fundamental change disappears before the evidence of such unmatched perfection, past, present and future. Clearly England stands to lose more, must surrender more if innovation is tried than other nations whose condition is less fortunate. If men live in awe of their own blessings, they will hardly lead reform against what is already ideal. They will see no purpose in refined theories or abstract speculation as to possible improvement of what is evidently the result of the direct intervention of Providence in human affairs. Indeed, such minor blemishes as might be admitted to exist in the English scheme of things have been the result of "fanciful alterations and wild experiments," the rage of clumsy and unskillful improvements introduced in later ages. The venerable edifice of antiquity which has come down to the eighteenth century has been merely confused by rash and inexperienced workmen, "and its majestic simplicity exchanged for specious embellishments and fantastic novelties." [84] Let there be no more of these foolish intrusions of the imperfect. The British constitution "should be, like the ark of Israel, inviolable and untouched." [85] Writing in 1737, Chesterfield finds the government so nicely established that he sees no reason to call for any change in its balance: "I apprehend no danger this century," he says, and urges upon the care and attention of posterity the preservation of "our happy constitution," advising them "to be watchful of any the least innovation in any part of it." [86] The great man's advice was hardly necessary. Questions of importance touching reform were scarcely tolerated before the reign of George III; any other scheme of things was apparently unthinkable. In the year 1760, the only debate in the House of Commons was "whether our success was owing to our unanimity, or our unanimity to our success." [87] The literary class, from whom some adverse criticism of the prevailing order might have been expected, was in fact little inclined to raise disturbing questions. Under the leadership of Johnson, "the most abnormally English creature God ever made," [88] the men of letters seemed content to accept the state of things in their day as entirely reasonable. Some, like Fielding, might see abuses in certain details of administration or practice, but for the most part the world of Johnson, Richardson, Smollett, Sterne, Goldsmith, and the blue-stockings was accepted by them as the only world conceivable. Miss Talbot, writing to Mrs. Carter in 1761, will not so much as allow the main pleasure of complacency, which is to marvel that things are so ideal. "Have I not already warned you," she asks, "not to wonder at anything that is good and right in the reign of George the Third, and in the victorious year 1761?" [89]

III · METAPHYSICAL
OPTIMISM

Nowadays the term optimism suggests the hope of coming prosperity and general good, a confidence that things will improve if they are bad, or the belief that what is already good will continue, with more of the same in the future. This simple form of optimism naturally follows from "Complacency" and is inherent in the enthusiastic applause given by the English to their way of life in the eighteenth century. Another form of optimism extends to the world as a whole and asserts with Hutcheson that "the good of every kind in the universe, is plainly superior to the evil." [1] Although a certain amount of pain, death, and disorder is admitted in this view, yet "there is an over-balance of happiness in the sentient beings of this visible world . . . beauty, order, pleasure, life, and happiness, seem to superabound." [2] In fact it was an early opinion of Adam Smith that if the whole earth were taken at an average, "for one man who suffers pain and misery, you will find twenty in prosperity and joy, or at least in tolerable circumstances." [3]

But the eighteenth century expressed a paradox called "Metaphysical Optimism," a denial of hope and joyous confidence, as both Voltaire and Johnson pointed out. This form of optimism declared that everything is for the best in the best of all possible worlds and that whatever is, is right. Such a position was not based, however, on the belief that there is no evil in the world. On the contrary, as Lovejoy says, the metaphysical optimist was so far from asserting the unreality of evils as to be occupied mainly in showing that they were necessary. To say that this is the best of all possible worlds is not to say that it is an absolutely good world; the optimist implies only "that any other world which is metaphysically capable of existence would be worse." He does not show how little good there is in the world of reality, but how little of it there is in the world of possibility.[4] He will say, in the first place, that if there seem to be evils in the world, they are not so numerous or so important as they appear to be, and on closer consideration "will be found scarce worth taking notice of." [5] Actually it is only the ignorance of man which makes him think that he sees faults or deficiencies of goodness in the world. Men are not competent judges of the entire scheme of life; often certain details are denounced as unjust or evil when "some unknown relation, or some unknown possibility, may render what is objected against, just and good; nay good in the highest practicable degree." [6] As Shaftesbury says, a "mind which sees not infinitely, can see nothing fully" in the universe; such a mind "must therefore frequently see that as imperfect, which in itself is really perfect. . . . The appearances of ill . . . are not necessarily that ill they represent to us," which may really be good.[7] If therefore we could view the entire workmanship of God and could understand the connections and mutual relations of things, "it would appear that the world is as well as it could possibly be; and that no evil in it could be avoided, which would not occasion a greater by its absence." [8] For the world must be understood as the product of a comprehensive plan by God in which everything is the result of divine intention. Nothing happens by chance, but only in accord with the great plan of government fashioned with consummate wisdom and "admitting no events but what are comprehended in the original plan." [9] The individual man must not consider the world from his position as a single part of an harmonious whole. What would suit the world if God had made it a mere collection of separately considered units will not serve when it is seen that He chose to create a general union subject to certain definite laws.[10] Man must not make the mistake of referring all things to his individual self, since he is only a small part of the great scheme. He should rather be thankful that the universal plan of God has not called him to occupy an even lower and weaker place:

> Presumptuous man! the reason wouldst thou find,
> Why formed so weak, so little, and so blind?
> First, if thou canst, the harder reason guess
> Why formed no weaker, blinder, and no less! [11]

Whatever man calls wrong "May, must be right, as relative to all." [12] Man is "as perfect as he ought" and he will see that if rightly understood, "partial ill is universal good." [13]

What is needed then is a view of the whole work of God's creation, which when seen in its entirety will show that present evils could not be prevented without causing even worse imperfections, that actually a certain amount of evil may be necessary for the production of good in human affairs, and that in the end it must be admitted that all is for the best as it is. Lovejoy observes that complete optimism is "equivalent to the doctrine of the Conservation of Evil, metaphysical, moral, and physical; the sum of imperfection in the parts must remain constant, since it is in the realization of just that sum that the perfection of the whole consists." [14] It therefore follows that "the prevention of all the present evils in any conceivable manner, would have been of worse consequence than the permission of them." [15] These evils could not have been prevented without the loss of a greater good; "for ought we know," says Bishop Butler, interpositions "would produce greater evil than they would prevent; and prevent greater good than they would produce." [16] It is rash for blind men to wonder at the dispensations of Providence, which are what they must be. "A golden age would to man be more poisonous than Pandora's box; a gift, sweet in the mouth, but bitter, in the stomach." [17] The truth is that even the infinite power of God could not produce a world in which good is exclusive of evil; many imperfections "will unavoidably insinuate themselves by the natural relations and circumstances of things, into the most perfect system of created beings, even in opposition to the will of an Almighty Creator, by reason they cannot be excluded without working contradictions." [18] This recalls too the celebrated paradox of Mandeville, "private vices public benefits," which seems to mean that what evil there is, is necessary in order to produce what good there is. Mandeville is very hard on those who unreasonably desire to have the nation opulent and flourishing without at the same time submitting to those vices and inconveniences which no government on earth can remedy and which have always been inseparable from the greatest kingdoms and states in the past.[19] Just as it is true that "Pride and vanity have built more hospitals than all the virtues together," [20] it must be admitted that the necessities, vices and imperfections of man are the motive forces behind all worthwhile human effort:

Hunger, thirst and nakedness are the first tyrants that force us to stir: afterwards, our pride, sloth, sensuality and fickleness are the great patrons that promote all arts and sciences, trades, handicrafts and callings; while the great taskmasters, necessity, avarice, envy, and ambition, each in the class that belongs to him, keep the members of the society to their labour, and make them all submit, most of them cheerfully, to the drudgery of their station.[21]

It would seem then, that a certain amount of suffering by individuals is necessary for universal happiness; pain must have its special value and use, like an alloy "cast into the universal mass of created happiness, and inflicted somewhere for the benefit of the whole." [22] Indeed, if the larger view be taken, things which men are inclined to see as evil are not evil at all; they may be means of accomplishing wise and good ends, perhaps the only means by which these good ends could be accomplished.[23] The larger view might show that the disorders objected to could "be consistent with justice and goodness, and even to be instances of them." [24] Providence thus acts kindly toward men where they most complain, and casual evils are seen as necessary concomitants of some mechanism whose intention is the good of the whole.[25]

In the *Rambler* for July 7, 1750, Johnson implies that metaphysical optimism is at an end; the controversy as to whether external evil is real no longer exists, for it is universally confessed "that life has many miseries, and that those miseries are, sometimes . . . equal to all the powers of fortitude." [26] Condemnation of the notion that all is well regardless of appearances also occurs later in the eighteenth century,[27] along with some ingenious ridicule of the so-called benevolence of the divine intention:

> Each rule of Nature's an unerring rule,
> And when she makes, she always means a fool.[28]

None the less metaphysical optimism is found related to Adam Smith's "invisible hand" working for the general good, as well as to such opposites as Blackstone's conservatism and the idea of progress in Priestley and Price. As Pope had proclaimed self-love and social love to be the same,[29] so Adam Smith discovers that those who seek their own selfish ends are led inevitably to contribute to an end which was no part of their intention. Self-interest is the natural law, which if allowed to operate without interference will do most for the general good; individual effort for selfish ends becomes part of that Providential order which works out for the good of all in the end, in spite of some apparent evils in details. Blackstone in turn encouraged the student of English law to have faith in Providence and to abandon any critical search into existing institutions. The movement of history had already been determined by a wise Deity which operated through a mysterious and powerful purpose which was gradually improving everything by itself. Man's own conscious intervention could avail nothing; it might indeed interfere with improvement which had been laid out already according to a plan. Man should not meddle therefore with apparent evils and inconveniences, lest by his interference he somehow disturb the inevitably beneficent processes of a wise Providence.[30]

A similar idea in the mouth of a radical reformer might have implications directly opposite to the conservatism of Blackstone. Priestley, enlarging upon the *Doctrine of Philosophical Necessity*, finds that since everything is working for a better state than the present, it follows that whatever happens is part of a plan to change everything into something better than what now is. Therefore all apparent evils are really subservient to and will terminate in, the general good. Discord only seems discordant and is in reality harmony and ultimate good. Likewise, since all is for the best and under the guidance of God's infinite benevolence, it also follows that what every man does toward his own improvement and progress is good and useful, a part of what God has intended in His plan for the general good. Man then becomes an instrument in hurrying along the process by which everything is getting better.[31]

The conservative interpretation by Blackstone is more central to the eighteenth century than the reforming zeal of Priestley. Lord Kames is typical when he says, "Let us not attempt to correct the works of God: the attempt will betray us into absurd errors." [32] No other conclusion remains for man beyond the self-evident one "that whatever God does, we must conceive nothing could have been better; howsoever 'tis brought about, no means could have been more proper; and whensoever it comes to pass, no time could be more convenient." [33] This view is especially suitable to the theologian, who is ever inclined to praise "the salutary nature and sanctifying influence of affliction," [34] against which men are accustomed to utter their senseless murmurs. The moral is to say to oneself that resignation is best and that one should accept the particular place to which one has been assigned in the universe without complaint.[35] As Parson Adams says to Joseph Andrews when Fanny is carried off, "you are to consider you are a Christian, . . . no accident happens to us without the Divine permission, and . . . it is the duty of a man, and a Christian, to submit." [36] The true believer "need not shudder or be grieved at the cup of affliction, which your father gives you to drink; for though it be bitter at the top, yet the sugar is at the bottom of the cup." [37] Let there be no harsh judgment of God's doings, no quarreling or questioning what man cannot know; "stoop down and stand in awe; *Be still, and know that he is God.*" [38] The individual has no choice but to be content and cheerful in whatever state he finds himself. He will be wise, as William King says, to adapt his choice to things as they are.

The way to be happy is to realize that things themselves are necessarily fixed by certain laws which cannot be changed; all that remains is that one's choices and "elections be altered, in order to make them conformable to things, i.e., to the will of God." [39] Complaints and efforts to bring about changes in the world are finally not called for. Pope has assured men that they are as blest as they can bear to be and that whatever is, is right. He comforts them that happiness does not depend on one's station in life; God has not placed contentment in externals, and "Bliss is the same in subject or in king," [40] provided that each acts his part in the universal play. Shaftesbury in defining the hypothesis of perfect theism, concludes that whatever the order of the world produces is on the whole both just and good. Therefore "whatever hardship of events may seem to force from any rational creature a hard censure of his private condition or lot; he may by reflection . . . come to have patience, and to acquiesce in it." He may go even further in his reconciliation and "may make the lot itself an object of his good affection." [41] He will then see the folly of complaint and will not be part of any ill-advised or discontented schemes for changing what is as it should be.[42]

IV · REALISM

THE GREAT CHAIN OF BEING

We ARE LED to the Great Chain of Being and the third general division, called "Realism." Those who believed in the chain of being supposed a completely rigid and static scheme of things. For them the reality of life showed man as a unit in an endless progression from nothing up to God, a "distinguisht link" as Edward Young said, "Midway from nothing to the Deity!" [1] The universe was a system "whose very essence consists in subordination; a scale of beings descending by insensible degrees from infinite perfection to absolute nothing." [2] Every unit in the scale has to be in its rightful, assigned place in order to sustain the vast, magnificent whole. Every distinct class, order, or species of beings, "is as full as the nature of it would admit, and God saw proper. There are . . . perhaps so many in each class as could exist together without some inconvenience or uneasiness to each other . . . we have the highest reason to conclude, that every thing is as perfect as possible in its own kind, and that every system is in itself full and complete." [3] So it is and so it must remain; if the chain be broken in any degree, the entire structure is destroyed.

> From Nature's chain whatever link you strike,
> Tenth, or ten thousandth, breaks the chain alike.
> And if each system in gradation roll,
> Alike essential to th' amazing whole,
> The least confusion but in one, not all
> That system only but the whole must fall.[4]

It follows that the philosopher of Ecclesiastes was right: there is not and never will be anything new under the sun.[5] Men must

look realistically at things as they are and see that no possible alteration could be made without projecting greater inconveniences
into the general scheme of things. We are again in the
company of the metaphysical optimist. There is no absolute evil at
all but only a comparative evil; things are more or less perfect
when compared with each other.[6] Actually the so-called evils of
imperfection arising from the necessary inferiority of some units in
the general structure in comparison with others "can in no sense be
called any evils at all." [7]

Now while the pure theory of the chain of being did not specifically mention the dominant social order of the eighteenth century, it could by analogy be made to justify a society of carefully
ordered ranks and classes. Its implications for the suppressed classes
were clear enough: they could not hope to improve their situation
without disturbing the order of the chain of being. The person
above must quit his station before anyone from below may rise up
to it. Each degree of possible difference allowed by the scale can
have only one representative at a time. There is only one inexor-
able conclusion to be drawn by the man who is dissatisfied with his
place in life:

Know then that it was necessary that you should either be what you are,
or not at all. For since every other place and state which the system or
nature of things allowed, was occupied by some others, you must of
necessity either fill that which you are now in, or be banished out of
nature. For, do you expect that any other should be turned out of
his order, and you placed in his room? That is, that God should exhibit
a peculiar and extraordinary munificence toward you to the prejudice
of others. You ought therefore not to censure, but adore the divine goodness, for making you what you are. You could neither have been made
otherwise, nor in a better manner, but to the disadvantage of some others,
or of the whole.[8]

It is easy to exaggerate the influence in actual affairs of such a neat
explanation of the prevailing social order; still it suited those
whose interest was best served by keeping things as they were.
Much of its terminology and social implications passed into common usage and thought, even though the philosophical back-

ground of the idea was not influential. Blackstone speaks of the necessity for due subordination of rank and a gradual scale of authority and dignity proceeding from the peasant to the prince, and rising like a pyramid from a broad foundation to a single point.[9] Josiah Tucker finds in human nature itself a natural subordination which enables men to fall into the mutual dependence and connection of ranks and stations which God has evidently intended for the stability of the whole.[10] The poet Thomson in his eulogy of English liberty, praises the wisdom of England's "matchless orders" and "The calm gradations of art-nursing peace." [11] The constant recurrence of certain words and phrases implies belief in a stable, fixed gradation of society. While these expressions and their underlying assumptions might have been derived from feudal days and not from the chain of being,[12] they are well suited to the analogy between social order and the great, unbreakable chain. The words rank, station, and order, and the words higher, middle, and lower or inferior as applied to areas of society suggest the assumption that there are and should be, regularly established, recognizable and fixed levels, so well defined as to have each its own name, and so separated as to have a distinct set of qualities and characteristics appropriate to each.

If, then, society is like the great chain of being, it is clear that every link, every person, must accept the place and the accompanying task to which he has been assigned. "In the great social chain every link is united. . . . Were this chain broken, society would be dissolved, and anarchy must ensue." [13] It is unjust and unreasonable for any creature in the great chain to complain that it is inferior to another; all are good in their particular places and answer to the design of the creation if they remain where they are and do not interfere with the general plan. We may rely again on Pope for the classical statement of this view:

> What if the foot, ordained the dust to tread,
> Or hand to toil, aspired to be the head?
> What if the head, the eye, or ear repined
> To serve mere engines to the ruling mind?

Just as absurd for any part to claim
To be another in this gen'ral frame;
Just as absurd to mourn the tasks or pains
The great directing Mind of All ordains.[14]

All honor then to the man who supports the duties of his station "and is properly employed in that part of the great system of society, which the wisdom of providence has allotted him." [15] The Church itself was emphatic on this point; the Anglican catechism realizes too that "Order is Heav'n's first law" and enjoins upon the faithful the need of each person to do his duty in that state of life to which God has been pleased to call him.[16] A man so disposed toward his duty will find ample scope for virtue regardless of social rank. Hume shows comfortably that while those in the lower ranks do not have a chance to exhibit all human virtue, they may yet exert the fine qualities of "patience, resignation, industry, and integrity." On the other hand, those who occupy higher stations "have full employment for their generosity, humanity, affability, and charity." But if a man lies between these extremes, "he can exert the former virtues toward his *superiors,* and the latter towards his *inferiors.*" Thus provision is made for all proper moral qualities within the present dispensation.[17] "Cease, then, nor Order imperfection name," and let there be no more irrelevant complaints that life should be other than it is.[18] The doctrine of the chain of being suggests that man has considerably exaggerated his importance and dignity in the universe. He is no such high and important creature as he thinks. If his place in the world is in reality low, it will be found no lower than is suited to the inherent weakness and depravity of the individual man. Here the realistic observer of human life is once again joined by the theologian who has never been one to flatter the vanity of imperfect creatures.

THE CONTEMPTIBLE NATURE OF MAN

It is difficult to see why man should have come to entertain such swollen illusions of his own importance. He has persuaded himself that all things are to be measured by their usefulness to him, whereas,

the superiority of man to that of other terrestrial animals is as inconsiderable, in proportion to the immense plan of universal existence, as the difference of climate between the north and south end of the paper I now write upon, with regard to the heat and distance of the sun. There is nothing that leads us into so many errors concerning the words and designs of providence, as that foolish vanity that can persuade such insignificant creatures that all things were made for their service; from whence they ridiculously set up utility to themselves as the standard of good, and conclude everything to be evil which appears injurious to them or their purposes.[19]

The actual nature of man is in keeping with his relatively insignificant place in the universal plan. Whether man is corrupt because of his inferior station, or whether his station is low in keeping with his many weaknesses, the fact remains then, and must be admitted by anyone who faces the reality of human life, that men are weak and faulty by nature.

The theologian finds man still related to the gross materials out of which he was made. The Bible has said that God created man out of the dirt of the earth, the most vile and base thing in the world. If such is the origin of man, why should he be so vain? "Whereof art thou so lofty, thou stinking weed and dirty slime?" What cause is there to be proud, "thou dust and ashes? Why dost thou magnify and advance thyself thou silly wretch of the earth? Why dost thou not hold down thy peacock-tail, beholding thy foul feet . . . the vileness of thy state and condition?" [20] Again Scripture describes man's nature as miserably corrupted, compounded of the evil qualities of the worst of created beings, "in which do concenter the fierceness of the lion, the craft of the fox, the unteachableness of the wild ass, the filthiness of the dog and swine, the poison of the asp." [21] Swift himself opens one of his sermons with a summary of the Biblical view of the nature of man and his life on the earth. The Bible

is full of expressions to set forth the miserable condition of man during the whole progress of his life; his weakness, pride, and vanity; his un-

measurable desires, and perpetual disappointments; the prevalency of
his passions, and the corruptions of his reason; his deluding hopes, and
his real, as well as imaginary, fears; his natural and artificial wants; his
cares and anxieties; the diseases of his body, and the diseases of his mind;
the shortness of his life; his dread of a future state and his carelessness
to prepare for it: And the wise men of all ages have made the same
reflections.[22]

This condition of man "is the saddest case one can be in out of
hell." [23] It had its origin in the sin of Adam which transmitted guilt
and corruption to his posterity; "we putrified in Adam, as our
root," [24] and have since remained "nothing but pollution," defiled
in nature, "having a backwardness to all good, and a readiness to
all evil." [25] An examination of the heart and soul of man shows
"that he is, by nature, *unbelieving, proud, self-willed, disobedient,
impatient, angry, envious, full of hatred, malicious, revengeful.*" [26]
Thus the sin of our original father has made "the whole world an
infirmary, and every individual person a leper." [27]

It would seem from these unqualified theological assertions that
Locke was not entirely successful in relieving mankind from the
dark cloud of the Christian doctrine of total depravity; if man
could believe that his mind was at birth only a blank tablet, then
he could hope to write there a good record, and by the exertion of
his natural powers he might immeasurably improve his ideas and
his conduct.[28] But the theological insistence on man's inherited
corruption continued to deny this hopeful view. So also did the
skepticism of Mandeville, Hume, and of Swift in his secular writings, seem to bow before the evidence of reality. These and un-
counted miscellaneous writers were forced by experience and the
history of all ages to admit that little could be hoped for from a
creature so consistently wicked and foolish as man.

Swift seems, especially in *Gulliver's Travels,* to aim at a relentless catalogue of all that is weak and contemptible in human nature. From the picture of man's ridiculous vanity in Lilliput,
through his grossness in Brobdingnag and his final humiliation
below the beasts in Houyhnhnmland, man is shown by his various

actions and sayings to be stupid, cowardly, violent, cunning, malicious, treacherous, revengeful, sensual, cruel, gluttonous, avaricious, and endlessly deceitful. The King of Brobdingnag is forced to conclude "the bulk of your natives to be the most pernicious race of little odious vermin that nature ever suffered to crawl upon the surface of the earth." [29] Mandeville, too, while less afflicted with sadness and bitterness than Swift, adopts the disillusioned or even cynical view of human nature which was typical of enlightened skeptics and conservatives, especially since the example of Montaigne.[30] In the *Fable of the Bees* and his commentary on the text, Mandeville asserts that selfishness is the key to all human actions and that individual men are the victims of all of the seven deadly sins in varying degrees of intensity, mingled with ignorance, folly, credulity, hypocrisy, and selfish materialism. Hume also finds human follies to be numberless, and individual men the victims of as many varieties of knavery, selfishness, short-sighted folly, and avarice as there are individuals. A long procession of other writers throughout the eighteenth century testify to the ignorance and moral depravity of men; [31] they find human nature erroneous and imperfect, blind and blundering at the best.[32] Johnson finds the depravity of mankind "so easily discoverable, that nothing but the desert or the cell can exclude it from notice. . . . What are all the records of history, but narratives of successive villanies, of treasons and usurpations, massacres and wars?" [33] Most men are found not to be very wise or very good, and "human infirmity is as universal as the human race . . . even the wisdom of man is only a lesser degree of weakness." [34]

One human trait in particular is noted by Hume, Johnson, and others which makes the task of governing this problematical creature the more difficult. This is "that narrowness of soul" which makes men prefer what is present to what is remote. Human passions always plead for what is near at hand; [35] thus men act against their own interest and are led toward what they suppose their interest to be, more "by passion, by sensual appetite, by caprice, by any thing, by nothing, than by reason." [36] Every man knows, says

Johnson, that it is desirable to have health, knowledge, and plenty in life, yet individuals are constantly endangering these goods for temporary and immediate satisfactions. It is not easy to enter any house "in which part of the family is not groaning in repentance of past intemperance, and part admitting disease by negligence, or soliciting it by luxury." [37] Such is the way of the mass of mankind who "will always regard the present moment, and be blind in respect to distant consequences." [38]

The result is that any government is likely to be unpopular which sets out to do what is best for all. It must constantly oppose the inclinations and judgments of the people and must compel irrational, ignorant, and dishonest men to behave for the good of society as they are neither wise nor honest enough to behave if left to themselves.[39] The governor then resembles a jailor whose conduct is forced on him by the criminality of those in his charge. It is clear that man was never intended to be independent; his nature demands subjection and subordination; his welfare depends on a ready compliance with what has been devised for his own good,[40] since he cannot know what is best for him throughout the days of his vain life.[41]

The form of government known as democracy, therefore, which makes the largest assumptions of human capacity, is the one least likely to succeed. While it is true that "humanly speaking" inconveniences are inevitable in any government whatever,[42] democracy is as good as no government at all. It presupposes a virtue in men which does not exist; [43] it trusts human nature so far as to lay any scheme of things at the mercy of accident.[44] Nothing proves this so clearly as the operation of democracy in parliamentary assemblies. Swift observes of councils or assemblies of any sort that they commonly pass with majorities a kind of result or opinion which a man of common prudence would be ashamed to advance in ordinary conversation. The most reasonable propositions are commonly rejected by such assemblies, which adopt "opinions ridiculous, foolish, and absurd, with conclusions and actions suitable to them." [45] In all such numerous bodies, there are men who have no judgment, others who have no conscience, more who are selfish and lacking in public spirit: in short, men with all the weaknesses and corruptions which are seen to be inseparable from human nature.[46] If it be asked why men of virtue and principle are not or may not be elected to parliament so as to make democracy workable, Horace Walpole answers that "corrupt members must be the consequence of corrupt constituents. The people had not virtue, nor their leaders patience to profit of, or wait for, so constitutional a remedy." [47]

If democracy will not serve, then perhaps some other form may be found by which men will be obliged to curb their weaknesses for the common good. But it turns out that any form of government must be composed of persons who are themselves subject to the corruption of human nature against which all government is a safeguard. Governors of any kind are simply men who exercise power over other men as imperfect and vicious as themselves. In order to achieve this power, individuals have always betrayed selfish ambition, treachery, violence, and corruption and have maintained themselves in power by the same means. All human government is therefore contaminated by the means used to establish and maintain it, by the inherent depravity of those who wield and those who are subject to its power.[48] Politically, Hume says, every man must be supposed to be a knave who is governed only by self-interest; a government can conduct society only if it persuades men that their self-interest is best served by justice.[49]

Those who hope good things for men, who imagine that they can be led to a better way of life, must therefore follow the example of the English constitution; De Lolme says that this constitution is most likely to insure the general happiness in that it has taken men as they are and has not insisted that they exceed their natural abilities.[50] In the end no improvement can be hoped for in the external affairs of men unless it comes from within themselves; the virtue and sobriety of individuals is the greatest service to the state. It is not political institutions then, nor the accepted establishments of the past which are to blame for the evils and inconveniences of human life. The depravity and imperfections of human nature are the fault, although men are reluctant to admit this and are inclined to blame their woes on institutions.[51] Therefore, "one sure step towards the reformation of the world, is to begin the reformation in ourselves." [52] Toward this end Christianity makes the greatest contribution, aside from its sanctions of rewards and punishments for which statesmen are traditionally so grateful. Christianity improves men, hence it must improve the situation of any government: "For by diffusing a spirit of sobriety, industry and simplicity, of concord, justice and fortitude; by thus exalting and perfecting human nature, it makes society to consist of members who form, as it were, a superior class of beings." [53]

But the improvement of human nature through Christianity or any other inward reform is a remote, Utopian ideal; meanwhile the affairs of a creature so low in the chain of being and himself so corrupt and depraved must be conducted as best they can. The conservative implications of this view of man and his place in the universe are clear. It is impossible even for God Himself to give perfect institutions to an imperfect creature; the inferiority of man's station in the universe renders all of the evils of government and religion inevitable. These evils could not have been prevented without loss of greater good or the admission of even worse evils, or in the last analysis by not creating such beings as men at all in such a world as this.[54] Men must simply face realistically their earthly predicament. It is their destiny to have visions of perfection which they cannot possess and of virtues which they are incapable of attaining. They are the unfortunate middle species, composed of flesh and spirit, with all the imperfections of one hampering the aspirations of the other, doomed to perpetual uneasiness and dissatisfaction.[55] It follows that such a creature is incapable of attaining any high degree of political virtue or wisdom, and that it is foolish to hope for great improvement in political behavior or the organization of society. Since men are clearly not supposed to be angels, it is vain to expect them to act as if they were. Let us therefore "avoid the error of imagining that by an alteration of the form or mechanism of government we shall put an end to those limitations of human nature which are essentially unalterable, because they are inherent in the scheme of the universe which required just such a creature, as well as other kinds, to make it complete." [56] That change in this or that detail of the present arrangements will bring about a satisfactory improvement is then illusory, not to say dangerous.[57] Political evils cannot be removed by men as their nature now is; therefore "we ought quietly to submit to these evils, when they do not arise to any intolerable degree." [58]

As for the form of the actual government which men ought to accept, it must be based on the realistic acceptance of the need of men for subjection; they will respond only to be being beaten or bribed into obedience [59] and the liberal plans of such a visionary as Price, for example, are ridiculous as all high-minded schemes must be. They are based on such a pyramid of "ifs" that frequently they beg "what reason and experience cannot grant." [60] The disillusioned Mandeville finds the best constitution one "which provides against the worst contingencies, that is armed against knavery, treachery, deceit, and all the wicked wiles of humane cunning, and preserves itself firm and remains unshaken, though most men should prove knaves." [61] Government becomes then a protection against human weakness instead of the means whereby the fullest development of the individual person may be achieved. Since men are narrow of soul and are themselves grounded in the particular, in the moment and in the affairs of the moment, so also must government be realistic and base itself in the immediate truth and reality which is before it. Human meanness and narrowness is part of this realty which must be dealt with. In this view all government exists for conservative reasons; by definition and intention it tries to keep order and maintain the *status quo,* to see that weak men are not seduced into disturbing what is established in order to pursue any of the foolish illusions which are for the moment more attractive and promising, to see that their inherent corruption does not bring on even worse evils than those which have always

afflicted them. Such is the limitation of man's hope while he remains "The glory, jest, and riddle of the world." [62]

THE MISERY OF MAN'S LOT

Conservatism is seen to follow upon a realistic acceptance of the
narrow and defective nature of man. It follows as well upon a realization that life suffers from an inherent perverseness and malignity which is bent on making all human beings miserable. Here the
theologian once more is at one with the skeptical observer of life.
The more sober eighteenth century divine never tires of saying
that man is born to trouble as the sparks fly upward. When the
silly creature first appears in this world, it comes "weeping and
crying, poor, naked, weak, and miserable." It is able to do only one
thing for itself: it can weep. This it does when it first knows the
world, and this it is called upon to do by the nature of things
throughout its existence.[63] Thus do human creatures show by
the first action in life that this is indeed a valley of tears, in which,
until they are released by merciful death, the poor, banished children of Eve must add their cries to the piteous litany of human
agony which forever implores the mercy of Heaven. Life is "short,
uncertain, frail, inconstant, deceitful and miserable" where men
languish in misery like guilty persons in a prison.[64] Every human
being, from the palace to the cottage, groans under a thorn of uneasiness; "none wants a cross of one sort or another." [65] Some endure lingering diseases that unfit them for active life; others suffer
acute torments from the stone, gout, an ulcer, a broken limb or
other tormenting accident; still others mourn the loss of a beloved
parent or child, are miserable over some disgrace of fortune,
wretched poverty, losses through trade, the calamities of war, the
ruins of a fire; others writhe under the lash of conscience, filled
with horror and despair at their own crimes and the fear of God's
vengeance in the next world.[66]

We hear on every side the complainings of the afflicted, the murmurings
of the discontented, the repinings of the poor, the vexations of the disappointed, the cries of the sick, and the groans of the dying. What is the

world but . . . a place of weeping? Whilst sorrow cometh upon sorrow faster than Job's messengers of evil. And who are exempted from the general lot? [67]

God has contaminated and ruined human life as a punishment for sin, so that men would be certain not to desire its prolongation, and would be willing to consider it only as a preparation for a better life to come. A Christian must therefore see that there is nothing in this life worth living for; all is transition, danger, nothingness.[68]

Yet so vain and deluded are men that they fix their desires upon things of this earth under the illusion that the achievement or possession thereof will make them happy. They pursue profit and riches, pleasure, honor and grandeur; they seek wisdom, beauty, favor, friendship from the men of this world only to find in the end that all is vanity.[69] What seemed so delightful in imagination is unpleasant in possession. "Where they expected to have found a paradise, they find a desert." [70] Then, too, even when the reality is equal to men's first hopes, in a short time their feelings and inclinations change. "New wants and desires arise; new objects are required to gratify them; and by consequence our old dissatisfaction returns, and the void, which was to have been filled, remains as great as it was before." [71] Some one thing is forever missing and has been so for all human beings since the discontented behavior of Adam; the truth is that "if man were set again in Paradise . . . all the pleasures there would not keep him from looking, yea, and leaping over the hedge a second time." [72] He would think once more that happiness could be found in created things, and again would "pant after the dust of the earth." [73]

Men are thus led astray by their illusions and refuse to accept the reality of life. If their eyes were at last to be opened, they would see the things of earth for the vanities they are, and would bow before the judgment of Providence, which has assigned calamity to the sons of men according to its own wise aims.[74] Clearly the present life was intended as a school of discipline, a probationary period in which by the endurance of affliction, hazard, and difficulty men might develop the virtue and piety needed to qualify for a future state of security and happiness.[75] Since the human condition was designed to be one of suffering and trial instead of happiness, "why should we repine then at the common burthen of our nature, why murmur at the just and salutary dispensations of Providence?" [76] Let the human race submit to its ordeal and welcome death, the period to its woes, as a sign of the favor and mercy of God.[77]

The evidence of reality forces itself as well upon the observer of life who is not himself a theologian. "My view is to write history," says Raynal, "and I almost always write it with my eyes bathed in tears." [78] The work of a sombre mind like Johnson's is colored by a profound sense of the tragedy of human existence. Though Walpole might call him an "old decrepit hireling," a man "of the narrowest notions and most illiberal mind," [79] yet Johnson may be heard with respect for his relentless enmity to illusion. In *Rasselas*, Imlac makes the classical statement of our earthly dilemma: "Human life is everywhere a state, in which much is to be endured, and little to be enjoyed." [80] Throughout the essays of the *Rambler* and *Idler* particularly, Johnson exhausts the synonyms of misery in presenting a scene of misfortune, calamity, and danger. Life is short, but while it lasts, it offers more pain than pleasure; it is a chaos of unhappiness, a confused scene of labor, contest, disappointment, and defeat. Something is always wanting to happiness in such an abode of sorrow, so that human wishes are vain and "life protracted is protracted woe." To leave one set of evils is only to assume the incumbrances which cannot be avoided in some other condition; it is fortunate that nature has permitted man a short absence each day through sleep, for life is to most "such as could not be endured without frequent intermission of existence." [81] This is especially true of intelligent and sensitive men; they see not only the obvious facts of terror and distress which prey constantly on the human heart, but the coming of future calamity as well. Such men are glad "to close their eyes upon the gloomy prospect, and lose in a short insensibility the remembrance of other's mis-

eries and their own." [82] As time continues and one disappointment
follows another, men see the approach of death; all know that "we
must soon lie down in the grave with the forgotten multitudes of
former ages, and yield our place to others, who, like us, shall be
driven a while by hope or fear about the surface of the earth, and
then like us be lost in the shades of death." [83] So the inevitable
overtakes all the generations of men "and the grave continues to be
filled by the victims of sorrow." [84]

The same tragic view emerges from the pages of a variety of
eighteenth century observers. "I mourn for millions" says the poet
Edward Young:

> In this shape, or in that, has fate entailed
> The mother's throes on all of woman born,
> Not more the children, than sure heirs of pain.[85]

The list of human ills is endless "And sighs might sooner fail, than
cause to sigh." [86] Even Mary Wollstonecraft in more realistic moments sees life as a labor of patience, a conflict; the world is a vale
of darkness as well as of tears, where the human understanding
is deluded with vain shadows and where the most we can hope for
is an interval of peace now and then, a kind of watchful tranquillity liable to constant interruptions.[87] It seems "as reasonable to
hope for a year without winter, as for a life without trouble," [88]
and all of the natural misery to which man is born is made worse
by futile lamentation or his own perverseness.[89] No condition is
exempt from trouble and suffering,[90] and even a great king's mistress will say that this is true. The celebrated Pompadour herself
is moved to reflect on the strange mutability of human affairs, the
small resources in the human heart that make for happiness, the
great alloy of pain and misery which offsets what pleasure there is,
the failure of the very kings to escape the common lot.[91] Hume
finds that even virtue, not to say any particular situation in life,
will not insure happiness or make envy appropriate:

though virtue be undoubtedly the best choice, when it is attainable; yet
such is the disorder and confusion of human affairs, that no perfect or

regular distribution of happiness and misery is ever, in this life, to be expected. Not only the goods of fortune, and the endowments of the body
. . . are unequally divided between the virtuous and vicious, but even
the mind itself partakes, in some degree, of this disorder, and the most
worthy character, by the very constitution of the passions, enjoys not always the highest felicity. . . . Is it not certain that every condition has
concealed ills? Then why envy anybody? . . . Everyone has known ill;
and there is compensation throughout. Why not be contented with the
present? . . . Custom deadens the sense both of the good and the ill,
and levels everything. . . . Expect not too great happiness in life. Human nature admits it not.[92]

Those who view life more particularly in its details are of the
same mind. A vast amount of physical and mental suffering is
endured by men in their daily lives; [93] the miseries of poverty,
ignorance, hard labor, and bodily affliction, the evils of malice,
violence, ambition, and envy, the horrors of war and other public
and private calamities are visited alike on the just and the unjust.[94]
When Gulliver reviews the last century of English history, it appears to the king of Brobdingnag as a "heap of conspiracies, re-
bellions, murders, massacres, revolutions, banishments, the very
worst effects that avarice, faction, hypocrisy, perfidiousness,
cruelty, rage, madness, hatred, envy, lust, malice, or ambition
could produce." [95] No wonder that the philosopher, brooding
upon the origin of evil in the universe, must conclude that "not
even one of a hundred thousand is truly happy." [96]

But again there is always hope, and men continue to persuade
themselves that happiness and peace may still be found in this or
that object of their desire. This eternal energy in the human breast
alone makes life endurable. A credulous attention to the whispers
of fancy, and the expectation that life will fulfill its early promises
are necessary to every condition, yet these illusions are themselves
more valuable than the gifts of fortune which are never the satisfy-
ing rewards that we have promised ourselves.[97] Scarcely does man
achieve his desire than his pleasure ends, for "in pursuit alone it
pleases." [98] Man is forever promising himself that things will be
better, but with the coming of age he grows wiser:

> All promise is poor dilatory man,
> And that thro' every stage: When young, indeed,
> In full content, we sometimes nobly rest,
> Unanxious for ourselves; and only wish,
> As duteous sons, our fathers were more wise:
> At thirty man suspects himself a fool;
> Knows it at forty, and reforms his plan;
> At fifty chides his infamous delay,
> Pushes his prudent purpose to resolve;
> In all the magnanimity of thought,
> Resolves; and re-resolves: then dies the same.[99]

It is fortunate that the young are thus able to deceive themselves, says Johnson, for "the miseries of life would be increased beyond all human power of endurance, if we were to enter the world with the same opinions as we carry from it." [100] Life is then a scene of delusion "a series of misadventures, a pursuit of evils linked on all sides together. In the beginning it is ignorance, pain is in its middle, and its end is sorrow." [101] Man is caught like a fish upon a hook. Death allows a short line and so "we flounce, and sport, and vary our situation: But when we would extend our schemes we discover our confinement, checked and limited by a superior hand, who drags us from our element, whensoever he pleases." [102] It is certain therefore, that those who make their happiness depend on the success of the usual human efforts in public or private affairs, will be doomed to a life of disappointment and misery.[103]

The commonest of the many forms of self-deception by which men try to avoid admitting their predicament lies in envy of the situation of others, or at least the desire to possess a quality or thing which someone else has. Men tell themselves that if they had the wealth, talent, leisure, or power of a certain man whom they know, then all would be well at last. But this, too, is an illusion, for no one can tell the hidden inconveniences of another's life: riches bring vexation and anxiety, power is full of complexities, leisure is often wearisome. Superior talents and high achievement are the target of malignity, obstinacy and avarice; in the mass of mankind, "many need no other provocation to enmity than that they find themselves excelled"; whoever aspires to distinction by his merits has in almost every other man a rival and an enemy, so that his pleasure is lessened or destroyed entirely.[104] But still deluded hope has an answer, and "would take the riches and power, and leave behind the inconveniences that attend them." Nothing is more common "than a man to wish himself in another's condition; yet he seldom doth it without some reserve." He would not be so old as the object of his envy; he would be less sickly, less cruel, less insolent, vicious, or oppressive. Even in their own judgment then, discontented men are not so unjustly dealt with: "For, if I would not change my condition with another man, without any exception or reservation at all, I am, in reality, more happy than he." [105] Since therefore, man has more pleasure in expectation than in fulfillment, and since he would not change his place for that of another because the place of no other is perfect either, then he should learn at long last "that the cup of felicity, pure and unmixed, is by no means a draught for mortal man." [106]

Another favorite hope is that great improvement will be brought about by some special institution, but this too is an illusion. Even the church must consider the world for what it is and not what it ought to be. The church must not try to carry men too rapidly forward in search of the good life, lest it offend their follies and prejudices.[107] Just as most human foundations sooner or later corrupt their own ideals and principles, so the Church, especially when it is nationally established, begins in time to suffer from the very evils which it was founded to cure. The pure ideal of the original institution is mixed with the selfish pursuits of its members; knaves and fools will sacrifice the establishment to their own avarice and ambition, and it will be corrupted for the worst purposes of the worst men.[108]

What is the lesson of these sad reflections? For the theologian as well as for the secular observer, the moral is that man must endure his lot and give up the idea that changes in details will make life any happier. The danger is simply that, since nothing is likely to become any better, innovation may make things even worse. Let the Christian prepare himself to receive afflictions, is the advice of the Rev. Philip Doddridge; let him moderate his desires in this life and form his scheme of happiness only for another world in which it cannot be disappointed.[109] The only cure for our evils and perplexities lies in "an absolute acquiescence and complacence in the will of God"; [110] to accept the measures of Providence and to accommodate ourselves to that portion of happiness which has been set before us "is one of the strongest symptoms of a well-constituted mind." [111] As we grow older we shall find relief in piety, and while patience may not lessen the torments of the body it will at least bring peace of mind.[112] The nearest approach to happiness,

> . . . is an humble mind,
> To all the ways of Providence resigned.[113]

The moral of acceptance and resignation applies with special force to government and political affairs. It is simply impossible to prevent all irregularities in civil government, or to remedy them as they arise.[114] Political evils, like all others, arise from the nature of things and of man himself. If institutions are changed to conform to some set of objections, then the new institutions which result from the changes are in their turn liable to a new set of objections just as valid as the old.[115] It is absolutely certain that "whoever is governed, will, sometimes, be governed ill." [116] Adam Smith finds that "the violence and injustice of the rulers of mankind is an ancient evil, for which . . . the nature of human affairs can scarce admit of a remedy." [117] Blackstone sees that legal decrees often interfere with and contradict each other for various reasons, or in the end "because of the natural imbecility and imperfection that attends all human proceedings." [118] To expect "ministries without faults," says Mandeville, "and courts without vices is grossly betraying our ignorance of human affairs." [119] The most that human prudence can do, "is to furnish expedients, and to compound as it were with general vice and folly." [120] More than this may well increase the disease instead of curing it, or "introduce new, and worse evils, by attempting to remove the old

ones." [121] Here we encounter the familiar English dread of innovation,[122] the complacent belief in England's ideal constitution,
and the fears of the metaphysical optimist. Burke shows that the
constitution stands on a nice equipoise, but with precipices and
deep waters on all sides. "In removing it from a dangerous leaning
toward one side, there may be a risk of oversetting it on the
other." [123] There is even some use in the cynic's aphorism which
says "that the chief excellence of any form of government lies in
the possibility of another being worse." [124] And the optimist opposes hasty changes on the ground that since whatever is is right,
the present inconveniences are part of the rightness of the scheme
of things and can be removed only on peril of introducing far
worse imperfections than ever.

Thus though every hour teems with revolutions, these are rarely
for the better, or the best.[125] Anyone who seeks happiness "by
changing any thing, but his own dispositions, will waste his life in
fruitless efforts, and multiply the griefs which he purposes to remove." [126] Complaints then are the strivings of fools,[127] and men
should accept the sensible conclusion of Matthew Bramble that
what cannot be cured, must be endured.[128] The hope for England
in the eighteenth century was that she would never lay claim to
the famous Italian epitaph: "I was well, I would be better, and
here I am." [129]

The conservative thus allows himself to be defeated by the realities of life, which in turn follow from the realities of weak and
corrupt human nature. The conservatism of Swift shows the implications of a low view of human nature with special force. Swift
points out what is wrong in the affairs of men and shows what
changes should be made toward improvement.[130] He then admits
that his reforms have no chance whatever in view of the stupidity,
wickedness, and irrationality of human nature; so he has done
with all visionary schemes forever. The same is true for those who
face life as it is lived in its details. Such men are not like one who
stirs uneasily under a nightmare and by his effort dissipates the
tormenting vision; for them, no amount of uneasy struggle against

the reality of life will ever avail. It is not an incubus from which one will awaken in safety and relief, merely through fear and desire. The more reality is studied by the conservative cast of mind, the less hope there is of overcoming the obstacles to improvement, the more acceptance there is of what seems inevitable. Reality compels acceptance of itself by force, and the realist is willing to compromise with the way things are and to hope for very little change to the better. He knows that the order of things which he might wish to set up to replace the present defective order will bear within itself its own share of evil or inconvenience, which will merely substitute itself for the evil and inconvenience that is now complained of. Why not leave things as they are and avoid the trouble and suffering involved in fault-finding and sweeping changes? So the realist's admission that things are wrong paradoxically supports the existing order in its wrongness. His own disillusionment and sad bowing to stubborn fact are in turn a part of that reality, of that strange perverseness and malignity in things which forbids their own betterment. Hopeful change is prevented by admitting the presence of the evils against which change is invoked; the admission forbids improvement by giving as its reason the nature of reality, the way things and men actually are, which will go on as before no matter what is done to outward arrangements. That things are wrong is therefore no discovery of any particular age, but a realization once more of the human predicament which, by definition, will continue through all times and in all places.

THE FUTILITY OF INTELLECT

It follows that intellectual constructions and ideal schemes for the improvement of the world have no chance of success whatever. The truth is that principles which are speculatively perfect often turn out in practice to be harmful or at least unworkable. The straight lines of human thought are seldom reproduced by living institutions at any time; [131] the eighteenth century, with a seventeenth century view of man and distrust of the nature of things, was especially convinced that "nothing is more fallacious, or so apt

to lead astray, as theoretic reasoning." [132] The very term "speculation" had become an opprobrious epithet, about which a mediocre
poem might be written. This harmless term was once held in great
esteem, but now

> Whatever wild fantastic dreams
> Give birth to man's outrageous schemes,
> Pursued without the least pretence
> To virtue, honesty, or sense,
> Whate'er the wretched basely dare
> From pride, ambition, or despair,
> Fraud, luxury, or dissipation,
> Assumes the name of—speculation.[133]

Chesterfield doubts the advantage to society of "the most learned,
theological, philosophical, moral and casuistical dissertations." [134]
A surer guide is the general opinion of mankind, the common sense
arrived at by a reasonable view of experience.[135] Swift shows how
the Brobdingnagians, though ponderous and slow, had reduced
their principles to the simplest, most rational, most practical form,
having luckily not the least conception of "ideas, entities, abstractions, and transcendentals." [136] The Academy of Projectors at Balnibarbi presents a series of fantastic schemes for the improvement
of society; all are ruinous in practice, showing the folly and danger
of theoretical innovations. Gulliver finds that the only people able
to live normal, wholesome lives are those who go on sensibly as
their ancestors have done, operating within what is, without being
led astray by illusions of an ever-receding perfection. After all,

What signify lucubrations, and refinements, which apply not to life?
Theories, for the most part, are the legitimate offspring of dullness,
fostered, in the bosom of ignorance and pride, and flung on the world
at large, without design and generally without effect. Let the formal
fabricators of system and paradox, however, amuse themselves as much
as they please, in spinning out their idle, insipid abstractions; I pity the
man who can bestow a thought not intimately connected with practice.[137]

But it is not only that speculation as such is inferior to experience and practice; it is of limited value because once more the
mind and nature of man are full of error, weakness and corruption.

Theories assume that men act rationally and honestly, but experience shows that they do not act in this way. Hume recalls that saints do not inherit the earth, that abstract reasoning from principles is unsuited to the imperfection of man.[138] Therefore reality not only does not, but cannot, correspond to theory at any level. What happens is that reality is constantly forcing the abstraction to descend to its own level. Sir William Temple's fine analogy is quoted in the eighteenth century:

Quarrels with the age, and pretences of reforming it, end commonly like the pains of a man in a little boat, who tugs at a rope that is fast to a ship. It looks as if he meant to draw the ship to him; but the truth is, he draws himself to the ship, where he gets in, and does like the rest of the crew.[139]

This conflict between theory and reality was found to apply with unusual force to politics. Hume asserted that the world was still too young to establish any general rules in politics; not only is reasoning itself still imperfect in this science, but in less than 3,000 years, men have not accumulated enough materials to reason upon. He admits that there is some advantage in knowing what the perfect constitution for a society is, so that the real constitution may move toward the ideal as best it can. But political projectors as a class are harmful or ridiculous at best.[140] Those charged with the actual governing of affairs do well to ignore "obstreperous fumblers that must still be meddling and fingering, and spoiling every thing within their reach." [141] Human affairs simply refuse to correspond to the designs of such planners. Political events baffle our highest expectations and constantly produce effects which could never have been foreseen.[142] Hence "government is formed better from experience than theory." [143] It is never theoretical, either in its origin or its practice. It develops historically out of human conduct, "from particular conjunctures, from combinations of circumstances infinitely varied, from accident." [144] Long before the date of philosophy, political forms arose from the instincts, the actual circumstances of men, and not from their speculations. Movements are made with blindness toward the future, "and nations stumble upon establishments, which are indeed the result of human action, but not the execution of any human design." [145] If reflection is to be made on government, it should not compare the present arrangements with a speculatively perfect model, but with the actual chance of getting something better.[146] Governors ought then to confine themselves to the question posed by Burke, that most powerful opponent of the metaphysical in human affairs. The question is, "How does the institution work?" That it is an anomaly, an illogical contradiction of other practices, becomes irrelevant. Logic applies to reasoning, not to political affairs; these care nothing for symmetry or consistency, but only utility.[147]

This anti-intellectualism in politics was in keeping with the eighteenth century English view of the existing constitution. "Our constitution," says Chesterfield, "is founded upon common sense itself, and every deviation from one is a violation of the other." [148] Despite all the lavish praise of the beauty and perfection of the English constitution, extending in the case of Burke to a kind of Platonic idealism at times,[149] the constitution in its actual workings was often illogical and grossly inconsistent. The British willingness to accept facts without too much inquiry into their reasons or meaning [150] led them, as Burke said, to "choose rather to be happy citizens than subtle disputants." [151] Paley repeats the familiar figure of the ancient house. The constitution is like an old mansion which has grown up, not according to any regular plan, but with additions and repairs to suit the needs of its successive proprietors. Such a building lacks the elegance and proportion of a modern edifice, the external symmetry which "contributes more perhaps to the amusement of the beholder, than the accommodation of the inhabitant." [152] Actually, the most useful features of this house may seem to be the most grotesque and disproportioned. Witness the anomalous representations in the House of Commons which seemed to call for reformation. Absurd as it was to the speculative theorist, none the less the House "is practically found to answer every purpose of its intention." What is denounced as the worst absurdity is in fact the most beneficial influence.[153] The English constitution shows beyond all others, therefore, that politics must deal in what is expedient and useful in actual affairs, not in what is philosophically sound. The eighteenth century English politician knew how to avoid the philosophical search for truth which would have involved him in constant warfare with the complex details and demands of circumstances and public opinion.[154] Here the conservative temper of the rising industrial and moneyed class of Whigs—men of an eminently practical spirit—was supported by the influence of Locke's empiricism. While Locke had his own theories and tended to undermine old theological beliefs and seemed to defend revolution, none the less his empiricism was a part of, if not a cause of, that respect for facts and realities as against abstract, a priori reasoning in politics which even Priestley later on condemned.[155] By making sense experience the test of truth, Locke greatly narrowed the possible sphere for the operation of theory and seemed to justify a practical, unintellectual approach to government.

If it is true that brilliant reasoning or theoretically perfect ideas are of little value, then it would seem that great individual talent is not necessary in the governing of mankind. Actually "great geniuses are likely to do more harm than good," if there should happen to be too long a succession of them in one government; "woe be to the country, which happens to be cursed with a successive race of heroes." [156] Great talent may be abused and the "perverted excellence" of conspicuous abilities may well be the ruin of the country.[157] The eighteenth century called for quite a different set of qualities in its governors. Hume would be satisfied with "a great deal of virtue, justice, and humanity, but not a surprising capacity." [158] There was even something to be said, according to Shelburne, for simple indolence under certain conditions. Honest affections, plain sense, and common honesty are other homely qualifications which the governing of men requires in place of brilliant intellect.[159] Such a minister as the Earl of Bute might have his modest attainments excused, because "in this country, integrity and upright intentions in our governors are of far greater importance to us, than the most distinguishing parts, or liveliest genius." [160]

As Lecky says, in no other great nation were the practical qualities needed for successful government so commonly exhibited as in eighteenth century England: the qualities of patience, moderation, compromise, distrust of speculation and change as such, realistic facing of necessities as they arose, and a disposition to judge measures by their actual results—all were conspicuous in this period.[161] Even George III might be praised for his possession of some of these endowments. He seems to have represented the feelings of most of his people and to have been popular, as Leslie Stephen says, by showing "those qualities of dogged courage and honesty, shading by imperceptible degrees into sheer pigheadedness and insensibility to new ideas, upon which we are accustomed, rightly or wrongly, to pride ourselves." [162] Certainly George exhibited to an amusing degree that anti-intellectualism which accounted for so much of the conservatism of his time. Once when Henry Dundas was trying to explain to George that as king he had a dual capacity, to administer the laws and to assent to laws passed by parliament, the king cried out, "None of your Scotch metaphysics, Mr. Dundas, none of your damned Scotch metaphysics!" [163] From the king on down, the eighteenth century seemed to have chanted this refrain: "From all heroes, philosophers and geniuses, Good Lord deliver us!"

Yet the fact that general ideas and their brilliant inventors were in practice found to be unworkable or unnecessary was not the only objection to them. They might also be dangerous. The philosopher Whitehead has shown that a general idea is always a danger to the existing order because it can be used as the basis for endless specialized objections to things that are wrong. Hence the almost fanatical distrust of a minister like Walpole, for example, of philosophers or schemers who had new ideas for improving things.[164] Men like Johnson also disliked speculation which raised certain fundamental questions to which no final answer could be given; we do not and cannot know the answers to such awkward queries, so perhaps it is just as well to leave things as they are. Thought upsets peace,[165] and the mind may very well be led to a place where it can no longer accept its old beliefs. The foundation of everything is lost and the conservative mind has no further securities. Then too, since the conservative mind tends to be pessimistic about the chances for getting something much better than what now is, it would hesitate to embark on a sea of speculation which by its own definition could not lead to anything better than what it had to rest upon before the new search began. The best course is to stay with the realities of the moment, which are as good as any others are likely to be, and which are at least known. There is no telling how far new theories and ideas will go toward revolution; if they are pushed too far or too suddenly they introduce "the utmost confusion into human affairs." [166] It may even be dangerous to apply reason in any form to political affairs:

> 'Tis not for slaves on civil rights to dwell,
> To reason with a despot's to rebel.[167]

The people's heads may be filled with ideas of abstract rights and original compacts leading them to confound the duties of rulers and subjects; they grow inclined to dictate when it is their duty to obey.[168] It may be true that speculative truth, which

"greatly contributes to the perfection of human nature, may yet be recovered, in some cases, at too dear a rate. Whatever unsettles the foundations of government, affects the well-being of society, or *any way disturbs the peace and quiet of the world,* is of very destructive consequence; and the man who should retrieve fifty such truths, at the expense of one faction, would . . . be a very pernicious member of society." [169]

Let the English therefore not demonstrate that they are " 'Of schemes enamoured and of schemes the gull.' " Let them not "risk the possibility of deteriorating our condition by the rash application of empirical nostrums and elixirs." Otherwise they, too, may find the Italian's epitaph appropriate for their own grave: " 'I was well: I endeavoured to be better; and here I lie.' " [170]

The preference for fact over theory is finally related to a charac-

teristic English tendency: adherence to, and belief in, what has
come down from the past. In the realm of speculation, all abstract
systems were on the defensive after Montesquieu had drawn attention to the historical method, showing that laws, governments, and
customs were not universal and absolute truths, but were relative
to the time and place of their origin and growth. While this did
not prevent Rousseau and Godwin from writing, it was agreeable
to the English way of looking at things. The historical method
became the vogue in England and elsewhere; Blackstone made the
study of law simply a branch of the study of history [171] and before
long the historical method justified a respect for tradition and the
past which ended in Burke's famous doctrine of prescription. This
gave to the written law a permanent force which could not endure
change.[172] The sense of a stable and continuous social order grew
out of the interest in history and respect for the past. Such a by-
product as antiquarianism for example, intensified the conservatism which naturally follows from devotion to what has gone before; in the eighteenth century "men soon began to love the times
whose peculiarities they were so laboriously studying." [173] Thus
the belief in fact, in things as they are, develops a love of things
as they are and a desire to keep them so. Veneration of the past,
respect for the growth of institutions, regard for precedent—these
encourage a general dislike of new ideas.[174] As society grows older
or feels that it is older and has a past to refer to, it is likely to dwell
upon this past and refer to it for guidance. Certainly any appeal to
facts necessarily relies on the past from which all known facts
come. Man can be sure only of what has already happened, what
has been accepted as true before, what has been effective up to this
time. The best thing is to go on with what has seemed to suit the
people so far; past success is proof of present and future usefulness.

It is not surprising then that few books of political theory were
written in eighteenth century England. Some justify existing practices and facts, others find fault with details of behavior by those
in power; none are of a high speculative order before the late cen-

tury. Political theory was found to be undesirable, unworkable, and in fact unnecessary. If unopposed, the dangers of new theories and ideas were so great as to threaten actual revolution. But even if a writer did not recommend the overthrow of society in favor of a new order, he could be dangerous if he so much as inquired into or questioned the way things were. A writer like Voltaire, who urges the application of reason to custom or to institutions, was by definition a dangerous man. Conservatism flourishes when men do not think about their beliefs and loyalties, when they do not make unfavorable comparisons and discover faults. These activities are the symptoms of restlessness and energy of mind, and create the atmosphere in which revolutions are born.

But even allowing for the free play of speculation, what evidence is there that any new scheme will be more useful than what has stood the test of time? Experience shows that theoretical plans are unworkable and of no practical use outside their application to the stubborn facts of reality. The empiricist knows how hard it is to reach that improved state which is supposed to follow from adoption of some new plan; it is not only difficult but in the end futile, so that men are best advised to continue with what is known and tried by experience. And if political theory is thus bad and useless, for eighteenth century England it seemed also unnecessary. The moral, philosophical, and theological beliefs of the time took care of the need for developing a coherent political science. The political arrangements of the world were already sufficiently justified and explained by the general concepts of the world, of man, and of the nature of man. These already established systems or attitudes ruled out the need for change, so that thinkers were not called upon to set up a theory in order to explain what was taken for granted as proper and inevitable.

V · FEAR OF CHANGE

THE LAST of our categories is fear. Conservatism is vigilant and cautious when necessary to preserve the order in which it believes. Just as some Englishmen were complacent about the constitution, others were fearful and started with alarm over any possible danger to "this fair structure, the work of ages, and the nearest approach to perfection of any human establishment from the beginning of time." [1] But the principal fear was felt by those who stood to gain most from continuing the *status quo* and to lose most by its overthrow. They naturally wanted to go on enjoying their property and power, undisturbed by the less fortunate masses. Their fear was partly related to a low view of average human nature, which led them to distrust the undisciplined mob, and partly to anti-intellectualism which opposed education for the lower ranks of society. They relied on a most limited education for the poor and sought the powerful assistance of the church to keep the potentially dangerous part of society in contented submission to their lot.

At the head of his essay in the *Covent Garden Journal* for June 20, 1752, Fielding takes as his motto the words of Horace, "I hate the Mob." He has been for some time worried over the disproportionate power and influence achieved by this "fourth estate" which threatens to disturb the balance of the constitution. He fears its headlong, unthinking brutality and coarseness, its hasty and ill-considered violence, its envy and belligerent hostility to the rest of society, its bold, pushing insolence and ever-increasing indifference to the rights of others. [2] Numerous riots and mob outbreaks in the eighteenth century seem to justify conservative fear lest the lower classes should one day take the law into their own hands.

The chapter "Of Riots, Routs, and Unlawful Assemblies" in Hawkins's *Pleas of the Crown* covers 12 folio pages and deals with this question in 59 sections, covering every possible contingency that an officer might face in keeping the peace.[3]

Apparently the mob was likely to give vent to its feelings on any provocation. Births, marriages, deaths, victories, holidays, executions and other more seriously important occasions were the signal for riots or other violent public demonstrations. The trial of Henry Sacheverell in 1710 caused immense excitement; the use of calicoes or linens from India in place of British goods inspired a fierce outbreak in 1719 by the Spitalfields weavers; the execution of Jack Sheppard in 1724, as well as the public death of other popular malefactors, inspired riots for possession of the body; riots occurred in 1736 when certain contractors announced the intention of hiring Irish workmen at lower than regular English wages; violent demonstrations in favor of Wilkes in 1763 and 1768, on behalf of Admiral Keppel when he was acquitted in 1779, and against Catholic toleration in the notorious Gordon riots of 1780 took an alarmingly destructive form. Similarly, the holidays of January 30, May 29, and November 5 rarely passed without some violent popular excitement.[4]

Such things made it seem to those already disposed to think so anyway, that " 'the gross body of the people are weak, ignorant, injudicious, capricious, factious, headstrong, self-willed.' " [5] Basing his views largely upon the Bible, Francis Atterbury decides that the people "are foolish, sottish children, void of understanding, wise for wickedness, and ignorant for good." Though they are deaf, blind and senseless "nevertheless they are all tongue, noise, and clamour." They have the voice of "ignorance, mischief, and confusion," which Atterbury for one cannot believe is really the voice of God.[6] This "miscellaneous, noisy herd," [7] this "vulgar Mass," [8] this "rabble just ripe to rebel," [9] this vile populace or dregs of a country" [10] is denounced with every epithet of abuse which eighteenth century mistrust, contempt, fear, and disdain is able to muster. We are told that the masses of men are base, ignorant, selfish, avaricious, servile, corrupt, credulous, unjust, cruel, blind, precipitate, ferocious, undependable, licentious, disorderly, unstable, wild, headstrong, rash, hasty, desperate, foolish, conceited, furious, unmanageable, dangerous, capricious—a sheeplike, many-headed monster compounded of folly, and the everlasting dupe of villainous faction.[11]

The result in action of these qualities is "idolatry, rebellion, murder, and all the wickedness the devil can suggest . . . irreligion, profaneness, sedition, slaughter, and confusion." [12] The rage of the people, says Sir William Temple, is like the sea which may overthrow a country with suddenness and violence,[13] nor "can the sea be more violent than an enraged people." [14] Large bodies of men, according to Paley, "are subject to sudden phrenzies." Opinions may be circulated among them without proof or examination, and "passions founded upon these opinions, diffusing themselves with a rapidity that can neither be accounted for nor resisted, sometimes agitate a country with the most violent commotions." [15] The people are suicidally inclined to want what will ruin the country and themselves.[16] Then, too, they are never satisfied with one concession but will demand more until all power is in their hands.[17] They are capable of entirely destroying the work of ages, so that it is dangerous to grant them anything when they are in the mood to dictate to the government.[18] As Blackstone shrewdly observes, the game laws which forbade use of arms by the bulk of the people arose from fear of what an unthinking multitude might do if allowed to use weapons of destruction.[19]

DISTRUST OF DEMOCRACY

Such a view of the people as a beast implied profound distrust of democracy. Clearly "the vulgar" were not to be trusted with learning or liberty beyond certain well-defined limits. "The mass of the people often seemed so depraved that even their best friends and most sympathetic students saw in them a terrifying threat if intrusted with initiative." [20] Universal suffrage was out of the question. The day set aside for voting would become a scene of riot, drunkenness, and confusion, as hordes of low-class workers, soldiers, sailors, rogues, thieves, and smugglers would be let loose to give free expression to their views.[21] It would be difficult to prevent tumults and outbreaks from spreading throughout the kingdom under this system,[22] which in the end would prove to be useless and detrimental even to those who voted.[23] An ignorant populace is unqualified to decide on measures of government; [24] they cannot judge for themselves nor can they direct their own conduct in political affairs.[25] They are easily misled by popular incendiaries or mistaken zealots in the cause of democracy,[26] and when under such influences, as Horace Walpole says, they will "do more harm in an hour, . . . than a king can do in a year." [27]

Aside from the extreme forms of despotism, then, pure democracy must be counted the very worst form of government.[28] It would result in elevating to power the individuals who represented the worst qualities of the mob as a whole,[29] and the masses would soon find that they were no happier than before. For, says Adam Ferguson, "the power of the people is not the happiness of the people. Corrupt and vicious men, assembled in great bodies, cannot have a greater curse bestowed upon them, than the power of governing themselves." [30] It is best if the few are given charge of the many, the few who have superior wisdom and knowledge, men of "undoubted substance, and real property"; for this reason Josiah Tucker favors confining the right to vote to ten-pound householders and estate holders.[31] Hume in the end expects nothing from democracy but incessant dispute and civil war, from which the nation will have to take refuge in absolute monarchy, "the easiest death, the true *Euthanasia* of the BRITISH constitution." [32]

If it is so dangerous to give freedom or power in any degree to the populace, it follows that they must be held severely in their places. Property must get power into its hands and the ignorant masses must remain contented and submissive; their education must be carefully designed for the special duties in life to which the poor should be reconciled and which, with the help of the church, they may be persuaded to accept without complaint.

Society must inevitably be divided among the ruling and the ruled, for equality and independence are forbidden by the law of nature.[33] The question is, who shall rule and who shall consent to be ruled? Once Locke had asserted that government existed largely for the protection of property, the question was suitably answered for the privileged classes in the eighteenth century. "Dominion follows property," says Mandeville;[34] and for Blackstone the protection of property by government had the sanction of the laws of Nature and of God.[35] The Whig oligarchy considered the government as a means to the preservation of their own holdings, without consideration for any possible rights of the unpropertied.[36] If as Hume asserted, property must be stable and fixed by general rules,[37] they have the greatest right to power whose property is greatest and who therefore have the greatest reason for keeping society at peace and in order. It is fundamentally absurd to pretend that the weak should govern the strong, that the foolish should control the wise, or that those who have no property should dictate to those who are so privileged.[38] "What ridiculous vanity is this . . . what folly, to imagine that men, who have no interest in the state, but the profits of their daily labour, should be more anxious for the well-being of their country, than those, who have vast properties to take care of," who sustain the burdens and taxes of the nation.[39] Thus the holders of stock in the general enterprise are the only ones entitled to the protection of the state; those who do not have any stock in the social company, that is those who have no property, have no legal claim to a share in the profits. They can look only to the moral support of their superiors, who will bestow charity upon them if they work hard in their respective places and maintain the general peace.[40]

Thus everyone has his assigned place in society, an idea which the propertied classes were willing to inherit from an earlier age without including the corresponding duties and compensations which justified rigid status before the Elizabethan age.[41] The result was that a man who had no property found himself helpless and immobilized, virtually imprisoned, and denied opportunity to improve his situation. There were no efficient means of communication, no decent roads or forms of transportation to encourage moving from place to place. The mass of the people was too ignorant, impoverished, and scattered to be able to do much for itself.[42] Political practice encouraged such rigidity and isolation. The powerful justices of the peace were not interested in freedom of movement and did what they could to promote local isolation and fixity.[43] The system of poor relief gave to each parish the charge of all paupers who lived there and assured to the poor that they would get at least physical subsistence if they stayed in their own district. To this sanction of immobility were added the Settlement Acts, which demanded that all parish paupers be removed to or settled into the places of their birth or legal residence only. The joint tendency of poor relief and the Settlement Acts was to reduce the laboring poor to a state of almost complete geographical and social immobility; they were thus kept down at the bottom of society where they were expected to stay and work for the benefit of the whole.[44]

But the various expedients for keeping the lot of the laborer a hard one were not the result merely of capricious cruelty. They were said to have been demanded partly by the economic good of society as a whole and by the well-known moral laxity, laziness, and vice of the great majority of mankind.[45] Mercantilism, the prevailing economic doctrine for much of the eighteenth century, was less concerned for human welfare than for the prosperity and power of the state. It held that a nation could be strong and wealthy even though most of the people were poor and ignorant; in fact, the general prosperity depended on the willingness of most men to endure a life of labor, ignorance, and privation. The man who worked with his hands had to be poor so that the nation could be rich; he had to work hard so that his country might be strong.[46] The community is thus forced to make great demands upon the most indigent of its members. Too much should not be done by society to remove the hunger and the drudgery of these low ones; such a course "tends to destroy the harmony and beauty, the symmetry and order of that system, which God and nature have established in the world." [47] This is a familiar echo of that metaphysical optimism which is not to be questioned. If it should occur to some members of the laboring poor that by their own efforts they might be able to improve their situation, they must expect to feel the lash of Mandeville's indignation at such an attempt to pervert the interests of society as a whole. Mandeville on one occasion was

credibly informed that a parcel of footmen are arrived to that height of insolence as to have entered into a society together, and made laws by which they oblige themselves not to serve for less than such a sum, nor carry burdens or any bundle or parcel above a certain weight, not exceeding two or three pounds, with other regulations directly opposite to the interest of those they serve, and altogether destructive to the use they were designed for.[48]

Once more we encounter the low view of human nature in the further reason advanced for keeping the poor hard at work. It seems that the masses cannot be trusted to avoid debauchery and improvidence unless they are forced to work constantly at low wages. The virtues of thrift and diligence must be imposed on weak individuals who, if left to the dictates of depraved human nature, will be lazy, drunken, and debauched. Long hours, low wages, a severe workhouse system were justified on the ground that the laborer was naturally a wicked and lazy fellow who could be kept out of mischief only if he had no leisure and who would work only if threatened with starvation.[49] Brutality, insolence, debauchery, extravagance, drunkenness, improvidence, and idleness are constant charges brought against the laboring classes.[50] The work of the world has to be done, but the masses in their depravity will do it only under the threat of starvation; it follows that the laboring poor should get just enough to keep them from starving but not so much as to let them save anything.[51] Their wants must never be entirely satisfied and they must not be allowed to keep what they have won from the soil.

> Ah! well they know, that if the poor
> Were cloath'd and fed, they'd work no more,
> That nothing makes mankind so good,
> So tractable, as want of food,
> And like those frugal politicians,
> Who take their maxims from physicians,
> Think starving is the best foundation
> Of popular subordination.[52]

Even their profligacy was to be denied the poor; it, too, was a luxury reserved for the upper classes. Chesterfield took the view that a due subordination of inferiors to superiors would be totally destroyed by "an equality of profligacy." [53] Something quite different was called for from the large majority of mankind.

John Brown, in writing his famous *Estimate* of contemporary manners and principles, does not see fit to trouble himself about the behavior of the common people. These do not lead or govern, so they have no influence on the strength or weakness of a state.[54] Actually it is not necessary to spend much time in a moral treatise dealing with the duties of the lowest part of society. Such duties are so well-known, so simply stated and easily understood, that there is no need for their elaboration even if the poor were to read bulky treatises on morality.[55] The "lower sort" should cultivate the virtues of gratitude and respect toward the upper classes who employ them and give them the means whereby they live and uphold society.[56] Let them be patient, industrious, benevolent, cheerful, obedient, frugal, modest, resigned, and contented in that station to which they are called.[57] The persuasion that all is governed for the best will result in the principal virtue desired in a meanly situated person: contentedness. This may be defined as

such an acquiescence of the mind in that portion of outward things, which we possess, upon a persuasion of its being sufficient for us, as makes us well pleased with the condition we are in, and suffers not the desire of any change, or of any particular thing we have not, to trouble our spirits, or discompose our duty.[58]

This moral is enforced by the story of Sarah Meanwell and John Goodchild, contrasted with the career of Richard Coreworm and an assortment of his villainous associates. Sarah and John enjoy happy lives because they are obedient, religious, and faithful in performing the duties of their station; they are docile, amiable, and diligent in trying to deserve the esteem of worthy persons and are appropriately rewarded.[59] They show as they are supposed to do, that the English lower classes "possess a spirit of justice and order, superior to what is to be observed in the same rank of men in other countries." [60] The English poor see the propriety of Blackstone's admonition "to be decent, industrious, and inoffensive in their respective stations." [61] Like good soldiers, they devote themselves "to a quiet, conscientious and faithful discharge of the duties" assigned to their several offices and relations in life.[62] They succeed in the area of life in which they find themselves, and, as Steele admonishes them to be, they are as virtuous as the faculties and opportunities bestowed by Heaven and fortune will permit.[63]

Thus the controlling classes in the eighteenth century seemed to have those beneath them in a condition agreeable to everyone who mattered. Liberty and ease of life were reserved for those in power, and the many below were persuaded or forced to accept what could not be avoided. Mandeville said very shrewdly that "we seldom call any body lazy, but such as we reckon inferior to us, and of whom we expect some service." Children do not call their parents lazy, nor servants their masters; if a gentleman is so lazy that he will hardly put on his own shoes when he is in perfect health, still he is not considered lazy if he can afford to hire a servant to do it for him.[64] So also Horace Walpole observes that *authority never measures liberty downwards. Rarely is liberty supposed to mean the independence of those below us; it is our own freedom from the yoke of superiors.*" [65] The historian is right in saying that

Probably at no time in the whole history of England was the national attitude toward the laboring classes so heartless and inhuman as it was in the first half of the eighteenth century, at no time was the working man so completely at the mercy of his employer, at no time were the interests engaged in exploiting him so completely in control of every possible avenue of escape for him. Church and state alike were in the hands of his masters.[66]

But the man who was low in society was not kept there entirely by force; if he accepted his position largely without rebellion it was partly because he had been educated for it, in so far as education was possible for him at all. He was also consoled or persuaded that he had much to be thankful for in a life which was not as bad as he might think if he adopted the realist's view of the inherent misery in all human affairs. Then too he was assured by the church that even though his life now were hard and bitter, he must not repine, for resignation here would mean eternal happiness hereafter.

For more than sixty years after the death of Queen Ann, the history of education in England was uneventful. The government did nothing to support popular education, since this was held to be outside its duty; further, education might unfit the poor for the life which was to be their portion.[67] "Learning and liberty," says Soame Jenyns, "are excellent things; but, like tea and brandy, they are extremely pernicious in the hands of the vulgar, from the mischievous use which they are sure to make of them." [68] If the lower sort were educated beyond the most necessary rudiments, they would be unwilling to endure the drudgery to which they were born and the necessary work of the world would never be done.[69] They should therefore be kept from every thing "that might raise their desires, or improve their understanding." [70] It serves no useful purpose if a servant has the wit to see that his master is a fool.[71] Hannah More was opposed by some of the farmers in Somersetshire, because they "did not want their ploughmen made wiser than themselves." [72] The best course is to train up the poor very early in life to industry and obedience, so that they will accustom themselves to the low forms of labor which they are called upon to do. As Mandeville says, "Men who are to remain and end their days in a laborious, tiresome and painful station of life, the sooner they are put upon it at first, the more patiently they'll submit to it forever after." [73] Education is not only unwise from a social and political point of view; it is in a sense a cruel deprivation:

Ignorance, or the want of knowledge and literature, the appointed lot of all born to poverty, and the drudgeries of life, is the only opiate capable of infusing that insensibility which can enable them to endure the miseries of the one, and the fatigues of the other. It is a cordial administered by the gracious hand of providence; of which they ought never to be deprived by an ill-judged and improper education. It is the basis of all subordination, the support of society.[74]

Yet it was considered not unsuitable that voluntary organizations might be formed which would make it their business to offer the rudiments of education to the laboring poor, although as Swift said, "their education is of little consequence to the public." [75] Charity from the higher stations to those below was praised on high authority as a means of reconciling the necessarily low to their duties. Warburton heroically accepts the charge of the Common Father of Mankind, who has recommended the poor to the care and protection of the upper classes.[76] This benevolent care might, and often did, take the form of voluntary subscription to the charity schools. These institutions were at once a means of virtuous action for the privileged and a device for keeping those obliged to attend them in their useful stations far down in society. The curriculum was sharply confined to what was useful in the lives of future servants and laborers. As Hannah More said, "I allow of no writing for the poor. My object is not to make fanatics, but to train up the lower classes in habits of industry and piety." [77]

Once again the influence of Locke, hero and villain of so many studies in the history of eighteenth century ideas, leads to the discovery that the masses could be conditioned to perform their duties without complaint. If the mind at the outset is blank, it can be filled with whatever society might need. The poor then, could be made by education into anything that society needed them for: in this case for contented servants and laborers. Warned by the unrest of the seventeenth century, the ruling classes wanted to make sure of social discipline among the poor whose development, if left to itself, could not be trusted.[78] The charity schools as a result were not asked to develop a child's intellectual powers or to enlarge his opportunities; they were not to offer a liberal education. They existed largely to teach the virtues of submission to superiors and diligence in assigned tasks—virtues suited to those who were destined by God to live by the sweat of their brows. Humility and acceptance of poverty were instilled by the issuance of coarse, plain uniforms. These were without gaiety or color, ornament or decoration, which might make for vanity of appearance. Prayers and hymns were added to the curriculum to inculcate meekness, obedience, and contentment as well as gratitude for the Christian generosity which had given the children such good fortune in allowing them to attend school.[79]

The actual course of study in the Charity Schools was called "The Literary Curriculum"; it consisted of religious instruction, the three R's, and vocational training. Religion was learned from the Bible, Church Catechism, and prescribed prayers; moral applications of the Creed and the Ten Commandments were made in such a way as to encourage the virtues of meekness, gratitude, and subjection. Reading, as such, also was based on the Catechism, Book of Common Prayer, the New Testament, and the Old Testament in that order. *The Whole Duty of Man* was often given as a present when children came to the end of their school years, suggesting that this was the kind of reading which should be done in later life. Writing was not taught at all until reading was considerably advanced; it was then confined to simple passages from Scripture or Aesop's *Fables*. Arithmetic was the most advanced course, offered only when reading and writing had been perfected. This study also was sharply limited, going only far enough to show how simple accounts might be kept. Vocational instruction for the girls was confined to what would prepare them for domestic service; for the boys, outside the commoner forms of apprenticeship, instruction might lead to sea service or navigation. For a time, there was a tendency to permit a certain amount of singing in the schools, but this was generally dropped on the ground that it smacked of the politer forms of education and was therefore out of place in a charity school.[80]

The result of this discipline pleased the bishops and those whom they represented in society. The children learned no unbecoming airs and were accustomed to the meanest services in life, which they learned to perform willingly.[81] "Religion and labor" said the Bishop of Bristol, go hand in hand together in these schools to the general edification.[82] Society is "hereby made more secure, easy, and delightful, and the best foundation is laid for peace, order, and good government." [83] The Rev. Samuel Glasse, Chaplain in Ordinary to His Majesty, is emotionally stirred at sight of the annual meeting of the children educated in the charity schools around London and Westminster. Any human heart must be sensibly affected "by that appearance of decency and propriety, of simplicity and regularity, of humility and due subordination, which prevails in the surrounding assembly." [84] At a similar meeting the Bishop of Winchester praises the education offered to children of the necessitous poor. Their hands are trained to the useful arts of life and their hearts are given the conviction "that their best dependence is on the blessing of God: which by faith and holy fear, by upright dealing, by honest and sober diligence, they shall derive upon their future labours." [85]

Education could be thus effective in persuading the laborer to accept his place in the world. But the man low in society might be consoled by another thought: perhaps *he* was the fortunate one, better enabled to lead a virtuous life of health and peace than the man of higher privilege. Adam Smith says that while some men seem to have been left out in partition of the good things of earth, the truth is that "in what constitutes the real happiness of human life, they are in no respect inferior to those who seem so much above them." [86] In the course of time, Mandeville says, the poor man becomes so inured to hardships that he does not know they exist in his life.[87] If he is allowed to go on in blissful ignorance he will develop into a better and happier man in every way than his more sophisticated master. If, from those who cannot read or write, we take at random a hundred men over forty and contrast them with an equal number from the privileged classes, Mandeville is sure that among the illiterate we shall meet with more union and neighbourly love, less wickedness and attachment to the world, more content of mind, more innocence, sincerity, and other good qualities that conduce to public peace and real felicity, than we shall find among the latter.[88]

The truth is, therefore, that those who have no revenue but their bodily labor "enjoy as much cheerfulness, contentment, health, gaiety, in their own way, as any in the highest station of life." [89] The poor laborer has good health, the finest of earthly blessings; he can sleep calmly without fear of thieves and needs no potions to induce unconsciousness; his children are numerous and healthy, a great help to parents who are untroubled by ambition or desire for place. In time of political upheaval the poor are un-molested so long as they are quiet and do their work; they live at all times in peace, untroubled by envious rivals, unhated by rave-nous competitors.[90] They enjoy in common with all men, the gen-eral blessings of God upon the world—the sun, air, and beauties of nature.[91] If they will consider all these advantages of their station, and then compare them with the miseries of high place, the poor will see that, as a matter of fact, they are the chosen people of God. The upper classes endure the afflictions of idleness, languor, dis-sipation, and ensuing ill health. They suffer all manner of diseases unknown to the poor. "Business, fear, guilt, design, anguish, and vexation are continually buzzing about the curtains of the rich and powerful," so that they cannot sleep without some dose or other.[92] Likewise the rich are full of wants and desires of power and wealth which prevent them from enjoying what they have. They are sad and ungrateful to God. They often owe their wealth to meanness, dishonesty, and corruption—a thousand vile shifts of wicked thieving and scoundrelism torment their consciences; knowing that no single good human quality is needed to attain riches and power, they are incapable of using the one advantage of their wealth, which is to do good for other people.[93] Their minds are perplexed and they suffer from the malice of calumny and slan-der to the perpetual disturbance of their lives.[94]

Actually there is every reason why the poor man should be more virtuous than his theoretical superior. His temptations do not begin to be as severe, and his vices are less pardonable. He has no time for idleness and so is not so easily led into evil ways; his passions are not inflamed by excess and he is untroubled by any of the allurements to wickedness. Nothing lies in the way to divert the poor from simple, clearly defined duty. The work of salvation is easier for them, their reward in Heaven is more certain if they perform their task. Consequently their neglect of what is expected of them will be less excusable and will meet with fewer allowances from the judgment of God.[95] The evidence of life in the world therefore joins with the demands of the Christian dispensation to assure the poor laborer that he has nothing to complain of, that in fact he has all the advantage on his side. Let him then heed the classical admonition of Wilberforce to the lower orders,

that if their superiors enjoy more abundant comforts, they are also exposed to many temptations . . . that "having food and raiment, they should be therewith content", since their situation in life, with all its evils, is better than they have deserved at the hand of God; and finally, that all human distinctions will soon be done away, and the true followers of Christ will all . . . be alike admitted to the . . . same heavenly inheritance.[96]

THE INFLUENCE OF THE CHURCH

The ideas that underlie English conservatism finally lead us to the enormous influence of the church in preserving the existing order. While it seems especially appropriate to study this influence under the heading of "Fear," we have at no time been free of the assistance given by the church to those who feel that things should be, or may as well be, left as they are. The complacent ones who say that the English constitution is supernaturally perfect are enthusiastically supported by the highest ecclesiastics; these urge the people to submit to a state of things which hardly admits of improvement [97] since, as Edward Young says,

> Our constitution's orthodox
> And closes with our creed. . . .[98]

The metaphysical optimist is upheld by the pious view that the world is governed by a just and benevolent God Who has ordained all things in His infinite wisdom for the best, so that evils and inconveniences should be borne as part of what is decreed from above. The realist's low view of human nature and of the human predicament on earth is seconded by the theologian's conviction of man's depravity and his consequent exile in a lifelong vale of tears. Anti-intellectualism as well finds an echo in the English church's dislike of free-thinking, deism, skeptical philosophy, or indeed of sharp argument or intellectual controversy of any sort in religious matters. Such activities might stir up no end of those dogs who were taking their ease in eighteenth century England. Hume is very hard on the clergy of the established church for their age-long opposition to liberty of thought, a liberty which he says they have found incompatible with their own desire for power; hence their invariable alliance with a strong government.[99] Fielding allows Parson Adams to express a similar idea more amiably to Joseph Andrews. Adams is much concerned over a boy's morality and would educate him with care for his immortal soul. "I had rather he should be a blockhead than an atheist or a presbyterian," these being no doubt the horrible alternatives if the lad should grow up in complete freedom of thought.[100]

Although the *status quo* had little to fear from the deists, who were by no means revolutionaries, yet this class of men were generally denounced or ridiculed throughout the century.[101] Skeptical philosophers who write against the religion of the country in a popular vein were held to be extremely dangerous. "Philosophy will never do for the vulgar," who must be bound by prejudice and not be trusted to get the right ideas for themselves.[102] Aside from the fact that there was no political or social discontent to support a theoretical religious controversy,[103] it is clear that neither the orthodox clergy nor the rational deists wanted to carry the argument too far. The deists considered the religious superstition and theology of their time ridiculous, but they were glad enough to leave the established church more or less as it was. A kind of intellectual indolence prevented deism from pushing its views to so logical a conclusion as to damage seriously an institution which was useful to the well-being of society. As Gibbon said, to the statesman a creed is equally useful whether true or false; let the Roman practice prevail whereby superstition is accepted by the people, doubted by the philosopher, and used by the politician.[104] The futility or danger of theological argument was doubtless the reason for suppressing the annual convocations of the clergy at York and Canterbury. From 1741 to 1855 the clergy were deprived of their only chance to meet and discuss vital questions of doctrine and practice. Enough trouble had been caused by the Bangorian Controversy over Bishop Hoadly's individualism; it would be easier and safer not to have any occasion on which the vigorous clergy could air their views.[105]

But conservative fear lest there be an effort to change the social order from below was most comforted by the influence of the church. This was true partly because of the inherent distrust of change by an established church, either outside or within itself; partly because it was to the temporal interest of the establishment to ally itself with that state power most likely to insure the establishment's own safety and continuance; and partly because of the doctrines of reward and punishment, as well as Christian submission to hardship in this life, the tendency of which was to persuade men to endure patiently their earthly lot and not to rebel against the prevailing social order.

The Book of Proverbs warns the people that they should "meddle not with them that are given to change." This means not to give aid "to the measures of those who would, on slight pretexts, subvert all established order, and throw every thing into confusion." [106] No institution could be more faithful to this charge than the established English church of the eighteenth century. The "Preface" to the *Book of Common Prayer* shows the ancient view when change of any kind is suggested. "Innovations and new-fangleness" in matters of church ceremony are always to be avoided, but the church has not been unwilling to yield on occasion to the need for change. On the one hand experience has shown that "where a change hath been made of things advisedly established (no evident necessity so requiring), sundry inconveniences have thereupon ensued, and those many times more and greater than the evils that were intended to be remedied by such change. . . ." Yet since the particular forms and ceremonies of the church are in themselves indifferent,

it is but reasonable, that upon weighty and important considerations . . . such changes and alterations should be made therein, as to those that are in place of authority should from time to time seem either necessary or expedient. Accordingly we find, that . . . the church . . . hath yielded to make such alterations in some particulars, as in their respective times were thought convenient; yet so, as that the main body and essentials of it . . . have still continued the same unto this day, and yet do stand firm and unshaken, notwithstanding all the vain attempts and impetuous assaults made against it by such men as are given to change.[107]

The tone of this passage suggests the attitude from which the conservatism of the church grows. There is a patient weariness in the wording here which accepts the need of making some changes from time to time. It is the patience and weariness of one who knows from long experience that the change proposed will not do much good. There is also the recognition of an illusion which the church knows cannot be realized, but which must be given its poor human chance to improve things. The church in its long age and wisdom knows better than to believe in change, yet from time to time it gives in so as to quiet restless and deluded men who are simple enough to think that anything can be done to make that better which was not intended ever to be good. The church has gone on for centuries watching the hopeful new become the unsatisfactory old, to be replaced in turn by new which becomes unsatisfactory as well. It is too old not to see the folly of constantly repeated, forever renewed human illusion. It goes on, trained by the centuries to patience, weariness, and pity, retaining as much as it can of the old which was once new and which will do just as well over the ages as any of the new things designed to bring about improvement. It is therefore in the nature of the church and its attitude, its age, its role and place in the affairs of men, to be conservative and patiently attentive to purposes which make the pitiful changes men try to advance seem irrelevant and absurd.

This will be the view of any established church, but it is especially typical of eighteenth century England. The church at this period was, as Lecky so well says,

of all institutions the most intensely and most distinctively English. . . . Its love of compromise, its dislike to pushing principles to extreme consequences, its decorum, its social aspects, its instinctive aversion to abstract speculation, to fanatical action, to vehement, spontaneous, mystical, or ascetic forms of devotion, its admirable skill in strengthening the orderly and philanthropic elements of society, in moderating and regulating character, and blending with the various phases of national life, all reflected with singular fidelity English modes of thought and feeling.[108]

Certainly the church shared the English pleasure of the time in itself. The Archbishop of York was probably speaking for most of his clerical brethren in praising the English church as the purest, the most orthodox in faith, the freest from idolatry and superstition as well as from freakish enthusiasm among those then extant.[109] It was written of the Duke of Beaufort, that

> He loves the church, because that church is pure,
> No tawdry proud coquet, no prude demure;
> A modest, heav'n born, all-accomplished maid,
> With every grace of holiness array'd.[110]

In Swift's opinion, the system of episcopacy in the established church is "most agreeable to primitive institution, fittest of all others for preserving order and purity, and under its present regulations, best calculated for our civil state." [111] If the establishment is so well adapted to the requirements of the age, then it does not need to be changed radically, and all well-intentioned persons ought to belong to it without question. Burke gives his approval to the fact that the English church had changed its modes and

fashions very little since the early Renaissance.[112] Even such a re-
quirement as the demand for subscription from dissenters, which
had long since ceased to have any force and was no longer considered to be a test of anyone's opinions, was still kept up for form's
sake "because it might be some trouble to amend it." [113]

But what if it be admitted that the established church is not perfect after all? Bishop Hoadly pleads effectively for its acceptance
by all Christians on the ground that if the idea of an established
religion is a good one, which most Christians will agree to, then
it should be taken and conformed to, even though not everyone
considers it perfect. It is impossible to frame an establishment
which will not be considered defective by some persons; nevertheless their objections cannot be given as a reason for not
conforming to what is already set up. If a national church is a good
thing to have, then "the rule must be, that it is the duty of all
Christians to comply with it, if no sinful terms of communion be
required of them; unless you will lay all establishments open to
infinite divisions, and frustrate the very end for which alone they
are designed." [114] This is typically conservative reasoning. Weakness or imperfection in the prevailing order is no argument for not
accepting it. Why try to set up anything which is supposed to
conduct human affairs, if imperfection itself is never to be tolerated? The fact of instituting anything in society means that its
imperfections and weaknesses are set up and established with it.
The alternatives are to propose something perfect, which is impossible, or to conform to what is established. If one still objects
to prevailing abuses, he may set up his own institution which will
suit him better, but which, being also human, is open to further
objection and replacement by what is, by definition, also imperfect.
Swift agrees with Plato that men ought to worship the gods according to the laws of their country; otherwise they may endanger the
public peace by opening the door to discontent and faction.[115]
Even if a man sees that some other form is actually better than the
established one, he should think twice as to whether his opinions
may do more harm than good:

are not the majority of men more strongly attached to the religion than the government of their forefathers? Will it serve my country to introduce discontent of any species? May not those innovations in religion, which discontent may introduce, lead to all the evils which are caused by frenzy and fanaticism? [116]

An establishment thinking well of itself, considering its safety and continuance as necessary to the national good, was anxious to make a close alliance with secular power. Its own well-being depended on the favor of civil government, a favor which the church obtained by behaving in such a way as to recommend itself to the ruling classes. Adam Smith remarks that "the Church of England in particular has always valued herself, with great reason, upon the unexceptionable loyalty of her principles." [117] Lecky is probably unjust in saying that "Anglicanism was from the beginning at once the most servile and the most efficient agent of tyranny. . . . No other church so uniformly betrayed and trampled on the liberties of her country." [118] Yet "the Church of England was the central institution of Toryism . . . the body of clergy in the Church of England held Tory principles in overwhelming measure." [119]

Not only did the old doctrine of passive obedience linger on, but the church in its daily practice called for loyalty to the governing powers almost as an article of faith. In 1712, a generation after the fall of James II, Berkeley could still teach that loyalty is a moral virtue, that rebellion is criminal in the subject, that men should consider the rule against resisting the supreme civil power as unalterable as a proposition in geometry.[120] If loyalty is a branch of natural religion therefore, "the least degree of rebellion is, with the utmost strictness and propriety, a sin." [121] Although Hume was saying that the doctrine of passive obedience "is so absurd in itself, and so opposite to our liberties, that it seems to have been chiefly left to pulpit-declaimers, and to their deluded followers among the vulgar," [122] yet the powerful influence of such a work as *The Whole Duty of Man* was on the side of authority as of divine origin. The people were told that since those in authority on earth are God's vice-regents, it is an affront to the majesty of God "for sub-

jects to contemn and vilify their sovereigns, to expose their faults
and uncover their nakedness, and lampoon and libel their persons
and actions." [123] The Rev. Edmund Gibson, chaplain to the Archbishop of Canterbury, preaches from the text "Thou shalt not
speak evil of the ruler of thy people"; he proceeds to show that
complaint against a ruler "is contrary to reason, religion, and the
avowed doctrine of the Church of England." [124] A book of *Private
Devotions* anticipates even an unwitting fall into the sin of discontented criticism. Under the heading of self-examination as to
breaches of duty are found lists of various offences by consulting
which a man may remind himself of all the things he might have
done wrong, and so make sure that he does not overlook any possible offenses on his part. Among others are:

Not reverencing our civil parent, the lawful magistrate. Judging and
speaking evil of him. Grudging his just tributes. Sowing sedition among
the people. Refusing to obey his lawful commands. Rising up against
him, or taking part with them that do.[125]

The very devotions and prayers spoken within the church edifice often seemed to uphold the reigning powers as if they were in
turn a part of the church. *The Book of Common Prayer* makes civil
rebellion seem like heresy within the church by joining them in
one supplication: "From all sedition, privy conspiracy, and rebellion; from all false doctrine, heresy and schism; from hardness of
heart, and contempt of thy Word and Commandment, Good Lord,
deliver us." [126] This would seem almost by prior agreement to be
a balancing of, or repayment for, the actual law which says that
"Seditious words in derogation of the established Religion are in-
dictable, as tending to a breach of the peace." [127] The Church
prayed fervently as well in times of crisis or danger, lest the forces
of evil and rebellion prevail against the obvious forces of right and
peace, the sovereign and his government in England. Such a period
of crisis came with the American Revolution, at which time the
Church prayed with typical devotion to its principles:

Be thou to us a tower of defence against the assaults of our enemies . . .
and so bless the arms of our gracious sovereign, in the maintenance of

his just and lawful rights, and prosper his endeavours to restore tranquility among his unhappy deluded subjects in America, now in open
rebellion against his crown, in defiance of all subordination and legal
government, that we being preserved by thy help and goodness from all
perils and disasters, and made happily triumphant over all the dis-
turbers of our peace, may joyfully laud and magnify thy glorious name;
and serve thee from generation to generation, in all godliness and
quietude.[128]

Thus the support of the *status quo* by the church extended to
the very foot of the altar. A number of commentators have used
the figure of a police force to describe the established church in
this period, as if God, religion, and the church were all a part of
the civil constabulary whose object was to "maintain public peace,
in behalf of the existing order." [129] Laws passed at the Restoration
and the Glorious Revolution combined with books of religious
propaganda like the *Whole Duty of Man* to fix the alliance of the
church with royalty and nobility against the aspirations of those
who might lead another Puritan rebellion. The Act of Uniformity
in 1662 and the demand for an Oath of Allegiance in 1690 deprived the Church of England of some of its ablest and most energetic men; it had little left of spiritual fire and zeal, but much of
self-seeking "moderation" and time-serving.[130] The Test and Cor-
poration Acts were effective for the preservation of the civil as well
as the religious establishment and were defended in the eighteenth
century on that ground.[131] Swift was even sure that the voting
franchise should be confined to professed Anglicans, it being "absurd that any person, who professeth a different form of worship
from that which is national, should be trusted with a vote for elect-
ing members in the House of Commons." [132] As for *The Whole
Duty of Man,* the national church was for more than a century
devoted to it. The "whole duty" referred to was especially applied
to good subjects in the lower areas of society; these were constantly
urged, in one form or another, to stay contentedly in their places
and to do their assigned duties while looking for adequate reward
to another life than this.

Theory and practice both seem, then, to point to a mutual dependence between the church and civil authority. Every church officer from the lowly missionary who took the teachings of Christ seriously to the highest bishop who sat in the House of Lords had to give evidence of his devotion to the existing government. Recommendations of a clergyman for missionary service abroad were required to give information on the usual points of character, learning, and piety, as well as on "his affection to the present Government . . . his conformity to the doctrine and discipline of the Church of *England*." [133] The same was true of anyone who wished to be a bishop, or who being a bishop, wanted a see with a larger income. The independence of such men was sharply curtailed by the need of remaining loyal to the reigning powers, not so much to the king under the early Hanoverian rulers, as to rival Whig and Tory ministers. The point is illustrated by Robert Walpole when on May 24 and June 1 of the year 1733 he was able to rely on the bishops to save him from defeat in two critical divisions in the House of Lords. He received twenty-four out of the twenty-six votes of the bishops, offering a moral which was pressed home by a popular ballad. This urges Walpole to

> Consider the church is your rock of defence
> Your South Sea escape in your memory cherish,
> When sinking, you cry'd 'Help, lords, or I perish!' [134]

It seemed that all ordinary human motives called for a career of subserviency to the ruling class; the clergy, especially those in higher places, could hardly be expected to take a very noble view of their profession. To take one's faith seriously was to leave the road to preferment or to be branded an "enthusiast" or fanatic. The clergy as a whole therefore, became a subsidiary part of the aristocracy, a section of the upper classes who were told off and assigned to look after piety and popular good conduct, just as others were expected to look after civil affairs or the military establishment. All was designed to maintain the system of property and order which the revolution of 1688 had so gloriously affirmed.[135] Nor was the general attitude modified as the industrial revolution moved forward, and a new group of men began to reach out for power. The church found again that it could arrange itself so as to suit the ideas of the laity.[136] As R. H. Tawney says, "Religious thought was no longer an imperious master, but a docile pupil." [137] The doctrine of self-interest was accepted as the outward sign of a Providential plan which if left alone, as a metaphysical optimist would have it, was bound to work out all things for the best. The church in this view does not have to set up an independent standard of values to curb the operations of men in business and the affairs of society. There was no conflict between the church and the natural, wholesome economic ambitions which were doing so much for progress. Religion was no longer the critic and accuser of the established order "but its anodyne, its apologist, and its drudge." [138] Its support of a conservative order presents that great paradox in the history of ideas that Whitehead found so striking. The clergy are seen to fall in with the practices of their day when the ultimate ideas of which they are the professed guardians are a perpetual criticism of current behavior. The church in eighteenth century England had fallen into the hands of the very persons who would have supported the persecuting emperors when Christianity was struggling for life.[139]

The attitude of the church toward the upper classes required that it help conservative fear to prevent trouble from below. To perform what was expected of it in this field, the church emphasized two of its oldest doctrines: rewards and punishments, and the Christian duty of contentment and submission. It should be observed once more that these teachings are not considered so necessary for the upper classes. It was not absolutely essential that Shaftesbury, Bolingbroke, and Chesterfield should be devout or should look for their happiness in another world. They might safely be allowed their little heresies, so long as they did not contaminate the poor by presenting these ideas in a popular form.[140] After all, such men may be as irreligious as they like, because in any case they will never rebel against the existing order. Their irreligion is not a danger to the *status quo,* whereas irreligion among the lower sort is a very real danger. Here there really is some reason to object to the way things are, and a corrective is needed to hold the lower classes back from making trouble. From this point of view, religion is not an end in itself in human affairs, but is useful only with respect to the way things are. It is invoked in direct proportion to the social grievance of the person who is supposed to need it. Therefore what religion is supposed to accomplish toward the assuagement of conservative fear is not needed by those who are already comfortably rewarded in this world.

Conservatives tend to become moralists, because morality asks how one is to make people behave properly. Since the maintenance of things as they are depends on keeping the people in line, the conservative naturally allies himself with a moral system or a religious creed which has doctrines capable of persuading people not to make trouble. The best persuasion of this kind is the tangible one of rewards and punishments, men being the limited, literal, and crudely motivated creatures that they are. The conservative's low view of human nature again explains even more fully his reliance on the fear of God's punishments. The bulk of mankind are not deterred from breaking the law by fear of the gallows alone; unless they also fear God's retribution, they cannot be controlled.[141] "For restrained, one way or other men must be; otherwise a general scene of disorder and confusion would soon appear." [142] Sacheverell was of the opinion that only "the affrighting representations of hell and a future judgment" were sufficient to hold in check the "ungovernable, headstrong, brutal force, human nature and passion carries in it." [143] So necessary to keeping men in subjection is the doctrine of rewards and punishments,[144] that the existence of a state for any length of time unsupported by this sanction "would be nothing less than a miracle." [145] The office of a church minister in any well-conducted state is therefore evident. It is simply to "reform the manners and awe the violent nature of man by religion; by that means assisting the magistrate in preserving peace and order among the people." [146] In the very first year of his reign, George III seemed, by his admonition to piety and good manners throughout England, to admit that he could not hope for a successful reign without the aid of popular belief in another world where rewards and punishments will be sternly distributed. The king's proclamation of October 31, 1760, was to be read by every minister four times a year, in the hope of discouraging the people from all manner of offenses, "and to keep them in awe by all the means which the civil or religious laws of his country can devise." [147] Wilkes was perhaps right in speculating as to whether the divine or the politician has more frequently relied on the doctrine of rewards and punishments to make converts to his views. "I own," he says, "that I am rather inclined to the politician." [148]

From the very outset, Christianity preached the need of human acceptance of affliction without complaint. Christ himself gave the example to his followers, who were comforted throughout the ages by "assuring themselves that the more troubles, afflictions, imprisonments, and persecutions they suffer, the more they resemble our Lord and Master." [149] The early church held to its doctrine of unquestioning obedience and submission even after the Roman Empire had begun to inflict its worst persecutions. In the very reign of Nero, St. Paul preached the doctrine of passive obedience, and "at a time when Rome was swarming with Christians, the most horrible persecutions were endured without a murmur or a struggle." [150] By the eighteenth century however, Christianity had long been in a position to do a certain amount of persecuting itself and was closely allied with civil authority. Far from being a menace to existing government, Christianity was useful to it by means of a doctrine which had at first made the inflictions of government endurable. Now the same admonition could be used to make sure that the secular purposes of the government were not disturbed by discontent from below. The virtue desired in the lower sort was variously described as contentment, humility, meekness, industry, Christian fortitude, diligence, faithfulness, honesty, patience, or any of the qualities striven for in the charity schools. All of these terms were reducible to this idea: one should do his duty without complaint or high expectations in this life regardless of circumstances. The popular books of piety defined the fundamental terms with an accuracy which could leave no doubt as to their meaning. Patience is nothing else "but a willing and quiet yielding to whatever afflictions it pleases God to lay upon us." [151] Similarly, contentment receives with serenity whatever God considers wisest and best:

Contentment . . . is only solicitous to adorn that particular station, which heaven hath assigned it with proper duties. . . . It cheerfully follows where Providence leads. . . . It never utters one murmuring word, or indulges one repining thought on the miseries of its condition and station. . . . It puts the most favourable construction upon every sinister event, and studies what good it can produce from it. It makes the very best use of present events, and regards every thing future with a calm unconcernedness.[152]

This is not far from metaphysical optimism, emphasizing the wisdom of God which is certain to order all things for the best. Since it is impossible for God to appoint anything harmful for us, then discontent with our condition "is doing all in our power to introduce confusion into his all-wise government, and to destroy that harmony and beauty of which he is the author." [153] Further, to say that we are displeased with the condition which God considers the best for us, is "to say that we are wiser than God and know better than He what is good for us." [154] Since "perfect goodness is at the head of the world," [155] it is both wicked and foolish to repine at our lot,[156] and a gross folly "to murmur at those stripes which are meant so graciously." [157] Therefore we "are not to regard how mean and obscure our situation is, but only how well we discharge the duties of it." [158] In his private devotions, a man should ask himself the questions which will show how well his corrupt nature has learned this vital lesson of humility and submission. He should look into his own unworthiness and make sure that he has patiently borne all the afflictions which God has allowed quite properly to be visited on such a corrupt being. Has he obeyed God's commands and done his duty with contentment in his station? Has he spent his time well in thinking God's thoughts, or must he ask himself: "Hast thou preferred thy reason to God's revelation? Or, loaded thy memory with wicked thoughts, or romances and idle tales?" [159] If he is of the meaner sort in society, the unworthy individual should utter this prayer "to be said by such as are *poor* and *low* in the World":

O God, I believe that for just and wise reasons thou hast allotted to mankind very different states and circumstances of life; and that all the temporal evils, which have at any time happened unto me, are designed by thee for my benefit: Therefore, tho' thou hast thought fit to place me in a mean condition, to deprive me of many conveniencies of life, and to exercise me in a state of poverty; yet thou hast hitherto preserved and supported me by thy good providence, and blessed me with advantages above many others. . . . Inspire me with diligence and industry in my calling . . . let me chuse rather to be poor than wicked, and to want anything rather than thy blessing. For which end, cloathe me with a meek, and quiet, and humble spirit, and a thorough contentedness in my present circumstances; that I may neither dare to repine at my own condition, nor envy the prosperity of others.[160]

If these are the proper teachings of Christianity and if they are accepted by those for whom they are intended, it must be admitted that "nothing produces contentment in the lowest situaions so effectually as true religion." [161] Burke indeed denies that Christianity is used only to keep the vulgar in subjection, and says that it applies fully as much to other classes.[162] Even royalty is supposed to be content in that station to which it has pleased God to call it,[163] so that the tendency of the Christian idea of submission to support a certain social order may be thought of as accidental and not part of its declared purpose. Any Christian church might then, by appeal to rewards and punishments and the need of contentment, support a given society in its classifications without seeming to exist for precisely that purpose. It is left for the English church to say in so many words, in its official teaching, just what the moral and social effects were which the public religion was designed to achieve. These lines stand as a classical aid to the *status quo,* the perfect means of quieting the uneasiness of conservatism lest anyone should start trouble from below:

Q. What is thy duty towards thy neighbour?

A. . . . to love him as myself, and to do to all men as I would they should do unto me; to love, honour, and succour my father and mother; to honour and obey the king, and all that are put in authority under him; to submit myself to all my governors, teachers, spiritual pastors, and masters; to order myself lowly and reverently to all my betters; to hurt no body by word or deed; to be true and just in all my dealings; to bear no malice nor hatred in my heart; to keep my hands from picking and stealing, and my tongue from evil-speaking, lying, and slandering; to keep my body in temperance, soberness, and chastity; not to covet nor desire other men's good, but to learn and labour truly to get mine own living; and to do my duty in that state of life unto which it shall please God to call me.[164]

Such language will tend not only to keep people from disobedience, but also to prevent them from even thinking or feeling the kind of thing that makes for discontent and rebellion. To accept humbly, to obey without question or resentment, not even to want anything that one does not have, not to resent the superior position of others—these exhortations will prevent the mere possibility of any effort to undo the existing social order which is to be accepted without question. Religion is thus made to tell man that there is no point in trying to change a scene of appointed suffering and evil; at the same time it offers a means of comfort, of patient endurance of the very evil and suffering which it says cannot—and from its point of view—should not be avoided before a better life in the future is earned. The man low in society is not supposed to draw any conclusions as to injustice in this world. The fact is that conclusions of any kind are not for this life; this is not the end, so its logic or justification cannot be found in life on earth now, but must be expected elsewhere when conclusions are drawn on the basis of evidence gathered on earth.

So long as the established religious institution of a nation teaches such doctrines, the conservative need not fear the lack of those wholesome restraints upon the vulgar which are needed for peace and order.[165]

VI · THE LESSON OF
MODERATION

THE VARIOUS attitudes and feelings to which we have given the names of Complacency, Metaphysical Optimism, Realism, and Fear, have for their final implication a conservative moderation. A complacent man well satisfied with the way things are in a society which rewards him handsomely will not desire any violent or sudden change. A man who believes that everything is intended for the best according to a universal plan whose details are not always understandable to human ignorance will tend to be conservative. One who believes in a fixed, unalterable set of ranks or gradations in society such as exist in the chain of being as a whole will not advocate changing or rearranging what is decreed as it is for the harmony of the whole. Another who takes a low view of human nature and its possibilities will demand strict subordination and will see no point in changing one scene of the operation of human depravity for another. Again one who believes that the reality of life is necessarily defective, either because imperfect man makes it so, or because experience has simply shown that it is so, or because Providence has decided that it should be so in preparation for another life—such a man will be conservative. Another who holds that there is no point in setting up abstract ideals or intellectual constructions which have no chance of practical success, save to disturb the prevailing order, will also tend to distrust new plans for change. All these views of human affairs are prominent in eighteenth century England and help in various ways and degrees to make up what is called conservatism. And fear lest there be an effort to change society from below was present throughout the century, especially in the later decades. This feeling was assuaged in part with the help of the church, which exercised its proper influence in preventing the fear from being realized.

The moral of it all is to avoid overzealous feelings and enthusiasm, especially in religion; to distrust all extreme parties or factions in the state; and finally to observe a happy moderation far from extremes of any kind, and so help to maintain that peace and order which eighteenth century England had achieved and desired to keep undisturbed.

The term "enthusiasm" meant a variety of those extremes of inspiration or zeal which were distrusted by the conservative temper. We find the usual array of epithets applied to something which this articulate age did not believe in or which it feared. We are told that enthusiasm rises "from the conceits of a warmed or over-weening brain" [1] and is indulged by "men of heated imaginations and weak judgment." [2] In the clergy it may take various forms of fanatical and deluded action over the most trivial points, and as Voltaire himself said, it may cause more trouble by quarreling over a minor detail of a monk's habit than all the philosophers put together.[3] Men allow themselves to be bewitched by a "prepossessing panic"; they easily catch the contagion from other religious enthusiasts, the evidence of the senses is lost, the imagination is inflamed, and in a moment they have "burnt up every particle of judgment and reason." [4] They fall the victims of those "narrow principles, those bigoted prejudices, that furious, that implacable, that ignorant zeal, which had often done so much hurt both to the church and the state." [5]

Shaftesbury recommends humor and ridicule as salutary correctives of the extremes of enthusiasm; [6] since "nothing is ridiculous except what is deformed," this particular excess will respond to raillery.[7] Hume favored a greater skepticism, and distrusted people who believed in anything strongly, since they might at any time become fanatics. As Beattie said, the skeptic would substitute "for the sanguinary principles of bigotry and enthusiasm

. . . the milky ones of scepticism and moderation." [8] Hume feared that enthusiasm might produce "the most cruel disorders in human society." [9] Its victims unsettle and subvert other men, "filling their heads with abundance of foolish notions and scruples in religion, which are dangerous to government, and the public peace and happiness." [10] Swift pointed to the martyrdom of Charles I as an example of what happens when religious enthusiasts disturb the community with their fanatical zeal. "This was the folly and madness of those ancient puritan fanatics," [11] showing that "men who fight more from impulse than reason, and are guided rather by blind temerity than regular discipline, are the most inhuman of all victors." [12] The English are wise then to follow their sensible religious establishment and to be unwilling to exchange their blessings "for the arbitrary persecuting zeal of hot-headed fanatics." [13] It is clear that in the church as well as in the state, "no evil is more to be feared than a rancorous and enthusiastic zeal." [14] When John Cartwright first began to plead for parliamentary reform, he was regarded as little better than insane and "was honoured with the appellations of projector and enthusiast," [15] as if these terms represented all that language could be made to express of ridiculous delusion and outlandish fanaticism. As Lecky says, there were not many saints in eighteenth century England; that moderate and sensible age would have been ill at ease in their presence.[16]

Yet extreme enthusiasm is no worse in religion than in politics. Actually, "all excessive zeal, injures the cause it means to serve." [17] As the century moved forward and the lines of difference between Whig and Tory grew more and more indistinct, it was common to denounce what was called the spirit of party or faction as the source of political evil and discord in the state.[18] The Whigs in power were very much like the Tories in desiring to unify the country and be rid of former discords; the general prosperity and happiness would best be served by dissolving all parties and healing all divisions.[19] Swift had pointed out early in the century that the spirit of party was the "root of all our civil animosities." [20] It weakened the effect of governmental action by obstructing every effort to organize public affairs,[21] and in its most licentious form it was called "faction," having as its object to defeat the ends of civil liberty.[22] Indeed the very devil seemed always busy on the side of faction, "England's bane and worst disgrace," the "unhappy source of all the nation's woe!" [23] History has shown no greater evil or heavier calamity than the distraction caused by this spirit of party discord.[24] Warburton sees in faction a certain hypocrisy which under the cloak of good intentions deceives the country to its ruin:

Faction, which accumulates all the evils of dissention in one; and fraught with the disposition of the worst citizens, impudently pretends to all the qualities of the best. Faction, which scruples no shape however venerable, no name however sacred, to draw the deluded people to second her private and corrupt purposes, masked over with pious zeal for religion, and disinterested love of our country.[25]

It would perhaps not be asked of all men that they join Horace Walpole in saying, "I have seen too much of parties, to list with any of them." [26] Yet they might agree with Pope that "Whate'er is best administered, is best." [27] William Penn's advice came down into the eighteenth century, showing that in the end it was best never to mention politics at all, not to speak of favoring one faction or another. He left the charge to his children not to meddle with "the public, neither business nor money." They should also "meddle not with government; never speak of it; let others say or do as they please." The best thing is to "know God, know yourselves; love home, know your own business, and mind it, and you have more time and peace than your neighbours." [28]

Happily for England, these admonitions and warnings against the dangers of faction were effective at the time. Moreover, the tendency of power is to calm the overenthusiastic, and in England membership in the House of Commons had a chastening effect. Lecky quotes with approval a famous remark by Canning, suggesting that the flambuoyant Wilkes would have lost much of his popularity if he had actually gone to Parliament from the first. Canning said calmly, "I do not fear firebrands in this House: as soon as they touch its floor they hiss and are extinguished." [29] There was doubtless hearty agreement with the writer addressing the city of London in 1762: "From faction, dilapidations, and knight-errantry, Good God, deliver us!" [30]

The classical virtue of a neoclassical age is, then, moderation, as called for by its dominant conservatism. Bishop Hoadly considered it the duty of all men to consult the peace and concord of society, and never to give the least occasion to public disturbance.[31] They are to cultivate moderation which

signifies an easiness and gentleness of mind, disposing men, not only to be contented and quiet themselves, but to be pliable and yielding to those around them, in order to the general good; a temper always ready, by all reasonable methods, to promote and establish the happiness of themselves, and of the world about them.[32]

Men are too ignorant, life is too difficult and dangerous for headlong or precipitate action of any kind; we should "proceed with caution and circumspection" and should curb rash desires and expectations.[33] If a man insists on having a cause or party, Shenstone says that "moderation should be his party." [34] Nothing good is to be said of extremes, not even of extreme advantages, according to Montesquieu. He is sure that mankind will always be happiest "in the possession of moderate advantages of all kinds, whether they be personal endowments, or the gifts of fortune, or the blessings arising from society or civil government." [35]

The devotion of the English to a mixed form of government showed their belief in this principle. Mixed government settles far from the extremes of any single form such as monarchy or democracy, which if allowed to develop unchecked or unbalanced would clash with the practical needs of life, which are never so simple as the single form supposes. Again English history showed the way to a lesson which the eighteenth century, proud of its ability to learn from experience, took to itself. This was the lesson of the revolutions of the seventeenth century: that of the Puritans showed the danger of democratic extremes, while the Glorious Revolution of 1688 discredited once and for all excessive devotion to monarchy.[36] The two extremities of democracy and tyranny were then feared above all.[37] Even such a liberal and advanced book as Priestley's *Essay on the First Principles of Government* frequently uses the terminology of caution, speaking of "Christian moderation," "British principles," "due caution," "gradual alterations," and "this age of moderation and good sense." No wonder that Burke should find that "extremes, as we all know, in every point which relates either to our duties or satisfactions in life, are destructive both to virtue and enjoyment." [38] Hume for his part was always "more fond of promoting moderation than zeal," [39] for moderation was bound to be of advantage to every establishment in promoting eventual acceptance entirely. "The transition," he says, "from a moderate opposition against an establishment, to an entire acquiescence in it, is easy and insensible." [40] As for actual change in public affairs, it is best to "cherish and improve our ancient government as much as possible, without encouraging a passion for . . . dangerous novelties." [41] The truth is that all change in politics is more difficult and disturbing than in private life. Good policy seems to require that if there must be innovations, they "should deviate as little as may be, from the present forms of government, and cause no *remarkable* changes in the external policy, and long established customs of the *English* nation." [42]

A story is told of the irreverence of the democrat Thomas Hollis, the moral of which may be taken as the final lesson of conservative moderation. Hollis is supposed to have engraved on a picture showing the body of Christ being removed from the cross, this profane anecdote:

A certain gentleman, perceiving his son held, and was desirous to publish some opinions contrary to the established creed of his church, pointed to a crucifix, and said to this young man, BEHOLD THE FATE OF A REFORMER! [43]

Eighteenth century followers of the Crucified One were sure that there was nothing inconsistent in avoiding a similar fate for themselves. They were satisfied with their own interpretation of his doctrine and the establishments that had grown up in and before their time. They bowed to Swift's quoted admonition in his sermon "On the Martyrdom of King Charles I": " 'Obey God and the King, and meddle not with those who are given to change.' " [44]

VII · SIGNS OF CHANGE

THE EVIDENCE for our view of English conservatism has been taken from roughly the first three quarters of the eighteenth century. The main ideas may be considered as holding their force at least until the generation before the French Revolution. Yet it was not long after the middle of the eighteenth century that signs of a new spirit began to show themselves. No doubt Mrs. Montagu would have regarded any new ideas as dangerous to the social order, but there is some truth in her timid, apprehensive letter to Mrs. Boscawen in 1757. She bemoans "the wretched state of the public," with war going on abroad, faction rife at home, the people greatly discontented. "Ah! poor England. The old King I greatly pity; is it *thus* his faithful subjects rock the cradle of declining age? . . . all is anarchy and confusion." [1]

As Chatham became triumphant in war and as England developed into a great world power it was evident that changing externals would force the need for reform of established English ways and institutions.[2] Larger affairs, and new expansion abroad as well as at home in the industrial revolution, greatly increased the complexity of political and social problems. Before this period the number of questions which had to be treated was comparatively small,[3] and a certain amiable do-nothingism could be counted on to work things out for the satisfaction of the few people who mattered. But as the reign of George III wore on, it became clear that "the old dilatory sleeping plan will no longer do." There was a time when it did not matter "whether our statesmen were asleep or awake," but life became too complex for inaction and ministers were forced to realize that a great change was coming over the country.[4] A spirit of inquiry into important questions, resulting in debate and a wider demand for a share in managing the public destiny, gradually overcame the old stagnant indifference to political questions.[5] If any single year is to be taken as the definite beginning of the new spirit, it may well be the year 1769. Much agitation occurred before this year, and throughout the 1760's many who formerly had thought their lives and positions secure began to feel that "the ground they stood on was a bog." [6] This was the beginning of open, popular meetings for the purpose of expressing opinion on great questions, certainly a sign of great progress in the democratic spirit. As Lecky says

the institution of public meeting, the creation of great political organisa-tions, the marked change in the attitude of constituents to their members, and the severe scrutiny with which the legal proceedings of Parliament were watched, were all signs of the growing ascendancy of opinion.[7]

The agitation of 1769–70 is the immediate sign of the spirit of dis-content which to Mrs. Carter "seems diffused through the nation, and it is terrible to think on what may be the consequences." [8]

Now such a liberal impulse toward questioning and reform did not grow up over night. It had doubtless been stirring in some men's minds for years. Actually there is in every age a certain amount of faultfinding in details, denunciation of the ins by the outs, objections of moralists and other viewers with alarm—the signs of restlessness and discontent, inseparable from the human predicament at any period of history. Much of this in England exists alongside a growing sharpness of objection to weaknesses in the prevailing order; it develops into a call for radical change and in some cases takes the extreme form of revolutionary de-mand for a new social order.

The poet of *Apology for the Times* in 1778 has perhaps, in his irritation with those who find fault with the *status quo,* over-simplified their activity. They are in his opinion a "stubborn restless crew" who are "never smiling in or out of place." Some-thing is always not just right to their view, "a cruel something poisons all their bliss"; they develop distorted notions and

twisted values, "plunge down a precipice to shun a feather." [9]
They have the overrefined eye of the anatomist of the state:

> With one vast piercing comprehensive view,
> Keen-ey'd he looks the constitution thro',
> Sees all her sound and all her rotten parts,
> And gratefully the mode of cure imparts;
> (Oust all the ins, and put the outs but in)
> That moment is reclaim'd the state of sin. . . .[10]

Much of the faultfinding which stirred the calm waters of the
eighteenth century is of this variety; yet more of it shows a fundamental quarrel with dominant men and principles. It is true that
the Whigs launched a regular campaign against the ministry in
1769 which they carried on for thirteen years,[11] but this does not
account for all of the criticism of those years nor for the sharp
reminders of existing faults which had already begun by the middle of the century. In 1749 David Hartley had drawn up an indictment of six counts against his age, leading him to predict the
downfall of existing government and religion in Christendom,
especially in England. Hartley finds an increase of infidelity and
atheism, especially in the upper classes; a growing lewdness in
these classes with an unbecoming self-interest; licentiousness
and contempt of authority in the lower sort; a worldliness and
neglect of duty among the clergy; and a corruption of youth by
poor education.[12]

SACRED INSTITUTIONS ATTACKED

If we ignore the political turbulence of the 1750's as being due
only to the rivalry of a few great houses,[13] we come upon John
"Estimate" Brown in 1757, denouncing all manner of national
weaknesses with emphasis on effiminate luxury. He concludes
that "our situation seems most dangerous: We are rolling to the
brink of a precipice that must destroy us." [14] After cataloguing
an impressive array of sins, Brown cries out, "Blush, *if ye can*,
my degenerate contemporaries!" [15] Attacks on corruption both in
and without the government may have owed something to Mon-

tesquieu's reservations and warnings amid all of his praise of England's institutions. He had been the first to cry "Wolf," and in the succeeding years had inspired a number of attacks on England by Englishmen who saw the beginnings of that loss of honor and virtue, that growing corruption of the legislative branch which Montesquieu had said would precede the ruin of England. These attacks took something of a regular form:

Luxury and vice permeating all classes of society; a legislature wallowing in corruption and venality; a supine administration intent on its own interests and its own way; court influence; a spirit of faction and extreme liberty amongst the people; an increasing public debt; a decadent agriculture; a standing army; these were the things that were accused of corrupting the very soul of the nation and its constitution.[16]

The famous and controversial *Letters of Junius* which appeared in the early years of the Whig attack on the ministry seem also to have gone to Montesquieu for inspiration. These are much sharper in tone than the earlier series, called *Cato's Letters,* which had appeared in English papers and journals, demanding greater respect for the liberties and rights of the people and urging progress within the existing scheme of things.[17] Junius used the exclusion of Wilkes from Parliament to attack the king and his ministers as well as the judiciary for what he considered flagrant abuses of power. He drew up a fierce indictment of existing grievances against the ins, exposing corruption, incompetence, abuses of privilege, and other varieties of misconduct. Junius is a kind of radical Tory and by no means a revolutionary, but after his bold and eloquent attack, complacency in power was bound to be less sure of itself.[18] Certainly the government under George III suffered from a very "outrage of abuse," which did all things possible "to vilify the persons of ministers, and render government contemptible and odious." [19] Even those loyal to George himself denounced his ministers as the worst and weakest men ever to mismanage and bemire a nation.[20] The king is supposed not to know the extent of the knavery, injustice, and folly which afflict his realm,[21] yet the truth is that from a condition of peace, victory and well-being at the outset of his reign, the country has fallen into discord [22] and is widely corrupted both by love of power and that "lousy disease," the love of money.[23] England has become a prey to vanity and dissoluteness, spiritual and intellectual meanness, a cynical materialism, a perversion of virtue and justice throughout society.[24] Dire prophecies are made as to the future with gloomy suggestions that well nigh any change would be an improvement.[25]

The weakness of ministries in the early years of George III shows how far England had come in so short a time from the serene and untroubled exercise of authority which had seemed so secure. No doubt the crises that George III had to face in the 1770's would have been severe even without the intrigues of his own and other factions. Yet so unstable had the once firm leadership become that in less than six years the nation was ruled by the union of Pitt and Newcastle, Newcastle alone, by Bute, Grenville, Grenville and Bedford, and finally by Rockingham; a total of six ministries in as many years.[26] Actually, when in 1783 Shelburne fell before the attack of Fox and North, a period of six weeks elapsed during which there was no government at all.[27] The temper of criticism grew more rather than less violent as Parliament came in for its share of abuse as a body of profligate, servile, and corrupt creatures of the ministry.[28] We shall not often find Burke in the role of one who wishes to emphasize England's weaknesses, yet in his "Thoughts on the Causes of the Present Discontents" in 1770, Burke is a faultfinding Whig who summarizes eloquently the case of those who say "the time is out of joint." In a work which aimed at exposing the court cabal, the double cabinet operating behind ostensible ministers to exert secret influence in a government supposed to be popular, Burke summarizes as follows:

There is something particularly alarming in the present conjuncture. There is hardly a man, in or out of office, who holds any other language. That government is at once dreaded and contemned; that the laws are despoiled of all their respected and salutary terrors; that their inaction is a subject of ridicule, and their exertion of abhorrence; that rank and office, and title, and all the solemn plausibilities of the world, have lost their reverence and effect; that our foreign politics are as much deranged as our domestic economy; that our dependencies are slackened in their affection, and loosened from their obedience; that we know neither how to yield nor how to enforce; that hardly anything above or below, abroad or at home, is sound and entire; but that disconnection and confusion, in offices, in parties, in families, in parliament, in the nation, prevail beyond the disorders of any former time: these are facts universally admitted and lamented.[29]

If all this be charged to that general faultfinding which is only to be expected, the same cannot be said of charges more directly leveled at once-sacred English institutions, nor of a new body of vigorously written liberal theory from the pens of Joseph Priestley, Richard Price, Catharine Macaulay and others. We may include Tom Paine if he is to be considered as an English writer addressing his native country from America in *The Crisis*. We should expect to see continued the sharp objections already aimed at the secret influence of the crown, with its dangerous expansion of the royal prerogative.[30] We find, also, severe challenge to the position of the gentry who fail to live up to the obligations which their privileges impose on them.[31] The seemingly unbecoming obsequiousness of Parliament to the king and his ministers is denounced as out of place for such "very silly, and very worthless mortals." [32] It is declared in 1774 that in no previous age or nation has the people's opinion of their governors fallen to a lower ebb; political and satirical writers do not hesitate to call the highest officials to their faces, "with their names printed at full length, rogues, whores, corrupters, plunderers, and enemies of their country." [33] Outspoken as the writers had become under George III, the age had heard nothing, before the publication in 1776 of Paine's *The Crisis*. The public is now offered a fierce and uninhibited vituperation against the *status quo*, especially where the affairs of England and America are involved. The entire 574 pages are alive with invective, much of it in italics and great capital letters; apparently the nature of what was said needed these conventional aids to emphasis. As if all this were being exposed for the first time, Paine tells of falsehood, tyranny, royal villainy, Hanoverian treachery, baseness, ingratitude, perjury, lawless power, violence, cruel oppression, venality, insolent contempt of the people, and pusillanimous wickedness. These crimes lead to misery, ruin, servitude, destruction, slavery, beggary, unnatural civil war, butchery, fraud, and the eventual perdition of the country.

Alongside such a fiery blast, the criticism leveled at the revolution of 1688, at the weakness of the church, even at the constitution itself, seems timidly mild. Even so England was not used to hearing that the Glorious Revolution had really deprived the people of political liberty,[34] or that it did not really intend to bring about any real reformation.[35] Nor had it been customary under the first two Hanoverians to say that the constitution seems "one of the most awkward and unmanageable fabrics which has ever been produced by human folly." [36] By 1768 it was all right to say with Priestley that the constitution is the best thing of its kind but that it needs gradual reformation.[37] In 1772 it was not radical to suggest that the true spirit of the constitution ought to be restored, "instead of bestowing studied praises upon it in the morning, and betraying and polluting it before midnight." [38] This was not the same as a despairing cry over the fear that "the diseases of our constitution are too many to yield to any remedy," while governmental corruption is so great.[39] Actually, it follows that if there is so vast an amount of corruption in government, the constitution must be itself at fault. It is difficult to see why Blackstone should have been so fulsome in his praise, when "there is hardly any thing in the condition, it ought to be in." [40] The only conclusion possible is "that the constitution is not what it should be, in spite of all the praise lavished upon it." [41]

And the same is true of that handmaiden of the state, the church. One of the most interesting books of the eighteenth century is *The Confessional* by Archdeacon Francis Blackburne. Here the church and its worldly compromises are scored in vigorous form. Like Whitehead, Blackburne believes that a true acceptance of original Christianity would overthrow the established churches. "A reformation that should reach to the extent of our deviations from the scriptures (and, when the door is once opened, who knows how far a reformation might extend?) would not stop at a few liturgical forms and ceremonies." [42] Such passages moved Priestley to praise Blackburne as one who shows what a sensible man can do even when allied with a binding, galling fixed establishment like the church.[43] Richard Price, who in this period might be joined with Priestley as Holmes and Brandeis dissenting, finds that established religions engender strife, "turn religion into a trade" and "produce hypocrisy and prevarication." [44] At least the time seems to have come when the church must submit itself and its ways to the new liberal, questioning spirit. Up to now, the establishment has fiercely defended itself against even the smallest alteration in its articles and practices.[45] It must learn to accept reasonable amendments and to admit that it is not perfect, to realize indeed that it will establish itself only the more firmly if it accedes to sensible criticism.[46]

It may be said that we are still at the level of temporary criticism of this or that single defect in the existing order. True liberal change may be held to depend rather on larger ideas for a general challenge to the rightness of the way things have always been done. If men grow optimistic as to the possibility of change for the better, or the value of efforts to improve things, we are on the way toward something quite different from the familiar conservative pessimism and caution. This general hope and belief in better things to come also began to show itself in this period before the outbreak of the French Revolution. The idea that "almost every thing, in the compass of imagination, is possible, by method and arrangement" [47] is a long way from the sober realism which says that there is no escape from the troubles of our proud and angry dust. Priestley is almost lyrically certain in 1768 that men face a glorious future for their world through the increase of knowledge, and that "whatever was the beginning of this world, the end will be glorious and paradisaical, beyond what our imaginations can now conceive." [48] The human mind is capable of limitless expansion and improvement; the human species in general is certain in the future to be enormously superior to anything known before.[49] Since future generations will be able to improve in every way upon the civil and religious institutions that are handed down to them, it behooves the present day not to throw too great obstacles in the way of posterity. All plans of policy should be such "as will easily admit of extension, and improvements of all kinds." All establishments should be only so fixed as is absolutely necessary, lest too great obstructions be thrown in the way of that inevitable improvement and progress which time must bring. All things are in a state of growth and must be free to expand; "let us be free ourselves" therefore, "and leave the blessings of freedom to our posterity." [50] Nearly twenty years later in 1787, Richard Price hails the rapid approach of the millenium.[51] Progressive improvement in human affairs is such that, even now, the life of man shows greater dignity than ever before; there are no limits to the expansion of knowledge and improvement. The world is simply outgrowing its evils and may anticipate a degree of light, virtue, and happiness never before known.[52]

If it is true that the world is rapidly ascending toward a higher life, men must be free to speculate and to develop all possible new ideas in order to hasten the general progress. Conservative anti-intellectualism is to be recognized for the backward, obstructive force that it is. The notion that theory cannot be translated into practice is shown to be "the expedient of knaves and blockheads." [53] The splendid new ideas of eighteenth century philosophers were opposed to the old conservative gloom,[54] and should be accepted as efforts toward the service and improvement of mankind. Rousseau's *Emile* for example, is in the opinion of its English translator one of those books which help the human species toward its eventual perfection. "Let us encourage, let us esteem, every one, who, like our author, ventures . . . to controvert the general opinions and customs of a misguided or mistaken world." [55] Men ought to be allowed, as Priestley said of dissenting ministers, to give their minds free play without being cramped or standardized; they should be made into wise and useful men, urged to inquire into new things "without any concern what may be the result of their inquiries." [56] All that matters is the general progress and improvement; the utility, the general advantage of a thing, its applicability to the largest number of men should alone decide its fate. [57] The time has come "when the minds of men are opening to large and generous views of things." [58] They are becoming more aware that they have certain "natural rights" and that they are equal to other men in society. [59] The common rights of the people and their interest are better understood. [60] The popular good is recognized as the end of society; "we are therefore obliged to consider ourselves as naturally equal, and to behave as such," since sovereignty is lodged equally with all men. [61] It is time to realize that only "by justice, equity, and generosity" can the nation be expected to flourish; [62] progress to better things will come through reason and free enquiry, not by violence and coercion, "but with the hearty concurrence, and at the requisition of the people." [63]

Clearly there was some approach to that level of abstract speculation, of general ideas at which conservatism has always started with alarm. Claims of natural right and equality imply that the people should be consulted as to their own welfare, and that if in their judgment they are being improperly governed, they should be allowed to replace their leaders, by force if necessary.

Now even in the days of the most complacent eighteenth century conservatives both Whigs and Tories had admitted that in some cases resistance to authority might be allowed. [64] As Hoadly remarked when trying to make up his mind on this question, "as all killing is not murther, so all resistance is not rebellion." [65] None the less if the Glorious Revolution of 1688 were to be defended at all, it had to be admitted that under certain conditions it was permissible for the governed to resist the authority of an unwanted tyrant, or at least to find moderate fault with his actions.[66] It is true that resistance should not be leveled against the lesser faults of the sovereign,[67] but should be reserved, as Hume says, for "the last refuge in desperate cases, when the public is in the highest danger, from violence and tyranny." [68] Yet Hume admits that the old doctrine of passive obedience is an absurdity and that there will come exceptional instances of tyranny and injustice which ought to be resisted in the public interest.[69] After all, the "prerogative of the king is no more sacred than the liberty of the subject," [70] and if a subject is convinced that the general good is not being served by the reigning powers, he should be free to resist and to introduce changes which he is sure will be an improvement.[71] Even under Bolingbroke's patriot king, or perhaps especially under him, the way is to be left open for complaints of abuses and redress of popular grievances without convicting the voice of the people as the king's enemy.[72]

If the right to resist could be admitted before the reign of George III, in the ensuing period of awakened liberalism it became a truism. By 1786 it could be asked,

Who differs now about the mere manner of administering equal right to all? Every one at present regards government as a trust, which must be carried into execution, according to known laws; a trust, which if unfaithfully executed, may be resisted; laws, that every one has agreed to, and all ought to obey for the common liberty of all.[73]

Even a conservative like Josiah Tucker could point out again that those in authority do not "Have any right *divine* to govern wrong"; [74] the people on their side not only have the right to prevent them from doing it, but it may even as Paley said, be their duty to resist authority when the public advantage is at stake.[75] It is still considered true in 1778 that resistance should be reserved for cases of extreme need.[76] Yet the idea of passive obedience is derided even more emphatically than by Hume; it is complete nonsense in view of the fact that the people are themselves the source of all power.[77] When rulers are wicked, the Biblical charge to obedience is invalid; it is a "manifest perversion of the text" to demand obedience without exception.[78] Actually the Bible in many places permits the deposition of tyrants, a thing which is approved by reason itself since the people are the source of all power which in turn has only their happiness for its end.[79] Consequently every man retains and cannot be deprived of "his natural right . . . of relieving himself from all oppression." [80]

Yet all this is not to say that the time has come in England when this right should be exercised and that the existing government is so intolerably vicious as to be endurable no longer. We have as yet heard no call for an outright revolution. The truth is, as Swift had said two generations before, that any people will revolt only under the most extreme provocation in fact, or under delusions fostered by wicked men for their own sinister ends.[81] This applies in particular to the English people, whose history shows that they will endure extreme oppression for long periods, before rising in protest.[82] Those among them who object to what is regularly established like to be sure that their objections will not disturb the general peace before they are offered.[83] This moderation, however, began to be questioned by such new democratic writers as Cartwright and Jebb.[84] Hume reported that "the frenzy of liberty, has taken possession of us, and is throwing everything into confusion." [85] Certainly the excitement engendered by the Wilkes episode and later on by the American Revolution released a surprising energy of liberal feeling. The Corsican struggle for independence under General Paoli found considerable sympathy in England, where refusal to interfere was roundly denounced when France took over the island in 1769.[86] With the island, of course, France acquired the infant Napoleon, destined to become the greatest enemy England had known in all her previous history.

For the first time in the eighteenth century, a number of liberal societies came into being which allied themselves with various forces of discontent and change. The Supporters of the Bill of Rights were founded in aid of Wilkes, professing to uphold the

Constitution of 1689. An outgrowth of this group was the Constitutional Society which became sympathetic to the American cause. The Society for Constitutional Information, with Cartwright, Jebb, and Capel Loft as members, was also friendly to America and was active in pushing constitutional reform. The Robinhood Society was an old organization (1613) founded to discuss religion and politics which became more liberal as the eighteenth century moved forward. Correspondence was set up between these predominantly London groups and similar societies in other cities in order to spread interest in their common causes.[87] That the people are the source and end of power,[88] that it is their right and their duty to protest and to refuse obedience when they are injured by authority and that they may resume power into their own hands if necessary—these ideas are of increasingly common occurrence in this period.[89]

What is left but to threaten revolution directly if the popular will is unsatisfied? The writer of *Political Essays* in 1772 quotes Rousseau and finds that much is to be said for periods of revolution and civil war, when in reality only a few of the privileged suffer, and when the times release immense popular energy and uncover much otherwise obscure talent.[90] James Burgh does not deny that revolutions are troublesome and dangerous, but this does not affect the right of the majority of the people to change their government at any time.[91] And Tom Paine, while he admires the English constitution as the noblest in the world,[92] sees it in 1775 perverted and abused so that all of the human rights, the privileges and liberties of the people based on reason, justice, truth, liberty and the other abstractions so dear to him, have been violated. The people are left with no choice but to extinguish the tyranny and corruption under which they groan by "another glorious and necessary REVOLUTION." [93] Paine is not alone in threatening so bold a course. Language is used in scornful condemnation of kings, and of George III in particular, such as would mean arrest and trial for treason in the next generation. It is asserted again that all kings who are not usurpers are appointed by the people and are in no sense anointed by God; this is true in spite of what is said by the clergy, who are nothing more than the creatures of kings.[94] The arrogance and despotism of kings are unwarranted by their actual quality. Since they are "always worse educated than other men, the race of them may be expected to degenerate till they be little better than idiots, as is the case already with several of them." When this happens men will be tempted "to assert their natural rights, and seize the invaluable blessings of freedom."[95] There can be no doubt that when kings cease to serve their declared purposes and fail to administer public affairs for the general good, allegiance is no longer required. A ruler who "fails to carry out his side of the bargain . . . is to be driven out of society like Cain."[96] As for the actual king of England, he will do well to remember the correct answer to certain questions: "What is a king of England? *A:* The first subject. What are the people of England? *A:* The sovereign power. Whose is the crown? *A:* Theirs who can give it away."[97]

A close scrutiny of the individual who was then king of England might very well lead to cruel satire of George's many unfortunate weaknesses. The volume of verse called *The Lousiad* some of whose poems had seen eight editions by 1789, devotes much of its energy to deflating what seems to the author an absurd flattery and adulation of a very stupid man. By the use of common and homely phraseology, Peter Pindar tries to fix George III much lower in the scheme of things than the "Lord's anointed" might wish. As we should expect, the democrat John Cartwright resents the prefix "his Majesty's" before the navy, army, revenues, courts, and kingdom, when it is so evident that the king as well as everyone else should think only of the common good.[98] George is likewise warned in highly threatening language that he must soon accede to the people's wishes and dismiss the corrupt and treacherous men around him. Otherwise,

they will be apt to exercise what God and nature have given them, the right of punishing unfaithful servants, and substituting others in their place. What will become of your majesty in this dreadful shock? I tremble to think of the consequences, when the people is ranged on one side, and your ministry on the other. It is not every one that will distinguish between master and servant in such rencounters.[99]

The king's habit of referring in turn to the people, army, and nation as "my" possessions, raises doubt as to the real owner of these things. The question may need a revolution before it is decided:

> Hark! the glad sounds revive of me, and mine,
> And stale prerogative of right divine!
> ONE REVOLUTION RAISED YOU TO THE CROWN;
> ANOTHER REVOLUTION MAY—DETHRONE.[100]

It is easy to see now that such a revolution was remote in the England of George III. Yet conservative fear is able to find reason for its alarms at almost any period of history. Leaving for the moment the agitation over Wilkes, it must be admitted that the people seemed at times on the verge of taking the law into their own hands. In 1767 popular discontent was violently expressed over disputed elections and the high cost of living. Grafton had brought on the violence of electioneering by his methods of obtaining a majority in Commons; this, joined with the bitterness over high prices for food then prevalent, caused an outbreak of riots and disorders in which lives were lost and military aid had to be summoned.[101] In 1769 it was reported that a general distrust of government had spread throughout England; the cry of liberty had gone forth, and riot marched in the face of day, defying authority, attacking public order and decency—all inspired by selfish and ambitious men who saw a chance to promote their own vicious designs.[102] This spirit of discontent in the year 1770 assumes the aspect of a kind of demoniacal possession, a devil which has to be cast out. The people have seen too great an increase of wealth for a few and of poverty for themselves to be willing to return to their former submissiveness and sobriety of temper. Hence their rebellious "demon." [103] By 1780, the year of the Gordon riots, there is evident a "corruption of manners, contempt of order, disturbing the public tranquility, violating men's properties, and insulting their persons in the open streets," along with a certain bold contempt for the law and a dangerous licentiousness among the common people, "who have no visible or honest way of getting their livelihood." [104] The ease with which great masses of men can be led into violent action in a time of discontent, even though the action they take is unrelated to their actual grievances, was dramatically shown in the notorious Gordon riots. The unprotected state of English life and property in this period emerges from accounts of these riots, showing that conservative fear might not have been entirely unfounded. Breaking out in protest against measures planned for greater tolerance of Roman Catholics, the riots, named after their leader Lord George Gordon, were responsible for the death of 285 persons and the injury of 173 others, not including those buried in falling ruins, others who drank themselves to death amid the general frenzy, or those who died of their wounds.[105]

OUTLETS FOR DISCONTENT

Yet when every allowance is made for popular discontent and the trend away from early Hanoverian stagnation and complacency, the truth is that England's growing liberalism found expression in so many other ways that a complete break with the existing order was never found necessary. For the energy which in other places expressed itself in revolution, the English found more than sufficient outlet in various movements of thought and feeling as well as political events. Among these we choose the humanitarianism of the time as seen in the antislavery movement; the Benthamite doctrines leading to legal reform; the ideas of Adam Smith and their counterpart in the industrial revolution; and the powerful impact of Wesleyanism upon religious thought and feeling. Among political events, our points may be sufficiently made from the Wilkes affair; the growing movement for parliamentary reform; the reception of the American Revolution; and finally as most important of all, the English response to the French Revolution. We shall find that in spite of, and partly because of the immense release of potentially revolutionary energy in these various forms, English conservatism held its ground and in the fateful days of the French struggle showed that it was stronger than ever.

After the long slumbers of England for two generations at least, with a period of rest from the troubles of the seventeenth century long enough to quiet nerves and heal wounds, the time came for a reawakening. In the later decades of the eighteenth century a sense of philanthropy, of justice, and altruism manifested itself in devotion to various humane causes.[106] Better government for India, the founding of missionary societies, the improvement of education, increase and betterment of hospital facilities, humane treatment of animals, the reform of prisons, and wiser treatment of the poor were some of the causes in which humanitarianism expressed itself.[107] We find occasional indignation at subhuman laboring conditions and neglect of the poor, after the manner of the copious protests in the nineteenth century.[108] With an almost Carlylean belief in our common humanity, a writer in 1775 is able to plead for the impoverished and underprivileged masses, in the name of "humanity, religion, compassion, virtue, honour, decency, love to our brethren, the very frame of our composition, and bowels of our nature."[109] The activities of the Clapham Sect were inspired also by philanthropic feeling. This was a group of fervent Christians who rose above the ordinary barriers of class, creed, nationality, and race to interest themselves in projects which they believed were for the common good. They met in the library of Henry Thornton at Clapham and included, among others, Granville Sharp, Zachary Macaulay, James Stephen, William Wilberforce, and, for all practical purposes, Hannah More.[110]

Much the most important and widespread of these humanitarian activities was the movement to abolish slavery. This is shown by a mere listing of the various men of influence and power who gave it their support at various times. Among them are John Wesley, Samuel Johnson, Granville Sharp, William Wilberforce, Jeremy Bentham, Tom Paine, William Robertson, William Pa-

ley, and the Abbé Raynal through the English translation of his
History of the Indies. After 1783 the tempo of antislavery agitation increased, with the help of James Ramsay, Thomas Clark-
son, Sir Charles Middleton, the Quakers as an organized group,
James Stephen, Zachary Macaulay, the poets William Cowper and
William Blake, John Newton, Hannah More, Bishop Porteus,
and, in its earlier stages, William Pitt the younger. In spite of
previous agitation, scarcely any action had been taken against
slavery or the slave trade until the end of the Seven Years War in
1763. Now the feeling against traffic in human beings grew and
might well have succeeded in abolishing the slave trade if the
American Revolution had not cut off the colonies, thus making
the illicit slave trade very profitable.[111] At least the Somerset decision in 1772 had abolished slavery throughout the British Isles
themselves, and encouraged the humanitarian forces by one considerable victory.[112] After the American war, the time was ripe
for organized effort and the leaders against slavery intensified
their attack. Typical of the intensity of their feeling and conviction were the writings of Granville Sharp, who had never ceased
to cry out on religious and humanitarian grounds against this
violation of the brotherhood of man. Anticipating the belief in
human dignity and oneness which inspired much of the great literature of the nineteenth century, Sharp called for a reformation
in England's attitude to slavery, an institution which was a violation of the dignity of man and which, if persisted in, was certain
to bring down upon the nation some severe retribution, "some
heavy judgment from Almighty God upon these kingdoms." [113]

At this same period was begun the program of legal reform advocated by Jeremy Bentham that was to be so influential in the
nineteenth century. While in its early phases Bentham's two-
point program of legal change according to the principle of utility and the systematic codification of civil and penal law was
not revolutionary, it became after the French Revolution the
basis for an attack on the whole political structure of England.
Benthamism became one with the liberal, democratic, reforming

spirit when its leader was converted to democratic radicalism by James Mill. In the late eighteenth century however, utility was not as yet radical save in the hands of Godwin, Paine, and Mackintosh for a time. Under Burke, utility was in the last degree conservative, and Bentham at the outset favored a high degree of necessary restraint and security rather than liberty and equality.[114] Like all English reformers, Bentham began by attacking specific abuses in the penal law, seeming to oppose only in detail the existing order, which in most ways was looked upon as satisfactory. Yet one feature of Bentham's program was almost radically upsetting, at least as it applied to courts and judges. Since the time of Solon in ancient Greece, a demand that the law should be systematically written down and codified, arranged logically and simply so that it could be known and understood by everyone to whom it applied—this demand has always been potentially disturbing to the *status quo.* To leave the law unwritten gives more power and influence to a special body or class which alone knows what the law is and can interpret it at will, not necessarily for the general utility. Law in this case is "common law," the ancient jurisprudence of the courts, known only to experts in its mysteries. Thus law, in order to serve the common good, the general utility, has to be drawn up and written down systematically. Not only must it be written, but simplified and expressed in such a way that anyone can consult it according to his needs. Bentham's plea for codification, then, would make the law enormously wider in scope and more liberal in application, so that it could not be used by a special body for its own purposes.[115]

The liberal economic ideas of Adam Smith also coincided with the enormous release of energy and human capacity in the Industrial Revolution which these ideas justified and encouraged. Yet in themselves the doctrines of Smith were politically and socially conservative.[116] He is not theoretically planning to reconstruct society nor does he seem to imply that the existing order is not the only one conceivable. The doctrine of letting things alone "implies acquiescence in the existing order, and is radically opposed to a demand for a reconstruction of society." [117] Smith's doctrines of free enterprise and unhampered trade did not cause a reform of practice, but were only a summary or justification of what was already being done and what had already been expressed to some extent in writing.[118] In politics Smith was highly doubtful of reform, after the manner of his friend Hume, remaining for the most part a skeptical Whig.[119] *The Wealth of Nations* as a whole was not far in advance of average opinion which supported the mild changes evidently necessary and possible in the late eighteenth century. "Any thinking man would find in it the ideas which he himself was already beginning to form, under the pressure of historical events, and with the tacit and permanent collaboration of all enlightened people." [120]

Yet if Smith did not encourage a new social and political order, the ideas to which he gave classical expression were an immense stimulus to new economic energy. If in politics the individual was not to show initiative, in free economic activity he was given every encouragement.[121] The vast new opportunities created by the immense commercial and industrial expansion of England made for a much greater social mobility; men could alter their social status by successful enterprise, and many did so.[122] The Industrial Revolution opened the doors to adventure, industry and enterprise, so that many individuals could rise by their own efforts. On borrowed money or small personal savings, men succeeded in the struggle upward by reason of enormous labor and determined ambition. They rose from their subordinate position in society, and became in time part of the *status quo* against which their ambitious energy had been a protest in the first place.[123] Although in the course of time the Industrial Revolution increased discontent by making the condition of the masses even worse, yet at the outset it gave a chance to "be something in society" to a large number of persons who might otherwise have grown rebellious, and so it offered a satisfaction to what might have been dangerous revolutionary energy.

Thus, aside from the fact that England had already had her

revolutions in the seventeenth century, she could maintain her conservatism, because another kind of revolution in the late eighteenth century released enough of her power, liberality, and inventiveness. Here in industry and commerce no change was too radical to attempt as England led the way from the old to the new machine economy. The industrial revolution gave to restless, adventurous, and inventive persons a completely free hand to conquer new worlds without in any way endangering the existing order. Actually, the scheme of Locke set up after the revolution of 1688, whereby government became the protector of property, made certain that what a man earned by his new enterprise in business he could keep. It insured the continuance of the power of the few over the many,[124] and had as its obvious corollary the let-alone principle as advocated by Adam Smith and others. Thus the men who might have had the restlessness, personal force, and discontent to start a political revolution against an order which had failed to give them full scope for their talents, now had abundant opportunity to show what they could do in the wide open industrial arena.

The same mixture of conservatism and radicalism is to be found in the powerful movement of thought and feeling called Wesleyanism. Wesley shows again that in the England of his day, unlike the situation in France,[125] one might be a reformer in one sense and a dogged conservative in another. Yet Wesley's triumph showed how great was the sense of moral and social evil in England, waiting only for an energetic leader to give it direction. Wesleyanism, too, released and inspired a vast amount of progressive energy.[126] The conscience of England was stirred and its better feelings touched so that an effort to improve social well-being was inevitable.[127] The Church of England was particularly affected by Wesleyan example. New devotion, fervent philanthropy, a high standard of clerical duty and behavior aided in changing completely the inertia of the established church.[128] Then, too, the theology of Methodism with its emphasis on the value of the individual soul, the need of the individual's effort to save his own soul, the possibility of Christian experience for all men regardless of station in life—these ideas were democratic in implication. That this was not lost on the upper classes entirely is shown by the well-known story of the Duchess of Buckingham and her letter to the Countess of Huntingdon, a supporter of early Wesleyanism. The Duchess, unable to forget her origin as the daughter of James II, although illegitimate, thanks the Countess for information as to Methodist preaching. Yet

these doctrines are most repulsive and strongly tinctured with imperti- nence and disrespect toward their superiors in perpetually endeavouring to level all ranks and do away with all distinctions, as it is monstrous to be told that you have a heart as sinful as *the common wretches that crawl on the earth*. This is highly offensive and insulting, and I cannot but wonder that your Ladyship should relish any sentiments so much at variance with high rank and good breeding.[129]

This assumption of equality appealed to the forlorn multi- tudes, the forgotten men who now were made to realize that they too were important and valuable in the eyes of God.[130] Wesley created the mood or context of liberal activity by this doctrine as well as by his preparation for democracy which went farther than he himself realized or perhaps desired. He believed that so- ciety would improve through transforming the individual from within, and to this transformation he contributed not only his spiritual doctrines leading to charity and brotherhood and coop- eration, but by the training given in school. The Methodists were among the first to teach writing to the poor as well as reading; public speaking, oratory, organization, leadership, training in the duties and responsibilities of citizenship were learned from the Methodists by a large number of people who had never had such opportunities before and who were destined to rise with their new economic and political opportunities. The Wesleyan move- ment itself was a "democracy of service, fellowship, aspiration and attainment." [131] Wesleyanism likewise encouraged the partic- ular virtues of sobriety and industry which were the mark of that middle class soon to become so powerful in England. The doctrines of hard work, individual effort and self-help were especially suited to middle class energy, which Wesley stimulated on all sides. The entire project of Methodism in method and content was a new enterprise in society, making for better and more vigorous citizens if not better rebels.[132]

Wesley himself gave the best example of his precepts in action by moving toward the solution of most of the important social problems of his day. He believed in individual effort especially in the relief of the poor. He gave away himself about £30,000 during his life for poor relief, and constantly agitated to persuade others to help the poor; he organized societies and set up loan funds for this purpose.[133] Wesley fought mightily against slavery, press gangs, war (which he abhorred), the hoarding of wealth, bribery and corruption at elections, rotten boroughs, cruel prison conditions, the mistreatment of Ireland, unhealthful conditions of life and work for the poor, lack of education, and in general the economic exploitation of the masses. He preached human brotherhood and demanded help and kindness of men to one another, along with all possible self-help and initiative. His threefold economic doctrine—earn all you can, save all you can, give all you can—is governed by Christian principles throughout.

Wesley therefore created an atmosphere which in the course of time extended beyond his first limits. He could not liberalize human action at one level without also preparing for its release wherever needed. Thus to claim initiative for the individual in religion and economics and humanitarian reform was bound to encourage political action.[134] The concealed logic of Wesleyanism was to attack the assumptions of eighteenth century conservatism at various levels. By encouraging the laboring masses to initiative and enterprise, Wesleyanism fought the idea that the masses were to remain poor and economically helpless. Individuals were encouraged to rise in life, so that the old social immobility was undermined. The movement also fought against the feeling of inferiority of the masses; it encouraged self-respect and the individual's effort to be important in society. It developed group action, spurred mental activity and a new feeling of responsibility instead of a dull acceptance of low status. Wesleyanism also made enthusiasm more respectable, creating the mood for energetic prosecution of new causes and ideas. It undermined the old Calvinistic assumptions that things are divinely ordained in a fixed way, and claimed that men were equal in spiritual status with the same chance for salvation. Wesleyanism combated also the Mercantilist views of the necessary exploitation of the lower classes, by suggesting a greater practical equality. Thus by making new values of the spirit and personality of man supreme, the movement was compelled by its character to be a liberal force.[135]

If the context of liberalism was created by these and other movements, the new spirit showed itself in external events as well. The most spectacular episode of the first years under George III was the affair of John Wilkes and the Middlesex election. Wilkes was arrested for seditious libel and although he was eventually elected to a seat in Parliament from Middlesex on four occasions the House refused to let him take his place. Wilkes was a man of lurid personal morality, a member of the Medmenham brotherhood and partaker of its secret debaucheries, personally ugly, foolishly extravagant and ostentatious in his behavior. On both moral and political grounds he outraged the complacent society of his day. It was not because of his vices, however, that Wilkes became the object of persecution, but because he became a symbol of resistance to tyranny and a center around which popular enthusiasm might gather. Even Burke admits this.[136] In addition to an obscene parody of Pope's *Essay on Man,* called an *Essay on Woman,* Wilkes had written for *The North Briton* articles that were liberal in character for that time. Here and elsewhere Wilkes struggled for certain fundamental rights and liberties—freedom of the press, trial by jury, the accountability, as Locke had ruled, of governmental ministers to the people, the punishment of abuse of power in ministers when this power has been obtained from the people. Wilkes ridiculed as well the administration of Lord Bute, denounced corrupt ministers, praised the American colonies and their aspirations, defended the revolution of 1688, denounced all signs of Tory Jacobitism, condemned the political spoils system, and after his arrest in 1763 identified his own problem with the general cause of popular liberty. Matters were brought to a climax with the publication of the famous *North Briton Number 45*. Here Wilkes stimulated the popular imagination by sharply demanding adherence to the constitution which had curtailed the prerogative of the crown and which had emphasized what was not to be forgotten, that the people also have their prerogative.[137] It was a cry for liberty not to be endured by the *status quo*. Like the American agitation in its time, the Wilkes affair forced a conflict over such fundamentals as the meaning of representation, taxation, and liberty, so that the Whig policy toward America could not be separated from the attitude to Wilkes and the radicals at home.[138] The existing order, in which conservative fear is always a strong influence, felt obliged to act. The last warrant issued for Wilkes's arrest says that he is to be taken into custody

for being the author and publisher of a most infamous and seditious libel, intitled the North Briton, number 45, tending to inflame the minds and alienate the affections of the people from his majesty, and excite them to traitorous insurrections against the government.[139]

Wilkes's subsequent adventures alternating between forced exile in France where he had fled to escape prison, and his repeated reelection to Parliament together with the refusal of the House to let him take his place all tended to arouse the people who saw in this treatment a threat to their own liberties:

The whole kingdom in a manner therefore took fire at once,—all joined in an unanimous protection of him, under the idea of defending, *in his person, their own liberties,* and the infringed principles of the constitution. The more government persisted in their attacks and persecutions of him—the more united, the more violent, the more inflamed the nation became.[140]

At Wilkes's elections, uncontrollable riots and tumults broke out, to the dismay of helpless authority. Aggravated by hard times and social distress, with many idle and reckless men at large, the spirit of insubordination and violence grew under this stimulus to popular enthusiasm.[141] For a time it seemed that all the bulwarks to order would give way, as the spirit of unrest increased nearly to the point of revolution. Nothing within the memory of social observers of the time had appeared so terrible and alarming as these outbreaks that surpassed the worst excesses of the Sacheverell mobs.[142] On the morning of the election which followed Wilkes's dramatic return from outlawed exile and his first defeat, the roads were lined with vast numbers of people. They took possession of all avenues leading to the place of election, and compelled all who tried to pass to declare for Wilkes and to wear a blue cockade with the name of Wilkes and number 45. For two days the town was at the mercy of his followers, and when he was returned by a huge majority, the excitement broke out again. The people paraded the streets and forced everyone to light up his house as if in celebration of a great national victory in war.[143]

Thus the affair of Wilkes and the Middlesex election kept alive the excitement which had been aroused in the nation by the treatment of the elder Pitt; in the popular view, Pitt had been robbed of a proper chance for national service by a selfish oligarchy and a foolish king who controlled a weak and corrupt representation. So also Wilkes was made a symbol of the frustration of the expressed will of the people by wicked ministers and a servile Parliament.[144] His case became very important in the liberal movement toward reform, far beyond the significance of Wilkes as an individual. His conviction for seditious libel led to Fox's act, demanding that a jury, not the judge, be given the final decision in accusations of libel. This and Wilkes's protection of the printers who had printed the House of Commons debates in 1771 greatly advanced freedom of the press. The press could become a means of public education and could show the people what was really going on in Parliament. The refusal of the House of Commons to let Wilkes take his seat, although clearly elected by a majority of his constituents, led to questioning of a body which could thus defy the popular will. Since the quarrel with America had already led people to examine the proper meaning of representation, the Wilkes agitation on somewhat the same issue was a help in an organized demand for reform of Parliament which continued in greater or less degree for the rest of the century. Even the personal extravagance of Wilkes and the impossible burden of debts accumulated by him worked for the good of the liberal cause. His difficulties inspired the formation under John Horne (later Horne Tooke) of the Supporters of the Bill of Rights (1769), who came to his aid because he was suffering in their view for the popular benefit. This group became in its time an important force, emphasizing once more that the troubles of Wilkes were means to a liberal end.[145]

The dangerous appeal by Wilkes to public opinion placed the Whigs in an awkward and contradictory position; their conservatism now violated the principles which their party originally had existed to uphold. The Whig revolution of 1688 established the party as upholders of fundamental rights, but having now been long in power themselves they represented the *status quo,* which it became their interest to maintain. They did not wish to reform their own regime by methods similar to those by which they had changed things under James II; this would interfere with their privileges; so they were determined to suppress any possible trouble such as they themselves had once made in preparing their own way to power. The case of Wilkes shows that they would rather violate a principle of 1688 by imposing their will on the electorate than allow the presence in Parliament of someone who might disturb the possession of what they had so long enjoyed. But they seemed to overreach themselves; for the times had changed sufficiently to make possible a serious and determined effort to reform Parliament and to correct the more glaring anomalies of the Whig era.

As England changed from an agricultural nation to a commercial one, the serious defects of her parliamentary representation

became more obvious. During the industrial revolution the weight
of population shifted from the south and east toward the north
and west, so that in the course of time the balance of representation was completely upset.[146] It was plain enough to a man with
Swift's sense of the absurd and his discernment of what is irrational and silly, that the system of representation was already
ridiculous in his time. In Swift's judgment decayed boroughs
ought to have been extinguished since the members returned
for them did not represent anyone at all, and since several large
towns full of industrious men were totally unrepresented.[147] Later
on the obstruction of the elder Pitt by Parliament, or by the men
who controlled it, led to considerable doubt as to whether the
House of Commons was a good representative assembly. Pitt
stirred the nation with his vigorous appeal, but he was unable
seriously to upset the rule of the parliamentary managers. He
could not create a situation in which actual reform became a
popular measure, since the means of communication were limited;
geographical disunity was so marked that it was very difficult to
diffuse political information or to make the nation familiar with a
new idea.[148]

Yet by the year 1774, the author of a *Review of the Present
Administration* speaks of agitators who are spreading false alarms
to create dissatisfaction among the people. They have followers
in England "where the most illiterate are taught to think it wisdom to speculate on political affairs, and are at liberty to form
their own notions and principles of right and wrong." [149] It is
certainly true that along with the usual denunciation of what
was wrong in the nation, the inequities of parliamentary representation had begun to be exposed.[150] The customary array of
vices, gambling, bribery, distress of the poor, and other national
scandals are insignificant compared with this one great evil of an
irregular parliamentary system.[151] Liberal writers like John Cartwright, Catharine Macaulay, James Burgh, and David Williams
make full and heated analyses of all the prevailing abuses and
anomalies of the representation. England is told that only the in-

terests of corruption are served, not those of the public.[152] The idea of Locke that a free constitution may render Parliament the representation of property and not of the free and virtuous people is denounced.[153] Along with the most specific recommendations as to how reform should be accomplished, the complacency of England is shocked by such an outcry over the existing falsehood, bribery, and corruption amid its unjust and unequal scheme ·of representation: "blush! blush! O England: shed tears of contrition! put on sack-cloth! and hide thy dishonoured head in the ashes of humiliation!" [154] The people are shown to be without any real control of their affairs; they are inadequately represented, they are not taken into account by their leaders who profit from the anomalies which victimize those for whom authority should be most solicitous.[155] The supposedly perfect constitution is shown to be a ptochocracy or government of beggars, since a few beggarly boroughs elect the most important part of the government; this in turn becomes a juntocracy with power in the hands of a minister and his crew, since the court directs the beggars whom they should choose.[156] The vaunted system of checks and balances is unsound, since there is no reason why there should be any curtailment of the power of the people.[157] Actually if the constitution is faithfully interpreted, it will be seen that it is treason to deprive any subject of his natural right to share in the legislature.[158] The fact is that hardly fifty members of the House of Commons can be said really to represent their constituents in the manner called for by the constitution.[159]

The times were equally fertile of plans for the improvement of all these things which were wrong. Three main tendencies may be distinguished, in the order of their radicalism. The conservatives, represented by Burke and Rockingham, hoped to reduce ministerial influence in Parliament and elections. Burke's bill for economical reform expressed their views which involved no change in the electoral system. A second group, regarded as dangerous by the first, favored a reformation of the existing electorate by such measures as shorter Parliaments, larger membership for the counties, and perhaps the abolition of some rotten boroughs. The vote would not be given to the unrepresented population at all, but the old electorate would gain greater control, especially in the counties. The third group of radicals offered a program completely departing from the old representation of property. At times expressing itself in extremely complicated and sweeping plans of reform, this segment of opinion wished to insure representation of persons and called for universal suffrage, annual Parliaments, the end of all ministerial corruption, the insurance to all men of their constitutional and in some cases their more revolutionary human rights. "Thus the three groups may be considered as demanding, respectively, reform through the existing parliament, reform through the existing electorate, and reform through the enfranchisement of the unrepresented population." [160]

In actual political affairs, the fight for reform waxed and waned. The question was whether the moderate economic reformers would have to give way to the demands of the more extreme parliamentary group. The radicals had from the outset achieved a greater respectability than might have been supposed possible. The Dukes of Richmond and Roxburgh, the Earls of Selkirk, Derby, and Effingham, the Lords Surrey, Kinnard, and Semphill, along with eminent commoners like Pitt, Granville Sharp, and R. B. Sheridan, associated themselves with the radical cause.[161] Yet many gave mere lip service to reform, thinking that they might use it for their own purposes. The official Whigs in turn simply wanted to obstruct in some way the corruption which the court and its agents could use against them.[162] The moderate economic reformers under Burke and Rockingham tried from 1778 to 1782 for the success of their program of economic reform. Once it was accomplished, they were satisfied to have stopped the worst forms of influence and corruption. To others was left the difficult task of achieving a sound improvement in the make-up of Parliament. The several societies and associations, enthusiastic and devoted individuals like Christopher Wyvill, and the parliamentary group under the younger Pitt continued the work begun by the earlier advocates of reform. The difficulty lay in the fact that the reformers could not trust the Whigs, who might declare in vague terms for reform but could never be persuaded to pass any important laws to carry it out.[163]

At this stage in 1782, young Pitt entered upon his public career as a declared champion of parliamentary reform. On May 7, 1782, Pitt moved in the House that a committee be appointed to inquire into the present state of the representation, to report back to the House, and to suggest steps for a solution of the problem. His move lost by only 20 votes, the best showing the reformers were able to make until 1831. Meanwhile the Society for Constitutional Information was more active than ever in its propaganda for reform. It tried to appeal to all classes down to the tradesman and artisan. The various county associations also got under way once more, with circulars, letters, and petitions. Counties and cities by the score aired their grievances and made their recommendations. Encouraged by this support, Pitt tried again on May 7, 1783. Yet the House refused even to vote on Pitt's resolutions directly, so small was the effect of popular demand. However, on the fall of the Fox-North coalition, Pitt became Prime Minister on December 19, 1783. By 1785 Pitt and the reformers thought that they were ready to make their most powerful move for victory. Preceded by the usual barrage of petitions from around the country, Pitt moved to introduce his bill on April 18, 1785. His moderate proposal called only for abolition of 36 rotten boroughs by purchase, and a redistribution of the resulting 72 seats among the counties and unrepresented or inadequately represented towns. Even this lukewarm bill was not permitted to be introduced, losing out by 74 votes. After three attempts, Pitt abandoned the cause and never again risked his position for parliamentary reform.[164] The question was kept alive through various other proposals in the next two years, and by 1788 the movement for reform was still general with much agitation continuing on its behalf.[165]

Reform was to some extent connected with England's dispute

with her American colonies; both things raised the question of representation and emphasized that the existing House of Commons was not really representative either of colonial interests or of the majority of Englishmen at home.[166] In any case the troubles with America released a flood of liberal opinion sympathetic with the revolutionary cause. This is not to say that the American war was generally opposed in England at the outset. As Thackeray reports, in 1775 the address in favor of coercing the colonies was carried by 304 to 105 in Commons and by 104 to 29 in the House of Lords.[167] English opinion was at first behind the government, with the country gentry, the universities, the church, and Wesleyanism strongly anti-American. For three years the majority on the address never fell below 150.[168] Until Burgoyne's defeat the American war was popular and the majority did not really oppose it until Cornwallis finally ceased to resist.[169] Again, sympathy with America was not always a sign of liberal republicanism. One who thought the behavior of England to America unjust, might still say, "I would not be understood to mean . . . that I am a friend to *Republican principles.* I detest them." [170] Others might attack the American war simply to discredit the king who was prosecuting it and to curb his influence. Some were angry at the incompetence which had missed so many chances of victory, and so they turned against the American policy.[171] Merchants and gentry who suffered economically from the war might find fault with the government's policy on economic grounds without any interests in the rights of man or political theory.[172] Some took issue with the war because they felt that actually England needed America,[173] that the despotic English policy would ruin both the colonies and the mother country,[174] and that America should be independent so that England might profit in trade with her, using America as a vast new market for English goods.[175] Burke, too, found that the colonies should be conciliated for reasons of expediency. As befits the realistic, anti-intellectual conservative, Burke hated all talk of abstract right to demand tribute from the colonies. In his opinion it was simply bad policy to alienate them; much profit had been gained from them in the past and would be gained in future if they remained contented.[176]

These views of realistic or self-interested conservatism, with other more moderate efforts to compose the differences between England and America on a Christian basis [177] or to see both sides of the dispute with some leaning toward the English side [178] are in contrast with a considerable body of more liberal opinion. This was said to have encouraged America to be firm in resistance to England which has seen "publications here in their favour, . . . speeches, protests . . . regularly transmitted in print, and sometimes in manuscript, justifying all their proceedings, ever since they have been in a state of revolt." [179] These publications are attacks on the English policy toward America, defenses of the American position, appeals to the traditional liberties guaranteed by the British Constitution, pleas for justice, moderation, and abstract human rights.[180] Most of these stop short of the denunciation of the government by the reforming James Burgh who scores the shameful mistreatment of the colonies,[181] or even of Wilkes whose speeches on America defend the justice of the colonial cause and find that it is also the cause of all free Englishmen.[182] None compare in eloquence or liberal fervor with the views of Thomas Paine in *The Crisis* and in *Common Sense,* which also found its way to England. Along with the familiar vituperation against all that England has done to America, *The Crisis* reprints the *Declaration of Independence* with Jefferson's revolutionary theories and charges against the king for all to see.[183] Paine calls upon English lovers of liberty not only to refuse to bear arms against Americans but to resist by force those authorities responsible for the impending ruin.[184] *Common Sense* demolishes all arguments for reconciliation with England, justifies America on all counts, and unites her cause with the universal desire for human freedom of which America is the greatest hope.[185]

But the most enthusiastic and popular of the English friends of America was Richard Price. His *Observations on the Nature*

of Civil Liberty appeared in February, 1776, and became enormously popular. Not only did Price offer an eloquent defense of
liberty and high praise of America's struggle on its behalf, he
showed as well how imperfect liberty was in England itself because of defects in representation. Thus the English at home were
shown to have much the same case against their governors as the
Americans. In a few days several thousand copies were sold. In
six weeks six editions had appeared, and a cheap popular edition
was brought out at sixpence to reach a wider audience. The then
enormous number of 60,000 copies were sold within a year of
publication, spreading Price's views about America "which every
popular fool in the kingdom, from his Grace on the bench, down
to the scullion in the kitchen, have times innumerable, chimed
through all their changes." [186] Nearly ten years later (in 1785)
Price published his *Observations on . . . American Revolution,*
a lyrical tribute to the idea of progress. Mankind is on the way
to better things and will not cease until the restoration of that
paradisaical condition described in the Mosaic History. America
offers the greatest hope of this upward trend; indeed Price feels
that "next to the introduction of Christianity among mankind,
the American Revolution may prove the most important step in
the progressive course of human improvement." [187] Let there be
established in America then, a system of perfect liberty with all
the old shackles of civil and religious tyranny thrown off; let the
fetters of reason be destroyed and let America be "a country
where truth and reason shall have fair play, and the human powers find full scope for exerting themselves, and for showing how
far they can carry human improvement." [188]

The American cause finally triumphed, and the feeling which
it had inspired in England expressed itself in other forms, particularly in favor of a change in parliamentary representation.
Soon the outbreak of the French Revolution in 1789 released a
new wave of liberal enthusiasm in England, this time far more
intense and widely expressed, since at first England herself did
not seem to be involved. The French outbreak made an enor-

mous appeal to the young in particular, for now all their visions and dreams seemed immediately possible. As Hazlitt said in *The Feeling of Immortality in Youth,* the inspiration of France excited an enormous hope in men just coming into their early maturity to whom the most inspiring and limitless prospects were suddenly disclosed. There seemed to be something in the air men breathed which gave promise of wonderful things to come:

> There seems an ardent spirit, to my mind,
> A revolution spirit, 'mongst mankind:
> A spark will now set kingdoms in a blaze,
> That would not fire a barn in former days.[189]

It was all so modern, and everything in the age seemed bound to be an exception to all other ages.[190]

Aside from this excitement of the new and promising and limitless, the French uprising appealed to many Englishmen because they thought it was like their own revolution of a century earlier and inspired by much the same ideas.[191] France seemed bent only on changing an absolute to a constitutional monarchy, in short on imitating England's example. Since this left nothing to be desired, it was only natural that France's effort should be applauded by a nation which had successfully endured a similar ordeal. And certainly any people who wanted to be like the English ought to be encouraged. In 1789 was published *The Bastille,* "as performed seventy-nine nights successively at the Royal Circus" in London. The title page tells of a speech inserted into the play, supposed to have been given to French troops on the destruction of the Bastille:

> The administration of the laws of England is the first boast of the inhabitants of that island.
>
> O my dear countrymen, what a rapturous prospect now opens itself to our view.
>
> Twenty-four millions of inhabitants, in the finest and most fertile country in the world, regaining at once their natural rights, and starting into liberty,—unspeakable delight; we shall henceforth share the palm of glory, and the blessings of liberty with the immortal sons of freedom— Englishmen! [192]

This feeling that the French and English revolutions, just a century apart, were more or less the same, continued from the formation of the National Assembly in 1789 to the flight to Varennes in June, 1791. For these two years, in spite of some excesses, the revolutionists tried to work out some constitutional government which both people and king could accept. The French seemed bent on following the example of constitutional progress and reconstruction which the English had offered before them.[193] As late as November, 1791, a liberal English visitor to Paris was able to praise the French constitution as a finished product superior to that of England:

You have read their new constitution: can anything be more admirable? We, who pretend to be free, you know, have no constitution at all . . . as to modern politics, and the principles of the constitution, one would think that half the people in Paris had no other employment than to study and talk about them. . . . You may now consider their government as completely settled, and a counter-revolution as utterly impossible.[194]

In 1791 also, a member of the Society of the Friends of the Constitution, one John Oswald, translated into English *The Spirit of the French Constitution* by Collot d'Herbois, which presented the new French dispensation as a model of tolerant and brotherly cooperation for the good of all.

Even some English statesmen expressed approval of the French Revolution at its outset. Parliamentary reformers were freshly inspired, and began to base their claims more on abstract rights and justice than on practical expediency. They made new converts among the Whigs and achieved greater dynamic force from their French inspiration.[195] In 1788 the English reform societies (which existed in most of the larger cities and towns) were encouraged by the centenary of the English revolution to keep alive the principles of 1688. The centenary was celebrated throughout the nation, especially by the London Revolution Society, which so awakened itself and clarified its principles that it was able to take the lead in corresponding with interested societies in France.

Copious exchange of letters continued until well into 1792. Mutual praise and congratulation, messages of good will, sympathy and hope continued back and forth so long as the French seemed moderate in their intentions. Later on, after the correspondence had ceased and the French Revolution had discredited itself by bloody excesses, the English reform societies were accused of violent Jacobin sympathies, of which there is no sign whatever among them.[196] Meanwhile prominent individuals such as Lord Lansdowne, Lord Stanhope, John Erskine, Pitt himself, Romilly, Sheridan and Fox expressed sympathy in varying degrees with the French Revolution. In his defense of the French patriots in February, 1790, Sheridan spoke directly after Burke in the House of Commons and said regretfully that he "differed decidedly from that right honourable gentleman in almost every word he had uttered respecting the French Revolution." [197] Fox too differed from Burke, and on that memorable and tearful occasion, May 6, 1791, he spoke the words which cost him the friendship of his great contemporary. He repeated that he thought the French Revolution "on the whole, one of the most glorious events in the history of mankind." [198]

As might be expected, the enthusiasm of contemporary poets, especially the young romantics soon to become famous, was marked from the outset of the French uprising. Burns, Blake, Mrs. Barbauld, Erasmus Darwin, Coleridge, Southey, Cowper, and Wordsworth were variously inspired by the events in France. Even Hannah More could hope for some good as a result of the lessening of human misery on destruction of the Bastille.[199] Cowper thought that Providence must have intervened to bring about so wonderful an event as the French Revolution. Of the Bastille he could say,

> There's not an English heart that would not leap
> To hear that ye were fall'n at last.[200]

Wordsworth has left the best record of his and other young men's feelings in *The Prelude*. In a passage later reprinted in *The*

Friend under the title "French Revolution As It Appeared to Enthusiasts at Its Commencement," Wordsworth tells of the thrilling assurance that the world was opening out into exciting promise of new things to come. Anything seemed possible here and now for all, and the world of ideal and remote beauty and goodness had at last come to be realized in the actual lives of men.[201] As late as 1793 in his *Letter to the Bishop of Llandaff* Wordsworth still defends the French Revolution, denounces Burke as an "infatuated moralist," and excuses the crimes of the Revolution as unavoidable in the overthrow of tyranny. A host of minor and now forgotten writers also continued to express belief in, or sympathy for various ideas and feelings associated with the Revolution. Holcroft, Bage, Mrs. Charlotte Smith, Thelwall, the Della Cruscans, and others held views which combined sharp criticism of the evils in English society with such ideas as the natural goodness of man, the basic evil of governments and laws, the right of the individual to throw off the restraints imposed by society, an emotional deism and a dislike of priests and kings which the French patriots had dealt with properly.[202]

Of far greater importance and immediate influence than any of these was the famous *Discourse on the Love of Our Country,* by the dissenting minister, Richard Price. Since Burke took it upon himself to answer Price in *Reflections on the Revolution in France* and was in turn answered by Paine and others, the original *Discourse* may be taken as the opening statement of a fierce debate between the new liberals in England and the tremendous forces of the conservative order. From the outset, as might have been expected, there was an affinity between dissent and the new revolutionary feeling wherever it showed itself, nonconformity suffering still from disabilities imposed by the *status quo.*[203] Price had already shown how strong this dissenting opinion might become in a man of great personal energy and integrity. Having celebrated the American Revolution, he now used the centenary of the English Revolution of 1688–89 as an excuse for high praise of the French uprising as well. In the first and succeeding edition of his *Discourse,* Price calls for the enlightenment of all men, that they may no longer endure the despotism which has deprived them of their rights. He restates the principles of 1688 and demands liberty of conscience in religion, the right of resistance to abused power, the right of free election of all governors with the corresponding right to discharge them for misconduct and to set up another government. He hails the two revolutions in America and France as worthy of universal rejoicing; blows have been struck against priestcraft and tyranny and men everywhere have been aided in the recovery of their natural rights. The French Revolution in particular is a wonderful event without parallel in history by which the spirit of liberty has been universally extended:

> . . . I see the ardor for liberty catching and spreading; a general amendment beginning in human affairs; the dominion of kings changed for the dominion of laws, and the dominion of priests giving way to the dominion of reason and conscience.
> Be encouraged all ye friends of freedom, and writers in its defence! The times are auspicious. Your labours have not been in vain. Behold kingdoms, admonished by you, starting from sleep, breaking their fetters, and claiming justice from their oppressors! . . . Tremble all ye oppressors of the world! Take warning, all ye supporters of slavish governments, and slavish hierarchies! Call no more (absurdly and wickedly) reformation, innovation. You cannot now hold the world in darkness. Struggle no longer against increasing light and liberality. Restore to mankind their rights; and consent to the correction of abuses, before they and you are destroyed together.[204]

In 1790 Burke replied with his *Reflections,* one of the classical utterances of conservatism. Some thirty-eight formal replies were written in answer to Burke, the most famous of which was that of Tom Paine, *The Rights of Man.* The efforts of Mary Wollstonecraft, James Mackintosh, and Joseph Priestley are less radical than the work of Paine, but are perhaps more typical of English liberal opinion for that very reason. Mary Wollstonecraft ridicules Burke's dislike of abstract theory, condemns his devotion to antiquity and tradition, denounces Burke's whole system as designed only for a few, and calls, on the contrary, for greater equality, for happiness as a proper hope for all men now, in this world. The great feminist pleads for respect for the rights of men, a wide diffusion of happiness and virtue, love for one's fellow men, fear of God, and the greatest happiness for the whole through the happiness of each individual.[205] James Mackintosh also addresses himself to Burke's anti-intellectualism and denies that the French Revolution was the result of schemes and theories conceived by a few individuals. He defends the French National Assembly against the charge of having given themselves to illusive theories and having surrendered real good to imaginary excellence. He sees no harm in using man's intellect to make things better than they are. "It is absurd to *expect,* but it is not absurd to pursue perfection," [206] so men may be allowed occasional ventures into what is yet unexplored in the interest of public happiness. Priestley, who was to suffer personally for his views beyond other liberals of his day, simply tells Burke in so many words, "What you admire I despise, and what you think highly useful, I am persuaded is very mischievous." [207] He praises the French National Assembly for making progress in necessary reform. He disagrees with Burke's view of the 1688 English revolution, finding in it a precedent for change and redress of popular grievances at the general will. He attacks religious establishments as unnecessary and injurious to true religion, not to mention the harm they do to the liberties of a state. Priestley predicts the fall of the English church before the new spirit of free and rational inquiry and offers his congratulations to the French nation, and the world: "I mean the liberal, the rational, and the virtuous part of the world, on the great revolution that has taken place in France, as well as . . . in America." [208]

THE RIGHTS OF MEN

All these answers to Burke are the mild suggestions of typically moderate Englishmen compared with the powerful outburst of Paine in *The Rights of Man.* It has been well said that Paine was the "natural link between three revolutions, the one which had succeeded in the New World, the other which was transforming France, and the third which was yet to come in England." [209] His work was widely diffused, not less than 100,000 copies being distributed in England and inspiring one of the great conservative witch hunts.[210] Paine wrote to defend the French Revolution just as Burke had written to condemn it. In his review of events to 1791, Paine excuses all actions taken, explains and exonerates the revolutionists' principles, praises the new French constitution in great detail for its rational contribution to liberty and human rights, and reprints all 17 points of the National Assembly's *Declaration of the Rights of Man and of Citizens*. He ridicules and denounces Burke especially for his view of the 1688 revolution as binding future generations and for his belief in the alliance of church and state. He devotes large areas in both Parts I and II of *The Rights of Man* to ridicule and condemnation of the weaknesses of the English government, to the corruption of its parliamentary representation, to the faults of the court itself which he describes as "treacherous" and "demented." Paine's own statement of purposes is a fair summary of the whole and of his own defiance to the forces arrayed against him:

If to expose the fraud and imposition of monarchy and every species of hereditary government—to lessen the oppression of taxes—to propose plans for the education of helpless infancy, and the comfortable support of the aged and distressed—to endeavour to conciliate nations to each other—to extirpate the horrid practice of war—to promote universal peace, civilization, and commerce—and to break the chains of political superstition, and raise degraded man to his proper rank;—if these things be libellous, let me live the life of a libeller, and let the name of libeller be engraven on my tomb! [211]

Although William Godwin was not writing to answer Burke or to defend specifically the French Revolution, his work must have a place in any view of English liberalism in this period. Leaving aside his novels, it will be enough to consider *Political Justice* (1793), by far the most radical book of any consequence published in England during the French Revolution. Here Godwin is briefly at one with the conservative realist in his dark view of present reality. Godwin also describes the unrelieved misery and injustice of the present which almost forbids any future good. Unlike the conservative who says that these things are in the nature of reality and cannot be fundamentally changed, Godwin says that these evils are unnecessary accidents of a previous faulty way of doing things: they will disappear as mankind moves on to perfection, if he will give himself to the development of reason and virtue. Man is formed by his intellectual and moral environment, which is modified through education, religion, social prejudice, and government. Ideally men should abolish all government, and so give human virtue free play to develop without interference. They can then proceed to their perfection through education and persuasion. These influences are so important because all of men's voluntary actions originate in their opinions. Let reason dominate opinion, and error in action can be eliminated. Godwin's faith in human reason and logic is at the very opposite pole from conservative anti-intellectualism. Truth becomes omnipotent in Godwin's scheme; it will lead men to that perfection which will once and for all show how unnecessary and harmful government, as such, can be. Open sincerity, free discussion, appeals to reason and truth will end all previous social evils. Godwin desires no religious establishments, no system of national education to render knowledge stereotyped, nor tyranny of any kind to impede the inevitable progress of man to his perfection. Let there be a free play of ideas and opinions in an ungoverned community and all will be well. Godwin rejects both sides of the revolutionary controversy of his own day: he has no time for social contracts or natural rights of man on the one hand, or for monarchy and aristocracy on the other. He despises all parliaments and their doings, but has no desire to lead a revolution when reason is bound gradually to bring about the perfect human state. He would break up society however, into small units like the parish and so avoid the danger of large national aggregates. As for human relationships, Godwin desires universal benevolence, with all men regarded for their merits as contributors to the good of the whole. The perfection and elevation of the race is what counts, and men should not have to love or be grateful to their parents or anyone else, save with respect to this idea. Eventually all property will become equal, the family will be abolished, everything will be held in trust for the benefit of mankind in an era of reason and virtue.

Compared with such an attack on every belief and institution revered by the society of their day, the mild desire for improvement by other English liberals seems harmless indeed. A number of years were to pass before Godwin was made to suffer for his impudence; he was not attacked at first because he had written a learned book, addressed to educated readers, and selling for three guineas.[212] While *Political Justice* as a radical document influenced a number of its author's young contemporaries,[213] Pitt and his advisers simply assumed that it could do very little harm among the masses because of its price and its intellectual difficulty. In any case there was nothing to compare with its radicalism among the numerous minor writers of the 1790's. Actually, in spite of the fact that there was supposed to be much subversive activity in England among all classes,[214] that the grievances of the worker in the industrial revolution made him begin to be conscious of possible political action in the reform societies,[215] and that the success of the French Revolution in 1792 made it seem likely that a similar uprising would occur in England,[216] the views expressed by the so-called radicals of the time were surprisingly harmless and moderate. A pamphlet called *An Exposition of the Principles of the English Jacobins* [217] breathes a spirit of tolerance and justice. The Jacobins desire greater economic and political equality, universal suffrage and equal representation, the redress of grievances by peaceful means, the social uplift of those who have had so far no chance in life, a wider and more genuine democracy, which at any other time in the reign of George III would not have been considered dangerous. We find some justification, in this period as well, of the right of revolution,[218] enthusiasm for the revolution

of 1688 as a precedent for the right of resistance,[219] and praise of
the French Revolution, its purposes and its example to England.[220]
Conservative anti-intellectualism is denounced and free speculation advocated.[221] Severe criticism is leveled at the undeserving
upper classes, at the reigning inequality of wealth and condition,
at the selfish opposition to change among conservatives, and at
the stupid adulation of royalty in England.[222] Coleridge and others
denounce repressive measures by the government against so-called
seditious publications and call for freedom of the press and other
basic English rights.[223] The bill to suspend the habeas corpus act is
denounced by Sheridan, who asks the restoration of those rights
and privileges of the people that never should have been taken
away.[224] Passive obedience and nonresistance are severely condemned;[225] the clergy, especially the higher ranks, are chastised
for worldliness and unchristian behavior;[226] Montesquieu and
Blackstone are ridiculed as romantic for their lyrical praise of the
English constitution in the face of its sordid reality;[227] and some
guarded praise is given to the political associations in England as
making the people more discriminating in judging political affairs.[228] Erskine seems to have aroused considerable enthusiasm
for his brilliant defense of Paine on the ground that an Englishman has a perfect right to find fault with the government and to
try as best he can to improve it. After his great speech of four hours
on behalf of Paine and again after his successful plea at the trial
of Thelwall, Erskine's horses were unhitched and his carriage
drawn in triumph by the people through the streets.[229]

All this is a long way from the actual revolution which conservatism so desperately feared or pretended to fear. The dreaded
outbreak seems never to have been nearer than what is suggested by
the naval mutiny in 1797.[230] Meanwhile the only continuing force
working for a planned change was the parliamentary reform movement. Christopher Wyvill and others went on pleading as before,
advocating this necessary change in the available means for expression of the people's will.[231] In Parliament itself, the agitation
fell upon deaf ears. One explanation of its failure to act was put

into the form of a conundrum: "Why is the House of Commons like an account-book? Because there are so many cyphers in it." [232] The official explanation was that the times were unsuited to such a reform, but the reformers were undaunted. In 1791 Thomas Hardy formed a new society to further this cause. *The London Corresponding Society* was soon in correspondence with twenty or thirty popular societies in various parts of England and Scotland, advocating universal suffrage and an honest Parliament. *The Society of the Friends of the People* also was founded in April, 1792, and asked Charles Grey to introduce a new reform bill in the House.[233] The Society's *Authentic Copy of a Petition Praying for a Reform in Parliament* was presented to the House on May 6, 1793. It was modestly and respectfully worded in its plea that Parliament reform itself. But it was all in vain. In spite of the support of Sheridan [234] and thousands of signatures on twenty-three petitions, Grey's bill lost in May, 1793, by a vote of 282 to 42.

VIII · CONSERVATISM
REAFFIRMED

WHEN EVERYTHING has been said for the new spirit of critical reform in the 1760's and 70's, the release of liberal feeling in humanitarianism, Wesleyanism, and the Industrial Revolution; the agitation over Wilkes, the reform of Parliament, the American and French Revolutions and all the miscellaneous criticism, constructive or destructive, which these various events and movements had called forth—when all this has been reviewed and every allowance made for its probable influence, the fact remains that at no time was the conservative order in any real danger. Its power remained undiminished and its fundamental attitudes unchanged or even intensified as revolutionary France made its entrance on the European scene. This would have been true regardless of the particular English party which might have found itself in power. The conservative position remained secure partly because mere complaint or attack against abuses was not in itself revolutionary; because most Englishmen would not have desired a complete break with the way things were; because the forces making for continuance of the old order, led by George III himself, became stronger than ever; because the attitudes of anti-intellectualism and dislike of theory were still strong enough to discourage speculation to the point of danger; because even the movements which might have been thought of as liberal in tendency were considerably less so in fact than they at first seemed; and because when the French Revolution began to enter upon its violent phase, the alarm of Burke spread to all the forces of conservatism more certainly than ever, so as to defeat whatever little progress liberalism had made and to bring about a reassertion of the attitudes of conservatism in a form more intense and pronounced than ever before.

De Lolme had singled out for praise the right of all Englishmen to say what they like. Since this enabled them to complain as they saw fit, they got into the habit of doing so from time to time without meaning much by it. In England there can be a great deal of agitation without much general or profound discontent. Unlike other peoples the English do not complain only as a last resort against oppression. Their outcries are "often nothing more than the first vent which men give to their new, and yet unsettled conceptions." [1] The fault-finding spirit produces "murmurers, complainers, presumptuous, self-willed, factious spirits," [2] but these are contemptible and petty in all ages and countries. In Rome too, there were "dozens of duodecimo Catilines, who buzzed conspiracy in every corner of the Forum"; malcontents can always work up a following "officious, and obscure; busy, and forgot." [3] It is true that mere attacks on corruption, objections to the way things are, condemnation of this or that abuse or evil in practice do not necessarily mean a break with the *status quo*. They mean rather that the existing order should conduct itself differently, better perhaps, but differently only with respect to the specific abuses that are pointed out. The special objections being met, there is no further demand that life be changed in its fundamental arrangements and attitudes. Such criticism seldom comes from an underlying philosophy or far-reaching plan of moral or social reform which would make impossible the recurrence of the abuses being condemned. Most criticism in the eighteenth century is of this kind. It proceeds from those not in power, in the attempt to throw out these who are in and to substitute themselves, who will in turn use power in the same way except that it is now for their own benefit. Thus most objections to the *status quo* offer no real threat to the way things are. Only an underlying change in philosophy, a new general idea or a renewal of an old one, has any real power to change the existing order.

We are brought back at this point to the general tendency of most Englishmen in the eighteenth century. As Smollett's "Dying Prediction" said, "At home you have a few radically discontented men, with a vast and undoubted majority, who are inviolably attached to the present establishment." [4] Blackburne had pointed out earlier, repeating one of his favorite ideas, that a serious reform under the leadership of an enlightened ruler would interfere too much with the interests of too many persons for a real chance of adoption. "The consequence . . . is but too visible, that all hopes of any real and lasting public reformation, are vain and void of foundation." [5] In 1779 William Eden could say that

notwithstanding all our animosities, it does not appear that there is, at this moment, any division within the bulk of the people respecting any assignable point of political controversy . . . the bulk of the people have no grievance, either real or supposed, respecting the great outlines and essentials of government.[6]

In 1780, *The Sense of the People*

expresses loyalty and affection to the king; necessary respect for, and proper confidence in, his ministers; a cheerful submission to the burthens which the exigencies of the state render unavoidable in situations of public distress . . . a ready obedience to the law, by which every blessing is made secure to us; and a fervent wish to see public authority and private liberty stand together on that broad and immoveable basis.[7]

Mrs. Carter is much relieved after the Gordon riots of 1780 to find that "the people of England are by no means so ready to be engaged in a rebellion, as some bad persons may have hoped, and some good ones have certainly feared." [8] Two years later the same devout woman comforts herself with the reflection that "by the blessing of God, on the good sense of the people of England at large, it will not be in the power of a ragamuffin mob to overset this kingdom, whatever powers of oratory may belong to their leader." [9]

NATIONAL AFFAIRS

Yet even if there had been a general disposition among the people to demand a new society, the main forces of conservatism were more than strong and active enough to insure their own continuance and see that England was governed in their interest. Most important was George III himself. As king he would have been and was regarded with the greatest reverence and respect even if he had not chosen to assert his power so arbitrarily. A petition from the freeholders of Middlesex asking the king to dissolve Parliament in the interests of justice was expressed in language of an almost obsequious deference.[10] Yet the natural and unsolicited reverence of the people was not enough; George was bent on following his mother's advice and being a real king as he understood the word. Kingship came to consist in direct interference with political affairs to a degree unknown since James II; this interference had as one of its purposes to make sure that no reforms, however slight, or obvious their need, would be permitted.[11] Adding his own humorless stolidity to the usual pomp of royal pronouncements, George would say, along with the English catechism, that he desired only "to do my duty and to shew by firmness in difficulties that I am not unworthy of the station into which it has pleased Providence to place me." [12] He was determined to show the world "that neither zeal, activity, nor resolution are wanting in me, when the times require it, to forward with the greatest expedition every measure that can be necessary for the security or honour of my dominions." [13] Such measures were never to be understood as calling for changes of any kind. Evidently George had learned his lesson from Blackstone very well:

I own myself a sincere friend to our constitution, both ecclesiastical and civil, and as such a great enemy to any innovations, for, in this mixed government, it is highly necessary to avoid novelties. We know that all wise nations have stuck scrupulously to their ancient customs. Why are we, therefore, in opposition to them, to seem to have no other object but to be altering every rule our ancestors have left us? [14]

To make sure that nothing hostile to his ideal was done, George interfered not only in elections to Parliament, but in the actual business of the House of Commons which he attempted to control by bribery and other influences. Between 1761 and 1780, the king threw himself into general elections "with all the zeal and energy of a party manager." [15] Violating the rule laid down by another of his heroes, Bolingbroke, that "the crown is never to meddle in an election," [16] the king personally canvassed Windsor in the general election of 1780 against the Whig Admiral Keppel.[17] The elections of 1779 to 1781 cost George over £72,000 in the effort to increase the number of his supporters in Parliament.[18] Much of this was spent in purchasing seats for individuals and in helping others to meet the expenses of election. In controlling the actual conduct of affairs in the House of Commons, George bribed right and left to insure his supremacy.[19] Once he had shaken off the Whigs, and Grafton had resigned in 1770, George was able to tyrannize to his heart's content. He controlled all details of government and asserted himself as if he were an absolute monarch, ruling his Tory supporters with a rod of iron.[20] In 1783 he sent round a card, warning that whoever voted for Fox's India Bill would be considered the king's enemy; by implication this meant that such a person could not hope for any office of honor or profit.[21] If the king had used all this power for progress and wholesome change, history might forgive his peculiar methods. But there is only too much truth in Laski's opinion of George III: "There is no question which arose in the first forty years of his reign in which he was not upon the wrong side and proud of his error." [22]

Meanwhile all who profited from things as they were continued to hold fast to the traditional scheme of things. The church in particular could be relied on to uphold property and order. No bishop was expected to complain about a system which bestowed rank, wealth, and power upon him. He might see clearly enough that the church ought to be changed in certain ways; but he could not be sure that a reform once under way would stop where he would like to have it stop. So he was inclined to go on with what he knew to be wrong in the interests of keeping his place, which might suffer if the whole system were extensively reviewed.[23] So also the legal profession, the municipal oligarchies, the official class, the landed and farming classes all derived advantage from

things as they were and could not be expected to favor change.[24]
The time never seemed just right to these various groups to under-
take a reformation, which if thorough and proper would be
certain to interfere with some point of their own cherished interests. If there had to be changes, they could be gradually and
prudently conducted from within by measures provided for in
the excellent constitution. Such measures, if really needed, would
be perfectly evident to any sensible man, so that no one would
have to be violent about them. Such matters "whenever they become necessary, cannot escape the notice of wise and able men,
by whom they will be at the proper time adopted, improved, and
established." [25]

If conservatism could find in the constitution all the necessary
means of wholesome change, its usual anti-intellectualism saw no
need for "the wild schemes of our political visionaries." [26] There
was even some talk of the danger inherent in a free press. After all,
individuals "ought not to be at liberty, by speaking, writing, or in
any other way whatsoever, to effect, or even attempt, the subversion and dissolution" of the government.[27] If the press is allowed to be unrestrained, it will be abused for the propagation of
falsehood, leading to the subversion of order and the dissolution
of manners.[28] Such a fear of criticism and of new ideas could see
even in Burke a serious danger. In 1780 he is addressed as a
troublesome and officious reformer of abuses, one given to creating
disturbances and upsetting the constitution.[29] As for the work of
Price, it is based on an idea of liberty which proceeds "either from
mischievous intentions or sheer ignorance." [30] His book, with all
of its "metaphysical distinctions . . . extensive calculations," fails
to contribute to the highest good of the state: peace and quiet.[31]
The whole thing is "altogether Utopian or visionary, can never
have any real existence; and if it could, would be attended by no
important benefit to mankind." [32] On the contrary, Price has made
a foul attempt on the peace of society and has blown up a flame
which "may expire only with the extinction of all for which a
wise man could wish to live." [33] The same is true of other works

of a philosophical nature whose tendency is to advance new theories dangerous to good manners and government. Their readers are made to consider themselves competent to have opinions on natural equality and the rights of mankind. They get a new idea of their own political importance; they question established laws and become superior to that wholesome philosophy which has ever urged them " 'to study to be quiet, and to do their own business.' " [34]

Yet it is clear in retrospect that anti-intellectualism need not have been so apprehensive, since neither Price nor his liberal contemporaries offered a very serious revolutionary threat. If Priestley may be used as an example, it is evident that he would justify revolt only in the case of such wrongs and oppressions as the entire world would agree were intolerable. Priestley urges slow and moderate progress through established channels against existing evils. He would do away with absolutely rigid and unalterable establishments and would invoke the right of revolution only under such a set of conditions—surrounded by reservations and exceptions— as even the most reluctant Tory would agree to. Priestley's assertion of the right of revolution against a bad government is preceded by six "if" clauses; these being met, he would allow "an injured and insulted people" to change their political arrangements.[35] Such occasions, as he admits, "rarely occur in the course of human affairs." [36]

THE SOCIAL ORDER

If men supposedly ahead of their times in the realm of theory do not pose a serious threat against the *status quo,* neither do the various movements in practical affairs now seem dangerous. Certainly the attack on slavery might be launched without danger to the social order. The slave-trading class was comparatively small and could be denounced for their sins to the moral satisfaction of the right people.[37] Yet in spite of the great speeches of Wilberforce and his supporters, abolition failed in this period. Parliament remained so conservative as to be unwilling to abolish a traffic which had been encouraged for a hundred years. The trade had many defenders, so it seemed best to postpone the question to a later and quieter time than the French Revolutionary period. Besides, it might be argued that abolition was a violation of property rights; if Parliament could do away with one form of property, no kind of property would be safe. On this ground Wilberforce lost again in 1791.[38]

Adam Smith and Jeremy Bentham, while liberal at the economic level or in legal reform, did not oppose the social order of their day. Smith is more interested in guaranteeing the security of property once it has been acquired than in promoting any large social emancipation. Bentham was far ahead of his age in the reform of law, yet in economics he simply followed Smith, and in politics remained authoritarian throughout this period. Like Burke, Bentham was interested in facts, in the utility of things, in individualism and empiricism and particular interests. Laws of nature, original contracts, natural rights and similar theories might be left to "philosophers, that is, to silly people in libraries." [39] So also the individuals who were conducting the Industrial Revolution or were profiting from the changes taking place in their day were not radical in any real democratic sense. They were liberal in that they wanted to get rid of existing restrictions and the prejudices which conflicted with their own interests.[40] They wanted to insure political power and a higher place in society for themselves. They would democratize society only so far as to include themselves in the dominant classes. Evidently then, if reform had been granted in Parliament in this period to include those rising to industrial power and wealth, the result would not have been to transform rapidly England's basic conservatism. The social analogy of the great chain of being would still have been valid if the industrial revolution permitted men to rise out of the lower orders into those above them. Such men did not lead a reform of the class system, but simply moved or changed their own position within it. The regular stations in the social chain of being remained; only individuals within them were allowed to move elsewhere without damage to the basic structure.

Wesleyanism, too, may be thought of as a force working for conservatism, in that it transformed the possible dangers of the industrial revolution into religious turbulence on the part of the masses of people who were not reached by the established church. Wesleyanism helped to drain off "the accumulations of fear, resentment, bewilderment and despair produced by social disorder, that are such potent revolutionary materials." [41] Men became more resigned in spirit and less resentful of their state, as well as positively enthusiastic about a definite idea. Methodism, because of its energy and enthusiasm on the positive side of religious inspiration, and because of its indignation and horror at English social, religious, and political corruption, served as an outlet for discontent and human aspiration after a better world—natural human feelings that might otherwise have taken the form of revolution, as is usually the case when men cannot go on in the corrupt world they occupy. But the energy and hope and the effort to make things better that may thus be released in revolution are, indeed, popularly expended in religious fervor as well as in fierce criticism of abuses. Hence the need to speak out concerning what is wrong and to hope for something better was satisfied in part in England by the opportunity offered by Wesleyanism. One sign of the very discontent of England became a means of preventing any serious effort to overthrow the *status quo* completely.

Aside from the nature and the therapeutic effect of Wesleyanism, John Wesley's own Toryism was sufficient to insure his support of the existing order. He did not favor democratic political activity and used his influence on the side of repressive conservatism. He was devoted to royalty, to the British kingship as a divinely sanctioned institution. He hated Oliver Cromwell in the approved eighteenth-century manner; he revered George III on moral and religious grounds. Although Wesley had no stated political philosophy, he distrusted political democracy, objected to the republican form of government, and considered democratic representation of the people fallacious. The many had no claim to be represented and no right to a share in the government. In ruling his own followers Wesley kept to this view and was at all times a benevolent despot.[42] He was enthusiastic in praise of the 1688 Revolution, was exceedingly proud of the constitution, and thought that the English were "actually possessed of the greatest civil and religious liberty that the condition of human life allows." [43] He denied and even ridiculed the idea of a social contract, justified the exclusion of Wilkes from Parliament, and denounced Junius as a poisoner of the public mind against the king. To change the constitution would be a sin in Wesley's eyes, especially if it were to be changed in favor of the untrustworthy masses. He took the conservative's low view of human nature and of reality, and discarded metaphysics and theories of new societies entirely. Meanwhile he was willing to work for the more generous operation of the society in which he lived and would be active in social kindness and benefaction, relying on the change inside the individual man to bring about a better world for all men. Until this should come about, Wesley's religion kept men in line by teaching that revolt against authority was wrong, and at the same time helped them to forget that they had any real political or social grievances.

Yet even if Wesley had never preached, it is doubtful whether the forces making for change in England would have been strong enough to challenge the conservative position. Certainly the movement for parliamentary reform seems now to have been so moderate as to offer no threat to the social order as a whole. Aside from the fact that Parliament itself could not be expected to change a corrupt system to which so many members owed the very seats and votes which they would have had to use to abolish the system, it seems that the nature of the reform movement, the men and associations most interested in it, and the limitation of its aims forbade the development of any real revolutionary tendency within it. The first efforts at reform were not really democratic, but were made on behalf of property. Existing conditions violated the principle that power should follow property,[44] so a number of the aristocracy, together with members of the artisan and trading classes, tried to get power equal to their importance and wealth.

Further, reform attacked only individual abuses and not the system which had developed them. To regulate certain evil practices is quite different from making a new distribution of power.[45] English reformers were thus limited in their aims for the most part, but no doubt they would have justified even a revolution by the typically English device of referring to precedent. They were much more inclined to invoke the principles of 1688 than the rights of man, and, like religious reformers, to demand that doctrine return to principles originally pure and not at all new. Hooker stated an age-long English conviction in praising those " 'who only reform a decayed estate by reducing it to that perfection from which it hath swerved.' " [46] This practice "of representing constitutional change as though it were the preservation or restoration of some older and purer tradition" [47] is one of the true signs of English conservatism. Persuade the English that a novelty is in reality a revival and all is well. Many of the eighteenth-century leaders of parliamentary reform did not go much farther than this. The fiery Wilkes whose difficulties stirred up so much trouble and alarm was by no means as liberal as his cries of "liberty" might suggest, since "liberty" in his sense had been a conservative cry since 1688. He was never so rabid as a comparable figure in France would have been. Cartwright also thinks of reform as a return to the principles of the constitution as amended in 1688.[48] Even Price did not wish to change the mixed English government into a democracy entirely, but "to restore it to purity and vigour" by removing its defects.[49] All this does not seem too far from the aims of Burke himself, who desired to keep the essential constitution and to remedy details of practice.

As for the various reform associations, even if it is admitted that they represented the thoughts of most Englishmen of their time in spite of their limited membership, yet they were not themselves agreed as to the need or wisdom of changes in the constitution. Most of the people were not demanding the suffrage and seem to have been indifferent to their political position; the associations, it was said in 1782, "did not constitute the thousandth part of the nation, and could not discover or express its inclination." [50] Actually only a few progressive thinkers believed "in more than a very limited extension of the suffrage." [51] As time went on, the record of the reform societies, even those composed of workingmen with everything to gain from real change, was a record of pathetic timidity and caution. The societies were unwilling to show themselves radical or extreme, as if the members were so much a part of and shared so much in the prejudices of the *status quo* that they did not want to undermine it seriously, save in a few details which showed how far they were from just and proper treatment. Their attitude is at once a result of the prevailing tone of society and a cause of it, as showing their acquiescence in the existing order and their share in its fear of violence and sudden change. Since what he had to deal with, then, was so comparatively weak and lacking in forceful conviction, "meagre Pitt" had no trouble in systematically defeating the various bills which were offered for reform of Parliament after his own lukewarm efforts at change. Pitt put down the reform movement on every attempt of its leaders to revive it, in 1790, 1792, 1793, and 1797.

Such was the moderation and hesitancy of what might seem extremely liberal English forces in the late eighteenth century. But the same cannot be said of those who spoke for the *status quo,* especially when the American and French revolutions were in question. Although these events aroused considerable sympathy and even enthusiastic hope in England, the sentiment against America was very great, and in the course of time it was overwhelming against the French Revolution. Leaving aside the well-known denunciations of Dr. Johnson and Wesley, who fail to see what America has to complain of, we find the Americans condemned as deluded fanatics and rebels, the victims of artful and designing men.[52] Americans are the rebellious sons of Belial, and England is justified by the Bible in taking up the sword against them.[53] They are guilty of unprovoked and outrageous rebellion; [54] they are the viperous, ungrateful recipients of unselfish bounty from

England,[55] which has a perfect constitutional right to act as she does toward America.[56] In short, America is selfishly rebellious and indifferent to the general welfare,[57] and England is completely justified in behaving as she has been forced to do toward such a treasonous and ungrateful people.[58] The forces of the *status quo* were not inclined to put up with any serious challenge to their supremacy and were quick to say No to claims from any quarter, lest the infection should become general.[59] There is much truth therefore in the Hammonds' belief that "England was . . . less like a democracy, and more remote from the promise of democracy when the French revolution broke out" than it had been when the church and the ruling families had led the Revolution of 1688.[60]

The analysis of conservatism and its ways which we have been following so far has taken form according to what seemed the principal ideas with conservative implications in the eighteenth century. The order which has resulted seems to be present in retrospect only; it is imposed from without, from a long-range view which is able to see details and to join them together in what seem to be their proper relationships. It would be a mistake to suppose that the sum of the ideas and attitudes which now seem to have made up English conservatism were ever deliberately formed in order to make a platform to which conservatives might subscribe. Until 1790 there was no definite conservative party and no consciously held body of conservative doctrine. Most conservatives thought as they did without wondering very much whether it was possible to think anything else, or whether it was desirable to draw up their views in an orderly form so that they might better be able to defend themselves and these views against some alternative which had to be taken seriously. But when the French Revolution broke out and gave to the genius of Edmund Burke its greatest opportunity, an issue was raised which definitely called into being a recognizable conservative body. As Lord Cecil says, "those who stood emphatically against the revolutionary movement made the party in politics which we now call Conservative." [61] The various liberal movements have turned out on examination to be much weaker than they seemed. The American war and other stirrings of democracy had already aroused strong reaction against any hint of republicanism beyond what was already allowed by the constitution. When a threatening cataclysm like the French Revolution occurred, it is no wonder that conservatism should strike out more powerfully than ever, since it had already been sensitive and vigilant to slight tremors below. It was able to overwhelm entirely the weak liberalism that showed itself, which liberalism in turn came to adopt the conservative attitude to the French outbreak and almost ceased to exist as such when England declared war on France.

The English attitude to the French Revolution in general passed through several stages. First came early approval of a blow to despotism which seemed like English efforts along similar lines; this was followed by increasing distrust, as the nature of the Revolution became more democratic; finally, war was declared and anything even resembling reform was violently hated and suppressed.[62] English conservatism in particular, which eventually came to mean the whole of England, asserted its own view in Burke's *Reflections on the Revolution in France* in 1790. Burke wasted no time in compromising with the French uprising. He denounced its tendency and predicted nothing but disaster for its future. The remarkable discernment of his prophecies became only more evident with time, and his work was the rallying point of English opinion as well as the classical statement of that conservatism which had dominated the eighteenth century and was now to show itself more completely in control of England than ever before. Burke was answered by thirty-eight works of varying degrees of liberalism,[63] but no one has troubled himself to count the number of those who wrote and spoke in agreement. His great summary of views long expressed or implied in his other works was the signal for a restatement of all the ideas and attitudes which have seemed most characteristic of eighteenth-century English conservatism. Burke denounced equality and defended rank in society; he upheld the value of religion in the state; he described society as an organism which changed slowly and depended much on what had come down to it from the past; he upheld prejudice and old custom as salutary; he condemned the violence and injustice of sudden reform; and he uttered a most scathing denunciation of theory as distinguished from practice, discrediting with all his force the "metaphysical" in human affairs. Following his leadership, English conservatism on all sides renewed and restated itself, its complacency, realism, and fear now more intensified, and seemingly justified, than ever.

We have already made ourselves familiar with the details of these attitudes in eighteenth-century England, their form and manner of expression. It should be sufficient now merely to sample their numberless reaffirmations in this period, to show that they were still held in characteristic form. Once more, then, we find that England is able to count on the friendship of God. She is the "heaven-favoured island," on whose behalf divine Providence has repeatedly intervened in order to preserve her from danger and to bring her to that overwhelming perfection which now makes her the admiration and dread of all nations.

Oh Britain! Britain! the wonder and admiration of Europe, enriched with every blessing! Thou privileged spot, of nature's vast domains, whose sons are valiant and brave, and whose daughters like polished stones, add strength and beauty to the state. May thy inhabitants ever be sensible of the goodness of Divine Providence, in constituting them members of thee! [64]

While it has always been true that nations are able to discover God on their side, the English have a way of expressing their own alliance with God which seems to imply that God has no choice but to declare himself in favor of such a virtuous nation and against what must be by definition the wickedness of any enemy England might have. At the end of an extravagantly patriotic "Serenata" in 1790, we find two stanzas of *God Save the King,* the second of which asks that God take appropriate action against England's foes:

> O Lord our God arise,
> Scatter our enemies,

And make them fall;
Confound their Politics,
Frustrate their knavish tricks,
On Thee our hopes are fixed,
God save us all.[65]

God's friendship in the 1790's continues to take the form of a shower of miscellaneous blessings. England is now at the height of her power; she is the richest, most beneficent, most free and happy country in the world; nothing is so good and perfect on the globe as England; she enjoys well-nigh every advantage which can be derived from society; she offers all that the most discontented being could wish for; her state is such as can scarcely be improved, such as to make real grievances nonexistent outside the corrupted brains of a few bigoted enthusiasts and fanatical innovators.[66] As Burke said of the people as a whole, "we fear God; we look up with awe to kings, with affection to Parliaments, with duty to magistrates, with reverence to priests, and respect to nobility." [67] Everyone is happy and satisfied amid such unprecedented evidences of divine favor. It might be said that "we love our king . . . we love our parliament . . . we love our religion . . . we love our laws . . . we love our constitution . . . and we love our country." [68] If all this is still more true than ever, it follows that it is to the interests of all including the lower classes, "to keep things as they are, because every change must be for the worse." [69]

These general blessings are once more crowned by England's matchless constitution. The passage of time has made this wonderful creation seem ever more admirable and more worthy of the devotion and loyalty which is bestowed upon it. The English now feel for it a kind of superstitious reverence. Its principles are immaculate and fundamentally incapable of improvement. It is the perfection, the summit of human wisdom, the most perfect work of fallible mankind, the best of constitutions since it has had so long a period in which to perfect itself. And even if it is admitted that the constitution might be improved, all necessary means are provided within itself, so that no external revolt is called for.[70] Therefore, Mrs. Carter wants to know, "What reason can there be to wish for a change?" [71] The great edifice of England's constitution has come down through the ages, and if it is to be remodeled or repaired, the most extreme caution must be used to make sure that the main outlines are preserved without injury.[72] The late examples offered by America and France should convince every Englishman aware of his own good fortune that he should resist any efforts at innovation.[73] Actually such necessary changes as were once called for to make the constitution perfect are now far in the past. England has had her revolution in the year 1688, so the work is finally accomplished. "We want no revolutional storm—the storm is over—the establishment is gained; now let us watch against every intruding foe, or any adventurous assailants that want to attack our interests." [74] The mighty Judge Braxfield may be allowed the final word to summarize English conservative complacency in the French revolutionary period. It is the classical statement of complete belief in what is: "The British Constitution is the best that ever was since the creation of the world, and it is not possible to make it better." [75]

Although "Metaphysical Optimism" as such is not prominent in the late eighteenth century, its conservative implications are maintained by allied attitudes. There is still a belief in the goodness of God who will be certain to work out all things for the best in spite of apparent injustices. The best example of the continuance of this attitude is offered by Hannah More in her tract *'Tis All for the Best*.[76] Here men are shown that there is no questioning the Providence of God; no matter how unjust or unfortunate life may be, all is for the best in the end. Men simply must believe that God's ways are not our ways and that we have no choice but to accept His dispensation without complaint.[77]

The various elements of conservative realism as we have understood them continue to be prominent. Something akin to the social implications of the great chain of being is present in the demand that ranks, orders, and stations be maintained, that a regulated and subordinate inequality is necessary in society, that there is a natural or social chain which connects all men together and which is wholesome if all links remain fast in their places and perform their specific duties. Subordination cannot be avoided, and so men should go on contentedly in their places.[78] The very name of the *Society for Preserving Liberty and Property against Republicans and Levellers* suggests how conservatism maintained its familiar concepts. If "levelling" is bad, it is so because it disturbs the idea of subordination, of ranks, of the high, low, and medium in life, gradations and inequalities which were regarded as so indispensable that society could not very well exist without them. "Levelling" is therefore an unforgivable offense against the prevailing order.

The conservative view of the weakness of man has also undergone very little change. We are told again that human nature by its weakness prevents anything from being perfect. Man is wicked and unclean, his nature frail and defective; his passions are base and dangerous, his vices the permanent cause of evil in the world. By far the majority of men are slaves and must be governed as such; they are devoid of virtue or wisdom, the victims of depravity and folly which render them incapable of doing anything without much weakness and error.[79] The same conclusion must be drawn from this as of old: Men cannot expect their works to be better than themselves; as a result, reforms will only make way for new defects and abuses, and efforts to change things in the face of the nature of man will continue to be like arguing in a circle.[80]

If little can be done in view of the continuing nature of man, so also does the unsatisfactory quality of human life make all plans for its improvement largely illusory. We hear again of the universality of pain, misery, and misfortune in life. Human existence is beset with dangers, and afflicted with calamities. The body is tormented by diseases, and the mind disturbed by unhappy reflections. Man's desire for happiness is forever frustrated, leading to a perpetual discontent because there seems to be no good in life without a mixture of evil. Since the nature of things cannot be remedied, there is no point in attempting reforms which avoid one set of evils only to bring on others which may turn out to aggravate and multiply the very things they were supposed to correct. Men are well advised therefore to bear the ills they have rather than fly to others that they know not of. Let them be sure that the old Italian epitaph need never be applied to them: "I was well—I endeavoured to be better—and here I lie." [81]

The anti-intellectualism which forbids hopeful theories and schemes for change or improvement in what by definition will never be perfect has been given in this period its classical expression by Burke. Throughout his *Reflections on the Revolution in France* Burke continues to plead for the conservative way. To preserve as well as to reform; to go slowly and to take time as an aid to improvement; to be patient, for patience is more effective than force; to make use of all past experience; to watch the effect of each step taken and to consult the wisdom and practice of former generations; to cherish long-established prejudices; to permit no haste or violence—such are his endlessly repeated admonitions. In particular Burke will not allow the fanciful innovations of speculators, however symmetrical or logical, to be hastily adopted. He believed that metaphysical truth might lead only to practical falsity, whereas the need was for compromise and balance, for moral computation, "adding, subtracting, multiplying, and dividing, morally, and not metaphysically or mathematically, true moral denominations." [82] If any proof beyond the lessons of long experience were needed to show the folly of surrender to theory, Burke found it in the ruined condition of France. Here one might conclude that the country "had been for some time under the special direction of the learned academicians of Laputa and Balnibarbi." [83]

Burke at once led the anti-intellectual conservatism of his age, and at the same time reflected it. From all sides we hear the conviction that "nothing valuable could be derived, from the chimerical reveries of metaphysical vanity." [84] It became axiomatic that history and fact must precede all doctrines and arguments, that experience must be preferred to speculation. The English people are repeatedly warned against fanatical theories and the metaphysical plans of crusaders. They are told to avoid at all costs new-fangled schemes, wild ideas, and a priori systems which are imaginary, unstable, dangerous. Extreme caution should obtain in all reforms, which must proceed by gradual degrees and not by theoretical experiments. All arrangements should be adapted to the present state of things, to the facts as they now are. Otherwise theoretical change will destroy the very liberty it means to preserve. And the horrible example of France is perpetually held up as a warning to the English. Here indeed they may behold the fate of speculative reformers, as William Windham said in opposing Flood's motion for parliamentary reform in 1790. It was his duty

to oppose the dangerous and progressive spirit of innovation;—I must still enter my protest against the strange mixture of metaphysics with politics, which we are witnessing in the neighbouring country, where it would seem as if the ideal world were about to overrun the real. In that country speculatists and theorists are now *frontibus adversis pugnantia*. Let us, in good time, avoid the infection. Sir, it is my firm opinion that there is no grievance existing in this country which we cannot correct, without calling in the advice of a theorist.[85]

Yet of all the attitudes most characteristic of conservatism, it was fear which dominated the French Revolutionary period in England. Mary Wollstonecraft was only summarizing the obvious in saying that "the fear of innovation, in this country, extends to every thing." [86] Any change was held to be ruinous to the public happiness; the slightest variation from established rules was sure to destroy the perfect English order. There was no telling what dreadful passions and baneful effects might follow from even the smallest innovation. Burke continued to warn against the "desperate enterprises of innovation" and Coleridge reported that a man who had wanted to call a ship of his the "Liberty" was urged not to do so since the word had a Jacobinical sound.[87]

In particular those who had most to lose from change, who had something they especially wanted to preserve, were most fearful of the revolutionary spirit which they saw, or imagined that they saw, in things that ordinarily they would never have noticed.[88] The governing classes were thrown into a panic and were convinced that an organized conspiracy against property and order in England was about to strike with an armed force. A certain amount of social unrest, discontent in both England and Scotland, bread riots, strikes, industrial agitations, along with the great success of Paine's writings, made it seem as if there were some ground for the fears of those in power.[89] The whole country was aroused and became a "scene of hostile array and preparation" against this formidable uprising against the existing order.[90] Mrs. Thrale speaks of the general agitation when Pitt reported that an army of 18,000 men had been organized to follow the example of France by force; fortunately 24 of the leaders had been secured; they would have to be adequately punished in order to "tame their frantic followers." [91] Such a spirit of democracy had gone forth, some people "say openly now that 'tis no treason to cry *George's head in a Basket.*" [92]

Yet other things were regarded as treason, and these far less harmful even than the loss of George's head. *The Association for Preserving Liberty and Property* set itself the task of halting all efforts at reform; it particularly directed itself against printed materials of a dangerous nature, and the meetings of clubs formed to seduce ignorant and credulous people and so to destroy the general happiness. All writers as well as printers, publishers, news-carriers or sellers of papers or books of a seditious or unconstitutional kind were to be held equally guilty. The king's own proclamation supported this attitude.[93] Booksellers were prosecuted for selling the works of Tom Paine.[94] All who spoke or wrote in favor of reform or who joined reform societies, however moderate, were suspected, and a number of the more prominent reformers were unsuccessfully tried for treason. The word treason had to be so defined as to include any effort, no matter how orderly or peaceful, to change English institutions. Even the peaceable reform of Parliament was used as an excuse to try Hardy, Tooke, Thelwall, and others until the courtroom proceedings became cruel farces, victimizing innocent men.[95] The trials which took place in Scotland under the notorious Judge Braxfield were particularly severe, both as to intention and result, giving Braxfield abundant scope for his classically reactionary views.[96]

Fear of dangerous writings or of attempts to change details of the existing order was related to conservative distrust of the people. Familiar charges were again heard against the undisciplined majority. This "swinish Multitude" in Burke's phrase, this mixture of the tiger and the ape as Voltaire had called them, was not to be trusted. In the number of the multitude were the deluded, the vile, the worthless, the ignorant, the credulous and desperate of men. Such are led away often by mere sound; weak, wicked, and mad as they are, they listen to inflammatory innovators, led astray in their feebleness and blindness of mind to give rein to inflamed passions and frenzy. Once roused to fury, a mob composed of such elements will be guilty of anarchy without restraint. Discord and devastation will ensue, the end of all peace, religion, and law must follow.[97] Hence Burke's conviction that it was almost one of the rights of men that their inclinations "should frequently be thwarted, their will controlled, and their passions brought into subjection. This can only be done *by a power out of themselves,* and not, in the exercise of its function, subject to that will and to those passions which it is its office to bridle and subdue." [98]

The conservative attitude toward the poor, the lower orders, is likewise unchanged from its earlier expression. The poor still need the consolations and sanctions of religion to make them contented and submissive. Poverty as such is still unavoidable in society, and nothing can be done to cure it without destroying society as well. No hope is held out for changes which will elevate the poor, and any inflammatory writings which say otherwise are false and delusive. To remove due subordination in society would be like persuading the feet on one's body that they should not obey the dictates of the mind, and should refuse to do their assigned tasks of wading through the dirt and carrying the weight of the rest of the body. Furthermore the poor are still better off where they are; they still enjoy better health and a greater share of happiness than those above them in life. Let them be quiet, civil, contented, and honest in their assigned places. As for education, no public measures are needed for it, since the charity and Sunday schools already do all that one can ask of a school in conveying a sense of religion and a love of order.[99] Bishop Horsley said he did not know "what the mass of the people in any country had to do with the laws but to obey them"; [100] if they did this without complaint, they did all that was expected of them and gave all the signs of life that were considered appropriate.

Finally, all these elements of conservative fear were intensified and seemingly justified by the revolution in France. The English were reminded that not so many generations earlier in their own history, an armed rebellion had successfully overthrown and murdered the king even as the French had done to Louis XVI. Observance of the 30th of January, the day of the execution of Charles I, had been established at the Restoration and had been used in succeeding generations by conservatives as a means of reaffirming the dangers of revolt and the necessity of moderation. Swift's sermon "On the Martyrdom of King Charles I" says that

By bringing to mind the tragedy of this day, and the consequences that have arisen from it, we shall be convinced how necessary it is for those in power to curb, in reason, all such unruly spirits as desire to introduce new doctrines and discipline in the Church, or new forms of government in the state.[101]

In the British Museum Catalogue are listed 225 sermons on Charles I's anniversary during the eighteenth century, most of them adopting the proper conservative tone and using the example of Charles as a defense of the *status quo*. While there was always opposition to the Charles I tradition in the period of liberal expression before the French Revolution, there was more sign that Charles was no longer regarded universally as a martyr and that he had become an object.of absurd, outmoded veneration.[102] The dissenters indeed were never convinced that their ancestors had not been justified in beheading Charles, who was demonstrably a tyrant and a betrayer of popular rights.[103] Wilkes also made bold to say in the House of Commons that the execution of Charles I had been a glorious deed, necessary to English liberty.[104] In March, 1772, Frederick Montague introduced a bill calling for the abolition of the observance of January 30. Opposed by George III,[105] the bill lost by a vote of 125 to 97.[106] The eighteenth century never lost sight of the evil of any form of strife which led to confusion, and, while any proper reason for continuing the January 30 tradition had long since passed, the observance of the day continued. The whole tradition was given a new vitality, along with all other conservative ideas and attitudes, by the French Revolution. Although Priestley could say that the thirtieth of January was a proud day for England just as July 14 was for France,[107] the more general attitude lay in Gibbon's simple statement: "I have never approved of the execution of Charles the First." [108] A resemblance was seen between France and the unhappy reign of Charles, and the people were warned to "let the recollection of these dreary times put us all upon our guard in admitting republican principles." [109] The sermons, especially in 1793, were so forgetful of logic as to express sympathy even for the persecuted Catholic clergy of France.[110]

But the English hardly needed the assistance of their own history to convince them of the horrible dangers of following the example of France. Conservatism formed itself as a particular doctrine or party at this time for the purpose of resisting Jacobinism, which it opposed with all its power.[111] While the dislike of France had been traditional for generations and the conflicts with that country had gone on almost without ceasing, the French Revolution now inspired an absolute horror of everything connected with France, extending even to a distrust of liberty itself because France seemed to favor it.[112] The English idea of national solidarity was upheld against the new French idea of equality and class war.[113] The English were warned by the example of France, which had put "arms into the hands and metaphysical ideas into the heads" of the people.[114] Let England avoid rash and inconsiderate reforms, sudden changes in what is established. Let the nation be prudent and cautious, holding fast to what is certain, and so avoid the tragic chaos of France.[115]

This may be thought of as the usual kind of sentiment against an enemy in war, since war was finally declared on France in 1793. But it had already been present in the early stages of the Revolution to some extent and became far more pronounced in the year 1792, which may be taken as the final turning point in the English view of the French Revolution. Hostility had been growing ever since the flight of Louis XVI to Varennes, but now definite steps may be seen leading to the declaration of war, the ultimate gesture of conservatism against a danger to itself. First came the September massacres of 1792, followed not long after by the execution of Louis XVI in January, 1793. In November, 1792, after Flanders had already been conquered by France, there was a breach of international agreements, threatening French aggression against Holland. The November decree said that the Scheldt and Meuse should be thrown open to navigation, although control of them had long been guaranteed to Holland by treaty. After the English protest against this decree, the French government invited all the nations of Europe to rise against their rulers, promising them the help of the French people if they did so. War seemed then an unavoidable necessity against a force threatening the entire social order of Europe.[116] Once war was declared there could no longer be any question as to the proper attitude toward France:

This is no time to speculate, but to act; to meditate novelties, but to support ancient possessions. . . . We have seen reformations grow into revolutions; and revolutions rush into the worst forms of anarchy . . . our highest duty and our dearest interests call upon us to guard with the most watchful attention against the introduction of French principles and French barbarities. . . . In the view of the miseries arising from vanity and irreligion, let us not forget how rapidly the scene of horror has been opened.[117]

Five years later Cobbett calls down the curse of God upon any Englishmen who would wish to reproduce in England the excesses of the French Revolution. God is asked to give a tenfold measure of their own medicine to such men. They should be afflicted with every curse of which human nature is susceptible and their entire race swept from the face of creation.[118]

THE REFORMERS

The result of this panic-stricken self-defense by the conservative order was to make all reform movements, however mild, impossible. Any effort to change anything was immediately branded with the red mark of Jacobinism. The attempt to abolish the slave trade had made considerable progress, but when France did away with slavery and the trade as part of her revolutionary legislation, Englishmen decided not to follow her example. The black revolt on Santo Domingo, inspired by the example of France at home, supplied new arguments against abolition to English conservatives. A policy of delay and postponement prevented any action, as Jenkinson and Dundas advocated "gradual" changes in the lot of slaves.[119] The reform of Parliament also became impossible. It was said that any change in the manner of elections or any effort to get full and equal representation would necessarily cause the same anarchy and revolution in England as France had endured.[120] Actually, in 1790, even before there had seemed good reason to fear the example of France, English conservatives used the Revolution as an excuse to vote down the mild reform measures of Flood.[121] The same excuse was used by the administration to protect itself from having its own abuses corrected, saying that such correction would be an attack on the constitution itself, with the usual results to be seen abroad. The reform societies which had corresponded with France were identified with the Jacobins, once the revolution had passed into its bloodier stages. The mere fact of having had an innocent correspondence with the French groups, long before it seemed harmful to do so, was made an excuse to damn the moderate English reform groups as dangerous and

Jacobinical.[122] The government took the field against the reform societies and organized groups all over the country, on behalf of church and king against "republicans and levellers." Newspapers were used for official conservative views; spies and agents were insinuated into the reform societies to report on their activities. The reformers found it in time almost impossible to meet in any hall outside private homes, and official witch hunts went on in every town of consequence in England.[123]

In the light of history, all this panic and agitation seems unnecessary in view of the remoteness of the vast majority of Englishmen from any thought of actual revolution. It was obvious to someone like Sheridan, even then, that the fear of actual sedition in England was much exaggerated by the government. The influence of French principles and the number of French agents trying to undermine the nation's peace and stability was far less than had been reported. Actually there was not a syllable of truth, according to Sheridan, in the reports of plots and conspiracies in England; these rumors were used to distract the attention of the people from the cause of reform and from the venal practices of those in power.[124] Sheridan seems to be right in view of the great moderation of English reformers and the reform societies, the actual loyalty of the great mass of Englishmen of all kinds, and the reaction against the French Revolution on the part of some of those who had been its most ardent friends in the beginning.

The English reform societies never seemed to demand anything more revolutionary than an honest Parliament which would represent the people as a whole and to which the people in turn could be loyal. No real threat of force ever existed from these groups, save from a few of the more radical individuals among them. Their declarations of principle, the toasts drunk at their meetings imply only the most sane and moderate desire for improvement on broad lines acceptable to any reasonable person. In no sense could these societies have been charged with threatening harm to the established order in church and state.[125] The final word in refutation of the case of conservatism against the reformers was spoken by Thelwall after his acquittal on a charge of treason:

I call Heaven, this court, and posterity to witness, that I am an enemy to all violence—my activity in those societies arose from an ardent wish to promote the happiness of my fellow creatures—my labours were constantly and unremittingly directed to inspire a love of peace and reverence for the laws. If my writings or expressions carried any appearance of intemperance, it was done with an honest zeal to prevent the effect of inflammatory speeches, and the propositions of violent measures, in those societies by spies and informers, who laboured to lead the unwary into snares.[126]

So also the fear that the undisciplined masses in England would rise in violence against the conservative order was without foundation. The people might very well have started trouble had they wanted to, but they did not want to. Coleridge reports that the multitude were "maddened with excess of loyalty." He appeals to any who can remember in 1818–20 whether, during the French Revolution, "the prevailing passion of the British nation, nay, of the British multitude was not an almost fanatical aversion to everything under the appearance of Republicanism." [127] In no town of any size could a man suspected of holding democratic views move abroad without "receiving some unpleasant proof of the hatred in which his supposed opinions were held by the great majority of the people." [128] Not one person in five hundred in England had any time for democratic or reform propaganda.[129] As for the average English workingman, he was as willing to accept the government and institutions of his country as the ordinary aristocrat. The workmen approved of all the repressive measures of the government, and, instead of pleading for liberty and equality, joined in the cry of church and king.[130] Actually what violence there was because of the excess of popular frenzy and indignation was on the side of church and king, so that Burke's *Reflections* were "at least as dangerous to peace and good order as Mr. Paine's *Rights of Man*." [131] The Birmingham riots in July, 1791, released a frenzy of destruction by the mob against everything unorthodox, including harmless and loyal dissenters like Priestley. The houses and possessions of suspected liberals and dissenters were burned, as the law turned out to be completely helpless to stem the tide of enthusiasm for church and king. Priestley lost everything in the fire, including vast amounts of manuscript embodying years of work. The authorities issued advertisements pleading with the rioters not to burn any more houses, since they would injure many loyal families and add to the burden of taxes which might seem more grievous to other friends of church and king.[132]

We have then the paradox that the fear of the mob which was so strong an element in English conservatism was especially unfounded at the very time when it was supposed to be most dangerous—in a revolutionary period when the mob might have its greatest chance to make itself felt as a destructive force. In the 1790's the English mob was in fact a conservative force; far from being a danger in its unthinking fury, it acted as a gratuitous means of maintaining the *status quo* by directing its frenzy against the liberal elements instead of helping these elements to change society.

Writing to Mrs. Gibbon in August, 1792, the historian is happy to realize "that the most respectable part of Opposition has cordially joined in the support of 'things as they are.' " [133] After the September massacres in 1792, men like Mackintosh ceased to vindicate Gaul and had no desire but to forget France.[134] The poet Cowper could no longer rejoice with the French Revolutionists, in his abhorrence of violence and his belief that reform of any kind should come from above to those below in society.[135] Coleridge and Southey and Wordsworth in the end had to give up also and to recognize that the French Revolution was not the signal for universal happiness they had first supposed.[136] Godwin, who began to feel the denunciation which he had escaped at first, summarizes the total collapse of any sympathy for the liberal movement in England by the year 1797:

The societies have perished, or . . . have shrunk to a skeleton; the days of democratical declamation are no more; even the starving labourer in the alehouse is become the champion of aristocracy. . . . Jacobinism was destroyed; its party as a party was extinguished; its tenets were involved in almost universal unpopularity and odium; they were deserted by almost every man high or low in the island of Great Britain.[137]

English conservatism had thus reasserted itself against the possible dangers of Jacobinism and, having entered upon war with its greatest enemy, enjoyed a power greater than any it had known even in the days when its own fears had more foundation than existed for them in the French Revolutionary period.

PART TWO

THE CASE AGAINST VOLTAIRE

IX · RELIGION
AS THE SUPPORT OF
GOVERNMENT

T HE ENGLISH "case against Voltaire" as a principal cause of the
French Revolution did not proceed indiscriminately from English
conservatism as here analyzed. It had its roots in one of the strongest beliefs of eighteenth-century conservatism, however, and may
be shown to follow logically from an idea which was so widely
held, as Wilberforce said, "that there can be no necessity for
entering into a formal proof of its truth." [1] This idea was that no
government could long maintain itself in peace without the support of some popular religious belief. For, in the absence of such a
belief, there could be no peace, prosperity, or happiness, no safety
of the permanent institutions of society, no true social order.
This was especially true of Christianity, which was considered the
most useful of all creeds to those in power. When it was shown
that Voltaire had undermined the power of Christianity in France
before the Revolution, he was blamed as the original cause of
the ruin which followed, since it was he who had removed the
surest support of the existing order.

The belief that religion strongly supports civil government was
found to have well-nigh timeless origins in the ancient classics.
The idea was discovered in Numa, Solon, Lycurgus, Plutarch,
Plato, and Cicero, who seems to have impressed the eighteenth
century particularly with his hope that all citizens would believe
in the Gods.[2] Yet Burke and his contemporaries might well have
appealed to mere English precedent for their convictions, since

English writers of the sixteenth and seventeenth centuries had also seen the need of religion in a well-ordered state.[3] The best contemporary French opinion was also available in the person of Montesquieu who saw that all religions "contain precepts useful to society," [4] and that since it was necessary for society to have something fixed, it might best obtain this stability from religion.[5] And as the French Revolution drew near, Jacques Necker also perceived *The Importance of Religious Opinions*. For "the maintenance of public order and the increase of private happiness . . . the aid of religion is absolutely necessary" to the sovereign and the laws. Religion seems to complete "the imperfect work of legislation," and to supply "the insufficiency of those means which government is under the necessity of adopting." [6]

Yet there was in reality no need of calling in outside authority: the English seemed incapable of imagining a state separated from the support of the church. Burke said that the English would prefer any superstition, however absurd, to downright impiety. Further, "Church and state are ideas inseparable in their minds, and scarcely is the one ever mentioned without mentioning the other." [7] Throughout the eighteenth century in any case, it seemed that whenever an English writer commented upon the essentials of sound government, he held religion to be indispensable, the surest means of strength and support to the civil power.[8] From the very beginning of society this alliance between religion and government was fundamental [9] so that it was held to be difficult, even "if it be possible, to name a government that ever subsisted long without some connection or alliance with religion." [10] Burke himself, long before he had the motive and the cue for passion provided by the French Revolution, insisted that any government would have to draw in an artificial religion of some kind as a necessary safeguard of its own stability.[11] It seemed then that from long experience and observation, "all wise legislators have laid the foundation of their laws in religion, being sensible, that no other foundation could be trusted." [12] Not only reason itself but "the experience afforded us by the history of every nation that has existed in the world" renders this an unquestionable truth.[13] England herself makes an appeal to wider experience unnecessary; for by her faithful attachment to the Christian religion she has become a splendid proof of what religious reverence can do for political order.[14] But there is no need for so pure an establishment as that of England; even in its most degraded condition, religion "has still given a confidence and stability to particular societies, which would have been sought in vain elsewhere."[15] It is better to have people profess a faith of some kind, even though it contains "useless and sometimes harmful superstitions," than to let them go on without any faith at all.[16]

It may be argued that all this shows only the opinions of conservative Englishmen who are pleased with the prevailing order in church and state and who say only what we should expect them to say. What if those who were notoriously irreligious themselves admit that religion is indispensable? Bentley points out that the good influence of religion on communities and governments is so obvious that the atheists object to it as they say, because it "was first contrived and introduced by politicians, to bring the wild and straggling herds of mankind under subjection and law."[17] The term "atheist" is taken among the more orthodox to mean deists and infidels in general.[18] When Warburton wishes to emphasize the intimacy between church and state, he calls in the ancient infidel, Critias of Athens. For "what would we more, when the adversaries of all religion, themselves confess this truth?" Critias describes the introduction of the belief in a God to " 'some cunning politician, well versed in the knowledge of mankind,' " who hoped thereby to terrify men from doing secret mischief or stirring up disorder.[19] Strangely the admission by infidels that religion aids the operation of government seems not to have deterred them from making war on it. They opposed it on intellectual grounds, yet they "who laboured to erase out of the mind all respect for religion, have acknowledged the importance and expediency of it." Such men as Bayle, Rousseau, and Gibbon all admit that religious belief helps to make government effectual.[20]

Bolingbroke in particular, who "with unwearied application and diligence, endeavoured to destroy religion from the minds of his countrymen, and of all mankind," [21] none the less asserted that "to make government effectual to all the good purposes of it, there must be a religion." [22] But the ultimate tribute comes from no less than Voltaire himself. If this man, the very essence of sneering infidelity and irreverence, should confess that the religion he seemed to despise was none the less needed by society, "what would we more" indeed? Yet few have made so clear an admission, that it is "absolument nécessaire pour les princes et pour les peuples que l'idée d'un être suprême, créateur, gouverneur, rémunérateur et vengeur, soit profondément gravée dans les esprits." [23] Human weakness and perversity are such, "qu'il vaut mieux sans doute pour lui d'être subjugué par toutes les superstitions possibles, pourvu qu'elles ne soient point meurtrières, que de vivre sans religion." Wherever there is an established society, a religion is necessary: for "les lois veillent sur les crimes connus, et la religion sur les crimes secrets." [24] This testimony of Voltaire's is translated and reprinted by the Rev. Andrew Fuller, who is scarcely able to believe the evidence of his senses that these really are the words of Voltaire.[25]

Testimony seems then to have been abundant from ancient times to the end of the eighteenth century, on the part of the reverent and faithful as well as the sworn enemies of the faith, that nothing supports the well-being and safety of society and its government so well as religious belief. Even though such belief take an absurdly superstitious form, it is held to be better for the effectual operation of government than unbelief and impiety. What, then, must be the influence of such a faith as Christianity? Experience has shown, in the opinion of Bishop Porteus, "that of all the religions that have ever yet appeared in the world, none were ever so well adapted to promote the welfare of society, and the great ends of civil government, as the Christian revelation." [26] There never was any religion so well fitted for the support of civilized government as Christianity,[27] which is and "must ever be the firmest bond for upholding the authority of the magistrate, and preserving the peace of society." [28] Christianity so strengthens the union of religion and civil government because it has a greater tendency than any other faith to preserve men from vice and to encourge them in virtue.[29] As the *Encyclopaedia Britannica* of 1797 points out, Christianity supports civil order because it is so favorable to "the virtue and the happiness of mankind." [30] It tends to check the weak nature of man, with the result that "the best Christian is the best member of civil society." [31] Again the testimony of an "atheist" shows how true this assertion is. Notorious for his dislike of organized Christianity because he thought that it had been corrupted by theology and so defeated in its chief design, Bolingbroke nevertheless admits that "no religion ever appeared in the world, whose natural tendency was so much directed to promote the peace and happiness of mankind." [32] The basic qualities that mark a Christian show how true this is. It must be remembered "that a conscientious submission to the sovereign powers is, no less than brotherly love, a distinctive badge of Christ's disciples." [33] One may even recognize a Christian by his superior equipment for excellent citizenship: his qualities of obedience and submission to authority. Rousseau himself believed that "Christianity inculcates servitude and dependence . . . true Christians are formed for slaves; they know it, and never trouble themselves about conspiracies and insurrections." [34] Christianity binds men in conscience to obey civil governors, lest in offending them they offend God Himself. No matter how evil the governors of the divine choice, "submission to God's appointment is required of us; and we should always prefer suffering to sin." [35] God did not intend to "bestow absolute perfection on any system of laws here below," and it is clear "that a wise man will hesitate, and a good man tremble, in taking any part in the subversion of the Government under which the providence of Almighty God has placed him." [36] The true Christian "will love the government and the laws which protect him, without asking by whom they are administered." [37] Actually, there is only one question for the Christian in the face of authority: "Who are the powers? And our duty . . . is to obey without resistance." [38]

In addition, the Christian religion has a final check on human impulse through its doctrine of rewards and punishments in an after life. The conservative usefulness of this doctrine was axiomatic. "Mankind can never be kept in subjection to government, but by the hopes and fears of another world; nay, the express precepts, promises, and threatenings of the gospel are requisite for this purpose. The unwritten law of nature is too pliable, too subtle, and too feeble." [39] Paley insists that "a person who acts under the impression of these hopes and fears . . . is more likely to advance both the public happiness and his own, than one who is destitute of all expectation of a future account." [40] Not only will future reward and punishment restrain men through fear, but it will console them with the hope that the inequalities of this life will be rectified in a future world. They will not then rebel against injustice and inequality. Christians forego the usual human impulse to envy or regret in the face of differences of rank or fortune or the burdens of oppression, and they learn "submission without meanness." [41] Such a plausible truth could not escape the eye of Voltaire. He regarded these principles as necessary for the preservation of the human species [42] and as providing a double restraint upon rulers and subjects alike. Belief in a God who rewards the good, punishes the evil, and forgives the venial is most useful to mankind: "C'est le seul frein des hommes puissants, qui commettent insolemment les crimes publics; c'est le seul frein des hommes qui commettent adroitement les crimes secrets." [43] Even in his own daily life the great infidel saw the usefulness of this belief in a future reckoning, as *The Monthly Review,* examining his *L'Evangile du jour,* suggests:

Concerning future rewards and punishments, the author says, 'he wishes his lawyer, his taylor, his servants, and his wife to believe them, because he will then be much less in danger of robbery and cuckoldom'; from which an inference follows which he has not drawn; either the doctrine of future rewards and punishments is true, or God has so constructed the world, that its well-being depends upon the belief of a lie.[44]

Now it follows that if religion, and Christianity in particular, tends to encourage a submissive and obedient attitude toward civil government, the decline of religious belief will remove one of the strongest supports of the existing order. Should the government be unpleasant to the people, they will rise up against it when restraint imposed by religious belief is weakened. Rulers of nations ought therefore to guard their people against infidelity. The spirit of opposition to government is the natural offspring of irreligion,[45] just as the spirit of submission is the fruit of devout faith. Experience has shown that the decline of religion is followed by the dissolution of states: "sap Religion and you sap the state." [46] Long ago Bacon had warned against even "innovation in matters of Religion," [47] as a first possible cause of sedition. The lenient attitude of toleration was also a possible danger, suggesting a "levelling republican spirit in the Church" which might lead to republicanism in the state. There is danger in the mere notion "that religion and government admit of improvement; much of their influence and efficacy depending on the persuasion that they are already perfect." [48] The attitude of skepticism, or the use of reason as opposed to revelation, is likewise dangerous and leads to discontent with established authority.[49] If even these remote beginnings of a questioning point of view are dangerous, such extremes as deism may well lead to rebellion against the reigning powers. In England, certainly, "the idea of a *Deist* and a good *Democrat* seemed to have been universally compounded," [50] and according to the *Anti-Jacobin Review* "the general habit of scepticism" produced by deistical writings "leads to the overthrow of all established governments." [51] Thus when the Christian religion, the very cement of the governmental structure, is renounced, "the peace, the order, the comfort, the security of civil government are for ever gone," and the way is prepared for every disaster feared by man.[52] The door is open to vice, disorder, and misery; confusion and violence will result and every evil work ensue.[53]

Once again the orthodox view is supported by a skeptical conservative. Gibbon has "sometimes thought of writing a dialogue
of the dead, in which Lucian, Erasmus, and Voltaire should mutually acknowledge the danger of exposing an old superstition to
the contempt of the blind and fanatic multitude." [54]

Finally, if those who wish to keep things as they are see that
they must have the help of religion in doing so, those who are
subversive must also realize that Christianity has to be undermined before their desired revolution can succeed. For "is not
every attempt to subvert this institution, or to turn the dispensers
of these ordinances into ridicule; is it not, in fact, a blow levelled
at the foundation of government?" [55] Common sense will dictate the abolition of Christianity to every political association
bent on a violent uprising.[56] Bishop Watson therefore warns the
people of England as to the procedure which revolutionists must
inevitably follow:

they will first attempt to persuade you that there is nothing after death,
no heaven for the good, no hell for the wicked, that there is no God,
or none who regards your actions: and when you shall be convinced
of this, they will think you properly prepared to perpetrate every
crime which may be necessary for the furtherance of their own
designs. . . .[57]

This obliteration of "the sense of Deity, of moral sanctions, and
a future world" is an invariable part of modern subversive prepara-
tions.[58] Pious citizens and good Christians are of no use to "these
emissaries of sedition," [59] who must needs mar "all sway, by
mocking sway divine." [60] This "rage of modern innovation" has
compelled those wishing to undermine the existing order, "to
deny the utility" of organized religion.[61] They have observed "that
the precepts of a Christian Church were absolutely incompatible
with the meditated horrors of Revolutionary atrocity," [62] and
have therefore deliberately set out to destroy the influence of
Christianity.

It is easy to apply this entire theory to the French revolutionists. Leaving out for the moment the long-drawn philosophic con-

spiracy, the means used by the active revolutionists to gain their
ends could have been of only one kind, to the horrified view of
conservative England. Members of the infamous Jacobin club
are represented as enjoying a review of their recent exploits and
looking eagerly to the future:

Second Jacobin: . . . The wisest thing we ever did was driving all
those priests, who were true Christians, out of the kingdom.—I hate
a Christian; their religion teaches them to honour their King, and to
submit to all who are in authority over them, and bear no malice or
envy in their heart. We worship men who have done all in their power
to abolish all religion; we cannot bring the people to our purposes
if they fear God and honour the King; to abolish both at once was
absolutely necessary—and what a glorious harvest shall we have if we
can blind the infernal English! [63]

It was then admittedly clear to the revolutionists, that "no other
means could be found—no casuistry—no sophistry could support
the abolition and destruction of earthly monarchy; but the denial
of heavenly supremacy." [64] And the national assembly recog-
nizing this, told the people that "religion was all a hum, and that
they would live as happy if they worked or danced, or got drunk
of a Sunday, as they would if they went to church morning and
afternoon." [65]

It was also natural to transfer these general considerations to
certain individuals who had been active in the French Revolution.
The English held that men wishing to overthrow government have
always been, generally speaking, unbelievers themselves,[66] and,
according to "the uniform tenor of historical record," popular
leaders of revolt have been singularly cruel and godless.[67] But it
was not enough for English observers to take into account the
merely active leaders. The roots of the French Revolution lay far
back in the life of a certain extraordinary man who made war
upon religion and who set in motion the forces which finally broke
out into rebellion:

With a strong disposition to evil, he was no friend to restraint of any
kind; so he abhorred all law but the law of liberty, which is no law;

and all government but the government of equality, which is no government: and as religion is the support both of law and government, he hated that worst of all.[68]

We must now inquire into the manner in which the condemnation of Voltaire developed from the English belief in the utility of religion. If the English believed that the Christian religion was indispensable to the support of government and that anyone trying to undermine that religion was automatically preparing the way for revolution, it must follow that Voltaire, who had been active in weakening French belief in Christianity, was at least a partial cause of the French revolution. His guilt became undeniable when the revolutionists themselves admitted their debt to his influence. And when the Abbé Barruel drew all these various threads together in his *Memoirs Illustrating the History of Jacobinism,* English conservatism was ready to believe anything he chose to say about Voltaire's authorship of the French Revolution.

X · EVIDENCE OF FRENCH INFIDELITY

In THE GENERATION before 1789, English observers of Parisian society often remarked on the indifference, if not open hostility, to religion among French men of letters. The "philosophes" seemed to recognize no authority in religious matters and tended uniformly toward "atheism." These English observations were applied with special force to the friends of Baron d'Holbach, who were considered as openly hostile to orthodox religious belief and influential in a manner most harmful to France. Englishmen who learned to know Diderot, D'Alembert, D'Holbach, Helvetius, and others of their circle, not to mention Voltaire himself, were never in doubt as to the determined enmity of these men to the "infamous thing" in the religion of France.

When the English disapproval of this anti-religious spirit finally converges on Voltaire at the end of the eighteenth century, it takes the form of an accusation of a deliberate conspiracy. Not only were these men personally unbelievers, but, led by Voltaire, they systematically set out to uproot all religion, and Christianity in particular from France. *The Monthly Review* in 1799 is probably exaggerating when it says that readers "for thirty years past, have been perfectly aware of the avowed, systematic, and ostentatiously notorious cooperation of the Encyclopedists to overthrow Christianity." [1] The truth is perhaps halfway between this view and the statement by the Rev. Henry Kett that a concerted plot was hardly noticed in England.[2] In any case the growth of infidelity and the enmity to organized religion in France were apparent to many English visitors who were able to see the evidence at first hand. Others learned of these irreligious forces through letters or works available to the English reading public. This early awareness of an anti-religious movement in France under the leadership of Voltaire is the first important step toward final condemnation of him as the cause of the evils allegedly resulting from French infidelity.

Warburton had noticed as early as 1746 that France and Italy were "overrun with the worst kind of Deism." [3] This came in time to be especially true of France, which was inclined to throw off Popery and to go to the other extremes of deism and infidelity. It applied particularly to the men of letters whose guilt seems to have been obvious.[4] So different was the tone of literary society in France from that in England that it was in a French writer's favor if he could show an infidel or even materialistic spirit. An open skepticism made one sure of welcome in the apartments of Mme du Deffand and Mlle de l'Espinasse.[5] Writers were ambitious to be shown as "esprits forts" and to share the acclaim given those who wrote down all religions without distinction.[6] Horace Walpole becomes very weary of this invariable spirit of unbelief, which he finds in its extreme at the Baron d'Holbach's dinners. To his friend George Augustus Selwyn, Walpole confides in 1765 that these meetings are at last more than he can bear:

I sometimes go to Baron d'Holbach's; but I have left off his dinners, as there was no bearing the authors, and philosophers, and savants, of which he has a pigeonhouse full. They soon turned my head with a new system of antediluvian deluges which they have invented to prove the eternity of matter. . . . In short nonsense for nonsense, I like the Jesuits better than the philosophers.[7]

Gray also learns of this French spirit from Walpole, and frankly admits that he is shocked by it. "As an Englishman and an Antigallican," says Gray, as if the second term naturally followed from the first, "I rejoice at their dulness and their nastiness." But their atheism "is a little too much, too shocking to rejoice at. I have been long sick at it in their authors, and hated them for it: but I pity their poor innocent people of fashion. They were bad enough, when they believed everything." [8] The austere conservatism of Gray's life would naturally lead him to disapprove, but the frown of Gibbon is more significant. It seems to suggest that the French infidels were going to an intolerable extreme, not to be endured even by one who became a notorious foe of Christianity himself. In 1763 in Paris, Gibbon, too, denounced the philosophers. He could not approve when "they laughed at the scepticism of Hume, preached the tenets of atheism with the bigotry of dogmatists, and damned all believers with ridicule and contempt." [9]

Of this impious circle, Diderot, author of numerous immoral and scandalous works [10] was, according to Sir Samuel Romilly, one of the most zealous in the spread of irreligion. Romilly spends some time with Diderot in November, 1781, and describes the man's fervor in the preaching of materialism. Diderot praises the English for having led the way to true philosophy, but they have long since been surpassed by the adventurous spirit of the French. " 'Vous autres . . . vous mêlez la théologie avec la philosophie; c'est gâter tout, c'est mêler la mensonge avec la vérité; il faut abrer la théologie.' " [11]

In the minds of those Englishmen therefore who were able personally to observe this trend among Parisian men of letters, there seems to have been little doubt as to the tendency of the new "philosophy." To them, a "philosophe" or "philosopher" in Paris just before the Revolution was any person who professed in writing to be skeptical in matters of religion.[12] Such men set up a new religion of their own "with doctrines opposite . . . to those of Christianity." [13] Walpole wearily tells Gray that the "philosophic" obsession is universal; "tout le monde est philosophe." [14] This set of wretches who have dignified themselves by the title of philosophers have achieved wide influence in France, where they have been "endeavouring to quench the light of the human understanding, to confound all the principles of morality, and to stifle all the natural feelings of the heart." [15] They have intro-

duced a system of gay morality "to disguise a system of wickedness and infidelity," [16] the whole designed to persuade the unwary "to wander over a wide stormy ocean without a pilot, and
without a leading star." [17]

It would have been serious enough to the conservative English
if "philosophy" had implied nothing more than religious skepticism. But whenever an Englishman was admitted into a select
circle in Paris, he soon found that some predominant spirit took
the lead, and "if he is ambitious of making a master-stroke indeed,
he may go the length to declare, that he has the honour to profess
himself an atheist. The creed of this leading spirit is the creed
of the junto; there is no fear of controversy." [18] Priestley found in
1774 that atheism was so prominent among the philosophers that
they considered Voltaire himself guilty of religious timidity if
not bigotry for the mildness of his views:

When I was myself in France in 1774, I saw sufficient reason to believe,
that hardly any person of eminence, in church or state, and especially
in the least degree eminent in philosophy, or literature (whose opinions
in all countries, are, sooner or later, adopted by others) were believers
in Christianity; and no person will suppose that there has been any
change in favour of Christianity in the last twenty years . . . not only
were the philosophers, and other leading men in France, at that time
unbelievers in Christianity, or deists, but atheists, denying the being
of a God. Nay Voltaire himself, who was then living, was considered
by them as a weak-minded man, because, though an unbeliever in
revelation, he believed in a God.[19]

Horace Walpole tells Gray in 1765, that one of the lady devotees
of the philosophers had contemptuously said of Voltaire, "Il est
bigot, c'est un deiste." [20] But the famous anecdote telling of Hume's
encounter with seventeen professed atheists at the table of Baron
d'Holbach dramatizes the philosophic pride of France in unbelief.
It seemed that what was so rare in the Englishman's experience as
to be quite incredible could be almost indefinitely multiplied
in Paris where the believer in God was very seldom encountered
in literary or "Philosophic" circles. Sir Samuel Romilly has preserved this incident, professing to have learned it from Diderot:

He spoke of his acquaintance with Hume. "Je vous dirai un trait de lui, mais il vous sera un peu scandaleux peut-être, car vous Anglais vous croyez *un peu* en Dieu; pour nous autres nous n'y croyons guères. Hume dina avec une grande compagnie chez le Baron d'Holbach. Il était assis a côté du Baron; on parla de la religion naturelle: 'Pour les Athées,' disait Hume, 'je ne crois pas qu'il en existe; je n'en ai jamais vu.' 'Vous avez été un peu malheureux' répondit l'autre, 'vous voici à table avec dixsept pour la première fois.' " [21]

Disapproval of French infidelity implied or expressed in the comments of most English observers is not unanimous among those who knew the "philosophes." The more liberal Englishmen who recognized the philosophic trend in Paris found themselves in harmony with its irreligious spirit. John Wilkes had been a fellow student of the Baron d'Holbach at Leyden and upon being exiled to Paris, Wilkes was received as an honored guest by the philosophic circle. He found himself in complete sympathy with D'Holbach, Helvetius, Diderot, D'Alembert and the rest.[22] On his part Wilkes enjoyed his intimacy with the freethinkers of Paris,[23] and after his return to England he continued to exchange letters with D'Holbach.[24]

Garrick is another who seems to have become intimate with the enemies of religion and to have maintained the friendliest relations with them.[25] Wilkes even acts as a messenger between Garrick and their common friends in the later days of his own exile in Paris. In January, 1767, he sends Garrick a packet "from our most amiable friend Helvetius," and assures the actor that he is greatly missed by his Parisian friends, especially by "Monsieur et Madame d'Holbach," who, along with the others, "vous font milles complimens." [26]

It seems not to have disturbed Garrick and Wilkes that the infidelity of their friends was gradually having consequences beyond itself which would appear dangerous to most English observers. For the "philosophes" were not content with their own infidelity: by their zealous endeavors they set out to encourage others to a similar disbelief,[27] which in turn led people to feel disrespect for their governors and to prepare themselves for the outright overthrow of existing institutions. Long before in the eighteenth century, Addison had commented on that monstrous species of men, the "Zealots in Atheism" who propagate their infidelity "with as much fierceness and contention, wrath and indignation, as if the safety of mankind depended upon it." [28] Such men continued to scoff at religion with "unwearied pains and assiduity" and to do all in their power to make "Proselytes to Unrighteousness." [29] In the case of the French "philosophes," this characteristic infidel effort "to make proselytes by their writings" [30] provided the real cause for alarm. They were like men afflicted with some contagious disease, who none the less ran out into the multitude "with the infernal design of communicating the pestilence" to others. Diderot attempts even to convert Sir Samuel Romilly from his "unhappy errors," and reads for his purpose a little work of his own: "a dialogue between himself and a lady of quality much attached to religion, whom he attempts to convince of her folly." [31]

The diligence of the infidels was such, their scornful warfare upon "everything that falls not under the notice of the senses" so zealously waged, that religion was seen to fall, in the eyes of Hume, into an "almost universal contempt . . . among both sexes, and among all ranks of men." [32] Infidelity seemed determined to rid the face of the earth even of the name of God.[33] Inevitably the reverence of men for those placed above them on this earth began to be weakened. D'Alembert himself ascribed the growing popular indifference concerning the birth of a future king to the effect of that "philosophy" which he himself was so diligent in teaching.[34] The French became worse subjects as they grew more "philosophic," so that other nations ought to oppose the French freethinkers: otherwise their people's morals will also decline and they will become worse subjects.[35] Lady Mary Wortley Montagu was so convinced of this danger that when visiting Florence, Italy, in 1751, she deliberately avoided the meetings of freethinkers at the house of Lady Orford. These people met weekly "to the scandal of all good Christians." Lady Mary refused to join them, because it was wrong to jest at ordinances which are so necessary to all civilized governments.[36]

The truth of the general conservative principle seemed clear long before the Revolution in France: in the spread of religious infidelity there lay the germ of irreverence for existing government and the danger of a general movement for change. Philosophy was subtly preparing the minds of the people for a new era; it was laboring to free mankind from all restraints, both human and divine,[37] so that France was bound to plunge headlong toward violent change. Smollett in his "dying Prediction" of 1771, saw that the French passion for abstract questions of religion and government made "a revolution, political, social, and religious . . . inevitable in France." [38] In 1781, eight years before the outbreak of the revolution,

The progress of philosophy in France had already begun to weaken the reverence of the people for their old despotic government, and to undermine the influence of the clergy. . . . I well remember a conversation I had with Captain Recarte . . . about the year 1781 . . . he remarked, that the minds of the people were in general prepared for a change. "Fenelon" said he, convinced us we were blind as to the nature and intent of government: *Voltaire* tore open our eye-lids, *Raynal* couched our eyes, and *Franklin* with his American sponge wiped away the corroding humour, so that we now see as clearly as you.[39]

Apparently then there was some knowledge among Englishmen before the French Revolution that infidelity was the accepted attitude among Parisian men of letters. It was easily seen that the philosophers were eager to spread their irreligious point of view among the people. It was also easily deduced that such an effort would endanger the existing order in church and state, so that the crumbling foundations of the old regime in France were no secret to English observers.

More important for the case against Voltaire is the belief that the spread of French infidelity was no accident, but the result of a deliberate plan to destroy all religion, and especially Christianity. Besides the outspoken unbelief of the "philosophes," other factors might well have suggested to the English that a subtle plot was in operation looking to the overthrow of the church in France. The production of the *Encyclopédie* and the concerted attack upon the French clergy were ultimately found to be deliberate steps in the subversive plan; Englishmen had some awareness of their implications, as well as of the meaning of Voltaire's activities in the last twenty years of his life.

In 1752 there appeared in London *"The Plan of the French Encyclopedia; or, Universal Dictionary of Arts, Sciences, Trades and Manufactures . . . ,* translated from the Preface of the French editors, Mess. Diderot and Alembert." As if answering in advance the objections of the orthodox, the editors praise Christianity as a faith sent down from Heaven, against which mere reason and philosophy can never prevail. The existence of God is readily admitted, the necessity of revealed religion is insisted on; no outright atheism or unreasonably impious language is used in this sensible and moderate plan for the progress of knowledge and science. This pretense was not long in being exposed by vigilant English conservatism. In 1763 Mrs. Carter denounces the Encyclopedists as men who undermine morality, break the connection between earth and heaven, and try "to cheat mankind out of all that is worth living for, and all that is worth dying for." [40] Actually the *Encyclopédie* had not proceeded beyond the article on "Geneva" before it was suspected of an effort to introduce and to spread religious skepticism. The Rev. Robert Brown, pastor of the English Church at Utrecht, edited in 1761 the *Lettres Critiques d'un Voyageur Anglois sur l'Article Génève du Dictionnaire Encyclopédique*. The purpose of these letters was to expose the *Encyclopédie* as a calculated attempt at spreading the subtle poisons of unbelief.[41] The offensive article on Geneva appeared in England in 1764 in a volume of *Miscellaneous Pieces in Literature, History, and Philosophy* by *"Mr. D'Alembert."* There could be little question in the minds of English readers as to D'Alembert's intention. His "Short Account of the Government of Geneva" [42] describes the religion of that city as well. Most of the clergy are said to doubt the divinity of Christ. There is of course adoration of one God, but a reverence for Christ and the Scriptures is perhaps the only feature distinguishing the Christianity of Geneva from pure deism. D'Alembert tries to glorify the ideal conditions in Geneva, where people have sense enough to pare down their religious belief to something like deism. The reader is supposed to infer then, that there is no advantage to a people in accepting Christianity without reservation.

In 1772 *Select Essays from the Encyclopedia* were published in London. A clear assertion was made in an "Advertisement to the Public" that much of the original work was irreligious in tone. All the articles "discovered to be offensive to religion, morality, and consequently to the welfare of society in general" [43] are now omitted, with the result that a generally orthodox and harmless impression is given to the reader. The real tendency of the original work was again made clear in 1781 through a translation of the *Private Life of Louis XV* by Moufflé d'Angerville. As early as 1753 it was easy to foresee that "a work of such extent, requiring a great number of assistants, would of course form a point of union for philosophers, who from this time would begin to grow into a sect and thus make one body." Their design was to dissipate prejudice, to destroy error, and to enlighten the human race. They developed a settled and regular system with indissoluble ties. They labored without intermission to spread their doctrine in all its forms. "They even insinuated themselves into the Schools of divinity, the foundations of which they sapped, by combating it even through the mouths of the students themselves." [44]

THE JESUITS ATTACKED

The attack upon the French clergy was not hidden in the pages of a learned work, but was so openly violent as to accomplish for a time the fondest hopes of the "philosophic" warriors. Their system called into question much of the authority and importance of the French clergy.[45] The Jesuits seem to have been singled out for particular abuse, as if the destruction of the remaining clerical orders depended on the suppression of this, the most powerful of them all. On his way to Paris in 1765, the Rev. William Cole hears loose and licentious talk both of the French religion and the clergy. The Jesuits are denounced as deserving the worst of fates, and the opinion is expressed that "their banishment was only a prelude to that of the other religious orders." As the abuse of clerical orders was exorbitant, so praise of Voltaire and Rousseau was proportionately high.[46] On meeting his friend Horace Walpole in Paris, Cole is shocked at the extent of this anticlerical feeling. On Cole's remarking that one saw few regular clergy on the streets, Walpole tells him that the clergy had been ordered by their superiors to keep within the cloister, lest their enemies be offended by their too open appearance in the world. Many of the younger monks had petitioned for leave to quit their religious habit.[47] The government ceased to support the clergy as before; they became generally less conspicuous on the streets and other public places. As people heard less of them, so less was thought of them.[48] In time, the priests were so neglected and despised that the few who were to be seen looked dreary and solitary, "their visages pale and sallow, with the blush of health and youth destroyed; at once disregarded by the vulgar, and contemned by the wise."[49]

The strong feeling against the Jesuits accounts partly for the fact that their friend and protector, the Dauphin, was "maligned, hated and abused by the Deistical Philosophers and their faction." Their joy on every intimation that the Dauphin would not recover from his illness was indeed a "shameful sight."[50] Sir Robert Talbot in 1771 sent back to England from Paris "all that has been published here for and against the Jesuits." He is amazed at the rapid and apparently helpless decline of an order once so learned and powerful. It is defended only by a few half-starved priests, fanatics, and dunces and has gone down so completely before its adversaries that the entire structure of clerical orders is threatened and, with it, the main support of the Romish church in France.[51] It is a matter for general European astonishment none the less that the Jesuits should have succumbed so rapidly, yet their enemies seem to have been "so numerous, so potent, and so implacable, that their destruction was inevitable." [52] More detailed information on the crusade against the Jesuits had reached England in 1766 with the publication of D'Alembert's book on the subject, *Account of the Destruction of the Jesuits in France*. Although D'Alembert professes to tell the dispassionate truth of the whole matter as befits an historian, it is not long before his true bias appears. He points out that the Jesuits made a serious error in attacking the *Encyclopédie* and its philosophers, and a completely fatal mistake in denouncing Voltaire. This celebrated individual proceeded to expose the Jesuits to public laughter. After he had made them ridiculous, they made themselves odious by their fanatical intolerance and persecution, their selfish, domineering, scheming, and factious behavior in the country as a whole. The people were irritated by the spectacle of an order supposedly pledged to humility and charity trying falsely to run everything and to control French affairs from the court to the provinces. Their just and salu tary destruction is owing to the philosophers: "The nation, and the philosophers at its head, wished the annihilation of these fathers, because they are intolerant, persecutors, turbulent and formidable." [53] D'Alembert also predicts that the fall of the Jesuits is only a prelude to the destruction of other religious orders in France and suggests, as a means of hastening this end, the revival of old laws forbidding entrance into monastic orders before the age of twenty-five.[54] In reviewing the French edition of D'Alembert's work in 1765, the *Monthly Review* mentions the author's prediction that the other monastic groups in France would now also be in danger.[55] More circumstantial information as to the fate of the Jesuits became current with the reprint in 1769 of a "Memorial presented to the late Pope, by the French ambassador, for the total extinction of the Society of Jesuits, and the secularization of all who composed it." [56]

The English were then to some extent aware of the desperate plight of the French clergy and the grievances under which they labored. "Philosophy" acquired boldness with its growing strength, and the clergy fought desperately to maintain their ancient power. As the illumination of the "philosophers" spread throughout France, respect for the clergy diminished and with their backs to the wall the Lord's anointed fought to postpone the inevitable.[57] Censures, decrees, suppressions were only of temporary avail, and such incidents as the cleverly impious thesis of the Abbé de Prades, which escaped the notice of the Sorbonne censors, delivered severe blows to the clerical cause. This latter affair showed the arrogance and cynicism of the enemies of the church, who made capital of the controversy which was distracting the orthodox in France between the Molinist and Jansenist groups. While those involved in this quarrel were concerned only with getting their views to prevail, the impious took advantage of their distraction to shake the foundations of religion itself. De Maupeou reports "a public thesis being maintained [by the Abbé de Prades] without opposition, in the first university of the Christian world, whereby all the false principles of incredulity are systematically established." [58] In addition to such devices, the "philosophers" had always the powerful weapon of their unanswerable ridicule, and "their chief priest" in particular was capable of such raillery as no parliamentary decree could extinguish.[59]

If these signs of a concerted attack on the Christian religion were clear, discerning Englishmen could see the underlying plan. The actual "works of the foreign infidels," composed in order to advance a plot against Christianity, seem to have made little impression in England.[60] But as early as 1762 attention was drawn by the *Annual Register* to the revelations of the *Lèttres critiques d'un voyageur anglois,* wherein it is shown that the French infidels are deliberately bent upon weakening and finally uprooting the tree of religion.[61] They proceed by subtle insinuations in their writings. Equivocal language is used so that by adroit suggestion more is conveyed to the reader than is literally said.[62] The *Annual Register* accepts this interpretation of the "philosophic" aims, speaking of a "club of pretended sages" who seem "to have formed a sort of confederacy against the cause of Christianity, and are not a little anxious about making proselytes." [63] They use a language which has a meaning of its own with metaphorical implications imposed on the literal sense,[64] thus heightening the impression that their war upon religion is carefully planned and safely concealed although effective. Their zeal has a vicious depravity in determining upon the ruin and annihilation of Christianity, for it will be satisfied with nothing less than complete destruction.[65] The war upon the clergy is, in turn, part of the larger fight against religion itself. The conspirators see that "the stroke that is apparently aimed at the members of a society overturns in its rebound the principles by which they profess to be regulated." [66]

Those who realized the extent of the plot against the very existence of Christianity could not fail to see the danger to established government. If the one follows naturally from the other, Walpole could not be long in discovering this amid his wide Parisian experience. He writes to the Hon. Henry Seymour Conway in 1765 from Paris, saying that he is sure of the philosophic danger to monarchy as well as to the church. The "philosophers" rejoice at the coming death of the Dauphin, having feared his friendship with the Jesuits. The term "philosophers" comprehends "almost everybody; and . . . means men, who, avowing war against popery, aim, many of them at a subversion of all religion, and, still many more, at the destruction of regal power." [67] Another observer at first hand who sees the coming end of the existing government as well as religion is the Rev. John de la Flechere, English clergyman following his vocation on the Continent. He writes to his friends, John and Charles Wesley, from Burgundy in 1778:

a set of freethinkers, great admirers of Voltaire and Rousseau, Bayle and Mirabeau, seem bent upon destroying Christianity and government. "With one hand (said a lawyer who has written something against them) they shake the throne, and with the other they throw down the altars! If we believe them, the world is the dupe of Kings and priests. Religion is fanaticism and superstition. Subordination is slavery and tyranny. Christian morality is absurd, unnatural and impracticable; and Christianity the most bloody religion that ever was. . . ." Popery will certainly fall in France, in this or the next century.[68]

The consequences of the "philosophic" spirit were also clear to those who read *The Speech of Anthony Louis Seguier,* translated from the French in 1781. Seguier expresses his alarm when a new edition of Raynal's *History of the Indies* appears. John Wesley had violently condemned this work in his *Journal,* April 26, 1778. He saw in Raynal's performance a danger both to Christianity and to monarchy, Raynal himself being "one of the bitterest enemies of the Christian Revelation that ever set pen to paper." [69] Seguier, before the French parliament, makes public his similar reaction. "Philosophy" is the enemy of all that is "most dear to the tranquillity and happiness of mankind." Raynal seeks to undermine "the sovereignty of earthly powers, and the Christian religion. . . . Kings are his tyrants, and the ministers of the church his hypocrites." [70] A close examination of Raynal's book would "display the general plan of subversion contained in this dreadful production," a work which is "equally contrary to the respect due the Divinity, and the submission we should be in to sovereign power." [71] Let men know therefore, the true intention of "philosophy," which would break the chain uniting the sovereign and his people, "even that which binds kings one to the other." [72]

There seems to be some evidence then that before the French Revolution the English had detected the plot against Christianity from which the Revolution was said to have sprung. At least two of the essential elements of the conspiracy, the *Encyclopédie* and the war on the clergy, were clear enough to English observers. Some were also able to see the consequences to the government of France implied in the impending fall of the church. It is Burke who tells the English once and for all in 1790 that infidel "philosophy" was a factor in causing the revolution in France. Indeed Burke had been himself much alarmed over the course of things in France long since, and on his return in 1773 from Paris, he had spoken of his fears and his opinions of the French infidels to the House of Commons:

> He pointed out the conspiracy of atheism to the watchful jealousy of governments . . . he was not over fond of calling the aid of the secular arm to suppress doctrines and opinions; but if ever it was to be raised, it should be against those enemies of their kind, who would take from us the noblest prerogative of our nature, that of being a religious animal. . . . "Already under the systematic attacks of these men, I see many of the old props of good government beginning to fail. I see propagated principles which will not leave to religion even a toleration, and make virtue herself less than a name." [73]

Thus Burke himself and his readers in 1790 were not entirely unprepared for the accusation which he leveled against the infidel "philosophers" as a cause of the French Revolution.

THE PERFIDY OF VOLTAIRE

Meanwhile, what of the archcriminal upon whose head the blame for all the disasters of France finally falls? It was not until some time after Voltaire's death in 1778 that even his long record of anticlerical activity weakened his immense European reputation as the great literary genius of the eighteenth century. The reader in the general literature of England in the eighteenth century comes upon references to Voltaire by the hundreds, many of them in high praise of his achievement. His work was enormously diffused in England, so that both his purely literary and his later "philosophical" works of an anticlerical bias were available to English readers.[74] Along with a great deal of admiring praise for what seemed admirable to the English in Voltaire's long career, there was an increasing awareness of his fight against organized religion in France and a growing fear of the dangers which such an hostility necessarily involved, especially if, as it seemed, Voltaire was part of an organized scheme to destroy Christianity. Thus all praise of Voltaire, no matter how high, must in the end have a religious qualification.[75]

As is to be expected, the *Plan of the French Encyclopedia* approves of Voltaire. It is sure that he cannot fail of a distinguished seat among "the very few poets of the first order" because of his "extraordinary genius." [76] Goldsmith in his brief memoir of Voltaire (1759) shows the Frenchman's great reputation as a man of letters, but makes little of his irreligion, which does not seem to become really shocking to the English before *Candide*. In 1762 the author of *Letters to a Young Nobleman* praises Voltaire as one of "the greatest men, whom France can at present boast to have given birth to." Nothing is said here of Voltaire's infidelity, and he is further lauded for his services in the cause of liberty. [77] In 1764 "the Chinese Spy" describes a visit to Voltaire, in which he finds new evidence of the abundance and versatility of Voltaire's genius, along with the immense circulation of his ideas. Nothing is said of irreligion. [78] In 1771 *The Universal Magazine* reprints, along with high appreciation of Voltaire's ability, his argument against complete atheism and materialism, which is so good as to inspire the regret that the energy of such an able writer has not been oftener used in the service of virtue and religion. [79] In 1774 the late Lord Chesterfield is quoted as saying that he had read all of Voltaire's published works more than once, including the *Siècle de Louis XIV*, which he had read four times. Chesterfield praises the *Henriade* as an epic poem, is astonished at Voltaire's versatility, thinking that there is no kind of writing in which Voltaire has not excelled. [80] By 1779 the English translator of Frederick the Great's *Panegyric of M. Voltaire* finds the general opinion of Voltaire's impiety to be low, yet he recognizes the spirit of Frederick's attempt to show that Voltaire was not really a danger to true religion but only to its shams and hypocrisies. Frederick professes, after quoting some sentiments of his own choice from Voltaire's works, to be unable to tell whether it is Voltaire or St. John who is speaking! [81] A fulsome tribute is paid in the works of John Andrews also, who says nothing of Voltaire's irreligion but who praises him on every score. The *Henriade*, the tragedies, and the histories are especially recommended. France should be proud of this great man, for "no country ever produced a more universal genius." [82] An amazing variety of excellent productions has been flowing from his "inexhaustible genius, during the space of more than half a century: a portion of time wherein he has indisputably reigned the most eloquent historian, the sublimest poet, in short, the most celebrated writer in all Europe." [83]

But the side of Voltaire's achievement which presented itself to the English in the most amiable and high-minded light was his effort for religious tolerance, especially his great defense of Calas, Sirven, and Montbailly. He is quoted and praised for his labors on behalf of tolerance against persecution; [84] his own letter "Concerning the Case of the Unfortunate Families of Calas and Sirven" is reprinted, thus presenting to the English reader the best side of Voltaire's work and personal character.[85] In 1776 in Edinburgh *The History of the Misfortunes of John Calas* was published, being largely a reprint of a *Treatise on Toleration* in which Voltaire had used the Calas case to make his charges against intolerance ring true. Six pages are given to a "List of the Nobility and Gentry who have subscribed to relieve the Family of Calas," including "Her Majesty," the Archbishop of Canterbury, twelve dukes, eleven bishops, representatives of all ranks of the nobility as well as prominent merchants and other distinguished Englishmen.[86] In a prefatory remark to an English edition of the *Treatise upon Religious Toleration*,[87] Voltaire is praised for his defense of the Calas family, which he "most humanely and generously undertook, with the magnanimity of a Demosthenes and a Cicero." [88] Such praise seems to suggest that if Voltaire had been thought of in England as attacking merely the Roman church and its excesses, the English would not have considered him a public enemy. In 1768 *The Dispute Between Mademoiselle Clairon, and the Fathers of the Church, at Paris*, "Said to be written by M. De Voltaire," was published in London. The title page notices that the book was condemned to be burnt by the common hangman, with this comment: "The reader will not wonder, that the church of *Rome* should condemn a book to the flames that so boldly exposes the arts and tyranny of Popery." The English seem inclined to welcome the destruction of what they regard as the superstition and error, credulity and ignorance fostered by the Roman church. In 1778 the effort of French writers to overcome these things is praised, along with special approval of Raynal for his exposure of the injustice, wickedness, and cruelty of the Church of Rome.[89] It is therefore a good thing that "many absurd notions and practices have been exploded and abolished." [90] Actually, it is small wonder that so many Frenchmen have become deists; Englishmen should not blame those who have not had the priceless advantages of living under the perfect English dispensation. Who can blame the French for their deism when from their very cradles they have been made the victims of "gross and palpable superstitions" so that they cannot distinguish between true revelation "and the fabricated superstitions of falsehood." [91]

If Voltaire is in the end to be blamed for causing the French Revolution and for hastening the decline of all supports of the existing order in Europe, it must be shown that he was attacking religion itself and Christianity in particular. Even though the English might theoretically admit the usefulness of an unsound religious superstition in maintaining order in a state, their dislike of what they considered a corrupt and dangerous perversion of true Christianity by Rome was strong enough to insure at least a toleration of Voltaire when he seemed to be sharing their own prejudices only. They would not be inclined to blame him for attacking something whose destruction might well have seemed to them good riddance. But it turns out that Voltaire's writings are recognized in conservative England long before the French Revolution to have been as much a disgrace as an honor to his country, and to have posed a serious threat, which may have been part of a deliberate plan, against the Christian revelation.

In the early 1750's Voltaire was already being denounced as one who despised revelation,[92] and John Wesley had begun to show contempt and detestation for "such a creature as Voltaire," an influence for vice and iniquity.[93] The appearance of *Candide* scandalized both Mrs. Carter and Mrs. Montagu who exchange letters about it. The book has an air of "impiety and profligacy that is shocking," and it is sure to "incline people to atheism." [94] It is provoking that "such an animal calls itself a philosopher" when it has no fear of God to make a beginning in wisdom. "This creature is a downright rebel to his God," [95] according to Mrs. Montagu, and her friend is unable to finish *Candide* at all, having found it so "horrid in all respects, that I threw it aside, and nothing, I believe, will tempt me ever to look into it again." [96] The good Lord Lyttleton has Pope and Boileau express his fears that Voltaire's influence will be most dangerous for human society by reason of the impious and immoral tendency of his effort to make vice agreeable.[97] Although Edward Young confesses to an admiration of long standing for Voltaire, he is forced to denounce "such bold trash" as *Candide*. His long diatribe against Voltaire in the poem "Resignation" was the result of a visit from Mrs. Montagu and Mrs. Carter who persuaded him to expose the wickedness of Voltaire.[98] This he does while regretting the perversion of so much that is to be admired in the French infidel, who is looked upon with a mixture of horror and admiration, so that "We shudder, whilst we praise." [99] There is a rumor in 1763 that Voltaire is about to visit England; Mrs. Carter is sorry to hear it. Her views in a letter to Mrs. Vesey show the combination of that admiration for his genius with regret as to its perversion which mark Voltaire's English reputation toward the end of his life:

If I happened to be accidentally in a room with Voltaire, I do not believe I should think it necessary to run out screaming fire and murder; but certainly from every society in which I had a casting vote, such a wretch would be infallibly excluded; and excluded particularly for the very circumstance for which he would claim to be admired, his being a *genius*. I must confess, that to me the idolatry of great talents applied to wicked purposes, is still worse than the idolatry of titles and riches, as their influence is more universally destructive.[100]

When the notorious "Philosophical Dictionary" is published in England at this same period, the editor feels obliged to refute some of the more objectionable passages, although true religion is only

strengthened by the attacks of infidels.[101] Particular exception is
taken to Voltaire's article on "Solomon" to which a note is written
denouncing the harmful effects of skeptical ridicule, the disregard
for common decency, the profanity and lewdness, and indifference
to virtue and religion in all such performances.[102] In commenting
upon the *Philosophical Dictionary* the *Critical Review* is once
again moved to praise Voltaire for his great genius, yet to condemn
him "for the prostitution of those abilities on trifling and obscene
subjects, for his prejudices against revealed religion, and for his
affecting on every occasion to ridicule the sacred writings, especially those of the Old Testament." [103] In *Humphry Clinker* (1771)
we learn of an old acquaintance of Matthew Bramble's who is
returning to Italy by way of Geneva "that he may have a confer-
ence with his friend Voltaire, about giving the last blow to the
Christian superstition." [104] By this time, Mrs. Carter is willing to
take on hearsay all evidence that Voltaire is an enemy to religion.
Writing to Mrs. Vesey in May, 1774, she has not seen Voltaire's
verses "nor ever wish to see any thing which attempts to destroy
the only hope which as you say 'makes this life supportable.' " She
has not in fact seen any of his late writings, "nor from the character of them, do I ever design it. I should as soon think of playing
with a toad or a viper, as of reading such blasphemy and impiety
as I am told are contained in some of his works." [105]

The honest Joseph Priestley despises the hypocrisy of such unbelievers as Voltaire who attack Christianity in a covert manner,
"pretending to believe what they really wish to undermine." [106]
By his "prophane jests" Voltaire has succeeded in making the
Bible something to be laughed at among modern European readers.[107] But the most complete exposure of the tendency of Voltaire's antagonism to religion was made in a *History of the Life
and Writings of . . . Voltaire,* published in England in 1782. The
great infidel had now been dead for four years and his life achievement could be more accurately estimated than ever before. It was
finally clear beyond doubt that a "blind and senseless rage against
the Christian religion" had animated Voltaire. He employed a

chain of calumnies and groundless insinuations in his attack on Christianity. Such works as the *Philosophical Dictionary, La Pucelle,* and *Candide* could not "be read without a blush even by men who are no strangers to vice and immorality." He was supposed to have been an apostle of tolerance himself, yet he was fanatically intolerant and zealous in the cause of irreligion.[108] His whole life was devoted to his vile crusade, "a man whose old age appeared heated with impious phrenzy, and who, the nearer he approached the tomb, seemed to manifest a more violent hatred against religion and its ministers."[109] In 1784 Mrs. Thrale finds herself in Geneva and discovers the works of Voltaire in the possession of the daughter of the house where she is staying. She charges the girl never to look again into such books which could bring only offence to God and sorrow to herself. "But how does one's abhorrence increase of these traitors to human kind! who rob youth of its innocence; and age of its only consolation: who spurn at offered salvation themselves, and turn others from the gate that leads to eternal life." All this seems to have been predicted in the Bible itself. "I hear the plague is got into Europe," Mrs. Thrale says, "and am little astonished at it; in the latter days come scoffers wars and pestilence."[110] The role of Voltaire himself in creating the plague is by now known to all men. In 1786 *The Political Magazine* prints some "Anecdotes of Voltaire," in one of which a dialogue is carried on between a workman and Voltaire. Voltaire denounces Rousseau as one devoid of honor and religion:

Workman: Without religion, Sir! It has been said, you have not much of that yourself.

Voltaire: No! Gracious God! Who can say such a thing?

Workman: All the world, Sir . . .. It is said, Sir, you have written very wicked books.[111]

It is one thing to say that Voltaire had attacked religion and had been especially hostile to Christianity. A far worse charge would be that he was acting with deliberate, far-seeing intent, using his genius in the service of a well-laid plot systematically to destroy Christianity with the help of numerous disciples. Such a plot would have the most serious consequences in church and state. As early as 1759, Voltaire's irreligion was described as "a state of formal rebellion and hostility against the administrations of infinite wisdom and goodness." [112] By the time of Voltaire's death it had been evident that "for several years past, there has been a set of pretended sages, who, . . . appear to have entered into a kind of confederacy against the cause of Christianity. To this sect of false philosophers M. de Voltaire is justly suspected to belong," by reason of his disgust with religion in general and his never losing an opportunity to ridicule or disfigure religion, the clergy, or the affairs of the church.[113] From his establishment at Ferney, Voltaire became the center of an impious flood of pamphlets, novels, and romances all designed to corrupt religion and the state. He was the leader of a band of infidels, a regular school of impiety which deliberately set out to discredit the worship of God and to deprive the people of their long-cherished convictions and devotions. In so doing Voltaire showed that he was the enemy of kings and of his country, since the religion he set out to undermine was the strongest support of the throne and necessary to the stability and happiness of the state.[114] Although the implications of Voltaire's crusade were antimonarchical, he was intimate with and influential upon such kings as Joseph II of Austria [115] and more conspicuously Frederick the Great of Prussia.[116] Small wonder that in 1785, by an arrêt of council, the first thirty volumes of Voltaire's works, printed by a foreign literary society, were suppressed in Paris. The arrêt says that "these works are suppressed, because inimical to good morals, and the authority of the laws." [117] It was simply evident that the first place among the infidel champions of modern times, who were deliberately trying to discredit Christianity, must be assigned to Voltaire for his ridicule of the Christian religion and its followers.[118] It was, therefore, the chief duty of a preacher to warn all parties against the specious and glittering principles of Voltaire.[119]

There is evidence then, that French literature or "philosophy" in general and Voltaire in particular were already notorious in

England for enmity to Christianity: the English even suspected a deliberate plot led by Voltaire to undermine permanently the institutions by which the Christian religion expressed and propagated itself in Europe. When in the course of time the entire blame for the French Revolution was laid at his door in England, the general opinion was already prepared to accept Voltaire's guilt and that of the individuals and groups who had helped to carry out his impious plan.

XI · THE FRENCH REVOLUTION
AND ITS CAUSES

THE REVOLUTION in France was not long under way before English opinion was saying that the great change had been prepared for by French literature. It was also agreed that the Revolution had come about after a strong movement against religion, the existence of which in France had long been known to the English. Others, led by Burke, held that the entire catastrophe was the result of a deliberate plot against religion, carried out in the hope that the fall of the church would destroy the existing government. The demon "philosophy" again was roundly abused, with Voltaire mentioned among its practitioners.

Everyone was willing to believe that the Revolution was partly the result of literary preparation; so vast an upheaval could hardly have been the work of sudden impulse. The immense inertia of life had to be prepared for motion, chiefly by stimulating the minds and feelings of the people. Condorcet saw the folly of attacking oppressors before having enlightened the citizenry,[1] a truth which did not escape those hoping for a change in France. The mere fact that books are abundant and studious habits general among a people already creates a state of mind hospitable to new ideas.[2]

The Revolution showed how true this was. The light of knowledge had penetrated to every class of citizens in France; the change began when men first were inspired to think for themselves, and the notorious abuses of the old regime along with other peculiarly French elements hastened the revolt. "When Bacon made his first experiments, when Montaigne doubted, when Bayle became the advocate-general of philosophy, they were preparing the revolution of France." ³ Originating in the "Cabinets of the literati" reason progressed to "the public at large." ⁴ Superior men spread abroad an abundance of useful truths, forming multitudes of disciples. An enlightened tribunal of public opinion was established; books crossed every frontier in the kingdom; they entered every house; and at length the tired Inquisition ceased to persecute them.⁵ Book societies and reading clubs were formed in France by which the most modern publications were made available to all who could read, and their most dangerous implications of skepticism and infidelity were emphasized.⁶ The French began to think about the mysteries of government; the *Encyclopédie* in particular inspired discussion of governmental topics and the true science of political rule.⁷ The revolution was taking place "in the minds of the people" long before it expressed itself externally in the violence of mobs,⁸ and for this entire change from the old order, France was "certainly indebted . . . to her authors only." ⁹

THE PHILOSOPHERS

By authors the English meant "philosophers," once the Revolution had declared itself. The term acquired an implication even more unpleasant than it had known before 1789, in view of the horrible atrocities committed in the name of the revolution and inspired by "philosophic" doctrine. The Lord Bishop of Ossory is sure that the system which had so suddenly overthrown every "essential good on which the welfare of mankind has hitherto rested," was the result of poisonous effusions from "philosophic" freethinkers.¹⁰ A government must have been strong indeed to have stood "against the undermining principles of French *philosophy*," ¹¹ which had blinded the people by false theories and aided their natural impetuosity to the ruin of their entire heritage.¹² The present calamities, the miseries and horrors now grown into such a plentiful crop, the rule of murderers, ruffians, and bandits, the consequent spread of vice, brutality, and ignorance, are all the natural result of modern "philosophy." ¹³ Mackintosh feels at first that "it is the glory of its admirers to avow" that the "philosophers" had prepared the revolution by their writings,[14] but he could attract few supporters to his view. The very term philosophy has become odious by its application to such perverted men, so that one may "dread the appellation of philosopher, as comprehending every thing absurd and pernicious." [15] To Burke, those guilty of the exhibition of July 14 "are capable of every evil . . . they are modern philosophers, which when you say of them, you express everything which is ignoble, savage, and hard-hearted." [16] And the Birmingham riots of 1791 suggest that the English were more apt to agree with Burke than with Mackintosh. The mob's common cry was "No philosophers—Church and King forever"; some persons painted upon their houses, "no philosophers." [17]

If French authors as the source of the Revolution were synonymous with "philosophers," this term was further concentrated upon certain individual writers. Gradually it is lost in the names of Voltaire and Rousseau and finally in that of Voltaire alone. But earlier in the period others are included. The *English Review* finds that "Turgot and other writers" helped to scatter the sparks of freedom.[18] Paine mentions Montesquieu and Raynal as well as Quesnay and Turgot who have aided the liberal cause "by their moral maxims and systems of economy." [19] Helvetius is added to those writers who inspired the formation of theories "absolutely atrocious and impracticable." [20] Burke sarcastically hopes that "handy abridgements of the excellent sermons of Voltaire, D'Alembert, Diderot, Helvetius, . . . are sent down to the soldiers along with their civic oaths. . . . I understand that a certain description of reading makes no inconsiderable part of their military exercises, and that they are full well supplied with the ammunition of pamphlets as of cartridges." [21] The "philosophers" whose guilt is most frequently referred to are D'Alembert, Diderot, and Helvetius, with some reference to Volney, Raynal, and Montesquieu.[22] An admirable list is offered by J. Courtenay, M.P., as he draws up the general English indictment of the group:

The luminous scrutinizing genius of Montesquieu; the splendid levity of Voltaire; the impassioned and fascinating eloquence of Rousseau;

the precision and depth of d'Alembert; the bold and acute investigations of Boulanger; the daring paradoxical spirit of Helvetius; the majestic sublimity of the systematic Buffon; the profound astronomical researches of Bailly; the captivating eloquence of Marmontel; the impressive condensed thoughts of Diderot;—all these with combined force assailed and unsettled the consecrated opinions of ages. The venerable gothic structure was shaken from its very foundations; the sacred edifice is now laid low, and the madness of democracy has vainly dedicated a temple to liberty on its ruins.[23]

Once it is established that the "philosophers" were guilty of preparing for the French Revolution, it is easy to discover how they went about the work of subversion. Actually the nature of things themselves dictates the method by which a government has to be overthrown. Religion alone keeps the multitude within bounds,[24] so that a rejection of God's authority will lead to revolt against the authority of man as well.[25] When the "philosophers" try to claim natural liberty against all kings and rulers and to assert equality of rights, they know full well that Christianity will never countenance such doctrine.[26] They are obliged to set up their own rule of faith and "under the specious pretext of banishing the too numerous ornaments of the Catholic practice, to shake the foundations of Christianity itself." [27] It is true that the English might have welcomed the decline of popery itself if the philosophers had confined themselves to that useful task.[28] But these public enemies used the falsity and crudity of the Roman superstition to discredit the doctrines of the true faith; they tried to show the people that since so much of their accepted religion was false, the rest of it could not be true. All religion was classed with superstition and Christianity itself was regarded as a fable, the same as any other faith.[29]

Since irreligion was the surest path to revolt then, the "philosophers" had to spread infidelity. They systematically ruined the religion of France, and when the Revolution itself broke out it soon made clear that its principles were irreligious. The English lost their colonies in America themselves because reverence for government had been weakened by publications which sneered at orthodoxy and the national church, while encouraging uncontrolled freedom of inquiry and thought in matters of religion.[30] A similar impulse, called by a different name, underlay the French revolt. The revolutionists saw at the outset that they had to neutralize religion. "They fell upon the church first, as the church stood most in their way. She was their greatest eye-sore." [31] The irreligious character of the Revolution was now so obvious as hardly to need proof. It was a fact "known to anyone in the smallest degree acquainted with the history of that miserable country." [32] The very basis "and essential principle" of the Revolution had been the total rejection of all religious reverence.[33] Infidelity and contempt for religion became the "main cause of the judgment which has fallen" upon France.[34] Taking their cue from the French authors who had for generations preached materialism, scoffed at the clergy and church, and ridiculed Christianity, the revolutionists made it a matter of principle to defy all previous concepts of proper belief and weaken the restraints imposed by devout faith; they got rid of everything that might deter the people from following their profane leadership; they ridiculed conscience and piety, and made infidelity the road to preferment; they put an end to religious and moral obligation from one end of society to another, with the result that their revolution developed into the most bloody, profane, and destructive of which there is any record.[35] All this is by way of contrast to the way things have remained in England. In 1792 a broadside was published called *The Contrast: English Liberty, French Liberty, Which Is Best?* This is decorated with two medallions symbolic of English and French liberty. Under the English medallion, which shows an idyllic scene of peace and justice, are listed the qualities which represent England: "Religion, morality, loyalty, obedience to the laws, independence, personal security, justice, inheritance, protection, property, industry, national prosperity, happiness." Religion is given as the first virtue, from which all the others follow. The French medallion shows a creature with snakes in her hair, a sword in one hand, a pike with a human head on it in the other, one foot placed on a prostrate body, with another dead body hanging from a lamp post in the background. Beneath this are listed, "Atheism, perjury, rebellion, treason, anarchy, murder, equality, madness, cruelty, injustice, treachery, ingratitude, idleness, famine, national and private ruin, misery." Here atheism is given first, as if all the rest were its progeny.

France was therefore undone, and by a vicious principle within herself. "It was the abundance of her iniquity," a kind of "inward ebullition, which like a subterraneous fire burst out and buried her Church and her Monarchy in one universal ruin." [36] And a complete ruin it certainly was. The revolution renounced every tie and restraint essential to the order and even the existence of society, down to the relation "between man and his Maker—between time and eternity." [37] The authority of God was cast off in the delirium induced by modern philosophy [38] and as the ultimate refinement of blasphemy, "the belief of a Supreme Being" was renounced in the form of "a National Act." [39] Belief in hell, heaven, the devil, and life after death was now a thing of the past in France:

> Damnation vulgar to a Frenchman's hearing—
> The word is only kept alive for swearing.
> Against futurity they all protest;
> And God and Heav'n are grown a standing jest.[40]

Nothing in the bloody history of the French Revolution seems to have horrified the English more than the complete separation of this life from the next. If any proof of the irreligious character of the French revolt were needed aside from the mere fact of its existence, it would be seen in the revolutionists' denial that there was a life after death. The special horror of the English seems to have been reserved for the calm assertion over the gates of French cemeteries that "Death is an eternal sleep." Here was the very summary of rebellious impiety, a statement in so many words that the new order in France would recognize no world but this and no authority beyond that of men. And what men indeed, now ruling in France. The Bishop of Moulin seems to have been the "vile wretch who first caused to be written on the gate of the burying ground *'this is the place of everlasting sleep.'* " [41] Such men believed as they did because in view of their lives and characters they had no choice:

> Well may you wish, O miserable men!
> Since cancel'd every sacred, awful tie,
> From the cold grave you ne'er may rise again,
> And all existence end when you shall die.
>
> .   .   .
>
> For hence the impious, petrifying creed,
> God has to man immortal life decreed,
> He who denies it is a wretch indeed.[42]

John Gifford describes what takes place at the burial of a human body under the new dispensation in France:

Posts, bearing the inscription "la mort est un Sommeil éternel," were erected in many public burying grounds. No other ceremony is observed with the dead than enclosing the body in some rough boards, and sending it off by a couple of porters (in their usual garb) attended by a municipal officer. The latter inscribes on a register the name of the deceased, who is thrown into a grave generally prepared for half a score, and the whole business is finished.[43]

It was as if the leaders of the revolution were "pointing to the silence of the sepulchre, and the sleep of the dead" by way of apology "for leaving neither sleep, quiet, nor repose to the living." [44] And all this by solemn legal decree! "The very existence of the soul after death . . . the very being of GOD" was denied by the National Assembly, and the inscription proclaiming the eternity of death ordered to be placed over "the gates of every churchyard in the country." [45] The legend may well stand as the epitaph of the revolution itself, a summary of what the philosophers had been teaching, of what kind of men were leading the revolution and what kind of deeds might be expected from them. "Those who consider death as an eternal sleep have nothing to consult but their appetites and their will; for, as their lot is to be like that of the brutes that perish, so also will their conduct naturally be." [46] At any rate it is all now clear what the philosophers had preached; no one need any longer suspect or suppose or conjecture. The legend that death is sleep for eternity sums up the theories of materialism; "the depositaries of the dead will not corrupt more by the exhibition of this desolating standard, than the libraries of the living by the volumes which hold out the same oblivion to vice, and discouragement to virtue." [47]

A dreadful warning for England lay in all these revelations, for even in England there was evidence that "a disregard to religion is the leading feature in every station of life." [48] It is unquestionable that a "dreadful flood of infidelity, atheism, irreligion, damnable heresies, looseness of principle and practise, contempt of God and religion, scoffing at the truths of God and serious Godliness, hath broke out in this age," and has extended itself from foreign parts to Great Britain itself."[49] Let the English realize the consequences before it is too late:

We see a nation, openly professing atheism and infidelity, groaning under all the miseries and distractions of anarchy, rebellion, and civil war; how ought we then to guard against all blasphemy and profaneness! —We see a nation, rejecting all religion, with famine and the sword stalking through the land, and spreading wide desolation and destruction; how ought we then to cherish religion, as the guardian and friend of civil society! [50]

And that the English people were such as would heed this warning, explains in part why they thought as they ultimately did of Voltaire.

A CONCERTED PLOT

It could hardly be argued, therefore, whether or not the French Revolution had its basis in irreligion. But there remained the possibility that it had all proceeded from a deliberate plan; that the philosophic enmity to religion was not merely a natural growth or reaction but the consequence of a far-reaching plot by a group of men who had planned the overthrow of Christianity at long range; that finally the entire catastrophe of the Revolution had been foreseen and deliberately prepared for, thus removing the faintest impulse to extenuation of its horrors, on the plea that it was a spontaneous protest against unbearable tyranny.

In the light of history this supposition now seems fantastic, yet it gained currency in England with the considerable aid of Burke's *Reflections* (1790), and by the year 1797 was a familiar explanation of the genesis of the Revolution. The English seem largely to have ignored Locke's simple assertion that "there is one only thing which gathers people into seditious commotions and that is oppression." [51] William A. Miles writes (1793) to a French acquaintance, that the original cause of the Revolution was "the scandalous rapacity and profligate manners of that pestilential and contemptible banditti of legalized plunderers—your nobility and clergy of the highest class." [52] As might be expected, Mackintosh sees nothing beyond the personal infidelity of the "philosophers." Their "political hostility" was directed only against the church and not against religion. He therefore thinks that "the supposition of their conspiracy for the abolition of Christianity is one of the most extravagant chimeras that ever entered the human imagination." [53]

A far more popular view held that the Revolution was the result of a concerted plot. The revolutionary edifice was the "accumulation of much toil and much time." It had formed the secret meditation of French philosophers and politicians, having been produced "to employ an expression of our English Horace, by The Patient touches of unwearied Art. Pope." [54] Traceable, according to John Bowles, to the "principles taught by Mr. Locke, respecting the Source of Power, and the Natural Liberty and Equality of Man," the Revolution came into being with the industrious propagation of these principles by "another sect of Philosophers, who laboured with dreadful success, to undermine the two great bulwarks of Society, Religion and Morals." The whole edifice was therefore "a deliberate, metaphysical, and cold-hearted rebellion." [55] Many respectable politicians concur in this view. They believe that

the French Revolution is nothing more than the result of the schemes of a set of designing men, who for the last thirty years have been deliberately undermining all principles whatever; first preaching finespun systems of morality and sentiment; then gently insinuating that such systems wanted not the aid of religion, or at least of revelation; and in the end finally aiming to overturn all subordination, all regular government, and it seems all regular society, along with every thing mankind had hitherto held most sacred. Accordingly, the ingenious personage who said in a public assembly "There is no God," was a legitimate descendant of others who had some time before said it "in their hearts." [56]

Given the existence of a deliberate plot, its method of operation would have to be obvious. Its natural prey was the Christian religion. With this bulwark gone, the way was open to any plan of subversion. The particular English observers who publicly announced this fact are of some interest. Aside from the hint of a conspiracy in the article on D'Alembert in the *Encyclopaedia Britannica* [57] there is the testimony of three bishops, of Edmund Burke, and the Abbé Augustin de Barruel, soon to become the central figure in the denunciation of Voltaire. Burke sees the "philosophical fanatics" having long entertained "the utter abolition, under any of its forms, of the Christian religion, whenever the minds of men are prepared for this last stroke against it." [58] Bishop Samuel Horsley of Rochester discovers that the overthrow of the whole worship of God and the effacing of his name from the world is a project "reserved for the accursed crew of French philosophers, turned politicians, at the close of the eighteenth century." Appropriately, the Bishop's indignation is expressed in a sermon commemorating the death of Charles I, on January 30.[59] The accusation of the Bishop of London is more pointed still. The "philosophers" have "waged open war with the gospel for near half a century," and have assailed it with every weapon furnished by "wit, genius, eloquence, ridicule, calumny, invective." At length they have been able to establish "a regular system and school of infidelity on the continent" and have avowed their grand object to be "the extirpation of Christianity from the earth, and the substitution of philosophy in its room." [60] A year later the Bishop of Ossory announces to his clergy that there has arisen "a systematic opposition as well to the faith, as to the morals of the Gospel" to distinguish the present age:

A new race of infidels and freethinkers have arisen to astonish and shake the Christian world. Inflamed with a frenzy of fanaticism, unknown to their predecessors of former ages, they have not only conceived, but executed the bold, and seemingly hopeless project, of forming themselves into a sect, acting together on a plan of universal proselytism, and combining for the final extinction of the Christian faith and name.[61]

The Abbé Barruel adds nothing new to this literal accusation. Yet he places before the English reader in his *History of the Clergy in the French Revolution* (1794) the first suggestion of his fanatical certainty that the revolution followed from a deliberate conspiracy. He traces the revolt to a set of men calling themselves "philosophers" who had "divided among themselves the task of overturning the throne and altars." [62] This emigrant French priest, fleeing for his personal safety to England, thus states the theme of his *Memoirs Illustrating the History of Jacobinism* (1797), the work which finally established the guilt of Voltaire as the founder of the revolution.

The Bishop of Ossory seems to have singled out one of the distinguishing marks of the plot in his view of the fanaticism of the conspirators against Christianity. It was a common English opinion that infidels were the greatest of all bigots themselves; that atheism led to superstition and fanaticism more certainly than did piety; that deists and philosophers were capable of inflamed prejudices and were intolerant, arbitrary, and violent in their zeal, in spite of all their talk against such vices in others.[63] All this applied especially to the anti-Christian plotters. Never before had such enthusiasm been shown, save by the preachers "of some system of piety." A spirit of "proselytism in the most fanatical degree" took possession of the plotters [64] and they set out to spread their impious design over Europe. The republic of Berne, Italy, Germany, and even England itself, were all included in "the comprehensive scheme of their malignant charity." [65]

Their method was to obtain command over public opinion and to achieve a kind of literary monopoly by a flood of impious and subversive literature. For years this notorious confederacy tried to undermine the Gospel openly "by licentious publications, in which the imagination, deluded by vicious pleasantry, and the passions, inflamed by every art of seduction, corrupted the judgment, and procured for sophistry an easy access, especially to youthful and unexperienced minds." [66] These writings they dispersed "with incredible assiduity and expence." They preached in the streets and public resorts of Paris as well,[67] but their chief ally was the "unbounded licentiousness of the press" which became "a most potent instrument of the Revolution." Pamphlets appeared with incredible frequency. In one week ninety-two were published; booksellers' shops were so crowded with buyers of this stuff that one could barely obtain entrance. These publications were sent out over the entire kingdom from Paris, apparently supported by an "unknown fund," since many people received them free of charge.[68]

A key to the spirit of this blasphemous enterprise is to be found in the private correspondence of the principal conspirators, particularly that in which Frederick the Great had participated. Burke shows that a part of the whole design was to obtain the favor of foreign princes with whom the plotters entered into correspondence. They could more readily bring about their desired changes, if they had royalty on their side. The letters between the cabal and Frederick show the spirit of their proceedings.[69] The relationship with Frederick was a very happy one on both sides, because of the king's notorious "enmity against the ministers of religion of every denomination." In fact, this hatred of religion, especially of Christianity was one of the chief bonds between Voltaire and Frederick. Their correspondence personified Christianity "in a variety of places, under the denomination of *the infamous*." [70] The letters that passed among Voltaire, D'Alembert, and Frederick had as their theme the destruction of Christianity, which they summarized in the favorite phrase of their letters, "écrasez l'infâme." [71] The record leaves no doubt as to the conspirators' secret mission; "the grand object they had in view was . . . the entire extinction of the Christian religion." [72] They were engaged in "a pre-meditated plot by all possible means to destroy the Christian religion." [73]

The overthrow of Christianity would have been horrible enough, if the schemes of the plotters had included this and nothing more.

But the enemies of religion necessarily are allied to the enemies of government, so that when the Revolution itself broke out after the antireligious preparation its true character soon became obvious: it was an attempt to overthrow all religion and all civil establishments so as to ruin every existing institution in church and state. Nothing less than universal anarchy was the goal. The original impious philosophers having aimed at the complete annihilation of religion,[74] their zealous pupils united with the despots of the Revolution and wrote into the legislative code of their nation "the most dangerous and destructive sophisms," seating "atheism and anarchy on the ruins of a throne," whose ancient princes had been proud of its foundations in the Christian faith.[75] The French Revolution is consequently unique among all the uprisings against an individual government in history. It

should be considered as an event altogether *sui generis*. It is the nature of this Revolution not merely to subvert the existing Government, but to overthrow every establishment, civil and religious; every institution, political and moral. . . . The tendency of this Revolution is universal. It is a contagion which human nature is everywhere pre-disposed to imbibe, for it acts directly upon the passions, vices, and infirmities of mankind.[76]

Only the dissolution of society, the subversion of government, and the extirpation of religion will satisfy the revolutionary leaders.[77] Other nations must face the fact that this revolt is an aggression upon their institutions as well as upon those of France. "The contest is between order and confusion, between humanity and cruelty, between justice and violence, between religion and impiety, between heaven and hell!"[78] The combined powers are therefore obliged in self-defense to oppose the revolutionary establishment of France. It would be fatal to give any sanction to this subversive code; once recognized this principle would expand to other countries and soon not a throne or a church would be standing in Europe. The sole hope lies in restoration of the French monarchy, if this menace and defiance of the whole world, this effort at the universal disruption of society, is to be nullified.[79]

The belief that the French Revolution was universal in its aim was already a part of English opinion, therefore, when in 1797 the Abbé Barruel proclaimed that there were men who had actually intended and planned that the Revolution should be exactly what he, and some English conservatives before him, had said it was: a universally subversive scheme. The fact that the elements of Barruel's entire interpretation of the French Revolution were already current in England by 1797, goes far to explain why his work was so enthusiastically received. It fixed the guilt upon Voltaire, whose war upon Christianity had set in motion the whole gigantic plot against every element in life tending to keep things as they were.

XII · THE APOTHEOSIS
OF VOLTAIRE

AFTER LONG preparation we come to Voltaire himself. If the English thought that the French Revolution was partly the result of deliberate literary preparation, they also believed that a central figure existed to whom the whole tragedy was due, some first mover or primary cause. By the year 1800 Voltaire had become the chief if not the only candidate for this doubtful honor. For some time he divided responsibility with other men of letters, but as the study of what had preceded the revolution went farther into the past, Voltaire was declared to be at the outermost point of the revolutionary movement.

Yet long before this view of final origins was accepted by the English, there was abundant opinion that Voltaire was the author of the tragedy being enacted in France. Such a view followed partly from the principle that an enemy of religion was necessarily a danger to the state. It was strengthened by the unqualified admission of the French themselves that Voltaire had prepared them for liberty. Their debt to him was publicly acknowledged in 1791, when his remains were transferred to the Pantheon in a ceremony which stands as one of the most extravagant popular tributes ever paid to a man of letters. This expression of gratitude became known in England, so that public opinion was further prepared to accept a final condemnation of Voltaire as the cause of the Revolution.

It is ironical that the French movement against religion which the English regarded with such horror should have come in some measure from England herself. The English might admit not too unhappily that such writers on politics and government as Sydney,

Locke, Milton, and Harrington had inspired the French to make progress toward the ideal of liberty which made England so enviable.[1] It is quite another thing to confess that Voltaire himself had praised England as the great modern preceptor to the world,[2] and was in turn praised for having gone to England for his own enlightenment and then having returned to share his English philosophic treasures with other Frenchmen.[3] Long before Voltaire's death, his English lessons had already begun to be too well learned in France. The Rev. William Cole saw the danger to Christianity in the preaching of Voltaire, Rousseau, and D'Alembert, "who are now retailing to the French the doctrines of our apostles, Shaftesbury, Hobbes, Tindal, Toland, Collins, Morgan and Bolingbroke." [4] These French atheists "indeed derive their pedigree from writers of the same stamp of this nation." [5] There is more truth in this than the Rev. William Jones would like to admit. He sees the whole French mischief as traceable to England, because there it was that reason "was first invested with the right of making its own religion." That other pernicious doctrine of "no power of government but from the power of the people" also arose in England, and modern France is simply carrying these ideas to their certain conclusion.[6] The whole abominable crew of modern philosophers, English as well as French, may now see their labors consummated and may assume due credit, such as it is: "Ye Shaftesburys, Bolingbrokes, Voltaires, and must I add the name of Gibbon, behold yourselves inscribed on the registers of fame with a Laplanche, a Chénier, an André Dumont, or a Fouche!—Do not blush at the association; your views have been the same." [7] And Voltaire himself has simply collected "all the antiquated objections of Collins, Tindal, etc., and dressed them up anew for the very same purpose for which they were first proposed." [8]

It seems paradoxical, too, that Voltaire, the alleged author of the Revolution, was in no sense a republican but an avowed friend of monarchy. Lecky has shown that "there is certainly no natural or necessary affinity between free-thinking in religion, and democracy in politics." [9] Hobbes, Bolingbroke, Hume, and Gibbon, while notorious in varying degrees for their infidelity to religion, were in the last degree political conservatives. In France itself the philosophical freethinkers were largely conservative as well; Rousseau, who had the largest theoretical influence on the actual revolutionists, was of all the "philosophers" the most conservative in religion. The difference between England and France was, however, that Voltaire and his friends could not utter skeptical views without becoming, though not intentionally, allies of the revolutionary party.[10] Actually, Voltaire had much in common with those English Tories who so fiercely denounced him as a danger to their world. He had no sympathy with democratic ideas of universal suffrage and political equality. He had the aristocrat's willingness to do all he could to improve the condition of the masses, without any belief in their ability to govern themselves. He favored some administrative reforms, and fought to weaken superstition, intolerance, persecution, and to put an end to all needless suffering. But his humor and skeptical good sense, his feeling for practical reality made Voltaire the direct opposite of a revolutionary. And this was clear even to many conservative Englishmen, who admitted that "Voltaire was no republican." [11] While his writings are "an appeal to the revolution which has been brought about, and which he had foretold," Voltaire, if alive would doubtless be of the aristocratic party.[12] He loved grandeur and royalty and was fond of signing himself the Count of Ferney.[13] Indeed in 1793, he "had been already accused of aristocracy," [14] and it is safe to say that if he could have lived to see what the National Assembly was enacting, he would have disapproved of such insanity.[15] In all probability Voltaire would have had trouble escaping the guillotine himself.[16] He was born under monarchy and for it, having no belief in the popular capacity for political liberty. In spite of his fanatical dislike of Christianity, he showed an "habitual indulgence towards reprehensible monarchs," and was indifferent to the natural rights of the people.[17]

Although Voltaire "neither foresaw nor wished for that revolution to which he prepared the way," [18] he none the less came to be regarded as its first cause. To some extent the reputation of Rousseau forced Voltaire to divide his terrible responsibility. Rousseau is mentioned separately from time to time and his characteristic ideas are recognized as the inspiration for the new French philosophy of government. The revolution came in part from "a college of metaphysical declaimers," bent upon experimenting with maxims which they drew from the *Social Contract*. Indeed, with the exception of Condorcet, "all the revolutionists of France . . . were the disciples of Rousseau." [19] The fact that the Revolution so obviously is indebted to Rousseau's *The Social Contract* makes it desirable for English readers to be acquainted with such an important work. It is accordingly translated in 1791 and offered to the public so that its message will be entirely clear.[20] Readers may then understand the work which more than any other has contributed "to excite the revolutionary mania by which Europe has been agitated." [21] Burke thinks it a matter of common knowledge that the leaders of the National Assembly dispute greatly as to "which of them is the best resemblance to Rousseau." The truth is "they all resemble him. . . . Rousseau is their canon of holy writ . . . he is their standard figure of perfection." [22]

Far more frequently Rousseau and Voltaire are considered together, when Rousseau is mentioned at all. M. Etienne Dumont, writing to Samuel Romilly (1789), is almost unique in his opinion that Voltaire's reign is a thing of the past and that posterity will be astonished at the fact of his once having been considered the rival of Rousseau.[23] A commoner English view is suggested by the poet Blake's lines on *The French Revolution*. He imagines La Fayette about to address the revolutionary army:

On pestilent vapours around him flow frequent spectres of religious
     men weeping
In winds driven out of the abbeys, their naked souls shiver in keen open
     air,
Driven out by the fiery cloud of Voltaire, and thund'rous rocks of
     Rousseau,
They dash like foam against the ridges of the army, uttering a faint
     feeble cry.

Fayette stands still and lifts his hands; all the officers crowd round him:
Over his head the soul of Voltaire shone fiery, and over the army
     Rousseau his white cloud
Unfolded, on souls of war-living terrors silent list'ning toward Fayette.[24]

Sheridan, speaking in the House of Commons, argues that the French Revolution itself is not to blame for infidelity, in spite of all the signs it has given of atheistic impiety. The tree was corrupted from the top first, and the people of rank and fashion in France, who were supposed to be more devout than the revolutionists, "were the genuine and zealous followers of Voltaire and Rousseau; and if the lower orders had been afterwards perverted, it was by their precept and example." [25] The Rev. John Moir tries to make up his mind which of the two great criminals is the worse, and decides that Rousseau has perhaps had a more pernicious influence than Voltaire. The great scoffer hated religion and attacked it out of the "malignant bias of his mind" more or less openly, but Rousseau insinuates his poisons more hypocritically under a guise of artlessness and innocence.[26] As for the French themselves, they seem to have given allegiance to both Voltaire and Rousseau,[27] and the ill-fated Louis XVI had designated their works as "the source of all his misfortunes." [28] Athanase Veau, deputy to the convention, goes so far as to propose the canonization of his heroes. Veau had recited several hymns upon the inauguration of the cult of reason at Tours in the second year of the French Republic. His "Hymne aux Grands Hommes" suggests that in place of the saints of the old order, a new group be raised up for veneration, including Voltaire, Rousseau, and Mably. Without Voltaire and Rousseau, reason would still be in the cradle and the earth would be shrouded in error.[29] If their suggested canonization is an extreme case, it seems clear that before the Revolution in France "Rousseau and Voltaire were the favourite authors." [30]

Eventually the English ceased to divide the blame so literally. Mirabeau indeed was said to be a combination of Rousseau and Voltaire by a contributor to the "Poet's Corner" in the *St. James's Chronicle*:

All men are alike, said the great Mirabeau;
Himself was like *two*—Voltaire and Rousseau! [31]

On the other hand Mary Wollstonecraft has "Voltaire leading
the way" among the writers "contending for civil liberty," with
Rousseau ranging himself "on the same side," apparently as one
who followed where a greater led.[32] George III himself suggests
best of all why the English leaned toward Voltaire as the author of
the Revolution, instead of to Rousseau. The one who was the
more cordially hated for his irreligion was more easily blamed.
Fanny Burney reports the king's opinion of the tendency of Voltaire's works: " 'I,' cried he, 'think him a monster, I own it fairly.' "
Of Rousseau the king spoke with more favor, "though by no
means with approbation." [33] Neither King George nor most of
his subjects who thought of such matters had Dr. Johnson's difficulty in comparing Voltaire and Rousseau. He considered them
so nearly equal in wickedness, that it was "difficult to settle the
proportion of iniquity between them." [34] Voltaire had a much
wider reputation as an enemy of Christianity than Rousseau, and
this goes far to explain the greater English willingness to believe
evil of him. There was still some question as to Rousseau's irreligion, but none whatever in the case of Voltaire. In fact Boswell
reports that in answer to his question, "Are you a Christian?" delivered "with a searching eye," Rousseau replied, striking his
breast, "Yes. I pique myself upon being one." [35] Further it would
not be difficult to produce from the works of Rousseau "a vast
majority of passages directly in support of Christianity itself,
compared with what are supposed to be hostile to it." Besides, it
was well known that Rousseau had incurred "the ridicule of Voltaire, for exalting the character and death of Jesus above that of
Socrates." [36]

Compared with Voltaire, then, Rousseau seems to be devout.
Boswell was careful to sound out the sage of Ferney on religious
matters. He learns it is true that the great infidel loves God and
is resigned to His will. But "he does not inflame his mind with
grand hopes of the immortality of the Soul. He says it may be; but

he knows nothing of it." Boswell asks for certainty's sake whether Voltaire is sincere in his belief and is answered, "Before God I am." [37] This is a much milder picture than the one which becomes so well known in England over the next generation. The mighty scoffer was in the end notorious as the enemy of all religions everywhere, detested and abhorred by sober and pious men of all nations.[38] One who spent several days with Voltaire reported that "he heard nothing from him but what had a tendency to corrupt the heart." [39] His passionate devotion to "philosophy" made his influence destructive of the consolations of religion, depriving men of guidance and comfort in times of weakness or sorrow. His irreligious fanaticism rose to the pitch of mania, and was more outrageous than that which he charges against his enemies, the priests. He was satisfied with nothing less than the corruption and seduction of men of all ages and conditions, including kings like Frederick the Great, nobles, and others in high places. He thus disturbed public order like any criminal, for Christianity cannot be uprooted without endangering the civil constitution, without releasing a wave of insubordination and crime. Voltaire's ridicule extended to all things generally respected by men, especially to the Bible, against which he railed throughout much of his depraved existence. Blessed with talents which might have brightened the lives of all men, Voltaire turned his great faculties to the disgrace of nature herself by the enmity of his mind to God and his frenzied attempt to ruin the common faith of his fellow men.[40]

In view of so long a record of infidelity, Voltaire was more likely to be held responsible for the French Revolution in England than Rousseau. This attitude was clearly defined even before the Abbé Barruel's *Memoirs* had fixed the responsibility of Voltaire permanently before English opinion. He was looked upon as the precursor not only of Mirabeau and Robespierre but of Tom Paine as well. Mirabeau's attendance at Voltaire's *Brutus* (1790) was reported in *St. James's Chronicle* with an account of the revolutionary demonstration which took place in the theatre. "Voltaire's

bust was called for, and supported by two National Grenadiers."
Mirabeau was seen in the house and a "deputation sent to him to
request he might come into the pit, where he was received with
the loudest plaudits," even as Voltaire himself.[41] As for the play
Brutus, the *British Critic* notes a passage which is almost the "very
language afterwards made use of by the hypocritical and bloody
Robespierre in his harangues." [42] Indeed when the French revolutionists distinguish between their view of the supreme being and
the orthodox belief in a God of retributive justice, their meaning
is made only too clear with the recent aid of Tom Paine. "It is the
Supreme Being of M. Voltaire, of M. Robespierre, and Mr. Paine,"
the same which this last gentleman has recommended to England
in his *Age of Reason.*[43] While Paine is simply repeating what has
been better said before by "Hobbes, Spinoza, Bayle, Voltaire,
Toland, Tindal, Collins, Morgan, Mandeville, Chubb," [44] yet he
takes rank beside Voltaire as one who has shed a great light among
mankind so as to "blind the unthinking part" of the human race.
Such individuals try to break up the happiest bonds of society and
to convert men back to the savagery of untutored Indians, all in
the name of "philosophy." [45]

Aside from these perceptions of what Voltaire had in common
with active revolutionists, there were unqualified statements before Barruel that the French calamity was to be traced to Voltaire
as its source. It was already seen in 1784 that Voltaire had exerted
an enormous influence for evil and had "brought about a melan-
choly revolution in wit and morals." True, he had promoted the
cause of reason and humanity as well as toleration; but "he too
often exerted himself in extending the principles of irreligion
and anarchy." [46] His satires on the clergy had rendered them
universally odious [47] and before the revolution "Voltaire was
more to be dreaded, than the prime minister." [48] The tendency of
his work was to subvert all law, order, and religion, to corrupt
the faith and morals of all ranks of society, and to hasten the rule
of insubordination and enmity to government.[49] French indebtedness to Voltaire was expressed in English with the translation of

Rabaut St. Etienne's *History of the Revolution in France* in 1792. Here the English are told again how much the Revolution owes to Voltaire. Indeed, St. Etienne asks every man of his generation, or at least those who "have learned to think for themselves, and to rise superior to prejudices whether they are not indebted for these advantages to Voltaire." As for the Revolution itself,

All the principles of freedom, all the seeds of the Revolution, are found in the writings of Voltaire. He had foretold it, and occasioned it. He incessantly undermined the ground on which despotism was ever building. Happy in being permitted by nature and time, to enlighten two generations! for freedom of thought keeping pace, day by day, with the errors committed by arbitrary power, the French arrived much sooner at the moment, when the minds of men were to undergo a total change.[50]

It would seem therefore that "if to any *one* man the present commotions of France be particularly owing, it is to Voltaire." [51] In the end, "if we would trace calamity to its source, we must be forced to confess that the flimsy writings of that wretched caviller Voltaire have *undone France*." This fact ought to be a lesson to other governments lest they allow impious publications to spread poison abroad and thus endanger the well-being of the state.[52] Voltaire is finally made culpable beyond extenuation by having foreseen the Revolution and having deliberately labored to hasten its outbreak. He is quoted as predicting the forthcoming change and envying the young who will live to see "charming things." There seems to be no doubt that "the efforts of Voltaire were purposely directed to produce the consequences which he foresaw: as to the *charming things,* they who have lived to see them will probably be inclined to seek a different epithet." [53]

Yet even if Voltaire had not wished to bring about the Revolution, the tendency of his life work was to undermine the social order and to make him the enemy of society at large. His contribution to the new era, whether deliberate or not, was magnificently recognized by those who profited from the change. They proclaimed him indeed "the God of their idolatry," [54] in a ceremony which has appropriately come to be known as the "apotheosis of Voltaire."

Condorcet's *Vie de Voltaire* gave the occasion for renewed interest in the great infidel's achievement. Under the leadership of Condorcet's organization, *La Société de 1789,* an agitation was begun to honor the remains of Voltaire. Since he had been the first to undermine the supports of despotism, it was appropriate that the Revolution should pay a debt inherited from the preceding generation. By the anniversary of Voltaire's death, May 30, 1791, the National Assembly itself had expressed interest in the plan to give some mark of public distinction to Voltaire's body, soon to be removed from the Abbey de Sellières after the confiscation of ecclesiastical property. On his death in 1778, Voltaire had been refused decent burial by the forces of intolerance and fanaticism. This wrong should now be rectified by a grateful nation which must see that without Voltaire the Revolution would have been impossible. Although three cities came forward to beg the ashes which were once unwanted, it was decided that his remains really belonged to the entire nation and that he should rest finally in the Pantheon of great men after suitable honors had been paid to him.

Voltaire's body was exhumed before the anniversary of his death; after a pause at Romilly while the celebration in Paris was being prepared, the coffin was placed upon an elaborate chariot brilliantly decorated with flowers. Everywhere along the way to Paris the great procession received the most distinguished honors; pilgrims flocked from far and near to give an ironically religious tone to the ceremony. The entrance to Paris was made at the Faubourg Saint-Antoine which was lined with enthusiastically cheering throngs, crying out for joy as if they were receiving the return of some God. The procession made its way to the Bastille, where Voltaire's body remained overnight under heavy guard.

Finally the festival in Paris itself was celebrated on July 11, 1791. A parade which was said to number 100,000 participants passed along an announced route lined with enormous crowds of people. The whole was of such size and complication that forty-eight masters of ceremony were chosen to help the national guard to direct the march. The official order of march contained twenty-eight different units, including representatives from all important walks of life, interspersed with groups of musicians to provide the beat for the solemn parade. A magnificent car of triumph had been especially prepared in antique and modern styles to carry the sarcophagus of Voltaire itself. Sustained on bronze wheels, the carriage rose high above the street and was drawn by twelve superb white horses harnessed in blue reins spiked with stars. The gorgeous and profuse floral decorations were surmounted by a figure of Voltaire, over which Immortality was represented as holding a crown of stars. On the sides of the carriage and throughout the length of the procession, inscriptions, posters, and signs proclaimed Voltaire's great contribution to the French Revolution, his indispensable preparation of mankind for liberty.

After making several stops, at the opera and the National Theatre particularly, the enormous cavalcade made its way to Sainte Geneviève. Scenes of frantic enthusiasm and emotion had marked its stately progress. Now at last, to the sound of all the musical instruments in unison and lighted by a thousand torches, the remains of Voltaire made their final entry into the Pantheon of Great Men. After the extravagant triumph of its journey from the Bastille, the sarcophagus lay at peace in the temple of revolutionary France. The people might there behold the receptacle of that very body which only thirteen years before had sought vainly for a place in the earth of Paris.[55]

Now a celebration of such magnitude and implications could hardly escape the attention of English observers. Leaving for the moment the comments of the many individual Englishmen who were in Paris on the occasion [56] or who formed opinions based on their reading, it seems clear that the reading public was aware of the Revolution's tribute to Voltaire. The English regarded the apotheosis as one of the really notable events of the Revolution,[57] and newspapers gave it wide publicity. Of twenty-seven English papers for July, 1791, which were examined, twenty-three carried some notice of Voltaire's triumph. Of these, nine gave only brief remarks, with few details.[58] Of the remaining fourteen papers, nine carried descriptions which made some selection among the details; [59] the other five accounts were highly detailed and circumstantial. *The Whitehall Evening Post,* July 16–19, devotes a column and a half to the apotheosis, repeating the French inscriptions as to Voltaire's authorship of the revolution and emphasizing the role of the Bastille in the celebration. *The Oracle,* July 19, gives a long and detailed description under the single-word heading, VOLTAIRE. *Lloyd's Evening Post,* July 18–20, has an excellent account covering over half a page in which the feeling of indebtedness to Voltaire by the Revolution is emphasized. *The Morning Herald,* July 19, has a long analysis of the procession, but adopts a tone of condescension and skepticism toward an affair which had provoked such enthusiasm among the French. The *Evening Mail,* July 25–27, gave the best account, offering under the heading, APOTHEOSIS OF VOLTAIRE, an elaborate and circumstantial description of the ceremony, adding its own comment upon the meaning of such a tribute.

The attention given to the role of the Bastille in the ceremony is of special importance for the "case against Voltaire." The English now see more clearly than ever that the French themselves considered the fall of the ancient prison as a symbol of the forces which Voltaire had set in motion. These forces were now able to triumph over the oppression against which the great infidel had struggled, and when the Bastille fell, Voltaire's battle against cruelty, fanaticism, and civil and religious bondage was at an end. His remains had to be honored on the ruins of the Bastille then, because his labor had prepared to make these ruins. *The London Chronicle* prints a declaration by the "Volunteers and Inhabitants at large . . . of Belfast" which had been agreed to on July 14, 1791, the anniversary of the fall of the Bastille.

It is good for human nature that the grass grows where the Bastille stood; we do rejoice at an event which seemed the breaking of a chain that held *universal* France in a Bastille of civil and religious bondage. When we behold this enormous misshapen pile of abuses, cemented merely by custom, and raised upon the ignorance of a prostrate people, tottering to its base, to the very level of equal liberty and common weal: we do really rejoice at this resurrection of human nature, and congratulate our brother man coming forth from the vault of ingenious torture and the cave of death.[60]

Comment upon and reaction to the apotheosis was varied in England. Those of liberal principles and sympathetic to the Revolution were inspired to imitate the honors paid "to the bones of Voltaire" and to choose for similar canonization men like Guy Fawkes, Wat Tyler, and Jack Cade.[61] There was even some praise of the new uses to which the Revolution had put the Church of Sainte Geneviève, formerly devoted to the purposes of superstition and now used to convey the names of great men to posterity.[62] A commemorative dinner on July 14, 1791, at the Crown and Anchor Tavern was even to be graced by a "relic" of Voltaire: "A gentleman is expected this day from Paris, who is to bring a jawbone of Voltaire, which the revolutionists have borrowed to partake, with Lord Stanhope's stone, of the Commemoration Dinner." [63] *The Oracle* itself felt that the apotheosis presented the triumph of liberty and the acknowledgement of its debt by a free nation. This day rendered "sacred to genius and literature" will inspire and "excite the emulation of a race of patriots," [64] who will find their imaginations elevated "to the high destiny awaiting them." [65]

Most independent English comment, however, took the form of fierce denunciation from those who disliked Voltaire on principle or who felt that honor to such a man meant the complete surrender of France to impiety and rebellion, atheism and anarchy. The French are evidently insane, suffering "under the immediate flagellation of Heaven" when they give themselves up to "public deification of that abandoned systematical professional infidel, Voltaire." [66] Only an "atheistic zeal" would pay honor to such a perverter of mankind.[67] The French leaders show what they are when they "honour and deify the poor corruptible remains of him, whose life was as impious and immoral, as his philosophy was false." [68] They perverted the sacred premises of the Church of Sainte Geneviève from the worship of God into a charnel house for those who blasphemed their creator and destroyed the peace of mankind. No sooner did these revolutionary leaders get power into their hands than they paid "more than mortal honours to the putrid remains of their reprobate master" and went on to destroy the national religion entirely.[69] To Burke such behavior is one of the signs of accepted atheism in France:

I call it *Atheism by Establishment,* when any state, as such, shall not acknowledge the existence of God as a moral governor of the world . . . when it shall generally shut up, or pull down, churches; when the few buildings which remain of this kind shall be opened only for the purpose of making a profane apotheosis of monsters, whose vices and crimes have no parallel amongst men, and whom all other men consider as objects of general detestation, and the severest animadversion of laws.[70]

It is as if the French had cried out "Give unto us Barabbas!" when they denied "the God of humanity" and carried out the apotheosis of Voltaire.[71] Now men may know once and for all what "Philosophy" means. It is to disbelieve in God, in heaven and hell. It is, says Hannah More, "to dig up a wicked old fellow's rotten bones, whose books . . . have been the ruin of thousands; and to set his figure up in a church, and worship him." [72] And men may also know how completely France has abandoned itself to this philosophy. The recent distinction paid to infidelity "was a full declaration of the principles as well as the intentions of the majority of the Assembly." [73] If people laugh at the simplicity of Rhenish peasants who honor a worthy saint, what shall they say to an assembly of legislators which "decrees a niche in the new temple of the Gods to a man who, while he lived, wandered from country to country, respecting neither the religion nor the manners of any of them?" [74]

The tendency therefore of the French nation and its Revolution is clear. The present policy seems to be "to encourage an open disdain of the sacred truths of religion." If not, why should they dig up the remains of the chief professor of "philosophy" from his unconsecrated grave and bring his moldering skeleton "in a profane triumph to their metropolis," there to inter it "beneath a dome, sacred to Christian adoration?" [75] By this act France shows that she has fallen before the enemies of religion and is unable to free herself from an impious bondage. She demonstrates that her Revolution was caused by a general retreat from religion and an alliance with avowed deists and atheists.[76] This is clear to Barruel himself who tells the English what the true meaning of Voltaire's triumph is:

Seventy years consumed in blasphemies, sophisms, sarcasms, falsehoods, and a virulent hatred of Christ and his saints, had placed Voltaire at the head of all the impious sects of the age. . . . The merits of the whole collective body of impiety had not as great a title to this new triumph as Voltaire himself. . . . All the impious wits of the day acknowledged him to be their father. . . . The triumph of Voltaire was the triumph of all the schools the declared enemies of Jesus Christ. All this had been sanctioned by the decrees of the national assembly. Impious deputies, jacobin clubs, hordes of banditti and their blind followers of impiety and profligacy without having the power or resolution to shake it off.[77]

France of the revolution has thus been revealed as "a mixture of impiety, levities, and pedantry." A pantheon is set up "for the remains of Voltaire, Rousseau, Mirabeau, and Marat," and religion is replaced by the goddess Reason.[78] It is this element of impiety which shows itself in "transferring the decorations of the altar to the tomb of Voltaire" and which in turn prevents the French Revolution from standing as one of the glories of the world.[79] Its real tendency can no longer be in doubt. A nation which denies God and honors Voltaire as the embodiment of its ideal must have sold itself entirely to the forces of evil. For he was a man "whose writings made a mockery of every religious faith," a man, "who had no one virtue, and whose genius was the powerful instrument of vice"; in this apotheosis he received the "veneration of a people whom he had corrupted." Such a ceremonial for such a person can only arouse horror, astonishment, and foreboding toward a nation guilty of "such a blasphemous insult on the Christian faith." [80]

So the reputation of Voltaire himself, by reason of this extravagant endorsement, becomes one with the ill fame of the French Revolution, for this revolt had taken him to itself as a hero. So also the Revolution in turn fell into worse disfavor because it became inseparable from the odious implications of the very name Voltaire. When Barruel's *Memoirs* appeared to denounce Voltaire as the cause of the French Revolution, its English readers were quite willing to accept his guilt as proved, once the apotheosis and its meaning had become clear to them.

With time the apotheosis passed into history and nothing remained save the resting place in the Pantheon. This seems to have become a permanent shrine to which English travelers came when visiting what were accepted as the standard sights of Paris The Pantheon was more likely to attract visitors and to become celebrated than the Church of Sainte Geneviève, now that the ashes of Voltaire and other heroes of France were buried there. Whether posterity abhors or honors their memory, "they will certainly not be forgotten." [81]

XIII · *BARRUEL'S* MEMOIRS ILLUSTRATING THE HISTORY OF JACOBINISM

ALL THAT HAS BEEN SAID as to Voltaire's supposed authorship of the French Revolution has been summarized by Barruel in his *Memoirs Illustrating the History of Jacobinism*. The protection afforded to government by religious belief; the anti-Christian movement prior to the revolution; the accusation that men of letters were precursors of the revolt; the concentration of the entire edifice upon Voltaire—these threads are now drawn together in a work which repeatedly blames Voltaire for the revolution. The author is sure that he is enlightening the world. His pages are full of repetition and emotional outbursts, glowing with a fanatical hatred of Voltaire and his disciples. Barruel seems to have a strong sense of personal injury, as if he were himself a martyr of Voltaire's persecution. Throughout four long volumes the writer's emotion burns fervently; he never loses sight of the enemy nor allows the reader to forget who are the accused and of what they have been guilty.

The Abbé Augustin Barruel was one of an immense number of refugee clergymen who found their way to England, "refractory priests" [1] who had refused to swear allegiance to the new French government and who would allow no change to be wrought in the church. By 1794 these priests numbered about 8,000 in England and the neighboring Anglo-Norman islands. In London alone about 5,000 had gathered, later to spread out over England as they found employment of various kinds. [2] The refugee clergy were "universally received not only with generous hospitality but also with beneficent kindness." The king gave the use of his house at Winchester for the reception of a thousand of them. Custom duties were remitted on the valuables brought over by individual priests and generous contributions were made by other Englishmen for this clerical relief.[3] For some time England had been more lenient with Catholicism. One reason was that popery stood as a firm conservative bulwark. The English governing class thought better of the Roman church as the French Revolution moved forward. Catholicism was opposed to radicalism and Jacobinism, now much more dangerous spectres than a possible return of the Stuarts to the English throne.[4] In any event the French refugee clergy were hospitably dealt with, Barruel being among the more fortunate.

The previous career of this French Jesuit recommended him to Burke and other English conservatives. Having felt the lash of persecution on himself, Barruel was not one to stand calmly by while the new order in France swept away the old foundations. He was active in the fight against "philosophy," having edited until a few weeks before his departure for England, the militant *Journal Ecclésiastique*. His contributions to this periodical were so fearlessly hostile to the revolution that Barruel was obliged to escape secretly from Paris and to make his way, without a passport, to England in September, 1792. His extraordinary energy continued to spend itself against the revolution. During his ten years in England he wrote two important books: *History of the French Clergy during the Revolution* which appeared in both French and English in 1794, and his *Memoirs Illustrating the History of Jacobinism* in 1797. The *Memoirs* were translated by the Hon. Robert Clifford, F.R.S., A.S., third son of the fourth Baron Clifford of Chudleigh. The papers of the Clifford family contain letters from Barruel showing his intimate connection with the Cliffords and his activity in the affairs of the emigre clergy. Robert Clifford, of this prominent Catholic family, had been educated at Liege and probably at Douay so that he was easily able to render the French work into English. His religious belief gave him a sympathy with Barruel's thesis as well, so that he was an important factor in the English publication of the *Memoirs*.[5]

The work itself is indeed a remarkable performance. Its central argument may be simply stated: the French Revolution was the result of a triangular conspiracy, anti-Christian, antimonarchical, antisocial, tending in the end to the universal overthrow of the existing social order. The origin of the entire scheme lay in the plot against Christianity, out of which grew the antimonarchical conspiracy, which in turn bore fruit in the schemes of German Illuminism for the complete subversion of European society. Freemasonry is also accused of having aimed at revolution, especially in its "occult" lodges. But our concern is chiefly with Voltaire and the anti-Christian conspiracy which Barruel never allows us to forget.

Barruel at the outset insists that he is dealing with a conspiracy and not an accidental, scattered feeling of irreligion. He insists on the deliberate element:

I not only mean to show that each individual had impiously written against Christianity, but that they had formed the wish, and had secretly concurred in that wish, to destroy the religion of Christ; that they had acted in concert, sparing no political nor impious art to effectuate that destruction; that they were the instigators and conductors of those secondary agents whom they had misled; and followed up their plans and projects with all that ardor and constancy which denotes the most accomplished conspirators.[6]

That it was a conspiracy will be proved from the intimate correspondence and published writings of the plotters. When the machinery of the plot is exposed, its secret language, the common union and perseverance toward the impious end clarified, surely no reader will be "so infatuated as not to see" that the destruction of Christianity was projected.[7] And particular attention will be given to the leader of this plot. Voltaire is the guilty one who so hated Christianity that he conspired deliberately to destroy it. Therefore to "unmask this dissimulating man shall be the leading object in the following Memoirs." [8]

Barruel loses no time in naming the chief actors in the plot and stating why each was involved in it. Voltaire was in England when he first decided to move against religion. He had flattered himself at the outset "that he should enjoy alone the glory of destroying the Christian religion, which was his sole object . . ." but he soon realized that he would need confederates. From those who were the admirers and disciples of his many "impious and obscene" writings, and who were called Philosophers, Voltaire first chose D'Alembert to aid in the attack: "and he could not have chosen better." [9] Plans were laid, and when Voltaire went to Berlin in 1750, Diderot and others joined in planning the *Encyclopedia* as "the grand arsenal of impiety." On the master's return from Prussia where he had included Frederick the Great (1752), the conspiracy was complete: its object was to destroy Christianity. The leaders corresponded frequently with each other and often used an enigmatical language whose peculiar meanings were known only to the plotters. They also called each other by special names, unintelligible to the public. These devices were used when it was feared that the letters might be tampered with.[10] The policy as repeated frequently by Voltaire was to *"strike but conceal the hand"* so that the criminals might be free, if undetected, to commit further mischief.[11] From the depth of his iniquity, Voltaire composed a watch-word or rallying cry to make very sure that the object of the plot should never be forgotten. Barruel is hardly able to contain himself as he reveals the conspirators' cry:

The words chosen by Voltaire must have been dictated by some fiend of hatred, or of frantic rage: And what words! [écrasez l'infâme!]. . . . they mean *Crush Christ, crush the religion of Christ, crush every religion that adores Christ.* Oh readers! restrain your indignation till you have seen the proof! [12]

Thus "the sophisters of impiety" joined in with the blasphemous cries of the Jews, " 'crucify him, crucify him!' " [13]

Now in order to get rid of Christianity, the conspirators had recourse to a series of concerted actions. The first of these was publication of the *Encyclopedia*. It was of course pretended that this was a compendium of general knowledge in the arts and sciences. But the plotters really aimed to present "all the sophisms, errors, or calumnies, which had ever been invented against religion" and yet to conceal these so artfully that "the reader should insensibly imbibe the poison without the least suspicion." [14] The compilation was rather for infidelity than science. A few religious truths were uttered, but only the more safely to cover up "their impious calumnies against religion." [15]

Part two of the subversive scheme called for suppression of the Jesuits. Their zeal and integrity were too much of an obstacle to the success of any "philosophic" plot. So with the connivance of the Duc de Choiseul and the infamous Pompadour herself, the suppression of the order was completed. Choiseul persuaded the council that it was necessary to destroy the Jesuits first if the state were to confiscate all religious possessions. Voltaire's own sentiments were typical. He *would willingly have seen all the Jesuits at the bottom of the sea, each with a Jansenist hung to his neck.* The order could not stand against such opposition, so religion sustained the blow intended by its enemies.[16]

The next move was the destruction of the other religious orders, now that the greatest of them all was no more. In reality this was no new project. It had already been conceived in 1745 by the Marquis d'Argenson, counselor of state and minister of foreign affairs under Louis XV, as well as a patron of Voltaire. Influenced by the ideas of this enemy of God, D'Argenson planned the destruction of every religious order in France:

The progress of the plan was to be slow and successive, lest it should spread alarm. They were to begin with those orders that were least numerous; they were to render the entrance into the religious state more difficult; and the time of professions was to be delayed until that age when people are already engaged in some other state of life. The possessions of the suppressed were artfully to be adopted to some pious use, or united to the revenues. Time was to do away all difficulties, and the day was not far off when, as Lord paramount, the sovereign was to put in his claim to all that belonged to the suppressed orders . . . the whole was to be added to his domains.[17]

Shorn of all material possessions and discredited by ridicule and calumny on the part of the conspirators, the religious orders would cease to support the crumbling structure of Christianity.[18]

So far the extermination of the infamous thing had proceeded according to plan. The fourth step described by Barruel was less successful. Voltaire saw danger to his henchmen if they lived and wrote openly in France. He had such ample reason to place his own person in safety that he established himself at Ferney where escape was easy in case of official persecution. But he had decided as early as 1760–61 to form a club, not unlike the freemasons. Members would be a select group of "philosophers," who would repair to some retreat where they might safely join the attack on Christianity. Voltaire therefore applied to Frederick for permission to found a little colony at Cleves, where he and his disciples would be free to speak the truth, without fear of governmental or ecclesiastical interference. Frederick is delighted with the plan, but the other "philosophers" are unwilling to sacrifice the attractions of Paris, even for so ideal a retreat. Voltaire holds out the enticement of their common purpose, but he cannot prevail against the superior delights of Paris. The colony is abandoned, but the war on Christianity moves forward with undiminished vigor.[19]

If the conspirators were not to retire into a more remote safety, they might well be insinuated into positions of distinction and influence at home. It was then decided to extend the empire of impiety by having the "philosophers" gain control of the French Academy. Voltaire and D'Alembert having become members, it was planned so to dominate the Academy that only a proved infidel could gain admission. Voltaire strained every nerve and stooped to any hypocrisy in order to secure the admission of Diderot. In the course of time all writers who had not in some way contributed to the anti-Christian movement were excluded from literary honors.[20] Anyone who defended religion was not acceptable. The Academy, thus renovated, became a more powerful weapon than Voltaire's projected colony would have been.[21]

Apparently the capture of the French Academy was only pre-

liminary to the next move in the series against Christianity. This
was the releasing of a flood of irreligious literature over Europe so
that the poisons of infidelity might be made available to all who
could read. For the last twenty years of Voltaire's life, Europe was
overrun "with most impious writings, under the forms either of
pamphlets, systems, romances, or feigned histories." The conspirators acted in concert, to produce, multiply, and distribute
these poisonous writings.[22] Voltaire was especially active in directing the attack. He even oversaw the particular witticisms and
epigrams of his disciples so that his matchless powers of ridicule
were used to full advantage in the conspiracy. Voltaire constantly
recommended the circulation of these books to his brethren at
Paris and "upbraided them with their little ardor in spreading
them abroad, while he himself dispersed them all around him." [23]
He asked Frederick also to encourage Berlin booksellers to reprint
"a few useful books" and to sell them cheaply enough to insure
readers. He asked the help also of Count Schouvallow in Russia
and of Prince Gallitzin at the Hague.[24] And this in the interests
of what was a literary attack, not solely on "the Catholic religion,
much less a few abuses. No; it is evident, that every altar where
Christ was adored was to be overthrown, whether Anglican, Cal-
vinist, or Protestant." [25]

Voltaire himself was not so much interested in contamination
of the multitude. He left this to his disciples, especially D'Holbach
and D'Alembert. His own real game was what he called "the better sort," people of wealth, power, or rank, and after them the
educated classes "and honest citizens ranking above what Voltaire calls rabble, footmen, cooks, etc. . . . the Anti-christian conspiracy first makes its progress . . . among princes, kings, emperors, ministers, and courts, among those, in short, who may be
styled the great." [26] He wished to corrupt society first at the top,
and by a subtle irony, the princes whose support he enlisted were
so foolish as to protect a plot against the altar, not realizing "that
the disciples of those same conspirators would conspire against
their thrones." [27] The implication is that Voltaire knew what the

result of royal infidelity would be. If he thought only of undermining the church itself and not ultimately the government, why
did he concentrate his impious crusade upon men who governed,
and others of "the better sort"? [28] Whatever his original motives,
he had by 1770 enlisted the help of Frederick the Great, Joseph II,
the Empress Catherine, the King of Denmark, the Queen of Swe-
den, her son, Gustavus III, the King of Poland and others of less
prominence especially in Germany.[29] The same was true, however,
of "the better sort" in France. The conspirators tried to place their
adepts in high positions, and by clever flattery and intrigues worthy
of any courtier, men of the proper impiety were insinuated into
the ministry. The supporters of this horrible plot were to be found
even among the magistrates, showing the great effectiveness of
the entire design.[30]

Barruel never tires of repeating the guilt of Voltaire. "From
his very birth, Voltaire's hatred against Christ had been at its
height. Scarcely had he known, ere he hated, scarcely hated when
he swore to crush, the God of the Christians." [31] Once the actual
plot was under way, Voltaire gave his entire life and talents to its
prosecution. In his last twenty-five years on earth, Voltaire had
no other object save "to vilify the wretch." He seemed determined
to "vomit forth himself" more blasphemies and calumnies against
the Christian God than had been uttered by all the infidels of
preceding history.[32] Voltaire had no particular system or doctrine
to preach; he wanted only to overturn the altar. All the divergent
threads of the anti-Christian conspiracy were united in him, "and
his heart may be said to have been their focus." [33] Though he
preached reason and toleration and humanity, he was able to call
for the strangling of the last Jesuit with the entrails of the last
Jansenist, calling this a fair compromise.[34] The ruler of hell itself
could not have been more ardent in stirring up his legions against
"the Word" than Voltaire was in stimulating his own creatures,
the men of letters of France, to share his infidelity and his impious designs. By means of his immense correspondence, Voltaire
encouraged and stimulated "whole legions of adepts from the east

to the west," [35] firing their zeal by his blasphemous letters. These writings must be seen and read to be believed. They show that "to extreme old age, his life was that of a legion of devils, whose sole and continued object was to crush Christ and overthrow his Altar." [36]

At the end of a life spent in such impiety, it was only to be expected that Voltaire should die in horrible agony. Barruel has done much to fix the classic myth of Voltaire's deathbed torments. He can barely find words to describe it, he says, for the historian of such a scene need not fear exaggeration. The dying atheist was a prey to "rage, remorse, reproach, and blasphemy." His death was "the most terrible that is ever recorded to have stricken the impious man." He tried vainly at the very last to be reconciled to the Church he had sworn to crush. He cried out in alternate supplications to God and blasphemies against Christ. He raved dreadfully and died in a paroxysm of curses and remorseful exclamations.[37] Such was the end of this man who swore, like a demon of blasphemy that he would *"Crush the Wretch."* So diabolically effective was his campaign, that kings and other great men applauded Voltaire. Little did they realize that this relish for poison prepared the way for revolution against themselves and all they stood for in the social order.[38]

We are led naturally to the central thesis of Barruel's entire work: the French Revolution was inherent in the plot against Christianity. It could not be avoided that those who made war on the altar should beget, and finally should become one with, those who could undermine the throne. The actual Revolution was no more than the practice of principles originally set forth by Voltaire and his disciples in their fight against Christianity. The Revolution itself shows how true this is by its obvious gratitude to Voltaire and others in the new worship of the Pantheon.

Barruel adds nothing to English opinion around him by saying that revolutions must be prepared for by influencing the popular mind. It is not surprising then, that the French Revolution was preceded by this essential anti-Christian conspiracy and that, after

long preparation, the movement against religion became a movement against monarchy. Barruel's object, now that he has out-
lined the anti-Christian plot, "will be to show, how the *Sophisters
of Impiety,* becoming the *Sophisters of Rebellion,* after having
conspired against every altar, conspire against every throne." [39]
The transition was already under way in the lifetime of the principal conspirators. Voltaire had said to his first adepts that not a
single worshiper must be left to the God of the Christians; they
had replied that not a single subject should be left to the kings of
the earth. From the mutual success of these two views the revolution was generated whose aim was to overthrow the altar and the
throne, not only in France but over the entire world.[40]

Such a transition from impiety to anarchy was an entirely natural one, since both movements shared the same principles of liberty and equality. Thus "to the plots contrived under the veil
of Equality and Liberty *applied to religion* . . . are to succeed
those begotten under the veil of *political* Equality and Liberty." [41]
Voltaire objected to the church because it opposed this principle.
Nothing was *"so contemptible* and *so miserable* in his eyes, as to
see one man have recourse to another in matters of faith, *or to
ask what he ought to believe."* [42] Just as the words reason, liberty,
and philosophy were constantly in the mouths of Voltaire and
D'Alembert, so were they used by the Jacobins who actually conducted the revolution. Men are supposed to be free and equal,
with reason as their sole guide. Since liberty and equality are to
reign, let all religions tending to subject reason and to hamper
man by authority be abolished. "Can the intelligent reader believe that this Equality and Liberty is not apposite to the war carried on by Voltaire against Christianity?" In fact, is there any real
distinction between Voltairism and Jacobinism? Do not the impious and bloody Jacobins attack the same religion of the same
Christ, of the same God, whom Voltaire and his impious clan had
sworn to destroy? [43] The school of Voltaire and the Jacobinical
den both operate under the mask of toleration, but "plunder, violence and death, have marked the toleration of the revolutionists,"

even as that of "the first conspirators whose language the latter had adopted." [44] Both made use of a literary attack upon the object of their persecution, the antimonarchists finding the writings of their impious predecessors most useful for their purposes. In fact the parallel between the two plots is so close that Barruel questions whether the overthrow of government was not the real object of the original anti-Christian plot.[45]

The active revolutionists themselves finally admit that without Voltaire there would have been no Revolution.[46] The Revolution honors Voltaire for the same thing that inspires Barruel to condemn him. The national worship is converted into something impious, for into one of the most magnificent of Christian temples Voltaire and Mirabeau are carried in triumph, making of this church "a den of thieves . . . the pantheon of the gods of the revolution." [47] If the Jacobin is asked why these men, including Rousseau, receive such honors, he will reply that while they are no more, their spirit lives on in their writings. This spirit fights more powerfully for the cause of Jacobinism than armed legions, and is the means whereby the Jacobins can "boldly proceed to certain triumph." [48] The apotheosis of Voltaire is then the final proof that the anti-Christian conspiracy was the germ of the Revolution which had to come out of such a movement against Christianity. The Revolution itself declares that it is only the logical execution of Voltaire's doctrines.

After exposing a double conspiracy against throne and altar out of which the French Revolution grew, Barruel is only beginning; this has consumed less than half his fanatical pages. The double conspiracy found a natural ally in certain lodges and secret societies whose tenets were a combination of the two master conspiracies. Freemasonry was the chief culprit; the whole "science of masonry, like the French Revolution" is reducible to the two words, *"Equality and Liberty."* [49] In the occult lodges this twofold principle is explained to mean war against the altars of Christ and the thrones of kings.[50] The oath taken in the final mystery of occult masonry is the very essence of Jacobinism itself. The com-

bined import of all the inner mysteries of the masonic degrees is
a summary of the subversive doctrine of the French Revolution;
the rights of man, liberty and equality, sovereignty of the people,
the law equivalent to the general will—these doctrines are the
same as those preached by Montesquieu, Rousseau, and Voltaire.[51]
Naturally, with so much in common, the followers of Voltaire
and masonry made an alliance. For years before the revolution
it was difficult to meet a "philosopher" who was not also a mason.[52]
And since all "sophistry" and "philosophy" derives ultimately
from Voltaire, it was appropriate that the masons should signify
their debt to him at their first and only opportunity. When Voltaire arrived in Paris at the very end of his life, the masons prepared a pompous festival for his admission to the mysteries. He
was flattered to learn that the masonic brethren had long been
his most zealous disciples, and that their secret was the same liberty
and equality which he had himself opposed to the Gospel and to
the so-called tyrants of the earth.[53] Thus were the unclean and
hateful birds of a feather united in one flock under Freemasonry.
All the forces tending to subvert the existing order were gradually
concentrated, and rebellion, fundamentally impious, was organ-
izing itself for war against European society.[54]

The final congregation of the entire rebellious movement is reserved for Mirabeau's Jacobin club. Here it is that Barruel's fantastic picture receives its final touches; the term Jacobin is defined
as embracing all the elements of impiety and anarchy which were
released in the Revolution. On his return from Berlin, Mirabeau
saw fit to add to the forces already in France the poisons of German
Illuminism. He felt that his country was at last ready for the light
of the German conspiracy, a thing of wickedness so abandoned as
to make all the French organizations "appear like the faint imita-
tions of puerility." [55] The German leader, Weishaupt, desired nothing less than the complete annihilation of the existing social order:
a universal frenzy of destruction which would leave no civilized
institution intact. Mirabeau saw that circumstances were now
favorable to the reception of Illuminism in France. Prepared by

Voltaire and Rousseau, the Jacobins were ready for the mysteries of Weishaupt, which would convert the French group "into the most abominable impiety and most absolute anarchy." [56] So Mirabeau calls them all together, the genesis of the French Revolution is complete, and the "history of Jacobinism" is finally illustrated. The adepts are convened in a temple formerly graced by the religious Jacobins, who now give their once sacred name to this horde of blasphemers. Soon all Europe recognizes by the term "Jacobin" a combination of all the plotters against Christianity, against the rule of kings, and against all civil society whatsoever.[57]

Barruel has finally a word for England in particular, a word of warning and of praise. Let England also beware lest the conspiracy endanger her God, her sovereign, and her laws. There is evidence that the revolutionary technique is being used in England even as it was in France. The same beginnings by impious and subversive literature, the same reading of Voltaire and other "philosophers" goes on. Subscriptions in aid of the works of Tom Paine, house-to-house canvasses on behalf of the most profligate and abandoned works by Voltaire, Diderot, and other deists and atheists, specious pretenses of enlightening popular ignorance— all this has come into being in the British Isles.[58] Barruel's warning was well timed, for it came not only after the English had been prepared to accept what Barruel says about Voltaire and the French Revolution, but in a year, 1797, when the condition of affairs was alarming. The war was not going well, invasion was threatened, the fleet had tried mutiny, and the general burdens seemed too heavy to be borne. The government's well-known panic in this period seemed justified in an atmosphere of general alarm.[59] Barruel not only gave a further reason for caution on England's part, but was shrewd enough to flatter England's sense of being a nation apart, a people superior to the crimes of France. While it was true that there was danger through impious writings, Barruel assured the English that they were too sound and sensible to become a prey to impiety. They had even repudiated their own infidels, those whom Voltaire had praised as the glory of Great

Britain. For "an Englishman's good sense does not allow him to hate religion, nor make an ostentatious display of impiety." [60] England's ruler in particular is distinguished in the revolutionary crisis for his consistent enmity to the infidels. The plans, records, and letters of the plotters never mention George III, and this silence is the highest encomium possible for so great a prince.[61] Barruel exonerates even the English freemasons. He finds them chiefly good and loyal subjects who believe that men should live as brothers, assisting each other equally and fraternally. There is nothing in their mysteries "tending towards the hatred of Christianity, or that of Kings." Their laws demand nothing save that English masons be honest men, with no adherence to the tenets of the French occult lodges.[62]

Thus the English were both prepared to hear, and were flattered to hear, what Barruel had to say. He assured himself of an interested audience, one likely to approve of an author who could say so literally what they long suspected to be true about Voltaire, and the French Revolution, and themselves. The *Memoirs*, like many another successful book, only summarized thought already in existence. Although it was shortly discredited by its own wild exaggeration and foolish emotionalism, it was addressed to a most credulous public, easily alarmed, and eager to hear an assured voice raised in telling them that their worst fears were justified. They were told that what they long suspected of the French Revolution was indeed true, save that they had made too mild an estimate of the tragedy and those responsible for it. Barruel simply resolved a chord of opinion which had been waiting for years to be completed. This harmony between him and his English audience does much to explain the otherwise astonishing reception of the *Memoirs*.

RECEPTION IN ENGLAND

Barruel's plea for an attentive audience was not in vain. The *Memoirs* achieved an extraordinary international reputation. On the Continent there had been some knowledge of the book before its publication. A prospectus prepared by Barruel had called forth so many letters, memoirs, and other books touching the German Illuminees that he was unable to use them all.[63] England and Germany received the actual publication of the *Memoirs* with particular interest. Robert Clifford testified that "an entire edition of these Memoirs was sold before the fourth volume reached the press." A second edition was withheld until all four volumes could be finished.[64] In view of the critical reaction in England, the *Anti-Jacobin Review* seems correct in saying that "few publications have appeared of late years—that have had so great a run, at least in England, as these Memoirs of Abbe Barruel." [65]

The success of Barruel's earlier philippic, his *History of the French Clergy during the Revolution,* perhaps helped to prepare for the wide interest in the *Memoirs*. The *History* appeared in London in 1793 and was translated into English the following year, appearing also in Dublin. An *Abstract* came out in 1795, and a third complete edition was published in London in 1800, followed by a fourth in 1801.[66] A selection from its recital of atrocities and horrors was published by Cobbett in his *Bloody Buoy* and reprinted in *The Calamities of France* under the auspices of *Every Man's Friend; or, Briton's Monitor*.[67] Another French edition had appeared at Brussels in 1794, followed by others at Paris in 1801 and 1804. Three German editions came out in 1794 also, and later, between 1814 and 1817, three Spanish editions. There was even a Portuguese and a Polish edition as well as one in America. Most numerous of all were the Italian reprints which numbered seven between 1794 and 1825, with an eighth as late as 1888.[68]

Barruel was then something of an international figure when the *Memoirs* appeared to create a far greater disturbance. Of this work three editions came out in England, the original French in five volumes, and two editions of Clifford's translation in four volumes.[69] To make purchase easier, Barruel made an *Abrégé* of the *Memoirs*, published in 1798–99.[70] Some of the author's enthusiastic champions also wrote what will be found to be abridgements of the *Memoirs*. Clifford, for example, gives a digest of the four volumes for those who have not seen them in his *Application of the Memoirs.* . . . The original edition was apparently sold only to subscribers,[71] so that an abridgement was needed for wider use. *The Gentleman's Magazine* assisted in spreading Barruel's account of the anti-Christian conspiracy in particular. A review of the *Memoirs* is quoted at length from *The British Critic,* and many of the essential points in the plot against Christianity, including Voltaire's part in it, are quoted or summarized.[72]

Surely Barruel could not have complained that there was a further "conspiracy" to deny him a hearing. In 1797 the *Memoirs* were a most timely response to the feeling then prevalent in England as to the French Revolution and its causes. Barruel was merely a part of the familiar conservative determination to fight anyone or anything suggestive of freedom or change in the existing order. The English were more than ever determined to oppose those given to change, more certain than ever that it was wisest to hold on to what was established and to put down those enemies and pests of the nation who would try to reform England's ways and so bring her to the situation of France. Therefore, "let the example of France be a warning to us to resist every attempt, every overture, towards change and innovation." [73] The design of authors must be "to preserve things as they are," to promote obedience to the laws, and to make sure that property remains secure.[74] Expediency demanded that those who favored free inquiry should be suppressed, that those advancing any new ideas in religion or politics should be silenced or discredited. In order to keep things in their old train, philosophers and other purveyors of general ideas had to be made antipathetic to the public. Barruel wrote in order to inflame and alarm the weak and simple of mind and was acceptable to a conservative period which found his charges to be useful for its own purposes.[75] The favorable reception of his work far exceeded the opposition of the unsatisfied.[76] It is by this favorable reception that the last word in the English case against Voltaire is spoken.

Barruel convinced his already sympathetic readers that the

French Revolution had sprung from a preliminary war upon religion; that this war was the result of a concerted plot led by Voltaire and abetted by the "philosophers"; and that the revolution was part of a universally subversive movement against all religion and government. Individuals differed in the extent of their acceptance of this. Some were so convinced of its truth that their comments merely summarize the main assertions of the *Memoirs,* serving further to extend the audience of that work. Others accepted it only in part or used its message to prove special arguments peculiar to their own interest. But scarcely anyone contests Barruel's charges against Voltaire. That the great infidel was in fact the originator of the anti-Christian conspiracy from which the French Revolution arose is the almost invariable opinion of everyone who mentions him at all in the closing years of the eighteenth century.

The first of Barruel's ideas certain to be accepted in England was that the discontented in France saw the need of undermining religion in order to make a political change possible. "The internal enemies of her constitution well knew, that to weaken the ties of religion was the sure way to overturn that constitution." [77] The most effectual means to produce the anarchy, confusion, and depravity which have disgraced the French Revolution was evidently to undermine belief in Christianity.[78] It was clear to the leaders that it is religion "which covers Kings with an impenetrable shield" and is therefore "the first victim to be immolated." [79] In the literature of the Revolution one finds an obvious attempt to use religious revolution as a means toward political change. This in turn explains the apotheosis of such a person as Voltaire, praising him because he was the man who had brought about the downfall of religion and priestly power, the first and strongest bulwark of despotism.[80]

All the ridicule, argument, mockery, contempt, and blasphemy against the worship of God and belief in His existence [81] are thus explained by the intention to found a new republic on a heathen basis. "All the world knows that the first Republicans were heathens: therefore, if the foundation of heathenism can be laid, a broad and easy way is open to a Republic." [82] Men have to be released from the check which Christianity exercises upon impulse and from the control imposed by its sanctions. Hence those responsible for the French Revolution, determined to "divest the mind of the controuling principle of religion, and to remove every check that might derive its force from the apprehensions of futurity." [83] They set out to relieve the wicked of all fear of God and to deprive the virtuous of their hope of future reward, to materialize mankind and release them from their duty to their Creator: all this as a means to overthrow political institutions on the ruins of worship.[84] So "philosophy," carrying on vast underground operations for years, decided to prescribe religion as an obstacle in its way.[85] The schemes of men bent on subversion do not allow for the encouragement of virtue and obedience; hence the sanctions of the world to come had to be removed. "Philosophy"

> . . . leaves for probity no room
> In this world or the world to come:
> Here decollates as useless lumber,
> There dooms it to *Eternal slumber*.[86]

The need of this warning upon religion is finally admitted by Mirabeau himself, as if to make it inevitable that the English should accept Barruel's thesis. Arising in the Assembly, Mirabeau *"began* with these memorable words: 'Si vous voulez une *Revolution,* il faut *commencer* par *décatholiciser la France.'* " [87]

In view of the nature of its preparation the French Revolution had to be precisely what it was. There is no need to be astonished at the atrocious violence of the revolt, for such was "the natural result of principles that had been long fostered, and of measures deliberately concerted with an express aim at this very object." [88] No sooner was the church declared independent of the state, "than a flood of vice inundated the land. The tribunals of justice received a shock, in the absence of every religious tie, and all conventions among men were weakened or rendered nugatory." [89] The spirit advanced until every restraint was thrown off and men rebelled against God and King alike.[90] The result was such "convulsions as scarcely ever shook the world in former ages." [91] The behavior of the French as they left their own country and passed through various German towns in the military struggle of the Revolution showed beyond doubt to the rest of the world the kind of influences which had formed the Revolution. The French progress was everywhere marked with rapine, blood, and violence, all clearly springing from want of religion. Monstrous cruelties, unmentionable atrocities, including the violation of women and the drowning of the children born from their abominable lusts—such are the crimes marked against France of the Revolution.[92] The sad truth is as always, that given the beginning, the end could not have been other than it was, full of atrocity and horror. What else could a nation expect which had shaken off the restraint of power and the awe of religion? It could draw no soothing comfort from a clergy which it had debased; "it could find no resource in . . . a legislature, which had Mirabeau for its leader, and Voltaire for its idol." [93]

Such is the result of prevalent atheism. It means inevitably such barbarity as that of the French Revolution, so let there be no doubt that atheism was the cause of this upheaval.[94] Malignant principles bear fruit in kind and the Revolution did no more than practice what men had been taught by the abandoned crew of philosophers. The wildest outrages of the Jacobins simply reduced to practice the speculations of the philosophic conspirators. "The writings of Voltaire had opened the way for the brutal power of Robespierre: and Marat and Danton did but spring from the ashes of Diderot and D'Alembert." [95]

So far Barruel's argument must have seemed obvious enough. But he was prepared to do more, to show the origin and progress of the entire movement against religion; to identify the guilty conspirators, as well as to show their deliberate planning of the overthrow of Christianity over a period of years, thus disclosing the exact manner in which irreligion was transformed into anarchy.

The English seemed glad to accept this as the final word on the revolutionary process in France, and Barruel was regarded as a public benefactor for exposing the entire conspiracy. He had done a service to the world, and his translator a service to the English reader in particular.[96] Indeed, "every friend of religion and moral virtue, of government and social order, of public and domestic happiness" must feel "greatly indebted to the worthy Abbe Barruel for the most important service he has rendered, in unveiling a system of iniquity, the most subtle, the most dangerous, the world ever saw." [97] In spite of certain lapses Barruel deserves high praise; his work as a whole shows "the hand of a master," and should be read and studied "by all who are interested in the great cause of God and man." The *Memoirs* stand as the "best historical and critical commentary extant (except the events themselves)," on Burke's *Reflections*.[98] Later on Barruel himself said that in 1790 "L'immortel Burke" had already seen the true origins of the revolution, and that everything written since that time on this subject had been only "un pur commentaire de son Texte." [99]

The English seem to have been particularly struck by Barruel's proofs, which they find highly convincing. A work by the Scotch Professor John Robison, *Proofs of a Conspiracy against All the Religions and Governments of Europe* (1797), dealing largely with Masonry and Illuminism is often mentioned also as supplementing and confirming his thesis.[100] These two writers have shown the existence of the conspiracy against Christianity "beyond the possibility of reasonable doubt . . . the *conclusion* remains established by the most incontrovertible proofs." [101] Unless one is "totally absorbed in prejudice," he cannot dismiss these proofs as an expression of party bias. Without them "it would certainly demand some stretch of credulity" to admit the entire conspiracy.[102] But Bishop Horsley feels that few histories are supported by such a mass of authentic documents as "the consentient narratives of Barruel and Robison." [103] These documents are "most authentic and impressive." [104] The whole is "judiciously methodized

. . . the style is spirited, the reasoning powerful, the proofs . . .
irrefragable." [105] As might be expected, Burke's tribute to the
Memoirs, only one volume of which he lived to see, is no less enthusiastic. He writes personally to Barruel, saying that he has
himself known five of the chief conspirators, and that he has certain knowledge, dating from 1793, that these men were "busy in
the plot you have so well described." [106] He is therefore delighted
with the *Memoirs;* the whole of this "wonderful narrative is supported by documents and proofs of the most juridical regularity
and exactness . . . the tendency of the whole is admirable in
every point of view." [107] Barruel is an ingenious writer who has
traced the plot against Christianity "with much accuracy" and has
proved his case beyond doubt.[108] Such sentiments are inspired by
a championship which was even militant when necessary. Along
with a general approval of the *Memoirs,* the *Anti-Jacobin Review*
had justly pointed out occasional misstatements and inaccuracies.
For this offense the *Review* is subjected to recriminations by Barruel and his violent supporters, who regard all adverse comment
as the hostile attacks of an enemy or rival.[109]

Some considered the *Memoirs* so important that they helped it
reach as wide an audience as possible. This is frankly the object
of the Rev. Lewis Hughes, to whom the Bishop of Bristol suggested
an abbreviation of Barruel's work, the size of which originally
confined it to a small audience. Mr. Hughes's *Historical View of
the Rise, Progress, and Tendency of the Principles of Jacobinism*
(1799) is accordingly based almost entirely on materials furnished
by Barruel. This work is given further publicity by review in the
European Magazine [110] and in the *British Critic* which points out
that Mr. Hughes may be read with advantage by those who cannot read the detailed exposition of the whole four-volume work.[111]
A similar service has been performed in the Rev. Francis Wollaston's *A Country Parson's Address to His Flock* (1799), which
outlines the conspiracy as described by Barruel and gives perhaps
more space to Voltaire than to any other element. This is also
reviewed in the *European Magazine* [112] which points out the em-

phasis of Voltaire. The *Universal Magazine* in fact quotes from
the pamphlet itself and chooses the very passage which deals most
harshly with Voltaire as the original criminal.[113] A third condensation of the *Memoirs* is given in the anonymous *Jacobinism
Displayed* [114] which often reproduces the very phraseology of Clifford's translation and proceeds again through every step in the
conspiracy. It is given a moderate endorsement by the *Critical Review*.[115] Perhaps the most representative digest of Barruel is that
of the Rev. Henry Kett, *History the Interpreter of Prophecy*
(1799), a work which saw five editions in six years, and wherein
the author quotes freely from the *Memoirs* and follows closely
the outlines of the conspiracy.[116]

Through two editions of the *Memoirs* themselves and by means
of these numerous summaries, the conspiracy should have become
known to a fair section of the reading public. But many other
agencies helped to spread the conviction that Barruel was right. Individual writers like Mathias pointed out that the *Memoirs* were
important in proving that literature can be a destructive as well
as a vital force. Certainly the grand triple conspiracy has shown
the force of literature "stimulated and conducted by an exter-
minating philosophy." [117] Readers of the *Biographical Memoirs
of the French Revolution* were also told briefly of the deliberate
combination against Christianity by Voltaire, D'Alembert, and
others [118] but with far less eloquence than John Bowles summoned
to his charges against the infidels. As the century ends, he finds
society in a shocking state of depravity in religion and morals,
brought on chiefly by a conspiracy against Christianity. A sect of
infidels for over half a century have been engaged in a daring
conspiracy against the majesty of Heaven, straining their faculties
to eradicate all sense of religion from the human mind, hoping
thereby to "leave the mind a total void of dark and hopeless atheism." This has been the chief source of those evils which afflict the
end of the eighteenth century.[119]

More effective than scattered individual writers in spreading
the gospel according to Barruel were the English clergy, especially

bishops in their *Charges* and other preachers whose sermons were published and who might expect to reach a certain minimum audience. It was from these various churchmen that the *Memoirs* received their heartiest endorsement to the public. The Rev. William Cole is especially convinced of the plot theory in his Fast-Day sermon of 1798. He denounces the "reprobate anti-christian philosophers" and their evil writings which "have undermined every principle of morality and religion." He is shocked at their systematic deliberation as they undertook the universal overthrow of religion, morality, political and social order. They carried on this "vast stupendous work of darkness" with sly caution, thus making it the more insidious and detestable.[120]

But the Rev. Mr. Cole's views have less authority than those of the Bishops O'Beirne, Watson, and Horsley. Bishop O'Beirne reaches an earnest audience when he addresses the Lord-Lieutenant and the "Members of the Association for discountenancing vice, and promoting the Practise of Virtue and Religion; in St. Peter's Church, Dublin." His sermon deals largely with the anti-Christian conspiracy and is especially severe on the flood of impious literature which trained up a new race in the contempt of ancient beliefs and nurtured the ferocious bands who have desecrated the finest inheritance of Christendom.[121] In his *Address to the People of Great Britain* (which saw fourteen editions in the year of its publication, 1798), Bishop Watson commends to their serious consideration the attempts by wicked men to rob them of their religion. Over seventy years ago certain men, the "philosophers," began especially in France and Germany, to make war upon Christianity. Until 1798 this design had continued, furthered by the writing of numberless books, "all stuffed with false quotations and ignorant or designed misrepresentations of scripture." Taking their ideas from the English deists, these writers are yet inferior to their English masters in learning and acuteness. The skill of these foreign infidels lies in "ridicule, in audacity, in blasphemy, in misrepresentation, in all the miserable arts by which men are wont to defend a bad cause." [122] Bishop Horsley is the most forcible of the Bishops against the conspiracy. He commends the ability and industry of Barruel and Robison in exposing this plot, "conceived in mere malice and carried on with steady and unrelenting malignity for half a century." So violent and relentless were these enemies of religion that if the very twelve apostles had lived in the time of Voltaire, D'Alembert and Diderot, they would have incurred "the reproach and insult of these Children of Hell." [123] Bishop Horsley also goes farther in denouncing the flood of impious literature than any other commentator on Barruel. In his view almost everything of consequence in the literature of France from 1750 to the revolution is part of the antireligious scheme. Every great literary undertaking, every large publication on whatever subject was in some way brought to bear on the defamation and discredit of the Christian religion.[124]

More useful than the clergy in spreading Barruel's message were the periodicals, sure of a devout and attentive audience. Even the *Critical Review*, perhaps the most resistant of all to Barruel's general doctrine, was able to accept the anti-Christian conspiracy, and with it, therefore, the guilt of Voltaire. While the whole of Barruel's complex structure cannot be accepted, it seems obvious that "there was a conspiracy of long standing to overthrow religion." [125] Mallet du Pan in *The British Mercury* also was convinced that for sixty years past opinions subversive of religion, morality, and society had been systematically spread in France. These opinions gave birth "to that crowd of fanatic pedants, sophists, and demoniacs, who from its origin seized upon the Revolution as by right of conquest." [126] While it is true that the original foes of religion did not foresee the effect of these ideas, they are none the less culpable: for "they sowed with poisons the field where the Revolutionists have reaped: they were the hounds that led and set on the tygers and panthers against the human race." [127] Other periodicals of a more conservative tendency such as the *Gentleman's Magazine* and the *European Magazine,* already referred to,[128] endorsed Barruel's message enthusiastically. The *British Critic* accepts the charge of a regular conspiracy ending in the French

Revolution, remarking with special heat on the watchword of the plotters, "Ecrasez l'infâme," and feeling that every good man "has felt ashamed to belong even to the same species of beings, with the monsters who could perpetrate such horrour." [129] *The Anti-Jacobin or Weekly Examiner* also gives currency to Barruel's thesis that the French Revolution had been prepared by the "philosophers," zealous as they were in their work of blasphemy.[130] *The Anti-Jacobin* suggests that a wide hearing would be gained for this testimony, in describing modestly its own immense success. Regularly the paper sells 2,500 copies a week, but since every family may reasonably be supposed to contain seven persons, the product of readers is 17,500. But these often make it a practice to lend their papers to neighbors, thus spreading the circulation to a grand total of 50,000 persons who have access to the excellent teachings of the Anti-Jacobin.[131]

The periodical most eager to convince the public of Barruel's veracity was the monthly *Anti-Jacobin Review.* Save for a few minor objections, this review accepted the conspiracy in its entirety.[132] In fact, so closely and zealously do the editors follow Barruel, especially in the anti-Christian plot, that they may also be added to those who brought out abridgements of the original work.[133] The *Review's* success before the public further shows the extent to which the plot theory was made available to readers. At the end of its first volume the *Review* is grateful to its followers for "the very liberal, and, we may say, very *extraordinary,* encouragement which we have experienced at their hands." That this is not idle boast will be admitted by the public "when informed that our sale . . . has mounted to *Three* thousand two hundred and fifty of each number." [134]

Through these various agencies Barruel's message seems to have reached a large section of the English reading public, to whom it was for the most part warmly recommended. Less favor was shown to Barruel's warning that the French uprising was only the beginning of a universally subversive move and that England should take care lest her institutions also fall. What was true of

France was not necessarily applicable to England; yet the warning was noted by some of Barruel's supporters. Among these John Bowles offers one of the most eloquent of the many denunciations aimed at the Voltairean system. He asks rhetorically concerning "philosophic" infidelity: "Can Hell's vast magazine of mischief contain a more potent engine of destruction than this horrid system, which tends to effect a complete subversion of every existing establishment—a total Revolution in the political and moral world?" [135] The allies in the war against France must realize that they oppose an enemy "whose obvious design it was to dethrone and murder all kings, to subvert every government and every social institution, religious and civil, and to revolutionize every country." France is in fact, an enemy "whose existence was incompatible with that of civilized society." [136] The enemy now threatening the English coast began their mad career with the "settled design of destroying all religion and all governments in the world." A few vain and self-sufficient men, falsely styled "philosophers" decided that they would achieve immortality "by projecting a regular and systematic plan for the abolition of everything, which . . . has been hitherto held sacred in society." [137] This obsession to effect the "overthrow of all the political and religious establishments of the earth—of the social order of the whole world" [138] is inevitable in a nation which accepts "philosophy" as a rule of life. This system is the

> . . . inveterate foe
> Of order, truth, and peace below
> Whose rancour never can be spent
> Till each rever'd establishment,
> Ecclesiastical and civil,
> Shall be sent packing to the Devil.[139]

The mischief wrought by the spread of this poison in Europe ought to be a warning "in the eyes of all those who enjoy the advantages of religion and good government . . . to stand upon their guard, and be prepared to counteract all similar machinations in their own, hitherto more fortunate countries." Indeed, every European country contains a number of men such as Barruel describes, "enemies to all religion, enemies to all government, except a mob-rule which will exalt demagogues to power." [140]

This last statement seems to include England as well. The already familiar picture of conservative alarm in the decade following the fall of the Bastille may be recalled to show how favorable circumstances were in England to reception of such warning. All kinds of imaginary designs had been at various times believed in. The fear of French principles and of anything like sedition continued long after the war with France had become unpopular. The spirit of alarm was encouraged by the government, either from a sincere belief that a revolution was possible in England, or as a means of making its policy against France seem justified. It was said that the French were trying to overthrow existing English institutions, just as Barruel himself claimed. The government used the help of clergymen, justices, and its own newspapers to keep the public in its nervous, alarmed state. Any sign of radicalism, any local disturbance was denounced as sedition or worse. In 1795, the attack on the king in his coach on the way to and from the opening of Parliament; the general popular distress; the food riots and demands for cheap bread; the discontent and opposition to war: all encouraged the fear that England was in no state to tolerate sedition of any kind. Hence the *Two Acts* (1795–96) which suppressed all large public meetings and unions discussing political questions save by special authority, and which made it treasonable to incite hatred of the government. Such measures were passed by immense majorities and enjoyed wide public approval. In 1797, the year of the *Memoirs,* further legislation was passed against secret societies. It was a generally alarming year, with the naval mutiny partly induced by seditious pamphlets. Conservatism stiffened after its fashion and buried Grey's moderate reform bill under a huge majority. The government was also alarmed by a rumor of French secret maneuvers in Somerset. A gang in league with disaffected Englishmen was reported to be working secretly from a mansion house at Stowey. Wordsworth and

Coleridge were supposed to have been involved in this move against the established order which came to nothing.[141]

All these disturbing facts were evidence even to the timid that England too had her share of these "enemies of religion and government." Witness the efforts to circulate Paine's *Age of Reason* and other works "of equally detestable tendency." Consider too the agitation for annual parliaments and universal suffrage, "the direct inlets to democracy."[142] Further, many members of the English upper classes are clearly tainted by French "philosophy," which was the first step to all the ruin and anarchy of France.[143] If men in England will tread the same steps, let them know "that they lead to the same horror, and the same remorse!" [144] Barruel and Robison have shown "the anxiety, dejection, wretchedness, and despair" caused by this vile impiety, and it can only be hoped that God will open the eyes of the deluded before it is too late.[145] In this one respect England is no better than France: here too "Atheism and Jacobinism walk hand in hand . . ." [146] More alarming than the spread of mere unbelief is the appearance in England of something like the actual plot against all religion and government. The English are therefore warned to

beware seriously of the ILLUMINATI. . . . Their main plan . . . is to bring God, Religion, and Goodness into contempt. . . . This is a war of Atheism, Wickedness and Licentiousness, against God, Goodness, and Good Order, and the battle must be fought out. . . . Remember that the Illuminati calculate upon the idleness of Englishmen. The Illuminati have sown their seed universally, and the weeds are springing up plentifully. . . . Remember they are *always* sowing, they never sleep; . . . if we do not be wakeful also—if we do not pluck up these foul weeds, these bad principles—if we do not probe the wound to the bottom, it will be merely skinn'd over, to break out again, to torment us and posterity.[147]

The destructive principles of these same Illuminati are spreading so rapidly that unless the government becomes vigilant to the utmost, it may be too late to ward off the enemy. The most dangerous of England's foes are not Frenchmen with arms "but Jacobins unarmed." [148] A letter to the editor of the *Morning Chroni-*

cle reveals the discovery of an actual society of Illuminees in England, and is especially grateful to Barruel and Robison for unfolding the real tendency of such an order.[149] How such a society might proceed in England is told by a versifier in the *Anti-Jacobin Review* who represents "A Jacobin Council" with the scene laid in "A Reading Room." The "Chairman" arises to speak:

> John Bull has a passion which most we detest.
> Of all countries on earth he loves England the best;
> Our efforts in private must all be combined,
> To banish this prejudice out of his mind:
> We must ridicule all that is sacred, and great,
> And sap the foundation of Church, Law, and State:
> No engine so sure as the means we'll employ,
> To ridicule first what we hope to destroy!
> To teach the young mind there's no life after this,
> No posthumous punishment—no future bliss! [150]

Bishop Watson has reason to believe that this very effort to poison the young mind has been going on in England. "Irreligious pamphlets have been circulated with great industry, sold at a small price, or given away." [151] Publications of nefarious tendency "have been universally diffused; the expiring opinions of some of our own infidels revived; people of all ranks infected, and the horrid monster of infidelity has walked with brazen front." [152] No pains have been spared to teach these wicked principles. "Heretical and seditious writings" were circulated "to poison the minds of the people of this country, especially those of the lower class, and to render them disaffected to our Constitution, both in Church and State." [153] The result is that a conspiracy like that of French "philosophy" has gained a footing in England. It is ultimately overcome before its evil can be accomplished, but, in the opinion of the *European Magazine*, William H. Reid's work on *The Rise and Dissolution of the Infidel Societies* (1800) proves that the fears of an actual conspiracy were by no means groundless. There was a regular plan of overthrowing the constitution and religion of the nation, set in motion by a diabolical cabal, now exposed by Mr. Reid.[154]

Even Barruel's extreme assertion then, that no country, not even England, was safe from the final consequences of the "philosophic" poison was accepted by the more credulous in England. Few public alarmists could have asked for a wider hearing than that given to Barruel's entire message.

XIV · VOLTAIRE CONVICTED

AND WHO is to blame if all these things are true? We are brought back to Voltaire, the malicious criminal grinning hideously, the father of the whole sanguine ruin which was the offspring of French infidelity and which threatens the very existence of civilization itself. If there was a war on religion in Europe during the eighteenth century, Voltaire was the commander-in-chief of the infidel forces; if this was based upon a deliberate, carefully planned conspiracy to destroy every altar then standing in Christendom, he it was who conceived and nourished the plot to its maturity; and if out of this conspiracy the French Revolution arose, which was the mere beginning of a movement for the universal annihilation of all existing institutions, it was only the inevitable fulfillment of what Voltaire had begun.

The note of irony again enters the final English estimate of Voltaire. At the end of the eighteenth century he is the undisputed leader of infidel "philosophy"; his exertions on behalf of impiety entitle him to this eminence which no "presumptuous competitor" may question.[1] His English reputation had reached its lowest point, yet it was admitted once more that Voltaire had derived his infidelity originally from England. "To the shame of England it must be recorded, that here he first conceived the project of overthrowing" Christianity.[2] Condorcet and Barruel both point out that "it was in this country . . . that he first made a vow to devote his whole life" to its subversion.[3] England's mild and tolerant laws permitted speculations from which no evil had as yet accrued; so Voltaire was free to furnish himself with the doctrines of English deism and to plan the speedy overthrow of Christianity.[4] But Voltaire's main desire was not so much to see Christianity

destroyed as to accomplish its ruin by himself. It was not enough
to put an end to popery; the decline of Christianity itself was his
object and his own unexampled vanity would be satisfied with nothing less than raising his own character on the ruins of a religion
which had stood for ages among the most enlightened nations
of the earth.[5] He saw that it had required the labors of a number
of Christ's apostles to found Christianity, but Voltaire felt himself
able to subvert it single-handed.[6] Two years after his English so-
journ, in 1730, he was already full of his design. M. Henault told
him confidently, "You may do or write what you please, you will
never be able to destroy the Christian religion." Voltaire replied
that "We shall see" and frequently was heard to say, "I am weary
of hearing people repeat that twelve men have been sufficient to
establish Christianity, but I will prove that one may suffice to
overthrow it." [7]

It may have been true that Voltaire was not a literal atheist.
Condorcet insists that Voltaire believed in God and at the time
of his death it was admitted by the *Annual Register* that the famed
unbeliever seems never "to have contracted the stupid frenzy of
atheism." [8] The *Analytical Review* is also careful to distinguish
between deism and atheism where Voltaire and Frederick are
concerned.[9] Yet if Voltaire did not go all the way to atheism, his
zeal in trying to destroy Christianity was equal to that of the most
intolerant religious bigot. He never tired of complaining that he
was being attacked and persecuted, yet no author ever set upon
and "persecuted others with more virulence and acrimony." [10] His
opposition to Christianity was "carried on with a degree of . . .
spite, bitterness, and bigotry, which has not been perceivable in
the writings of any deist . . . in the present age." [11] Voltaire
showed that an alliance between fanaticism and unbelief, between
bigotry and infidelity may exist, and that the zeal expended in the
cause of irreligion was not inferior to that of "the missionaries
of the Vatican, or . . . the disciples of Calvin and Luther." [12]
Indeed one might never conclude the effort to detail "all the in-
decorum which his hatred to religion impels him to exhibit

daily." [13] This fanatical zeal against religion accounts for Voltaire's thrusts at religious belief, no matter what the subject of a given work might be. He seems to have written almost nothing in prose "without bringing in by the head and shoulders some witticism or some declamation against religion." [14] It is common knowledge with what pleasure he diffused the poisons of his sceptical infidelity throughout all his works. His matchless talent for ribaldry and raillery, for impious laughter [15] was so delightful to him in use that he would often wander from his subject to create a situation in which he could indulge in some indecent scoffing at things sacred.[16] His entire work was planned toward discrediting religion, and he would stoop to the grossest falsehood in order to promote this end.

A horrible picture of Voltaire, the nature of his message and influence, is given in a poem called "The Vision of Liberty: Written in the Manner of Spencer." The poet describes the "House of Liberty" in the middle of which there stands an image of Voltaire:

> Wither'd his heart with fellest rage and hate,
> Shrivell'd and lean his carcase like an ape:
> And num'rous crowds upon the same did gape,
> As he all naked stood to every eye;
> Above an altar covered with crape,
> And formed of his books one might descry,
> Prophane and lewd it was, and cramm'd with many a lie.
> And still from 'neath the altar roared he,
> As from a bull lowing in cavern deep,
> "Come worship me, O men, come worship me;
> Spit on the cross, if Jesus take no keep,
> I promise you an everlasting sleep;
> The soul and body both shall turn to clay;
> Ye penitents, why do ye sigh and weep?
> Let not damnation's terrors you affray,
> Come learn my lore that drives all foolish fears away." [17]

Volumes would be required to trace Voltaire through all of the hypocrisies and deceptions that he published in this world. He is never so willing to stray from the truth "as when religion has any concern with the matter in hand. When this is the case, he is in danger of a lie at every step." [18] This is so well known that Cobbett can assume, "Those who have not had the patience to wade through the lies and blasphemies of Voltaire, know his principles from report." [19] He had no real program for establishing general liberty. While it is true that "ideas of civil liberty are scattered here and there through most of his works," [20] as a rule he gives praise to liberty "only so far as it might contribute to weaken the authority of the Church, and lower Sacred opinions." [21] Even his so-called intellectual and scientific interests were aimed at discrediting religious belief. On finding that some of his reading in natural history seemed to contradict the Mosaic accounts, Voltaire exulted in his letters over his discovery and urged on his colleagues to bring forward every fact that was hostile to the Mosaic history.[22] He was actually incapable of constructing or reforming in any real sense; his "professed aim was destruction." [23] This negative intention was the more dangerous, because Voltaire was a man of original and versatile genius and as such "entitled to the high admiration of mankind." [24] He was indeed the "giant of French literature," [25] a fact which makes the perversion of his talents the more lamentable and the more dangerous. The enemy of souls is of course, far too cunning to make use of weak and inadequate instruments for the extension of his designs.[26] Hence his use of Voltaire who could write in so pleasant a manner and concentrated a form as to make "infidelity easy to the meanest capacity." [27] Let the young and unwary then be cautioned against the subtle enticements of Voltaire's opinions made attractive by the distinction of his name and the charm of his expression.[28]

If he had been satisfied to try for the ruin of Christianity single-handed, Voltaire would have been culpable enough. In fact, he was alone in this impious warfare for a long time while others held off, remained lukewarm, disagreed with him, or deserted his cause. But "in the chaos of these divisions, *Voltaire,* away and in safety, kept up alone the fire of his artillery. He reanimated their zeal, preached harmony, and multiplied pamphlets!" [29] He did not rest until he had obtained able assistance in his undertaking. To insure his success he "called in aid from every other quarter in which his influence could operate." [30] He set about to form a definite plan or league for the destruction of Christianity and herein lies his worst offense. He "premeditated, pursued, and conducted methodically the project of subverting Christianity." He formed the "philosophers" into a sect, made them an organized power "which rallied youth around them, and which helped to produce the meetings, since converted into revolutionary arsenals." [31] The miscreant thus bent his persevering zeal to the formation of a conspiracy uniting "all the wit, the science, the philosophy, and the politics, not of France only but of many other countries, for the extirpation of the Christian name." [32] He admitted as his immediate assistants, "the cabinet-members of the impious council . . . Alembert, Frederick II, King of Prussia, and Diderot, men formed upon the principles, and . . . the previous instruction of the Arch-Infidel, their acknowledged chief." [33] The roles of these four men were sharply defined: *"Voltaire* was the chief; *Frederick the Second,* the protector; *D'Alembert,* the agent; and *Diderot,* 'the forlorn hope.' " [34] Between 1728 and 1752, when he returned from Berlin, the conspiracy was considered "as completely formed." [35] Abut 1750 the inundation of impious writings had begun and Voltaire led the way with "a dissertation every six months." [36] He superintended the *Encyclopedia* which marks the real maturity of his plot and in which he found "an extensive field for the display of his mischievous talents." [37] From Ferney, "he extended his influence into the interior of the capitol," and had the malicious satisfaction of hearing "his authority recognized from the borders of the Atlantic, to the distant regions which surround the shores of the Baltic." [38] He continually urged on his fellow conspirators to new exertions but shrewdly cautioned them not to show the hand which inflicts the blow. He perpetually enjoined secrecy, instructing his creatures "to act as 'conspirators, not as zealots.' " [39] He fashioned a kind of watchword, "écrasez l'infâme—which, shocking to relate, he dared to apply to the Author of our Holy Religion." [40] He meant by this expression that Christ was to be destroyed: "Crush him, then; crush him, crush him, is the conclusion of very many of the arch-fiend's letters." [41] The horror of orthodox Englishmen on learning of this dreadful war cry is told in a letter to Mr. Urban in the *Gentleman's Magazine*.[42] The writer had never felt any horror equal to that which rose on his spirit and burst forth at his lips on reading "what I can scarcely prevail on myself to write—the abominable name used by those *worse* than devils, Voltaire, Frederick, D'Alembert, Diderot, Etc. I firmly believe it to exceed in MALICE anything that ever was spoken by the Prince of Hell against his Almighty Foe." There seems to be no question then that "Voltaire was the father and founder of the conspiracy" and that he disseminated throughout Europe with the aid of his associates, "the impious and anti-monarchical doctrines" that so ruinously prevailed.[43]

Among the many dreadful consequences of Voltaire's infamous life, was the untold mischief wrought by his bad example to others. This may be seen in Germany and in England as well. The hateful doctrines of German Illuminism certainly owe much to Voltaire who began the movement against religion which finally developed into the "odious system" of the Illuminati.[44] Voltaire's methods were also adopted by English leaders of sedition who could do no better than follow the master infidel in pursuit of his same ends. His pouring forth of many books in order to mislead and pervert men's opinions was followed especially by English leaders of infidel societies. These men circulated cheap pamphlets in club rooms and formed actual reading societies in order "to enable the members to furnish themselves with the heavy artillery of Voltaire, Godwin, Etc." Lectures compiled from Voltaire's works and other notoriously infidel writers were delivered, so that others who might have remained in ignorance of these poisons should be misled and corrupted by them.[45] They went so far as to adopt one of the most impious of the Voltairean slogans which was particularly offensive to the devout English. A common toast among them was received with acclamation: *"May the last King be strangled in the bowels of the last Priest!!!"* [46]

If Voltaire's influence had ended with the harm done to religion, his life would have been damnable enough. But the effect of his work extended to the French Revolution itself. Even though Voltaire did not voluntarily set out to sponsor the revolt, he predicted it, regretted that he would not live to see it, and was sure that it was bound to come as a result of his beginnings.[47] His principles naturally led to the Revolution and he could not have halted the forces which he had unleashed.[48] The mildest estimate that can be given of him is that he at least made people unfit for oppression; he attacked those particular superstitions and prejudices "the ruin of which he thought necessary to pave the way to that of political truth." [49] Thus if he did not actually prepare the nation for liberty, he at least made it unfit for bondage. In actual fact, however, the revolution simply reduced to practice "the splendid theories of Voltaire." [50] . . . The structure of French liberty is a kind of play recalling the seven ages in the soliloquy of Jacques. The first act displays,

> . . . *Philosophic Infants,*
> Nurs'd by Voltaire and mewling for reform.

The others follow through the stages of Tiers-Etat, Citizens, Jacobins, Regicides; then a horde of half-famished *slaves* ending in the last scene of all which is mere,

> . . . barb'rous *anarchy,* mere savage life;
> Sans trade, sans laws, sans God, sans everything.[51]

Thus when *Gallia* received the monstrous birth of Jacobinism,

> Voltaire inform'd the Infant mind:
> Well-Chosen Nurse! his Sophist lore
> He bade thee many a year explore!
> He mark'd thy progress, firm tho' slow,
> And Statesmen, Princes, leagu'd with their invet'rate Foe.[52]

By his contributions to impiety and corruption of manners,[53] Voltaire gave the budding Revolution its first hold on life. It is small wonder, then, that those who actually carried out the massacres and atheism of the Revolution itself should have gloried in the title of "the disciples of Voltaire and Rousseau." [54] Since the Revolution is the work of "the sect of *Marat, Mirabeau, Voltaire,*" [55] the revolutionists do well to express their gratitude to the great unbeliever. He produced all that was to be seen in the actual rebellion; he was the first author of the Revolution, "for it is *the thought of the wise man that prepares political Revolutions.*" [56] Here then is the reason why Voltaire must be condemned. The English are warned that the beginners of specious measures of reform and change "are answerable for all those atrocities to which the worst men, who have intrenched themselves under their authority, character, and influence, may, in the usual and natural progress of such events, afterwards proceed." [57] Voltaire being admittedly the "beginner" of the entire subversive movement, the terrible responsibility for all the horror, misery, and bloodshed that have ensued rest squarely upon his shrunken figure. There is no doubt that

the works of *Voltaire* unchristianed the French nation, and produced all the horrors of their revolution: Try his principles by the effects of them. His tender love of toleration has ended in a worse than Decian persecution: his liberty has generated a tyranny more absolute and cruel than that of Turkey or Algiers; his declamations against Kings, as the enemies of peace, have produced such tumults and wars as never were known, and have nearly put the whole world into arms.[58]

In view of all these facts, "Could he have any satisfaction in looking back on such a life?" asks a writer to Mr. Urban.[59] The answer seems to lie in the manner of Voltaire's death, which had a morbid fascination for the English and which convinced them once and for all of his great wickedness. This concern with the manner of one's departure from life had long been important to the English. To go back no further than Shakespeare, we find in Henry VI, Part II, a scene describing the death of the wicked Cardinal Beaufort, who cries out in agonized remorse for his evil deeds, as befits a man faced at last with the inevitable reckoning. The King sighs,

Ah, what a sign it is of evil life,
Where death's approach is seen so terrible! [60]

Warwick adds on seeing that the Cardinal has breathed his last,
"So bad a death argues a monstrous life." [61] In *The Theatre of
God's Judgements* by Thomas Beard (1597) are given numerous
examples of men who fell away from religious faith and finally
died in torture of conscience, "in horrible griefes, terrors and
fearfulness," in despair, remorse, and agony. In their extremity,
those of wicked and faithless lives sometimes hanged themselves,
strangled themselves, or died amid the torments of their rotting
bodies, yelling out continuous blasphemies and infamous speeches
against God "with horrible howling and outcries." It is clear that
as one has lived, so must one die, and from the manner of one's
death may be seen the kind of life one has lived. God's vengeance
is certain against those who have lived beyond His favor:

But to him that liveth ill, death is an ever dying death: he lies tormented
with the pangues of the dying flesh, amazed with the corrosive fittes
of the mind, frighted with terror of that is to come, grieved with remorse
of that which is past, stung with the gnawing of a guilty conscience,
terrified with the rigour of a severe judge, vexed with approach of
a lothsome sepulcher. [62]

It seemed impossible for the infidel or the freethinker to maintain in the hour of death the insolence and pride of intellect which
had inspired his lifelong indifference or hostility to God and
religion. Until death stares the infidel in the face, he seems not
to realize that there are possible punishments in store for him.
It is assumed that a horrible death follows a lifelong failure to
believe that anything terrible is really going to happen after
death. Suddenly the unbeliever accepts and is afraid of what he
had never taken seriously before.

It is true, then, that a horrible death is in store for any man who
has lived a wicked life; this favorite orthodox view was common
in England throughout the eighteenth century and continued
unabated into the period of the French Revolution. [63] But all
this applied with special force to the wicked man who was in-

tellectually talented and used his gifts to arrive at false religious doctrine. In Voltaire's boyhood the idea was common in England that freethinkers begin to pay already in this life for their infidelity in that they cannot sustain their courage in times of illness. In the *Tatler* for February 17, 1710, Steele points out how common it is for a freethinker to be humbled and beaten down by sickness or sorrow and to attempt to make his peace with those truths which he had once so insolently denied, but, this is often denied him in turn by great agonies and horrors of mind. The mere titles of books later published by such groups as the Religious Tract Society emphasize the morbid conviction that infidels are bound to die in misery and remorse, their last hours poisoned by regret and self-accusation when it is too late. *The Confessions of an Infidel; The Last Hours of a Learned Infidel, and an Humble Christian, Contrasted; The No-Creed of Infidelity, Contrasted with the Faith and Hope of a Poor, Dying, Negro Woman; The Contrast; or, An Interesting and True Account of the Last Hours of a Learned Infidel and of a Learned Christian* all spare no pains to describe the miseries of infidels in their last moments, the horror of their guilty consciences, their tormented thoughts of eternal fire, their struggle to repent when they no longer can, their fears of avenging justice, their agonized shrieks to God to save them from inevitable damnation.

All this is placed over against the manner of departure from life enjoyed by the pious and good. The *Evangelical Magazine* informs prospective contributors that "anecdotes, remarkable providences, and the experience of dying Christians, if well authenticated, will always be acceptable." [64] A volume of such accounts was even possible, and the general interest seems to have warranted a "new edition," in 1789, of Richard Burnham's *Pious Memorials,* with the explanatory legend, "or the Power of Religion upon the mind, in sickness, and at Death: Exemplified in the *Experience* of many *Divines* and other *Eminent Persons* at those important seasons." The *Arminian Magazine* was able to conduct a regular department of "Experience and happy Death" wherein are listed persons whose edifying departure into eternity might well be an object lesson to the faithful.[65] Again the wicked are held up for the public instruction by way of contrast to an ideal demise. Men are warned to live justly by such accounts as "Awful Death of a Deist," "Miserable End of an Unbeliever," "Miserable End of an Infidel," "Account of the Life and Dreadful Death of a Notorious Backslider, "Death of a Libertine," and the like.

It is easy to see why the circumstances of Voltaire's death would seem of uncommon significance, and why Barruel's lurid account of it should appear entirely just and appropriate. If Barruel had not provided his classical version, some orthodox Englishman might well have arrived at something very much like it. Actually, notice had been taken in England of Voltaire's final illness and death long before Barruel's description of its horrors. As early as 1764, a review of the *Philosophical Dictionary* points out that whenever Voltaire becomes ill "his courage, or his philosophy as he terms it, entirely fails him, and he is as much afraid of hell-fire and the devil, as a child is apt to tremble at the mention of spirits and hobgoblins." [66] In the year of Voltaire's death, 1778, it is reported that in spite of his ridicule of the clergy and religion, "in sickness . . . no man is said to have ever betrayed more fear of the devil's class than M. de Voltaire. In such seasons, the most ignorant and mendicant priest can have a sway over him, which in perfect health, 'the infallible head of the church' would fail of." [67] By 1780, the tale of Voltaire's rising from a repentant sick-bed ready for more evil has become a figure of speech. At election time when everyone expects anxiously the dissolution of the old rascals in Parliament, there is a sudden onrush of goodness; political frailty "felt a sort of death-bed penitence; it was the hectic virtue of a moment: the panic however soon subsided; and, flushed with new hopes of protracted existence: the old septennial method-ist arose, like Voltaire from sickness, impatient for deeper vices, and anxious for more aggravated profligacy." [68] In 1781 the poet Cowper was reflecting in his poem *Truth* on the life of profane

ridicule led by Voltaire, and his inability to draw comfort from
it in the hour of trial:

> The scripture was his jest-book whence he drew
> *Bon mots* to gall the Christian and the Jew.
> An infidel in health, but what when sick?
> Oh—then a text would touch him at the quick.[69]

By 1782 the account of Voltaire's actual death bed agonies by
Dr. Tronchin was current in England through the *History of the
Life and Writings of . . . Voltaire* (1782). Here the legend of
the great scoffer's agitated consumption of his own excrement as
his philosophic calm gave way before the horrors of coming judgment was given its first but not its last endorsement.[70] In the same
year the *Gentleman's Magazine* recounts the dreadful last hours
of Voltaire in "An Authentic Account of the Last Moments of
Voltaire." [71] This periodical however, has some difficulty in determining whether the story is true, and decides two years later,
that "the idle tales that have been told about his last moments are
the more incredible," when it appears that his friends and relations report nothing said by Voltaire about religion.[72] In 1786 it
is reported that Voltaire's friends have covered up the true story
in order to make it seem as if he had died with perfect consistency
as befits a man with his opinions.[73] In the same year the translator
of Dom Chaudon's *Historical and Critical Memoirs . . . of Voltaire* makes a real effort to be dispassionate about the death of
Voltaire, warning that the version given by Chaudon is a preju-
diced one to be expected from a clergyman.[74] The actual text
follows the classical view, already beginning to be current: Voltaire
died in violent agitation and suffered dreadful agonies after vain
attempts to make his peace with God.[75] In 1789, however, D'Alembert's account of Voltaire's end as reported to Frederick the Great
gives the view of those who wished to think well of the infidel.
This account is nearer to that accepted by Voltaireans of the
present day, and of course says nothing about deathbed horrors.
D'Alembert shows how Voltaire tried to make his peace with the
church in order to get a decent burial, which finally took place at

the Abbey de Sellières.[76] In 1791, J. Milner, translating the *Pastoral Letter of . . . De la Marche . . .* , suggests that a partial version of Voltaire's death as later described in Barruel's *Memoirs* was already known in England to those who had read Barruel's earlier *Lettres Helviennes* (1784). In a note to the "putrid remains of their reprobate author," Milner says, "See an account of the terrifying and desperate end of this unhappy man (though but a month or two before he had endeavoured to reconcile himself to the church, and actually called for the sacraments) in the learned Abbe Barruel's *Lettres Helviennes,* vol. 2." [77] In the following year, however, "Lines written by Voltaire on his death bed" offer no suggestion of deathbed agonies. A simple poem is reprinted in French, expressing the devout conviction that God, who has been so good in life, will not see fit to torment Voltaire forever.[78] The feature of Voltaire's death scene which impressed Joseph Priestley was the immoral perjury of the unbeliever's profession of Catholicism in which he desired to die, regardless of his behavior in life.[79] By 1793 again, such a morbid curiosity and satisfaction was shown by the faithful in these details that "Coghlan's Catalogue" in the *Laity's Directory for the Church Service* could use it as promotional advertising for a book on Voltaire. Catholics are offered *"The Life and Writings of Mr. Arouet de Voltaire,* and the manner of his miserable Death," for two shillings.[80] Yet in the same year Stephen Weston finds that it is precisely Voltaire's death in which "every man would wish to resemble him; he slept away his life, and died without a pang." [81] In 1794 it is simply reported that Voltaire "died unbecoming the intrepidity of his doctrines," [82] and in 1796 attention is again called to his hypocrisy in professing the Roman faith when he thought himself about to die.[83] The same year discloses a number of references to Voltaire's death, showing the general and continued interest in this subject in England before Barruel's *Memoirs*. Voltaire's end is contrasted with that of a good Christian [84] and the usual account of his last illness is described as hackneyed, a "trifling, threadbare story" which is obvious enough and hardly needs to be repeated any further. "But, is it anything uncommon, that a man, who has lived a profligate life, should be stung with remorse upon the approach of death?" [85] Everybody knows that "infidels and ungodly men lose their courage when death and judgment stare them in the face" so it is not to be wondered at if Voltaire departed this life in the manner set forth by Dr. Tronchin.[86] His deism was unable to sustain him in the end, so he cried out in fear of hell and pled for continued life so that the day of reckoning might be postponed.[87]

By the year 1797 in which Barruel's *Memoirs* appeared there had then been current for some time in England a view of Voltaire's death which Barruel was now to fix once and for all in its final form, a version which is accepted by the devout and credulous to this day. It was now clear that if the accounts were true "of all the horrid departures from life, none were ever equal to that of Voltaire; in fearful apprehension of judgment, and in extreme despair." [88] The *Gentleman's Magazine* quotes Barruel's account and finds in it "a most instructive lesson." [89] Barruel's narrative, it is said, in fact but faintly describes the scenes which the deathbed of Voltaire is said to have exhibited.[90] The lesson to be learned from it may be driven home by contrasting Barruel's story with an account of the demise of poor Joseph, a half-witted errand man, who left the world in peace to the edification of all beholders. It may have been true that Joseph was stupid, but this was better than to be clever and to believe the wrong things.[91] So instructive and useful was this entire episode that the Rev. William Cole suggests "it may be of public utility to subjoin Barruel's account of the death of Voltaire." He then gives the story, omitting none of its horrors and lurid details.[92] The Rev. Lewis Hughes, confessedly abridging Barruel, recounts how Voltaire "died in alternate paroxysms of devotion, and impious rage: blaspheming his creator, and supplicating him for mercy." [93] Another close student of the *Memoirs,* the anonymous author of *Jacobinism Displayed,* tells that "the horrors he suffered were too great to be related . . . and he departed in the most extreme agony!!" [94] Evidently his philosophy could not aid him in his last agony and tribulation,[95] and he attempted a futile recantation at the last moment which ought to be a lesson to those who have been misled by his writings "lest they fall into the condemnation which their master seeks thus meanly at the end to avoid." [96] Thus for all the assurance with which Voltaire had expressed his perverted opinions they could not sustain him in his final moments, and his death as told by Barruel remains for all a fearful warning.[97] Even the versifiers of the time felt inspired by the compulsion of Barruel's account, so that the emotion of verse is added to the awesome description of Voltaire's dying torments. One effort is contributed to the *Anti-Jacobin Review* under the title "Eternity, a Poem: Addressed to Free-thinkers and Philosophical Christians," by John Jameson, D.D.F.A.S.S.;

> But when Voltaire a dreary deathbed press'd
> Not all the heathenish horde could sooth to rest.
>
> .   .   .
>
> He Jesus view'd with hateful envious eye,
> And *crush the wretch,* was still his impious cry.
> 'Twas still his cry, with worldly fame while flush'd:
> Too late he finds, himself alone is *crushed.*
>
> .   .   .
>
> Eternity, of mirthful days the sneer,
> Seen as at hand, o'erwhelms his heart with fear.
> From friends in guilt he solace seeks in vain:
> He views them only to increase his pain.
> Now he invokes, of other help forlorn,
> The object of his former hate and scorn.
> Then mad with anguish and despair, blasphemes;
> Or to his fellow-sophisters exclaims;
> " 'Tis you have brought me to this wretched state:
> Your praise more baneful than the bigot's hate"
>
> .   .   .
>
> Their dying chief they from all comfort bar:
> Even such the mercies of the wicked are.
> His keen remorse in vain they strive to veil:
> For well known facts belie their flimsy tale.[98]

It would seem from this and similar effusions that the orthodox derived more satisfaction from Voltaire's supposed recantation than from the actual recital of his terror on the approach of death. Their purposes were sufficiently served if it was clear that Voltaire could not maintain his lifelong tenets to the last. Another versifier, writing an "Imitation of the Thirteenth Satire of Juvenal" on this subject tells how

> . . . Voltaire, his life, his glory past,
> In death renounc'd his tenets at the last.
>
> .   .   .
>
> Lo there he lies, with guilt and terror worn,
> Despis'd, deserted, hated, and forlorn.—
> How chang'd from him, that kept the world in awe,
> Whose voice was gospel, and whose lip was law!
> Mark, where, convuls'd in grief and wild despair,
> He lifts to Heaven his first and stifled prayer,
> Mourns o'er the past, laments his present doom,
> But shrinks and shudders at the years to come.
> Adores in death that Godhead he denies—
> Ye Atheists tremble, and ye fools be wise.[99]

Barruel seems to have imposed his entire interpretation of Voltaire upon English opinion, even to the final hours of the great infidel's life. It is hardly necessary to trace the legend of Voltaire's final torments through its many repetitions in the nineteenth century; but its recurrence in the Germany of Hitler and Goebbels in our own time is worth our notice. There is a certain appropriateness in this that the most recent version of Barruel's grotesque performance should become part of Nazi propaganda. While not adopting the plot theory in Barruel's form, the Nazis used a variation of it in building up their case against Judaism and its alleged determination to conquer the world. In 1936 one Johann Georg Stakemann published *Voltaire: Wegbereiter der Französischen Revolution*. Here Voltaire emerges as a wretched spy and undercover agent for the freemasons and their secret plan to control the world; this was of course only one phase of the gigantic conspiracy of the Jews for universal domination. Voltaire is thus the whipping post of fanaticism in whatever violent form it has taken, even down to our own day. Once it was a frantic Jesuit and now it is a Nazi whose purposes are also served by telling us that Voltaire broke down in his last hours. Such are the strange bedfellows to be found in intellectual history. And along with the Nazis the orthodox are still fond of repeating the classical account along the lines established by Barruel. He is still believed in so far as there lingers among men a trace of the conservative beliefs and fears which he did so much to encourage, and his perfect response to and sympathy with which accounted for so large a part of the English case against Voltaire.[100] Certainly at the end of the eighteenth century Barruel's work was accepted in England as one of the most satisfactory and convincing estimates of Voltaire which had yet appeared. The *European Magazine* finds that "in a sketch of the progress of Voltaire through life, M. Barruel has given us one of the most able exposures of that man's inveterate and blasphemous spirit we ever met with." [101] Voltaire was never consistent in anything save in hating the gospel,[102] and his life work bore fruit accordingly. "He sowed unto the flesh and of the flesh he and his disciples have reaped death and corruption." [103] There was evil in him and all his works; his very appearance suggested one of the fallen. One who had seen his portrait when too young to realize "for whom it was painted," involuntarily cried, "That man looks like an odious devil." [104] Other men have lived wicked lives but none exercised such an evil influence as Voltaire:

> Others have been renown'd but he supreme,
> Deep-fraught with sin, and practis'd to blaspheme.
> Some flee, some slight, some war 'gainst themes divine:
> But he with impious worship mock'd the shrine,
> Troubled with feet unblest the fount of life,
> And tower'd a victor in the miscreant strife.[105]

The Earl of Exeter therefore does well to expunge "from his large and well selected library" the works of Voltaire and other unbelievers, and to burn them lest they contaminate others.[106] The

works of Voltaire have done harm enough with all the ruin of
modern times to be laid at their door, and the besmirching of
human virtue to be charged against them:

> Arise, *Voltaire,* proud conqueror, come away!
> High genius, art thou fall'n?—*Voltaire* laid low?
> No smile insidious on that victor brow?
> Arise, rejoice, review thy vassal-band,
> Who *wrought* the deeds, thy master-pencil plann'd!
>
> .   .   .
>
> Ask of *thy* faithful Satraps,—whence *arose*
> This full, this swelling, deep'ning tide of woes?
> *Who* subtly first the flame of discord fann'd?
> *Who laid, who sprang* the mine, which rent the land?
> Nor stay'd, nor spent its force, but smote around
> The nations; heedless of th'awakning sound!
> Who led *Philosophy,* the modest maid,
> To *Frederick's* pious court, or *Ferney's* shade?
> (There first the fiends their engin'ry prepare,
> In that Aetnaean forge, and school for dev'lish war!)
> *Who,* beauteous *Modesty,* thy blush profan'd
> As the vile jest his page dishonest stain'd?
> O sacred *Love, what* cruel hand unclean
> Shrunk thy pure bloom, and brutaliz'd thy mein?
> If life's best feelings lose their lib'ral flow,
> If *Honour* hide his once-unsullied brow,
> If *Loyalty,* from earth (like *Justice*) driv'n,
> Must refuge find,—should *Britain* fall,—in heaven,
> If cold self-interest canker ev'ry part.
> *Who spread* the lep'rous taint?—*who* froze the heart?
> These were *thy* triumphs!—Frenzy, death, despair!
> And—*thou enjoy'd'st them fully,*—lost *Voltaire!* [107]

So the English came to be convinced that Voltaire had gone
through life with a kind of diseased touch, contaminating everything and everyone that came near him. He left no human virtue
and, by his influence, no human institution unharmed. Therefore, "Good were it for that man had he never been born!" [108]

XV · CONCLUSION

THE ENGLISH CASE against Voltaire as one who caused the French Revolution by leading an attack on organized Christianity was a natural result of the conservative point of view in eighteenth century England. Not all of the elements of English conservatism as here analyzed are directly involved in the indictment of Voltaire. Yet English complacency and belief in the divinely given perfection of England naturally led to a disdain of what was not English. English nationalism and age-long rivalry inspired the distrust of and dislike for France and things French which is obvious in most classes throughout the eighteenth century. English complacency, too, was upset by an energetic challenge to its high opinion of itself and its ways on the part of France. While it is seldom stated in so many words, Voltaire suffered because of the means he took in *Candide* to achieve his end; after all Johnson also despised metaphysical optimism. But once the argument over metaphysical optimism had subsided in the later eighteenth century, it is rather to anti-intellectualism and fear that we must look for the roots of the English case against Voltaire, all due allowance being made for the traditional hostility to France that became more intense during the Revolution and the war itself.

It was not that Voltaire constructed a new theory of society and demanded overthrow of the existing order. On the contrary he was a well-known monarchist and himself distrustful of popular movements, of sudden and violent changes in a social scheme of things that had treated him generously most of his life. But he created an atmosphere of doubt and questioning, of thinking and criticising that was likely to be a disturbance. His weapons were distinctly intellectual and appealed to the mind in a pleasing, seductive way. He made others receptive to ideas and made the raising of questions more natural. The effect of his work was to set in motion certain trends of thought or attitudes of mind, the final goals of which he could not prophesy. The presence and activity of such a man must seem a danger to realistic conservatism which distrusts ideas not only because they seldom are useful in dealing with reality but because they cannot be controlled and may lead to results which no one has foreseen on their first expression. Voltaire was, then, the kind of man who caused others to think in certain ways and to ask certain things which ought never to be mentioned.

A far worse offense was his attack on an institution which conservatism looked to for the maintenance of its special dispensation. The presence of the church and its influence did more than any other single element to calm that fear which was found to be inherent in English conservatism. Voltaire was charged with depriving people of their beliefs in sacred things, of their consolations in this life, of their hopes and fears for the future which did so much to keep them in a state of mind favorable to the conservative desire to maintain things as they were. By undermining the church, Voltaire prepared for the overthrow of what the church existed to support. With ferocious skill and power, he made sure that certain beliefs which had long been depended on to keep the peace of contentment and subjection were no longer accepted without inquiry. English conservatism never forgave him, and when the French Revolution broke out, Voltaire was the inevitable target for the missiles thrown by disturbed complacency, pessimistic piety, realistic caution and panic fear.

BIBLIOGRAPHICAL NOTES
AND INDEX

BIBLIOGRAPHICAL NOTES

IT HAS SEEMED BEST not to draw up a formal bibliography for a work of this kind. The kind of material used would have little meaning for the reader if seen in a list entirely apart from the context in which it is used. Most of the references are to English works published in England in the eighteenth century. These are referred to as they are used, chapter by chapter. Since nearly all of the material then is English and taken from a clearly defined era, it has seemed unnecessary to give the place of publication or publisher for each reference. This is done only for books not published in Great Britain; otherwise it is thought sufficient to add only the date of publication to the author, title, volume, and page.

Spelling has for the most part been modernized. Since the eighteenth century was itself not always consistent in its practice in this matter, the present text cannot pretend to be uniform in spelling throughout. Yet every care has been taken to insure accuracy in the intellectual content of all quotations, and if excessive capitalization or other quaint practice has been modernized in the interests of clarity and ease of reading, this has not been done at the expense of fidelity to the original ideas. But since the ideas are most important, nothing is to be gained toward their clear exposition by retaining the curiosities of eighteenth century orthography.

I. INTRODUCTION

1. John Lord Campbell, *Lives of the Chief Justices* (1849), II, 335n.
2. N. H. Kennard, "Voltaire and England," *The National Review*, XIX (1892), 800.

3. 1927. For other support of the following analysis of conservatism see Quintin Hogg, *The Case for Conservatism* (London, 1947).

4. For the relationship of the Scottish philosophy to the kind of conservative anti-intellectualism under discussion, see the chapter on Dugald Stewart in Leslie Stephen's *English Utilitarians.*

5. J. W. Jeudwine, *Religion, Commerce, Liberty . . . 1683–1793* (1925), p. 1.

6. Josiah Tucker, *A Selection from His Economic and Political Writings,* ed. Robert L. Schuyler (New York, 1931), p. 238.

7. Horace Walpole, "Correspondence with the Rev. William Cole," *Yale Edition of Horace Walpole's Correspondence* (New Haven, 1937), II, 210–11.

8. Henry St. John, Viscount Bolingbroke, "The Freeholder's Political Catechism," *A Collection of Political Tracts* (1769), p. 269.

9. John Reeves, *Thoughts on the English Government* (1795), p. 8.

10. William Blackstone, *Commentaries . . . ,* ed. St. George Tucker (Philadelphia, 1803), I, 69.

11. W. E. Lecky, *A History of England in the Eighteenth Century* (2d ed., 1879), I, 452; cf. Leslie Stephen, *History of English Thought in the Eighteenth Century* (1876), II, 230–31.

12. George Pitt Rivers, *Letters to a Young Nobleman* (1784), pp. 333–34.

13. Sir William Temple, *Works* (1770), III, 46–47.

14. Soame Jenyns, *Works* (1790), III, 133.

15. Richard Price, *Observations on the Importance of the American Revolution* (1785), pp. 64–65.

16. M. Maty, "Memoirs of Lord Chesterfield," *Miscellaneous Works of Lord Chesterfield* (1777), I, 197–98.

17. Thomas Hardy, *The Patriot* (1793), pp. 17–18.

18. W. E. Lecky, *A History of England in the Eighteenth Century,* VI, 226.

II. COMPLACENCY

1. Jonathan Swift, *The Prose Works,* ed. Temple Scott (1898), VIII, 109.

2. William Warburton, "Sermons on the Rebellion," *Works* (1788), V, 214, 257–58.

3. William Vyse, *Fast Day Sermon . . .* (1778), p. 6.

4. *A Form of Prayer . . . Friday the 13th of December, 1776 . . .* , p. 8.

5. John Shebbeare, *One More Letter to the People of England* (1762), p. 4.

6. James Gough, *Brittania: a Poem* (1767), p. 20.

7. Joseph Priestley, *An Essay on the First Principles of Government* (1768), pp. 134–35.

8. John Campbell, *A Political Survey of Britain . . .* (1774), II, 2.

9. Horace Walpole, "Correspondence with the Rev. William Cole," *Yale Edition of Horace Walpole's Correspondence,* II, 89.

10. W. E. Lecky, *A History of England in the Eighteenth Century,* I, 80.

11. Benjamin Hoadly, "Defense of the Sermon before the Lord-Mayor," *Works* (1773), II, 100.

12. W. E. Lecky, *A History of England in the Eighteenth Century,* I, 71.

13. Henry Sacheverell, *False Notions of Liberty in Religion and Government* (1713).

14. J. L. De Lolme, *The Constitution of England* (1789), p. 342.

15. George Lord Lyttleton, "Dialogues of the Dead," *Works* (1776), II, 246.

16. Lord Hugh Cecil, *Conservatism* (7th printing, 1933), p. 25.

17. A. V. Dicey, *Law and Public Opinion in England . . .* (1914), pp. 82–83.

18. Tobias Smollett, *Roderick Random* (1911), pp. 300–301.

19. G. H. Guttridge, *English Whiggism and the American Revolution* (Berkeley, Calif., 1942), p. 33.

20. Edmund Burke, "Appeal from the New to the Old Whigs," *Works* (Boston, 1866), IV, 121.

21. John N. Figgis, *The Divine Right of Kings* (2d ed., Cambridge, England, 1922), pp. 263–64.

22. Edward Sayer, *Observations on Doctor Price's Revolution Sermon* (1790), pp. 17–18.

23. G. M. Trevelyan, "The Age of Johnson," *Johnson's England,* ed. A. S. Turberville (1933), I, 8–9.

24. Basil Williams, *The Whig Supremacy: 1714–1760* (1939), p. 1; cf. Nathaniel Buckington, Esq., Barrister at Law, *Serious Considerations on the Political Conduct of Lord North . . .* (1783), pp. 3–4; Leslie Stephen, *History of English Thought in the Eighteenth Century* (1876), II, 175–76; A. V. Dicey, *Law and Public Opinion in England . . .* , p. 77.

25. J. B. Bury, *The Idea of Progress* (1928), pp. 217–18.

26. William Blackstone, *Commentaries* . . . , II, 212.

27. G. H. Guttridge, *English Whiggism and the American Revolution,* p. 12.

28. M. Maty, *Miscellaneous Works of Lord Chesterfield,* I, 55, 111.

29. *Political Essays Concerning the Present State of the British Empire* . . . (1772), pp. 21–22.

30. Benjamin Hoadly, "The Happiness of the Present Establishment," *Works,* II, 113–14.

31. *Letters from Mrs. Elizabeth Carter to Mrs. Montagu,* between the years 1755 and 1800 (1817), I, 97n.

32. Adam Smith, *The Theory of Moral Sentiments,* 2d ed. (1761), pp. 89–90.

33. *Droit le Roy; or, A Digest of the Rights and Prerogatives of the Imperial Crown* (n.d.), p. 88.

34. N. W. Wraxall, *A Short Review of the Political State of Great Britain,* 6th ed. (1787), pp. 8–11.

35. James A. Farrer, *The Monarchy in Politics* (1917), pp. 30–33.

36. William Hawkins, *A Treatise of the Pleas of the Crown* . . . (1771), p. 60.

37. *Royal Perseverance: a Poem* (1778), pp. 5, 27.

38. *A Series of Letters between Mrs. Elizabeth Carter and Miss Catherine Talbot,* 3d ed. (1819), II, 194.

39. John Shebbeare, *One More Letter to the People of England* (1762), p. 35.

40. C. W. Everett, "Introduction," *Letters of Junius* (1927), p. xxvi.

41. Henry St. John, Viscount Bolingbroke, *On the Idea of a Patriot King* . . . (1749), pp. 224–25.

42. "The British Muse," *Universal Magazine,* XXX (1762), 39–40.

43. John Campbell, "Preface," *A Political Survey of Britain,* I, ii–iii.

44. *Political Essays Concerning the Present State of the British Empire* . . . (1772), p. 7.

45. John Brown, *An Estimate of the Manners and Principles of the Times* (1757), I, 69–70.

46. *Political Essays Concerning the Present State of the British Empire* . . . , p. 5.

47. William Shenstone, "Elegy XIV," *The Works in Verse and Prose of William Shenstone* (1764), I, 50.

48. John Campbell, *A Political Survey of Britain,* II, 143.

49. John Moir, *Obedience the Best Charter* . . . (1776), pp. 34–35.

50. David Hume, *Essays Moral, Political, and Literary,* ed. T. H. Green and T. H. Grose (1875), I, 475–76.

51. Sir James Marriott, *Political Considerations* . . . (1762), p. 24.

52. *Opposition Politics, Exemplified* (1786), p. 4.

53. John Moir, *Obedience the Best Charter* . . . , p. 31.

54. Benjamin Hoadly, "The Happiness of the Present Establishment," *Works,* II, 111.

55. George Heathcote, *A Letter to the* . . . *Lord Mayor* . . . , 2d ed. (1762), p. 77; cf. *Memoirs of Henry Masers De Latude,* "during a Confinement of Thirty-five Years in the State Prisons of France" (1787), pp. 19–20.

56. Leslie Stephen, *History of English Thought in the Eighteenth Century,* I, 361.

57. Percival Barlow, *The General History of Europe; and Entertaining Traveller* (1738–90), I, 7.

58. George Pitt Rivers, *Letters to a Young Nobleman* (1784), p. 232.

59. *An Apology for the Times: a Poem* (1778), pp. 49–50.

60. J. L. De Lolme, *The Constitution of England,* p. 540.

61. Gilbert Stuart, "Laws and Government of England," in Francis Sullivan, *Lectures on the Constitution and Laws of England* (1776), p. xxxii.

62. John Moir, *History of the Political Life and Publick Services* . . . *of Charles James Fox* (1783), pp. 132–33; cf. Adam Ferguson, *Remarks on a Pamphlet Lately Published by Dr. Price* (1776), p. 13; Edward Sayer, *Observations on Doctor Price's Revolution Sermon,* pp. 8–9.

63. Bernard Mandeville, *Free Thoughts on Religion, the Church, and National Happiness* (1720), p. 364.

64. George Heathcote, *A Letter to the* . . . *Lord Mayor* . . . , pp. 77–78.

65. John Campbell, *A Political Survey of Britain,* II, 281.

66. *Liberty,* Part IV, ll. 782–90.

67. George Pitt Rivers, *Letters to a Young Nobleman,* p. 74.

68. William Blackstone, *Commentaries* . . . , II, 217.

69. See especially the *Spirit of Laws,* Bk. XI, Chap. 6; Bk. XIX, Chap. 27; *Grandeur and Declension of the Roman Empire,* Chap. 8; *The Persian Letters,* Nos. 104, 136.

70. Stanley Pargellis, "The Theory of Balanced Government," *The Constitution Reconsidered* (New York, 1938), p. 46.

71. J. J. Burlamaqui, *The Principles of Politic Law* (1784), II, 95.

72. F. T. H. Fletcher, *Montesquieu and English Politics, 1751–1800* (1939).

73. *Liberty,* Part IV, ll. 815–17.

74. "Thoughts on the Constitution of England," *Universal Magazine,* L (1772), 113.

75. Edmund Burke, "Appeal from the New to the Old Whigs," *Works,* IV, 207–8.

76. *A View of the Internal Policy of Great Britain* (1764), p. 243.

77. Leslie Stephen, *History of English Thought in the Eighteenth Century,* II, 212.

78. Sir William Holdsworth, *History of English Law* (1938), X, 519.

79. John Brown, *An Estimate of the Manners and Principles of the Times,* II, 24–26.

80. John Campbell, *A Political Survey of England,* II, 285, 286n.

81. Oliver Mac Allester, *A Series of Letters* . . . (1767), I, 182.

82. *An Essay On Patriotism* (1769), p. 70.

83. James Gough, *Britannia: a Poem* (1767), p. 28.

84. William Blackstone, *Commentaries* . . . , I, 9–10; cf. *ibid.,* IV, 59, 98; V, 442.

85. Sir James Marriott, *Political Considerations* . . . , p. 74.

86. "Common Sense," *Miscellaneous Works of Lord Chesterfield,* I, 29–30.

87. *Thraliana* . . . , ed. Katherine Balderston (1942), I, 417.

88. G. M. Trevelyan, "The Age of Johnson," *Johnson's England,* I, 6.

89. *A Series of Letters between Mrs. Elizabeth Carter and Miss Catherine Talbot,* II, 210.

III. METAPHYSICAL OPTIMISM

1. Francis Hutcheson, *An Essay on the Nature and Conduct of the Passions and Affections,* 3d ed. (1742), pp. 186–87.

2. David Hartley, *Observations on Man* . . . (1749), II, 15.

3. Adam Smith, *The Theory of Moral Sentiments,* 2d ed. (1761), pp. 215–16.

4. Arthur O. Lovejoy, *The Great Chain of Being* (Cambridge, Mass., 1936), p. 208.

5. John Clarke, "An Enquiry into the Cause and Origin of Evil," *Sermons Preached at the Lecture Founded by the Honorable Robert Boyle* (1739), p. 195.

6. Joseph Butler, "The Analogy of Religion . . . to the Constitution and Course of Nature," *Works,* I (1896), 167; cf. *ibid.,* pp. 14–15, 164–65.

7. Earl of Shaftesbury, "The Moralists," *Characteristicks,* 5th ed. (1773), II, 363–64.

8. William King, *Essay on the Origin of Evil,* translated from the Latin by Edmund Law (1781), pp. 144–45.

9. Henry Home, Lord Kames, *Sketches of the History of Man* (1788), IV, 120–21.

10. William Warburton, "Sermons at Lincoln's Inn," *Works* (1788), V, 36.

11. Alexander Pope, *Essay on Man,* I, ll. 35–38.

12. *Ibid.,* l. 52.

13. *Ibid.,* IV, ll. 113–14; see also William Warburton, "A . . . Commentary on Mr. Pope's Essay on Man," *Works* (1788), VI, 17–168, in which Warburton praises the *Essay* from beginning to end and accepts its metaphysical optimism with all its implications. Later in the century, William Bowyer in *Miscellaneous Tracts* (1785) includes the famous passages from the *Essay* touching metaphysical optimism and related subjects in a prose rendering of a "Specimen of Pope's Essay on Man," pp. 504–9. See also "Didactic Pieces" in William Enfield, *The Speaker* (1786), p. 92, for quotations from Pope's optimism.

14. Arthur O. Lovejoy, *The Great Chain of Being,* p. 245.

15. Edmund Law, "Translator's Preface," in William King, *Essay on the Origin of Evil,* p. vii.

16. Joseph Butler, "The Analogy . . . ," *Works,* I, 171–72.

17. Henry Home, Lord Kames, *Sketches of the History of Man,* II, 217–22.

18. Soame Jenyns, "Nature and Origin of Evil," *Works* (1790), III, 37–38.

19. Bernard Mandeville, *The Fable of the Bees* . . . , ed. F. B. Kaye (1924), I, 7–8.

20. *Ibid.,* p. 261, "Essay on Charity and Charity-Schools."

21. *Ibid.,* p. 366, "A Search into the Nature of Society."

22. Soame Jenyns, "Nature and Origin of Evil," *Works,* III, 67–69.

23. Joseph Butler, "The Analogy . . . ," *Works,* I, 168.

24. *Ibid.,* p. 175.

25. Francis Hutcheson, *An Inquiry into the Original of Our Ideas of Beauty and Virtue* . . . , 2d ed. (1726), p. 303.

26. Samuel Johnson, *Works* (New York, 1903), I, 206–8.

27. See for example *View of the Internal Policy of Great Britain* (1764), p. 185; W. Belsham, "Remarks on Pope's Essay on Man," *Essays* (1799), I, 361.

28. Thomas Busby, *The Age of Genius: a Satire on the Times* (1786), pp. 11–12.

29. Alexander Pope, *Essay on Man,* III, ll. 317–18.

30. Daniel J. Boorstin, *The Mysterious Science of the Law* (Cambridge, Mass., 1941), pp. 63–83.

31. Joseph Priestley, "Dedication to John Jebb," and *passim,* in *The Doctrine of Philosophical Necessity Illustrated; Being an Appendix to the Disquisitions Relating to Matter and Spirit* (1777); *Letters to a Philosophic Unbeliever* (1780), Part I, pp. 72–78, 87–88; see also Richard Price, *Sermons on the Security and Happiness of a Virtuous Course* . . . (Philadelphia, 1788), pp. 52–54; Lord Monboddo, *Antient Metaphysics,* (1779–99), V, 116–44.

32. Henry Home, Lord Kames, *Sketches of the History of Man,* IV, 439.

33. Thomas Burnett, "The Demonstration of True Religion," *A Collection of the Sermons Preached at the Lecture Founded by the Honourable Robert Boyle,* (1739), III, 432.

34. John Witherspoon, *The Dominion of Providence* . . . , (Philadelphia; reprinted in London, 1778), p. 10.

35. Jonathan Richardson, *Richardsoniana: or, Occasional Reflections of the Moral Nature of Man* . . . (1776), pp. 205–8.

36. Henry Fielding, "Joseph Andrews," *Works* (New York, Bigelow, Brown, n.d.), II, 149.

37. Ralph Erskine, "The Militant's Song," *Sermons and Other Practical Works* (1777), II, 104–8.

38. Ralph Erskine, "Dark Providence Cleared in Due Time," *ibid.,* VI, 315.

39. William King, *Essay on the Origin of Evil,* p. 217.

40. Alexander Pope, *Essay on Man,* IV, l. 58.

41. Shaftesbury, "Inquiry Concerning Virtue . . . ," *Characteristicks,* 5th ed. (1773), II, 74.

42. For the view that metaphysical optimism is not to be interpreted so literally as to forbid change and reforms, see C. A. Moore, "Shaftesbury and Ethical Poets in England," *PMLA,* XXXI (1916), 320.

IV. REALISM

1. Edward Young, *The Complaint: or, Night Thoughts on Life, Death, and Immortality* (1742), p. 6.

2. Soame Jenyns, "Nature and Origin of Evil," *Works* (1790), III, 45–46.

3. Edmund Law, "Notes to William King's *Essay on the Origin of Evil*" (1781), p. 95.

4. Alexander Pope, *Essay on Man,* I, ll. 245–50.

5. Arthur O. Lovejoy, *The Great Chain of Being* (Cambridge, Mass., 1936), p. 244.

6. John Clarke, "An Enquiry into the Cause and Origin of Evil" (1719), *Sermons Preached at the Lecture Founded by the Honourable Robert Boyle* (1739), p. 170.

7. Soame Jenyns, "The Nature and Origin of Evil," *Works*, III, 53–54.

8. William King, *Essay on the Origin of Evil*, (1781), p. 125.

9. William Blackstone, *Commentaries* . . . , II, 157; V, 105.

10. Josiah Tucker, *A Selection from His Economic and Political Writings* (New York, 1931), pp. 477–78.

11. *Liberty*, Part IV, ll. 687–88.

12. See for example, the presence of similar ideas in Shakespeare: James E. Phillips, *The State in Shakespeare's Greek and Roman Plays* (New York, 1940).

13. *The Candid Philosopher: or, Free Thoughts on Men, Morals, and Manners* (1778), I, 244–45.

14. Alexander Pope, *Essay on Man*, I, ll. 259–67; John Clarke, "An Enquiry into the Cause and Origin of Evil," pp. 210, 241.

15. *Address to the City of London* (1762), p. 6.

16. Cf. Samuel Morton Savage, *Good Men Dismissed in Peace* (1762), pp. 8–9.

17. David Hume, *Essays Moral, Political, and Literary*, ed. T. H. Green and T. H. Grose (1875), 376–77.

18. For the changing implications of the idea of the chain of being later in the eighteenth century see Lois Whitney, *Primitivism and the Idea of Progress* (Baltimore, 1934), pp. 145–56; the chain of being shades into the idea of progress and becomes part of the new evolutionary theory.

19. Soame Jenyns, "Nature and Origin of Evil," *Works* (1790), III, 74.

20. *An Excellent Collection of Pious and Devout Meditations . . . by a Young Gentleman* (1782), pp. 33–34, 70–71.

21. Thomas Boston, *Human Nature in Its Fourfold State* . . . (New York: 1811), pp. 43–44; special reliance has been placed on this book as expressing common 18th century views, in that a new edition is said to have appeared every two years since the first was printed in 1720. See "Recommendation by Mr. Michael Boston, the Author's Grandson" in the edition from Falkirk, 1788, p. iii.

22. Jonathan Swift, "On the Poor Man's Contentment," *The Prose Works of Jonathan Swift*, IV, 202.

23. Thomas Boston, *op. cit.*, p. 109.

24. *Ibid.*, p. 104.

25. *Private Devotions for Several Occasions* . . . (1771), p. 388.

26. Thomas Haweis, *Evangelical Principles and Practice* (1762), p. 94.

27. James Hervey, "Theron and Aspasio," *Works* (1790), III, 229. For similar expressions concerning the baseness and corruption of man see Joseph Butler, "The Analogy . . . ," *Works* (1896), I, 102; John Witherspoon, *The Dominion of Providence over the Passions of Men*, (Philadelphia; reprinted in London, 1778), p. 10; Cornelius Murdin, *Three Sermons* . . . (1779), pp. 21–22.

28. Carl Becker, *The Heavenly City of the Eighteenth Century Philosophers* (New Haven, Conn., 1932), pp. 64–65.

29. Jonathan Swift, "Gulliver's Travels," *Prose Works*, VIII, 136; cf. Ricardo Quintana, *The Mind and Art of Jonathan Swift* (New York, 1936), pp. 69–72.

30. Louis I. Bredvold, *The Intellectual Milieu of John Dryden* (Ann Arbor, Mich., 1934), pp. 130–31.

31. Richard Hey, *Observations on the Nature of Civil Liberty* . . . (1776), p. 57.

32. Ambrose Serle, *Americans against Liberty* . . . (1775), p. 10; John Moir, *Obedience the Best Charter* . . . (1776), p. 38.

33. Samuel Johnson, *Works* (New York, 1903), IV, 25.

34. William Combe, *The Devil upon Two Sticks in England,* 2d ed. (1790), I, 134.

35. David Hume, *A Treatise on Human Nature,* ed. T. H. Green and T. H. Grose (1874), II, 300–303.

36. James Burgh, *Political Disquisitions:* . . . (1774), I, 1–2.

37. Samuel Johnson, *Works*, IV, 43.

38. Josiah Tucker, *A Selection* . . . (New York, 1931), p. 58.

39. Soame Jenyns, "Reflections on Several Subjects," *Works* (1790), I, 224–25.

40. Adam Ferguson, *An Essay on the History of Civil Society*, New ed. (Basil, 1789), pp. 400–401.

41. Hugh Blair, "On Our Ignorance of Good and Evil in This Life," *Sermons* (London; reprinted, Baltimore, 1792), I, 127.

42. *A Letter on the Behavior of the Populace on a Late Occasion* . . . , 2d ed. (1768), p. 23.

43. *The Rights of Citizens* . . . (1791), pp. 111–15.

44. John Moir, *Obedience the Best Charter* . . . (1776), p. 13.

45. Jonathan Swift, "Of Public Absurdities in England," *Prose Works*, XI, 179.

46. Soame Jenyns, "Thoughts on a Parliamentary Reform," *Works*, II, 244–47.

47. Horace Walpole, *Memoirs of the Reign of King George the Third* (1894), III, 255.

48. Soame Jenyns, "The Nature and Origin of Evil," *Works,* III, 119–21.

49. David Hume, *Essays* . . . , I, 117–19.

50. J. L. De Lolme, *The Constitution of England* (1789), p. 537.

51. Arthur Young, *An Enquiry into the State of the Public Mind amongst the Lower Classes* . . . (1798), p. 5; Sir Frederic Morton Eden, "Preface," *The State of the Poor* . . . , (1797), I, xxx.

52. *A Letter to a Layman, on the Subject of the Rev. Mr. Lindsey's Proposal for a Reformed English Church* . . . (1774), pp. 10–11.

53. William Newcome, *A Comparison between the Doctrines of Christianity and Those of Popery with Regard to Civil Government* (1767), p. 3.

54. Soame Jenyns, "The Nature and Origin of Evil," *Works,* III, 58–59.

55. Arthur O. Lovejoy, *The Great Chain of Being,* p. 205.

56. *Ibid.,* 203–4.

57. Nathaniel Buckington, Esq., *Serious Consideration on the Political Conduct of Lord North* . . . (1783), p. 47; Bishop of Bristol, *Sermon . . . in the Abbey Church, Westminster, on Thursday, January 30, 1783* (1783), pp. 18–19.

58. Soame Jenyns, "The Nature and Origin of Evil," *Works,* III, 16–17.

59. *Ibid.,* pp. 121–23.

60. George Pitt Rivers, *Letters to a Young Nobleman* (1784), pp. 50–51.

61. Bernard Mandeville, *Free Thoughts on Religion, the Church, and National Happiness* (1720), pp. 296–97.

62. Alexander Pope, *Essay on Man,* II, l. 18.

63. *An Excellent Collection of Pious and Devout Meditations* . . . , pp. 35–36.

64. *Ibid.,* pp. 69–71.

65. Thomas Boston, *Human Nature in Its Fourfold State,* pp. 44–45.

66. *The New Whole Duty of Man,* 22d ed. (1773), pp. 402–3.

67. Thomas Haweis, *Evangelical Principles and Practice,* p. 36.

68. William Holland, *Death to the Christian an Object of Desire* (1792), pp. 11–12.

69. Ralph Erskine, "Vanity of Earthly Things," *Sermons and Other Practical Works* (1777), I, 295–304.

70. Hugh Blair, "On our Ignorance of Good and Evil . . . ," *Sermons,* I, 124–25.

71. *Ibid.,* pp. 125–26.

72. Thomas Boston, *Human Nature in Its Fourfold State,* pp. 51–52.

73. Ralph Erskine, "Vanity of Earthly Things," *Sermons,* I, 311.

74. Michael Smith, *Twelve Sermons . . .* (1770), p. 212.

75. Joseph Butler, "The Analogy," *Works,* I, 106, 130–31.

76. Charles Churchill, *Works* (1774), IV, 147–48.

77. Samuel Morton Savage, *Good Men Dismissed in Peace* (1762), pp. 13–14.

78. Abbé Raynal, *Philosophical and Political History of the . . . Indies* (1798), III, 1. Although Raynal is a clergyman technically, it is not his cloth that inspires his sad view of life.

79. Horace Walpole, *Journal of the Reign of King George the Third . . . 1771–1783* (1859), I, 472.

80. Samuel Johnson, *Works,* VII, 43.

81. *Ibid.,* IV, 225.

82. *Ibid.,* p. 227.

83. *Ibid.,* pp. 184–85.

84. *Ibid.,* V, 21.

85. Edward Young, *The Complaint . . .* (1742), p. 12.

86. *Ibid.,* p. 14.

87. Mary Wollstonecraft, *Thoughts on the Education of Daughters . . .* (1787), p. 135.

88. "Misfortune," *The Hive; or, A Collection of Thoughts . . .* (1791), p. 143.

89. Robert Dodsley, *The Oeconomy of Human Life . . .* (1772), pp. 123–26.

90. Edward Harwood, *The Great Duty and Delight of Contentment* (1782), pp. 30–35.

91. *Memoirs of the Marchioness of Pompadour* (1766), II, 36.

92. David Hume, *Essays,* I, 229, and note 30.

93. David Hartley, *Observations on Man . . .* (1749), II, 361.

94. J. J. Burlamaqui, *The Principles of Politic Law,* 3d ed. (1784), I, 276–79.

95. Jonathan Swift, "Gulliver's Travels," *Prose Works,* VIII, 135.

96. William King, *Essay on the Origin of Evil,* p. 273.

97. Samuel Johnson, *Works,* II, 75; VII, 147.

98. Thomas Warton, *The Progress of Discontent* (1746), p. 134.

99. Edward Young, *The Complaint . . . ,* pp. 18–19.

100. Samuel Johnson, *Works,* IV, 142.

101. Robert Dodsley, *The Oeconomy of Human Life,* p. 103.

102. William Shenstone, "Essays on Men, Manners, and Things," *Works* (1769), II, 256.

103. Lord Monboddo, *Antient Metaphysics,* III, Book II, 281.

104. Samuel Johnson, *Works*, III, 96–97.

105. Jonathan Swift, "On the Poor Man's Contentment," *Prose Works*, IV, 208.

106. Robert Dodsley, *The Oeconomy of Human Life*, pp. 31–32.

107. Francis Blackburne, *The Confessional*, 2d ed. (1767), pp. 336–38.

108. Soame Jenyns, "The Nature and Origin of Evil," *Works*, III, 165–66, 169; "Disquisitions on Religious Establishments," *ibid.*, pp. 286–87.

109. Philip Doddridge, *The Rise and Progress of Religion in the Soul* . . . (1804), pp. 271–72 (first written in 1744).

110. David Hartley, *Observations on Man* . . . , II, 22.

111. William Melmoth, *Letters of Sir Thomas Fitzosborne* . . . , 4th ed. (1762), pp. 237–38.

112. Samuel Johnson, *Works*, I, 208; II, 91.

113. "Universal Discontent," *Universal Magazine*, XXXIX (1766), 263.

114. Joseph Butler, "The Analogy," *Works*, I, 170.

115. Benjamin Hoadly, "A Persuasive to Lay Conformity," *Works* (1773), I, 319.

116. Samuel Johnson, *Works*, XIV, 128.

117. Adam Smith, *The Wealth of Nations* (1899), I, 497.

118. *Commentaries* . . . , IV, 327.

119. Bernard Mandeville, *Free Thoughts on Religion* . . . , p. 355.

120. Henry St. John, Viscount Bolingbroke, *Letters, on the Spirit of Patriotism: on the Idea of a Patriot King* . . . (1749), pp. 90–91.

121. Josiah Tucker, *A Selection* . . . , p. 535.

122. William Connor Sydney, *England and the English in the Eighteenth Century*, 2d ed. (1892), I, 18.

123. Edmund Burke, "Thoughts on the Cause of the Present Discontents," *Works* (Boston, 1886), I, 520.

124. James A. Farrer, *The Monarchy in Politics* (1917), p. 23.

125. Edward Young, *The Complaint* . . . , p. 10.

126. Samuel Johnson, *Works*, I, 38.

127. Bernard Mandeville, *The Fable of the Bees* . . . , I, 36.

128. Tobias Smollett, "Humphrey Clinker," *Works* (New York, 1901), XI, 262.

129. William Knox, *Considerations on the Present State of the Nation* (1789), pp. v–vi.

130. See for example, his suggestions for change in England based on the lessons of Gulliver, "Gulliver's Travels," *Prose Works*, VIII, 6–7.

131. L. B. Namier, *England in the Age of the American Revolution* (1930), p. 212.

132. George Pitt Rivers, *Letters to a Young Nobleman*, p. 38.

133. *Speculation; or, A Defence of Mankind: a Poem* (1780), pp. 5–6; Thomas Busby, *The Age of Genius! a Satire on the Times* (1786), p. 34.

134. M. Maty, "Memoirs of Lord Chesterfield," *Miscellaneous Works of Lord Chesterfield* (1777), I, 184.

135. David Hume, *Essays . . .* , I, 460; Ricardo Quintana, *The Mind and Art of Jonathan Swift* (1936), p. 55.

136. Jonathan Swift, "Gulliver's Travels," *Prose Works*, VIII, 140.

137. John Moir, *Obedience the Best Charter . . .* , p. 21.

138. David Hume, *Essays . . .* , II, 174, 187; cf. Soame Jenyns, "The Nature and Origin of Evil," *Works*, III, 129, and note 30.

139. Quoted in John Brown, *An Estimate of the Manners and Principles of the Times* (1758), II, 27; John Almon, *Review of Mr. Pitt's Administration* (1762), pp. 21–22.

140. David Hume, *Essays . . .* , I, 156, and 480, note 81.

141. John Moir, *Obedience the Best Charter . . .* , p. 16.

142. William Miles, *Cursory Reflections on Public Men and Public Measures on the Continent*, 2d ed. (1790), pp. 4–7, 15.

143. W. D., *Second Answer to Mr. John Wesley* (n.d.), p. 17.

144. Richard Hey, *Observations on the Nature of Civil Liberty . . .* (1776), p. 49.

145. Adam Ferguson, *An Essay on the History of Civil Society*, pp. 186–87.

146. William Paley, *The Principles of Moral and Political Philosophy* (1785), p. 467.

147. W. E. Lecky, *A History of England in the Eighteenth Century*, III, 209–11.

148. "Common Sense," *Miscellaneous Works of Lord Chesterfield*, I, 24–25.

149. Harold J. Laski, *Political Thought in England from Locke to Bentham* (New York, 1920), pp. 273–74.

150. L. B. Namier, *England in the Age of the American Revolution*, p. 15.

151. Edmund Burke, "Speech on Conciliation . . . ," *Works*, II, 168–69.

152. William Paley, *The Principles of Moral and Political Philosophy*, pp. 465–66.

153. *A Dialogue on the Actual State of Parliament* (1783), pp. 34–35.

154. W. E. Lecky, *History of the Rise and Influence of the Spirit of Rationalism in Europe,* 2d ed. (1865), II, 144–45.

155. Joseph Priestley, *An Essay on the First Principles of Government* (1768), pp. 60–61.

156. Josiah Tucker, *A Selection . . .* , p. 484.

157. Richard Tickell, *Commonplace Arguments Against Administra-tion . . .* (1780), pp. 100–101.

158. David Hume, *Essays,* II, 378.

159. James Burgh, "General Preface," *Political Disquisitions,* I, xi.

160. *A Serious Address to the Vulgar* (1762), pp. 17–18.

161. W. E. Lecky, *A History of England in the Eighteenth Century,* I, 472–73.

162. Leslie Stephen, *History of English Thought in the Eighteenth Century* (1876), II, 203.

163. Quoted in Michael Mac Donagh, *The English King* (1929), p. 52.

164. F. S. Oliver, *The Endless Adventure* (Boston, 1931), I, 275–76.

165. Harold J. Laski, *Political Thought in England from Locke to Bentham,* pp. 262–63.

166. Richard Hurd, *Fast Day Sermon before the House of Lords,* Dec. 13, 1776 (1777), pp. 7–8.

167. *Royal Perseverance* (1778), p. 17.

168. Myles Cooper, *Fast Day Sermon,* Dec. 13, 1776, quoted by Earl of Abingdon, *Thoughts on the Letter of Edmund Burke . . . to the Sheriffs of Bristol . . .* (1777), p. 35n, 36.

169. Francis Blackburne, *The Confessional,* p. 349.

170. S. Foote, Jr., "Introduction," *Reform: a Farce, Modernized from Aristophanes* (1792), p. viii. For similar condemnation of the danger of theories and ideas and metaphysical schemes see Adam Ferguson, *Remarks on a Pamphlet Lately Published by Dr. Price. . . .* (1776), p. 14; Allan Ramsay, *Thoughts on the Origin and Nature of Government* (1769), pp. 9–10; *The History of the Reign of George the Third . . .* (1770), p. 336.

171. Daniel J. Boorstin, *The Mysterious Science of the Law* (Cambridge, Mass., 1941), p. 31.

172. F. T. H. Fletcher, *Montesquieu and English Politics . . .* (1939), pp. 75–78.

173. Leslie Stephen, *History of English Thought in the Eighteenth Century,* II, 445; cf. Leslie Stephen, *English Literature and Society in the Eighteenth Century* (1904), p. 183; Harold J. Laski, *Political Thought in England from Locke to Bentham,* pp. 162–63.

174. Ernest Campbell Mossner, *Bishop Butler and the Age of Reason* (New York, 1936), p. 147.

V. FEAR OF CHANGE

1. *The Question on Some Late Discussions Truly Stated* . . . (1764), pp. 54–55.

2. Henry Fielding, "The Covent-Garden Journal," *Works*, ed. Leslie Stephen (1882), VI, 132–33.

3. William Hawkins, *A Treatise of the Pleas of the Crown* . . . (1771), pp. 155–67.

4. William Connor Sydney, "King Mob," *England and the English in the Eighteenth Century* 2d ed., (1892), II, 192–216.

5. John White, *Free and Impartial Considerations* . . . (1751), p. 51, quoted in Francis Blackburne, *The Confessional*, pp. 320–21.

6. Francis Atterbury, *The Voice of the People, No Voice of God* . . . (1710), pp. 8–9.

7. *A Vindication of the Whigs against the Clamours of a Tory Mob* . . . (1765), p. 3.

8. *A View of the Internal Policy of Great Britain* (1764), p. 169.

9. *Thraliana* . . . , ed. Katherine Balderston (1942), I, 123.

10. J. J. Burlamaqui, 3d ed. (1784), *The Principles of Politic Law*, II, 130.

11. John Moir, *Obedience the Best Charter* . . . (1776), p. 58; *A Letter on the Behaviour of the Populace* . . . , 2d ed. (1768), p. 7; Henry Goodricke, *Observations on Dr. Price's Theory* (1776), pp. 107–8; *A Review of the Present Administration* (1774), p. 43; Adam Ferguson, *An Essay on the History of Civil Society*, new ed. (Basil, 1789), p. 282; George Campbell, D.D., *The Nature, Extent, and Importance of the Duty of Allegiance* . . . , 2d ed. (1778), p. 43; J. J. Burlamaqui, *The Principles of Politic Law*, II, 91; Josiah Tucker, *A Selection* . . . (New York, 1931), p. 515; *The Appeal of Reason to the People of England* (1763), pp. 32–33; *A Vindication of the Whigs* . . . (1765), pp. 3–4.

12. Francis Atterbury, *The Voice of the People* . . . , p. 6.

13. Sir William Temple, *Works* (1770), I, 32.

14. *A View of the Internal Policy of Great Britain*, pp. 225–26.

15. William Paley, *The Principles of Moral and Political Philosophy* (1785), p. 482.

16. Josiah Tucker, *A Selection* . . . , p. 550.

17. John Perceval, *Faction Detected by the Evidence of Facts*, 2d ed. (1743), p. 62.

18. *Ibid.*, pp. 135, 76.

19. *Commentaries . . .* , (Philadelphia, 1803), III, 411.

20. Wellman J. Warner, *The Wesleyan Movement in the Industrial Revolution* (1930), pp. 6–7.

21. Soame Jenyns, "Thoughts on a Parliamentary Reform," *Works* (1790), II, 238.

22. Thomas Gisborne, *An Enquiry into the Duties of Men in the Higher and Middle Classes of Society . . .* (1794), pp. 21–22.

23. John Shebbeare, *An Essay on the Origin, Progress and Establishment of National Society . . .* (1776), p. 34.

24. John Brown, *Thoughts on Civil Liberty, on Licentiousness, and Faction*, 2d ed. (1765), p. 119.

25. *A Letter to His Grace the Duke of Grafton . . .* (1768), pp. 5–6.

26. John Lind, *Three Letters to Dr. Price* (1776), p. 84; George Pitt Rivers, *Letters to a Young Nobleman* (1784), pp. 226–27.

27. Horace Walpole, *Memoirs of the Reign of King George the Third* (1894), III, 123.

28. Henry Home, Lord Kames, *Sketches of the History of Man* (1788), II, 230.

29. William Burke, *Letters of Valena* (1777), p. 59.

30. Adam Ferguson, *Remarks on a Pamphlet Lately Published by Dr. Price . . .* (1776), p. 5.

31. Josiah Tucker, *A Selection . . .* , p. 267.

32. David Hume, *Essays . . .* (1875), I, 126.

33. Allan Ramsay, *Thoughts on the Origin and Nature of Government* (1769), pp. 12–13, 15.

34. Bernard Mandeville, *Free Thoughts on Religion, the Church, and National Happiness* (1720), p. 144.

35. Daniel J. Boorstin, *The Mysterious Science of the Law* (Cambridge, Mass., 1941), pp. 168–69, 180.

36. Basil Williams, *The Whig Supremacy: 1714–1760* (1939), pp. 5–6.

37. David Hume, *A Treatise on Human Nature*, ed. T. H. Green and T. H. Grose (1874), II, 269.

38. Allan Ramsay, *Thoughts on the Origin and Nature of Government*, pp. 25–26.

39. John Perceval, *Faction Detected by the Evidence of Facts*, p. 109.

40. R. H. Tawney, *Religion and the Rise of Capitalism* (1929), pp. 188–89.

41. Wellman J. Warner, *The Wesleyan Movement in the Industrial Revolution*, pp. 7–8.

42. Leslie Stephen, *The English Utilitarians* (1900), I, 18.

43. Wellman J. Warner, *The Wesleyan Movement . . .* , pp. 8–9.

44. Dorothy Marshall, "The Failure of the Acts of Settlement," *The English Poor in the Eighteenth Century* (1926), pp. 225–45; Edgar S. Furniss, *The Position of the Laborer in a System of Nationalism* (Boston, 1920), pp. 145–46, 225.

45. *Ibid.*, p. 107.

46. Robert L. Schuyler, *The Fall of the Old Colonial System* (1945), pp. 8–9.

47. Joseph Townshend, *A Dissertation on the Poor Laws* (1786), p. 36.

48. Bernard Mandeville, "An Essay on Charity and Charity-Schools," *The Fable of the Bees . . .* , ed. F. P. Kaye (1924), I, 305–6.

49. Conyers Read, "Mercantilism . . . ," *The Constitution Reconsidered* (New York, 1908), pp. 71–72.

50. Edgar S. Furniss, *The Position of the Laborer in a System of Nationalism*, pp. 99–101.

51. Bernard Mandeville, *The Fable of the Bees . . .* , I, 192–94.

52. *Speculation: or, A Defence of Mankind: a Poem* (1780), pp. 48–49.

53. "The World," *Miscellaneous Works of Lord Chesterfield*, I, 214–15.

54. John Brown, *An Estimate of the Manners and Principles of the Times* (1757), I, 24–25.

55. Thomas Gisborne, *An Enquiry into the Duties of Man in the Higher and Middle Classes* (1794), p. 3.

56. Richard Watson, Bishop of Landaff, *Miscellaneous Tracts . . .* (1815), I, 466–70; *Elements of Morality for the Use of Children*, translated from the German of the Rev. C. G. Salzmann (1791), III, 93–95. See also the work of Hannah More and her sister, especially *Mendip Annals*, in which it is implied that the poor should be glad of the generosity and kindness of those above them in society.

57. *Elements of Morality for the Use of Children . . .* (1791), *passim*.

58. *The New Whole Duty of Man . . .* , 22d ed. (1773), p. 353.

59. *The Contrast: or The Opposite Consequences of Good and Evil Habits . . .* (1787), *passim*.

60. J. L. De Lolme, *The Constitution of England*, new ed. (1789), pp. 534–35.

61. *Commentaries . . .* , V, 162.

62. Jacob Jefferson, *The Blessings of Peace and the Means of Preserving It* (1763), p. 29.

63. Richard Steele, "On Ambition," *Selections from the Tatler, Spectator, and Guardian,* ed. Austin Dobson (1885), pp. 77–79.

64. Bernard Mandeville, *The Fable of the Bees . . . ,* I, 239.

65. Horace Walpole, *Memoirs of the Reign of King George the Third,* III, 24.

66. Conyers Read, "Mercantilism . . . ," *The Constitution Reconsidered,* p. 73.

67. W. E. Lecky, *A History of England in the Eighteenth Century,* VI, 276.

68. Soame Jenyns, "Reflections on Several Subjects," *Works,* II, 223.

69. Edgar S. Furniss, *The Position of the Laborer in a System of Nationalism,* pp. 148–49.

70. Bernard Mandeville, *The Fable of the Bees,* I, 185.

71. *Ibid.,* pp. 289–90.

72. Sir Charles Mallet, "Education . . . ," *Johnson's England* (1933), II, 212.

73. Bernard Mandeville, "Essay on Charity and Charity-Schools," *The Fable of the Bees,* I, 288.

74. Soame Jenyns, "The Nature and Origin of Evil," *Works,* III, 49–50.

75. Jonathan Swift, "Gulliver's Travels," *Prose Works,* VIII, 64.

76. William Warburton, "Charity Sermon . . . 1767," *Works* (1788), V, 512–15.

77. William Roberts, *Memoirs of . . . Mrs. Hannah More,* 2d ed. (4 vols., 1834), III, 133.

78. M. G. Jones, *The Charity School Movement: a Study of Eighteenth Century Puritanism in Action* (1938), pp. 4–5.

79. *Ibid.,* pp. 74–76.

80. *Ibid.,* pp. 76–84.

81. J. Wesley Bready, *England: before and after Wesley . . .* (1938), p. 167.

82. Thomas, Lord Bishop of Bristol, "The Gospel Preached to the Poor," *A Sermon . . .* (1765), p. 13.

83. *Ibid.,* p. 15.

84. Samuel Glasse, *Sermon . . . June 9, 1791 . . .* (1791), pp. 18–19.

85. Brownlow, Bishop of Winchester, *Sermon at Yearly Meeting of Children Educated in the Charity Schools . . .* (1790), pp. 15–16.

86. Adam Smith, *The Theory of Moral Sentiments,* 2d ed. (1761), p. 274.

87. Bernard Mandeville, "Essay on Charity and Charity-Schools," *The Fable of the Bees,* I, 316–17.

88. *Ibid.,* p. 308.

89. Francis Hutcheson, *An Essay on the Nature and Conduct of the Passions and Affections,* 3d ed. (1742), pp. 184–85.

90. Jonathan Swift, "On the Poor Man's Contentment," *Prose Works,* IV, 204–5.

91. Richard Watson, Bishop of Landaff, *Miscellaneous Tracts . . .* (1815), I, 460–61.

92. Jonathan Swift, "On the Poor Man's Contentment," *Prose Works,* IV, 205.

93. *Ibid.,* pp. 205–6.

94. *The New Whole Duty of Man . . . ,* pp. 240–41.

95. Jonathan Swift, "On the Poor Man's Contentment," *Prose Works,* IV, 208–9.

96. William Wilberforce, *A Practical View of the Prevailing Religious System of Professed Christians . . .* (Baltimore, 1833; first published, 1797), pp. 238–39.

97. J. Wesley Bready, *England: before and after Wesley . . . ,* p. 72.

98. Edward Young, *Resignation* (1762), p. 56.

99. David Hume, *Essays,* I, 135.

100. Henry Fielding, "Joseph Andrews," *Works* (New York, n.d.), I, 99.

101. Leslie Stephen, *History of English Thought in the Eighteenth Century,* II, 369–70.

102. John Pinkerton, *Letters of Literature* (1785), p. 373.

103. Leslie Stephen, *English Literature and Society in the Eighteenth Century* (1904), pp. 146–47.

104. W. E. Lecky, *A History of England in the Eighteenth Century,* II, 368, 524.

105. Basil Williams, *The Whig Supremacy: 1714–1760* (1939), pp. 79–80.

106. George Campbell, "The Nature, Extent, and Importance of the Duty of Allegiance," *Fast Day Sermon,* 2d ed. (1778), p. 12.

107. *The Book of Common Prayer . . .* (1791), p. 1.

108. W. E. Lecky, *A History of England in the Eighteenth Century,* I, 74–75.

109. Rev. Norman Sykes, "The Church," *Johnson's England* (1933), I, 15–38.

110. *An Apology for the Times: a Poem, Addressed to the King* (1778), pp. 37–38.

111. Jonathan Swift, "Sentiments of a Church of England Man," *Prose Works,* III, 54.

112. Edmund Burke, "Reflections . . . ," *Works,* III, 363.

113. *Considerations on the State of Subscription to the Articles and Liturgy of the Church of England* (1774), p. 43.

114. Benjamin Hoadly, "A Persuasive to Lay Conformity," *Works* (1773), I, 319.

115. Jonathan Swift, "Sentiments of a Church of England Man," *Prose Works,* III, 62.

116. Vicesimus Knox, *Essays Moral and Literary,* 12th ed. (1791), I, 76–77.

117. Adam Smith, *The Wealth of Nations* (1899), II, 331.

118. W. E. Lecky, *History of the Rise and Influence of the Spirit of Rationalism in Europe* (1865), II, 193.

119. G. H. Guttridge, *English Whiggism and the American Revolution* (Berkeley, Calif., 1942), p. 2.

120. George Berkeley, "Passive Obedience," *Works* (1901), IV, 103, 111, 114, 133–34.

121. *Ibid.,* p. 112.

122. David Hume, *Essays,* I, 142.

123. *The New Whole Duty of Man . . . ,* pp. 187–88.

124. Edmund Gibson, D.D., *Against Speaking Evil of Princes, and Those in Authority under Them: a Sermon . . .* (1705/6), p. 3.

125. *Private Devotions for Several Occasions . . .* (1771), p. 418.

126. "Litany . . . to be sung or said after Morning Prayer," *The Book of Common Prayer.*

127. William Hawkins, *A Treatise of the Pleas of the Crown . . . ,* (1771), p. 7.

128. *A Form of Prayer, to Be Used in All Churches . . . on Account of the Troubles in America* (no place or date).

129. Wellman J. Warner, *The Wesleyan Movement in the Industrial Revolution,* p. 34. See also Harold J. Laski, *Political Thought in England from Locke to Bentham,* pp. 121–22; W. E. Lecky, *A History of England in the Eighteenth Century,* II, 517; J. Wesley Bready, *England: before and after Wesley . . . ,* pp. 86, 95; Basil Williams, *The Whig Supremacy,* p. 73.

130. J. Wesley Bready, *England: before and after Wesley . . . ,* p. 25.

131. *A Brief Enquiry How Far Every Government Has a Right to Defend Itself . . .* (1736), pp. 19–20.

132. Jonathan Swift, "Of Public Absurdities in England," *Prose Works,* XI, 180.

133. "Proceedings of the Society" following Edmund Law's *Sermon . . . before the Incorporated Society for the Propagation of the Gospel . . .* (1774), p. 43.

134. Quoted in Norman Sykes, "The Church," *Johnson's England,* I, 17.

135. Leslie Stephen, *The English Utilitarians,* I, 39–43.

136. *Ibid.,* pp. 48–50.

137. R. H. Tawney, *Religion and the Rise of Capitalism,* pp. 190–91.

138. *Ibid.,* p. 193.

139. Ivor Brown, *English Political Theory* (1929), pp. 76–77.

140. Basil Williams, *The Whig Supremacy,* pp. 73–74.

141. Jonas Hanway, *Thoughts on the Importance of the Sabbath* . . . (1765), p. 30.

142. Jacob Jefferson, *The Blessings of Peace and the Means of Preserving It,* pp. 23–24.

143. Henry Sacheverell, *The Political Union, a Discourse Shewing the Dependance of Government on Religion* . . . (1710), pp. 10–11.

144. David Hartley, *Observations on Man* . . . (1749), II, 444; John Shebbeare, *An Essay on the Origin, Progress and Establishment of National Society* . . . (1776), p. 48.

145. *The Requisition of Subscription to the Thirty-nine Articles and Liturgy of the Church of England Not Inconsistent with Christian Liberty:* a Sermon (1771), p. 4.

146. *A View of the Internal Policy of Great Britain* (1764), p. 236.

147. Jonas Hanway, *Miscellanies* (1765), p. 18.

148. Quoted in George Nobbe, *The North Briton: a Study in Political Propaganda* (New York, 1939), p. 146.

149. *An Excellent Collection of Pieces and Devout Meditations* . . . *by a Young Gentleman* (1782), p. 333.

150. W. E. Lecky, *History of the Rise and Influence of the Spirit of Rationalism in Europe,* II, 152–53.

151. *The Whole Duty of Man* (1771), p. 35.

152. E. Harwood, *The Great Duty and Delight of Contentment,* (1782), pp. 6–8.

153. *Ibid.,* pp. 26–27.

154. *The Whole Duty of Man,* pp. 153–54.

155. Richard Price, *Sermons on the Security and Happiness of a Virtuous Course* . . . (Philadelphia, 1788), p. 71.

156. Bewick (John H. Wynne), *Tales for Youth;* in *Thirty Poems* . . . *Historical Remarks and Moral Applications in Prose* (1794), pp. 124–25.

157. *The Whole Duty of Man,* p. 36.

158. E. Harwood, *The Great Duty and Delight of Contentment,* pp. 24–25.

159. "Private Devotions," *The New Whole Duty of Man,* pp. 500–551.

160. *Ibid.,* pp. 466–67; cf. *The Great Importance of a Religious Life Considered,* 25th ed. (1780), p. 38.

161. John Liddon, *The General Religious Instruction of the Poor . . . a Sermon . . .* (1792), p. 14.

162. Edmund Burke, "Reflections . . . ," *Works,* III, 365–67.

163. George Lord Lyttleton, "Dialogues of the Dead," *Works* (1776), II, 163.

164. *The A.B.C. with the Church of England Catechism* (Philadelphia, 1785), p. 6.

165. Thomas, Lord Bishop of Bristol, "The Gospel Preached to the Poor," *A Sermon . . .* (1765), p. 10; Myles Cooper, "National Humiliation and Repentance Recommended . . . ," *A Sermon . . .* (1777), p. 23; J. Wesley Bready, *England: before and after Wesley . . . ,* pp. 95–96; C. A. Moore, "Shaftesbury and Ethical Poets in England," *PMLA,* XXXI (1916), 320–21.

VI. THE LESSON OF MODERATION

1. John Locke, "Of Enthusiasm," *Religious Thought in the Eighteenth Century,* ed. J. M. Creed and J. S. Boys Smith (1934), pp. 12–13.

2. *The Requisition of Subscription . . .* (1771), p. 8.

3. M. de Voltaire, *Letters Concerning the English Nation* (1926), p. 83.

4. Shaftesbury, "Letter Concerning Enthusiasm," *Characteristicks,* 5th ed. (1773), I, 43–45.

5. George Lord Lyttleton, "Speech upon the Repeal of the Jew-Bill" (1753), *Works* (1776), p. 32.

6. Earl of Shaftesbury, "Letter Concerning Enthusiasm," *Characteristicks,* I, 32. See his defense of his own dangerous raptures over the perfection of the world, "The Moralists," *Characteristicks,* II, 401, 408.

7. Earl of Shaftesbury, "On the Freedom of Wit and Humour," *Characteristicks,* I, 128.

8. James Beattie, *An Essay on the Nature and Immutability of Truth; in Opposition to Sophistry and Scepticism . . .* (1770), p. 146.

9. David Hume, *Essays Moral, Political, and Literary,* ed. T. H. Green and T. H. Grose (1875), I, 149–50.

10. *The New Whole Duty of Man . . . ,* 22d ed. (1773), pp. 365–66.

11. Jonathan Swift, "On the Martyrdom of King Charles I," *Prose Works* (1898), IV, 198.

12. John Moir, *Obedience the Best Charter . . .* (1776), p. 60.

13. Cornelius Murdin, *Three Sermons . . .* (1779), p. 15.

14. George Lord Lyttleton, "Dialogue of the Dead," *Works*, I, 104.

15. John Cartwright, "Introduction," *The People's Barrier . . .* (1780), pp. v, iii.

16. W. E. Lecky, *A History of England in the Eighteenth Century* (1879), II, 544.

17. Vicesimus Knox, *Essays Moral and Literary*, 12th ed. (1791), I, 57.

18. G. H. Guttridge, *English Whiggism and the American Revolution* (Berkeley, Calif., 1942), p. 13.

19. "Preface," *Memoirs of Edmund Ludlow* (1771), p. xii.

20. Jonathan Swift, "Sentiments of a Church of England Man," *Prose Works*, III, 74.

21. Jacob Jefferson, *The Blessing of Peace and the Means of Preserving It* (1763), pp. 26–27.

22. John Brown, *Thoughts on Civil Liberty, on Licentiousness, and Faction*, 2d ed. (1765), p. 14.

23. *An Apology for the Times . . .* (1778), pp. 24, 27, 51.

24. *A Political Analysis of the War*, 2d ed. (1762), p. 1.

25. William Warburton, "Sermons on the Rebellion," *Works* (1788), V, 227.

26. *Horace Walpole's Correspondence with George Montagu* (Yale ed., New Haven, 1941), II, 277.

27. Quoted by James Stewart, *Letter to the Rev. Dr. Price* (1776?), p. 18.

28. William Penn, "Advice to his Children," *Select Works . . .* (1771), p. 853.

29. Quoted by W. E. Lecky, *A History of England in the Eighteenth Century*, III, 130.

30. *A Continuation of the Address to the City of London* (1762), p. 63. For other warnings against divisions and factions, see "Discourse on the Happiness a State May Enjoy by Unanimity . . . ," *Universal Magazine*, XXX (1762), 1–5.

31. Benjamin Hoadly, "Persuasive to Lay Conformity," *Works* (1773), I, 321, 326.

32. Benjamin Hoadly, "Of Christian Moderation," *ibid.*, III, 659.

33. Hugh Blair, "On Our Ignorance of Good and Evil in This Life," *Sermons*, 16th ed. (London; reprinted, Baltimore, 1792), I, 128–29.

34. William Shenstone, "On Politicks," *Works* (1764), II, 153.

35. Montesquieu, *A View of the English Constitution* (1781), pp. 73–74.

36. W. E. Lecky, *A History of England in the Eighteenth Century*, I, 220; Benjamin Hoadly, "Of Christian Moderation," *Works*, III, 665.

37. *A Free Appeal to the People of Great Britain* . . . (1767), p. 30.

38. Edmund Burke, "Letter to the Sheriffs of Bristol," *Works* (Boston, 1866), II, 229.

39. David Hume, *Essays* . . . , I, 107.

40. *Ibid.*, I, 469–70.

41. *Ibid.*, I, 113.

42. Josiah Tucker, *A Selection from His Economic and Political Writings* (New York, 1931), p. 543. Cf. John Perceval, *Faction Detected by the Evidence of Facts*, 2d ed. (1743), pp. 163–64.

43. *Memoirs of Thomas Hollis* (1780), p. 473.

44. Jonathan Swift, *Prose Works*, IV, 201.

VII. SIGNS OF CHANGE

1. *The Letters of Mrs. Elizabeth Montagu* . . . (1813), IV, 27.

2. Sir William Holdsworth, *History of English Law* (1938), X, 125.

3. W. E. Lecky, *A History of England in the Eighteenth Century* (1879), I, 453–54.

4. *Political Essays Concerning the Present State of the British Empire* . . . (1772), p. 552.

5. William Connor Sydney, *England and the English in the Eighteenth Century* (1892), II, 266–67; Ramsay Muir, "Introduction" to George Veitch, *Genesis of Parliamentary Reform* (1913), p. vi.

6. *Political and Social Letters of a Lady of the Eighteenth Century, 1721–1771*, ed. Emily Osborn (1890), pp. 151–52.

7. W. E. Lecky, *A History of England in the Eighteenth Century*, III, 228, 174.

8. *Letters from Mrs. Elizabeth Carter to Mrs. Montagu* . . . (1817), II, 24.

9. *An Apology for the Times* . . . (1778), p. 16.

10. *Ibid.*, p. 12.

11. G. H. Guttridge, *English Whiggism and the American Revolution* (Berkeley, Calif., 1942), p. 35.

12. David Hartley, *Observations on Man* . . . (1749), II, 441–55.

13. W. E. Lecky, *A History of England in the Eighteenth Century*, II, 438, 464.

14. John Brown, *An Estimate of the Manners and Principles of the Times* (1757), I, 15.

15. *Ibid.*, II, 82.

16. F. T. H. Fletcher, *Montesquieu and English Politics, 1750–1800* (1939), pp. 161–62.

17. John Trenchard, *Cato's Letters* (1724).

18. *Letters of Junius*, ed. C. W. Everett (1927); F. T. H. Fletcher, *Montesquieu and English Politics . . .* , p. 173.

19. *Candid Thoughts; or, An Enquiry into the Causes of National Discontents and Misfortunes . . .* (1781), pp. 16–17.

20. "Preface," *Georgicon: an Imitation of part of Virgil's First Georgick . . .* (1778), p. vii.

21. *The Patricians . . .* (1773), pp. 32–33.

22. *The History of the Reign of George the Third . . .* (1770), p. i.

23. James Burgh, *Political Disquisitions: or, An Enquiry into Public Errors, Defects, and Abuses . . .* (1774), I, 267.

24. "Constitutional and Political English Catechism," *The Fugitive Miscellany: Part I* (1774), I, 65–71.

25. Richard Tickell, *Commonplace Arguments against Administration . . .* (1780), *passim.*

26. W. E. Lecky, *A History of England . . .* , III, 99.

27. James A. Farrer, *The Monarchy in Politics* (1917), p. 54.

28. Thomas L. O'Beirne, *A Short History of the Last Session of Parliament . . .* (1780), *passim.*

29. Edmund Burke, "Thoughts on the Causes . . . ," *Works*, I, 437.

30. *The True State of the Question* (1784), pp. 22–23.

31. *Observations on the Power of Climate over . . . Nations* (1774), pp. 109–10.

32. James Burgh, *Political Disquisitions*, I, 477–78.

33. *Ibid.*, I, 480.

34. David Williams, *Letters on Political Liberty* (1782), p. 20.

35. Catherine Macaulay, *Observations on a Pamphlet, Entitled, Thoughts on the Cause of the Present Discontents*, 2d ed. (1770), pp. 9–11.

36. David Williams, *Letters on Political Liberty*, p. 9.

37. Joseph Priestley, *An Essay on the First Principles of Government and on the Nature of Political, Civil, and Religious Liberty* (1768), pp. 128–29.

38. *An Essay on the Right of Every Man in a Free State to Speak and Write Freely, in Order to Defend the Public Rights . . .* (1772), pp. 46–47.

39. *An Address to Protestant Dissenters . . . with respect to the state of Public Liberty in General . . .* (London; reprinted in Philadelphia, 1774), p. 11.

40. James Burgh, *Political Disquisitions,* I, 81–82.

41. *Ibid.,* I, 376.

42. Francis Blackburne, *The Confessional* (1767), p. 361.

43. Joseph Priestley, *An Essay on the First Principles . . .* , p. 148.

44. Richard Price, *Observations on the Importance of the American Revolution . . .* (1785), p. 35.

45. *Queries Relating to the Book of Common Prayer . . .* (1774), pp. 36–42.

46. *Ibid.,* p. 4.

47. David Williams, *Letters on Political Liberty,* p. 76.

48. Joseph Priestley, *An Essay on the First Principles . . .* , pp. 7–8.

49. *Ibid.,* pp. 3–5.

50. *Ibid.,* pp. 137, 144, 183–87.

51. Richard Price, *The Evidence for a Future Period of Improvement in the State of Mankind . . .* (1787), p. 25.

52. *Ibid.,* pp. 5, 12.

53. David Williams, *Letters on Political Liberty,* p. 11; Catherine Macaulay, *Observations on . . . Thoughts on the Cause of the Present Discontents,* pp. 7–8.

54. Carl Becker, *The Heavenly City of the Eighteenth Century Philosophers* (New Haven, Conn., 1932), p. 103.

55. "Translator's Preface," *Emilius and Sophia . . .* , translated from the French of Mr. J. J. Rousseau (1783), pp. viii–ix.

56. Joseph Priestley, *Essay on First Principles . . .* , pp. 152, 78–79.

57. *Ibid.,* p. 17.

58. *Ibid.,* p. 188.

59. *Ibid.,* p. 41.

60. *Candid Thoughts . . .* (1781), p. 14.

61. J. J. Burlamaqui, *The Principles of Politic Law* (1784), I, 170; II, 38–39.

62. *An Address to Protestant Dissenters . . .* (1774), p. 23.

63. Joseph Priestley, *Letter to . . . William Pitt . . . on . . . Toleration and Church Establishments,* 2d ed. (1787), p. 46.

64. Leslie Stephen, *History of English Thought in the Eighteenth Century* (1876), II, 154–55.

65. Benjamin Hoadly, "Preface to the Measures of Submission," *Works* (1773), II, 7.

66. John Shebbeare, *One More Letter to the People of England* (1762), pp. 34–35.

67. J. J. Burlamaqui, *The Principles of Politic Law,* II, 126–27.

68. David Hume, *Essays Moral, Political, and Literary*, ed. T. H. Green and T. H. Grose (1875), I, 461.

69. David Hume, *A Treatise on Human Nature*, ed. T. H. Green and T. H. Grose (1874), II, 315–16.

70. George Lord Lyttleton, "Letter to a Member of Parliament," *Works* (1776), I, 103.

71. William Shenstone, "On Politicks," *Works* (1764), II, 150–52.

72. Henry St. John, Viscount Bolingbroke, *Letters, on the Spirit of Patriotism: On the Idea of a Patriot King . . .* (1749), pp. 156–57.

73. George Chalmers, *Opposition Politics, Exemplified* (1786), p. 4.

74. Josiah Tucker, *A Selection from His Economic and Political Writings* (New York, 1931), p. 412.

75. William Paley, *The Principles of Moral and Political Philosophy* (1785), pp. 425–27.

76. George Campbell, *The Nature, Extent, and Importance, of the Duty of Allegiance . . .* , 2d ed. (1778), pp. 12–27.

77. John Almon, *Letter to . . . George Grenville*, 2d ed. (1763), pp. 25–26.

78. Granville Sharp, *The Law of Passive Obedience* (1776), pp. 78–80.

79. *The Candid Philosopher: or, Free Thoughts on Men, Morals, and Manners* (1778), I, 61–62.

80. Joseph Priestley, *An Essay on First Principles . . .* , pp. 16–17.

81. Jonathan Swift, "On the Martyrdom of King Charles I," *Prose Works,* (1898), IV, 20.

82. Joseph Priestley, *An Essay on First Principles . . .* , pp. 33–35.

83. Theophilus Lindsey, *Sermon preached at . . . Essex House . . .* (1774), pp. 17–18.

84. John Cartwright, *Internal Evidence . . .* (1784); J. Bowles Daly, *Radical Pioneers of the Eighteenth Century* (1886), p. 129.

85. David Hume, *Letters* (1768), II, 191.

86. C. B. Tinker, *Nature's Simple Plan* (Princeton, N.J., 1922), pp. 51–56.

87. Dora Mae Clark, *British Opinion and the American Revolution* (New Haven, Conn., 1930), pp. 156–72.

88. James Burgh, *Political Disquisitions*, I, 3–4.

89. Earl of Abingdon, *Dedication to the Collective Body . . .* (1780); Earl of Abingdon, *Thoughts on the Letter of Edmund Burke . . . to the Sheriffs of Bristol . . .* , 4th ed. (1777), pp. 42–43; *The History of the Reign of George the Third*, p. 311; *The Fugitive Miscellany, Part I* (1774), pp. 85–87; *The Candid Philosopher*, II, 160–61.

90. *Political Essays Concerning the Present State of the British Empire* . . . (1772), pp. 67–73.

91. James Burgh, *Political Disquisitions*, I, 200.

92. Thomas Paine, *The Crisis* (1775), pp. 27, 63.

93. *Ibid.*, p. 158.

94. *Royal Perseverance*, (1778), p. 17n.

95. *An Address to Protestant Dissenters* . . . (1774), p. 9.

96. *The History of the Reign of George the Third*, pp. 326–27.

97. "Sketch of a Political Dictionary," *A Fugitive Miscellany, Part II* (1775), p. 92.

98. John Cartwright, "Introduction," *The People's Barrier* . . . (1780), pp. vi–vii.

99. *The History of the Reign of George the Third*, pp. 331–32.

100. William Combe, *An Heroic Epistle to an Unfortunate Monarch* . . . (1778), p. 14.

101. *The History of the Reign of George the Third*, pp. 255, 288–89.

102. *An Essay on Patriotism* (1769), pp. 51–53.

103. Thomas Bedford, *The Origin of Our Grievances* . . . (1770), pp. iii, 14–15.

104. *The Liberty of the Subject, and Dignity of the Crown* . . . (1780), pp. 1–3.

105. William Connor Sydney, *England and the English in the Eighteenth Century*, 2d ed. (1892), II, 211–12; Sir Walter Besant, "The Mob," *London in the 18th Century* (1925), pp. 484–93; John H. Jesse, *George Selwyn and His Contemporaries* (1844), IV, 328–33.

106. J. Wesley Bready, *England: before and after Wesley* . . . (1938), pp. 172–73.

107. Lodwick Hartley, *William Cooper: Humanitarian* (Chapel Hill, N.C., 1938), p. 19; Frank J. Klingberg, *The Anti-Slavery Movement in England* . . . (New Haven, Conn., 1926), p. 25.

108. *A Letter to William Beckford* . . . (1768), *passim*.

109. R. Potter, *Observations on the Poor Laws* . . . (1775), p. 31.

110. J. Wesley Bready, *England: before and after Wesley* . . . , pp. 302–4.

111. Frank J. Klingberg, *The Anti-Slavery Movement in England* . . . , p. 58.

112. *Ibid.*, pp. 38–40.

113. Granville Sharp, *The Law of Retribution; or, A Serious Warning to Great Britain and Her Colonies* . . . (1776), pp. 3–4. For other typical expressions of Sharp's ideas see *The Law of Nature and Principles of Action in Man* (1777); *The Just Limitation of Slavery in the Laws of*

God (1776); *Representation of the Injustice and Dangerous Tendency of Tolerating Slavery* . . . (1769).

114. Élie Halévy, *The Growth of Philosophic Radicalism* (1928), pp. 153–54, 45–54, 74–84. Cf. J. L. and Barbara Hammond, *The Town Labourer:* . . . *1760–1832* (1917), pp. 205–6.

115. Élie Halévy, *The Growth of Philosophic Radicalism*, pp. 76–78.

116. Glenn R. Morrow, *The Ethical and Economic Theories of Adam Smith* (New York, 1923), p. 43.

117. Leslie Stephen, *English Literature and Society in the Eighteenth Century* (1904), p. 186; *History of English Thought in the Eighteenth Century* (1876), II, 324.

118. See for example George Whateley, *Principles of Trade* (1774), p. 33, note 34.

119. Élie Halévy, *The Growth of Philosophic Radicalism*, pp. 140–49.

120. *Ibid.,* p. 107.

121. Wellman J. Warner, *The Wesleyan Movement in the Industrial Revolution* (1930), pp. 28–29, 139.

122. *Ibid.,* pp. 31–32

123. J. L. and Barbara Hammond, *The Town Labourer* . . . , p. 8.

124. *Ibid.,* pp. 323–24.

125. Leslie Stephen, *History of English Thought in the Eighteenth Century*, II, 453; Wellman J. Warner, *The Wesleyan Movement* . . . , p. 122; J. Wesley Bready, *England: before and after Wesley*, pp. 322–27.

126. Leslie Stephen, *English Literature and Society in the Eighteenth Century*, p. 143.

127. Maldwyn Edwards, *John Wesley and the Eighteenth Century* (New York, 1933), p. 147.

128. W. E. Lecky, *A History of England in the Eighteenth Century*, II, 627.

129. J. Wesley Bready, *England: before and after Wesley* . . . , pp. 211–12.

130. *Ibid.,* p. 222.

131. *Ibid.,* p. 268; Kathleen Walker Mac Arthur, *The Economic Ethics of John Wesley* (New York, 1936), p. 129.

132. J. L. and Barbara Hammond, *The Town Labourer* . . . , pp. 286–87; Wellman J. Warner, *The Wesleyan Movement* . . . , p. 58; Maldwyn Edwards, *John Wesley and the Eighteenth Century*, pp. 52–53.

133. Maldwyn Edwards, *John Wesley and the Eighteenth Century*, pp. 152–54.

134. *Ibid.,* pp. 202–3.

135. Wellman J. Warner, *The Wesleyan Movement* . . . , pp. 274–77.

136. Edmund Burke, "Thoughts on the Causes . . . ," *Works*, I, 500–501.

137. George Nobbe, *The North Briton: a Study in Political Propaganda* (New York, 1939), p. 213.

138. G. H. Guttridge, *English Whiggism* . . . , p. 69; Keith Feiling, *The Second Tory Party: 1714–1832* (1938), p. 114.

139. George Nobbe, *The North Briton* . . . , p. 220.

140. *Letter to the Honourable Mr. C——s F——x*, (1778), p. 34.

141. W. E. Lecky, *A History of England in the Eighteenth Century*, III, 135–37.

142. *Essay on Patriotism* (1768), pp. 49–51.

143. *History of the Reign of George the Third*, pp. 291–92.

144. George Stead Veitch, *The Genesis of Parliamentary Reform*, p. vi, "Introduction" by Ramsay Muir.

145. *Ibid.*, pp. 25–30.

146. *Ibid.*, p. 1.

147. Jonathan Swift, "Of Public Absurdities . . . ," *Prose Works*, XI, 182.

148. George Stead Veitch, *The Genesis of Parliamentary Reform*, pp. 23–25.

149. *Ibid.*, pp. 5–7.

150. George Lord Lyttleton, "Persian Letters," *Works*, I, 131–390.

151. John Almon, *Take Your Choice* (1776), pp. 14–47.

152. Catherine Macaulay, *Observations on . . . Thoughts on the Cause of the Present Discontents*, pp. 17–20.

153. David Williams, *Letters on Political Liberty*, pp. 22–24.

154. John Cartwright, "Address to the Gentlemen . . . ," *The People's Barrier against Undue Influence and Corruption* . . . , p. x.

155. James Burgh, *Political Disquisitions*, I, 37–49.

156. *Ibid.*, I, 49–50.

157. *Ibid.*, I, 116–18.

158. *Declaration of the People's Natural Right* . . . , pp. 17–19.

159. *Observations on the Power of Climate over . . . Nations*, p. 107; Cf. *Declaration of Rights* (1782), a large, poster-like page covered with medallions and designs, intended to show the need for reformation of existing corruption in Parliament.

160. G. H. Guttridge, *English Whiggism* . . . , pp. 120–21. For examples of moderate reform views see *Address to the Freeholders of Middlesex . . . December 20, 1779*, 3d ed. (1779); George Pitt Rivers, *Letters to a Young Nobleman* (1784), pp. 249–50, 342–58; Sir William Jones, "Speech to the Assembled Inhabitants of . . . Middlesex and Surrey . . .

May, 1782," *Works* (1799), VI, 715–24. Expressions of more extreme demands in varying degrees of complexity and radicalism may be found in John Cartwright, *The People's Barrier* . . . , pp. 75–141, 1–9, and *Letters to the Deputies* . . . (1781); James Burgh, *Political Disquisitions*, I, 72–197; David Williams, *Letters on Political Liberty* . . . , pp. 58–61; Catherine Macaulay, *Loose Remarks on . . . Mr. Hobbes' Philosophical Rudiments* . . . (1769); *Political Essays* . . . (1772); Jonathan Shipley, *The Principles of Government* . . . (1783); Joseph Williams, *Parliamentary Reformation* (1782).

161. J. Bowles Daly, *Radical Pioneers of the Eighteenth Century* (1886), p. 114; Richard Brinsley Sheridan, *Speeches* (1842), I, 44.

162. George Stead Veitch, *The Genesis of Parliamentary Reform*, p. 50.

163. G. H. Guttridge, *English Whiggism* . . . , p. 125.

164. George Stead Veitch, *The Genesis of Parliamentary Reform*, pp. 84–103.

165. Edward Porritt, *The Unreformed House of Commons* (1909), I, 11.

166. Robert L. Schuyler, *The Fall of the Old Colonial System* (1945), p. 55.

167. Thackeray, *The Four Georges* (New York, 1860), p. 158.

168. Keith Feiling, *The Second Tory Party* . . . , p. 126.

169. John, Earl of Stair, *The Claims of the Public* . . . (1785), p. 10.

170. "A Short View of . . . American Colonies . . . ," *The Remembrancer*, III (1776), Part II, 14–15.

171. Keith Feiling, *The Second Tory Party* . . . , p. 126.

172. Dora Mae Clark, *British Opinion and the American Revolution*, p. 177.

173. Samuel Estwick, *Letter to the Rev. Josiah Tucker* . . . (1776).

174. *The Annals of Administration* (1775).

175. T. True Britain, *Observations on American Independency* (1779).

176. See Edmund Burke's speeches on *American Taxation* (1774), *Conciliation with America* (1775), *Letter to the Sheriffs of Bristol* (1777). See the discussion of Burke by C. E. Vaughan, *Studies in the History of Political Philosophy* . . . (1925), II, 6–16.

177. Christianus, *The Voice of God* . . . (1775).

178. John Lind, *Remarks of the Principal Acts of the Thirteenth Parliament of Great Britain* (1775); William Pulteney, *Thoughts on the Present State of Affairs with America*, 5th ed. (1778).

179. *Experience Preferable to Theory* . . . (1776), pp. 72–73.

180. Here are a dozen or so of such publications showing in varying degrees a dislike of English policy or sympathy for American aspirations: Thomas Lord Lyttleton, "State of England, 2199" (1771), *Poems*, 4th ed.

(1780); W. D., *A Second Answer to Mr. John Wesley* (1775); *An Appeal to the Justice and Interests of the People of Great Britain* . . . (1775); *Tyranny Unmasked: an Answer to Taxation No Tyranny* (1775); *Lord Chatham's Prophecy, an Ode* (1776); *The Constitutional Advocate* (1776); The Earl of Abingdon, *Thoughts on the Letter of Edmund Burke* . . . , 4th ed. (1777), p. 41; William Burke, "The Letter of Valens" (1777); Francis Maseres, *The Canadian Freeholder* (1779); *A Political Mirror; or, A Summary Review of the Present Reign* (1779); *Considerations upon the French and American War* (1779); Thomas Day, *Four Tracts* . . . (1785).

181. James Burgh, *Political Disquisitions*, Vol. II.

182. John Wilkes, *Speeches . . . in the House of Commons* (1786), pp. 201, 359.

183. *The Crisis*, No. 84, August 24, 1776, pp. 527–31.

184. *Ibid.*, No. 5, pp. 27–28. For the view that "Englishmen were averse from imbruing their hands in the blood of their own relations" see John Moir, *History of the Political Life and Publick Services . . . of Charles James Fox* (1783), p. 86.

185. Thomas Paine, *Common Sense* (reprinted in London, 1776).

186. John Moir, *Obedience the Best Charter* . . . , p. 27. See also *Experience Preferable to Theory*, p. 1; Roland Thomas, *Richard Price: Philosopher and Apostle of Liberty* (1924), p. 74.

187. Richard Price, *Observations on the Importance of the American Revolution*, p. 6.

188. *Ibid.*, pp. 20–21.

189. Peter Pindar, *The Rights of Kings* (1791), p. 25.

190. Philip Brown, *The French Revolution in English History* (1923), pp. 35–36; Robert Bisset, *The Life of Edmund Burke* (1798), p. 467n.

191. Élie Halévy, *The Growth of Philosophic Radicalism*, pp. 186, 169.

192. *The Bastille* . . . (1789), p. 22.

193. George Stead Veitch, *The Genesis of Parliamentary Reform*, p. 109.

194. *The Letters of Joseph Ritson, Esq.* (1833), I, 203–4.

195. George Stead Veitch, *The Genesis of Parliamentary Reform*, pp. 109–10.

196. *Ibid.*, pp. 103–7, 121–25, 189–91, 220–29; Roland Thomas, *Richard Price* . . . , pp. 131–33.

197. Richard Brinsley Sheridan, *Speeches*, I, 517–19.

198. *The Speeches of the Right Honourable Charles James Fox in the House of Commons* (1815), IV, 215, 220.

199. William Roberts, *Memoirs . . . of Hannah More* (1834), II, 170.

200. William Cowper, *The Task,* V, ll. 389–90.

201. Wordsworth, *The Prelude,* XI, ll. 105–41.

202. See Crane Brinton, *Political Ideas of the English Romanticists* (1926), pp. 29, 45, 67, 73; Hoxie Neale Fairchild, *The Romantic Quest* (New York, 1931), p. 38; Allene Gregory, *The French Revolution and the English Novel* (New York, 1915), pp. 59, 180–90, 167–79; Lois Whitney, *Primitivism and the Idea of Progress* (Baltimore, 1934), pp. 238–76. While the novel *Dinarbas* by Ellis Cornelia Knight (1790) is not directly based on the French Revolution, its optimistic answer to Johnson's *Rasselas* may owe something to the spirit of the times.

203. Allene Gregory, *The French Revolution and the English Novel,* p. 42.

204. Richard Price, *A Discourse on the Love of Our Country* (1789), pp. 50–51.

205. Mary Wollstonecraft Godwin, *A Vindication of the Rights of Men, in a Letter to . . . Edmund Burke . . .* (1790), pp. 125–28, 141–43.

206. James Mackintosh, *Vindiciae Gallicae: Defence of the French Revolution . . .* (1791), p. 114.

207. Joseph Priestley, *Letters to the Right Honourable Edmund Burke . . .* (1791), p. 51.

208. *Ibid.,* pp. 51, 140.

209. H. N. Brailsford, *Shelley, Godwin and Their Circle* (1936), p. 63.

210. *An Impartial Sketch of the Life of Thomas Paine* (1792), p. 9.

211. *Complete Writings of Thomas Paine,* ed. Philip S. Foner (New York, 1946), I, 346. For other condemnation of Burke and pleas for semi-radical reform, natural rights of man, and renewal of 1688 principles, see Charles Pigott, *Strictures on the New Political Tenets of . . . Edmund Burke* (1791), *passim.*

212. H. N. Brailsford, *Shelley, Godwin and Their Circle,* p. 91.

213. B. Sprague Allen, "Minor Disciples of Radicalism," *Modern Philology,* XXI (1923–24), 277–301.

214. Robert Bisset, *The Life of Edmund Burke* (1798), pp. 550–52.

215. Philip Brown, *The French Revolution in English History,* pp. 62–72.

216. W. E. Lecky, *A History of England in the Eighteenth Century,* VI, 50–56.

217. R. Dinmore, Junior (Norwich, 1796).

218. *Memoirs of the Life of the late Charles Lee . . .* (1792), p. 184.

219. Lieutenant Christian, *The Revolution: an Historical Play* (1791), *passim.*

220. Joel Barlow, *A Letter to the National Convention of France . . .*

(1792), pp. 4–5, and *A Letter to the People of Piedmont* . . . (1795) *passim;* David Williams, *Lessons to a Young Prince* . . . (1790), p. 81; Charles Pigott, *The Jockey Club* . . . , Part I (1792), pp. 7–8.

221. J. Aikin, *Letters from a Father* . . . (1793), pp. 40–46.

222. Charles Pigott, *The Jockey Club* . . . , Part I, *passim; The Female Jockey Club* (1794), pp. 100–101.

223. Samuel T. Coleridge, *A Plot Discovered* . . . (1795), pp. 9, 13–14, 44; Hon. Thomas Erskine, *Declaration of the Friends of the Liberty of the Press* (1793); Robert Hall, *Apology for the Freedom of the Press* . . . (1793), pp. 15–28; Joseph Towers, *Dialogue between an Associator and a Well-Informed Englishman* . . . (1793).

224. Richard Brinsley Sheridan, *Speeches*, II, 438–59.

225. John Young, *Essays on* . . . *Interesting Subjects* (1794), p. 25.

226. *Advice to the Clergy* . . . *in the Manner of Dean Swift* . . . (1790).

227. David Williams, *Lessons to a Young Prince* . . . , p. 28.

228. Vicesimus Knox, "Preface," *Personal Nobility* . . . , 2d ed. (1793), p. xxii.

229. *Trial of Thomas Paine* (1792), p. 47; *State Trials for High Treason* (1794), Part III, pp. 106–8.

230. Philip Brown, *The French Revolution in English History*, pp. 155–57.

231. Rev. Christopher Wyvill, *A Defence of Dr. Price* . . . (1792). See also Joseph Gerrald, *A Convention the Only Means of Saving Us* . . . (1793); Thomas Oldfield, *History of the Original Constitution of Parliaments* . . . (1797); Charles Pigott, *The Jockey Club* . . . , Part III (1793), p. 217; David Williams, *Lessons to a Young Prince* . . . , p. 27; Robert Hall, *Apology for the Freedom of the Press* . . . , pp. 29–48; Henry Yorke, *Reason Urged against Precedent* . . . (1793).

232. "Ingenious Collection of Conundrums," *Wits Museum* (1790), p. 197.

233. George Stead Veitch, *The Genesis of Parliamentary Reform*, pp. 191–98.

234. Richard Brinsley Sheridan, *Speeches*, II, 232; III, 197–203.

VIII. CONSERVATISM REAFFIRMED

1. J. L. De Lolme, *The Constitution of England*, new ed. (1789), p. 533.
2. Alexander Gerard, *Liberty the Cloke of Maliciousness* . . . (1778), p. 18.

3. Richard Tickell, *Commonplace Arguments against Administration* . . . (1780), p. 21.

4. "Smollett's Dying Prediction," (1771), *Works* (New York, 1901), XII, 436.

5. Francis Blackburne, *Two Sermons . . . on a Fast Day . . .* , p. 19. These were probably given in 1758–59, and published after Blackburne's death, 1778.

6. William Eden, *Four Letters to the Earl of Carlisle* (1779), p. 17.

7. William Eden, *The Sense of the People* . . . (1780), pp. 30–31.

8. *Letters from Mrs. Elizabeth Carter to Mrs. Montagu* . . . (1817), III, 130–31.

9. *Ibid.,* pp. 169–70.

10. *The History of the Reign of George the Third* . . . (1770), pp. 315–21.

11. Edward Porritt, *The Unreformed House of Commons* (1909), I, 420.

12. *The Correspondence of King George the Third with Lord North* . . . , ed. W. B. Doune (1867), II, 257.

13. *Ibid.,* p. 161.

14. *Ibid.,* I, 89.

15. Edward Porritt, *The Unreformed House of Commons,* I, 410.

16. "The Freeholder's Political Catechism," *Political Tracts* (1769), p. 278.

17. Michael Mac Donagh, *The English King* (1929), p. 50.

18. Edward Porritt, *The Unreformed House of Commons,* I, 416.

19. James A. Farrer, *The Monarchy in Politics* (1917), pp. 6–7.

20. *Ibid.,* p. 43.

21. *Ibid.,* pp. 58–59.

22. Harold J. Laski, *Political Thought in England from Locke to Bentham* (New York, 1920), p. 215.

23. *A Letter to a Layman, on the Subject of the Rev. Mr. Lindsey's Proposal for a Reformed English Church* . . . (1774), pp. 20–21.

24. Edward Porritt, *The Unreformed House of Commons,* I, 457.

25. William Vyse, *Sermon before the House of Commons* . . . , February 27, 1778, p. 15.

26. George Campbell, *The Nature, Extent, and Importance, of the Duty of Allegiance* . . . (1778), p. 7.

27. *Experience Preferable to Theory* . . . (1776), p. 19.

28. *A Review of the Present Administration* (1774), pp. 7–10.

29. *The Sense of the People: a Letter to Edmund Burke* (1780), *passim.*

30. John Shebbeare, *An Essay on the Origin, Progress and Establishment of National Society* . . . (1776), p. 89.

31. *Experience Preferable to Theory* . . . , pp. 101–2.

32. *Ibid.,* pp. 16–17.

33. John Moir, *Obedience the Best Charter* . . . (1776), pp. 99, 101.

34. Bishop of Bristol, *Sermon . . . in the Abbey Church, Westminster, on Thursday, January 30, 1783* (1783), pp. 14–15.

35. Joseph Priestley, *An Essay on the First Principles of Government; and on the Nature of Political, Civil, and Religious Liberty* (1768), pp. 24–25.

36. *Ibid.,* pp. 31–32.

37. Leslie Stephen, *The English Utilitarians* (1900), I, 113.

38. Frank J. Klingberg, *The Anti-Slavery Movement in England* . . . (New Haven, Conn., 1926), pp. 87–90.

39. Leslie Stephen, *The English Utilitarians*, I, 133; Élie Halévy, *The Growth of Philosophic Radicalism* (1928), pp. 139–40.

40. Leslie Stephen, *The English Utilitarians*, I, 63–65.

41. Kathleen Walker Mac Arthur, *The Economic Ethics of John Wesley* (New York, 1936), pp. 126–27.

42. Maldwyn Edwards, *John Wesley and the Eighteenth Century* (New York, 1933), pp. 13–19.

43. John Wesley, *Some Observations on Liberty* . . . (1776), p. 35.

44. Wellman J. Warner, *The Wesleyan Movement in the Industrial Revolution* (1930), pp. 20–21.

45. Leslie Stephen, *The English Utilitarians*, I, 85–86.

46. Quoted in Keith Feiling, *A History of the Tory Party: 1640–1714* (1924), p. 29.

47. Lord Hugh Cecil, *Conservatism* (7th printing, London, 1933), pp. 24–25.

48. John Cartwright, *The People's Barrier against Undue Influence and Corruption* . . . (1780), p. 47.

49. Richard Price, *The Evidence for a Future Period of Improvement in the State of Mankind* . . . (1787), p. 31n.

50. David Williams, *Letters on Political Liberty* . . . (1782), pp. 36–37.

51. Dora Mae Clark, *British Opinion and the American Revolution* (New Haven, Conn., 1930), pp. 175–76.

52. "His Majesty's Most Gracious Speech . . ." (November 20, 1777), *Votes of the House of Commons* (1774–77), pp. 3–4; Cornelius Murdin, *Three Sermons* . . . (1779), p. 23 James Stewart, *Letter to the Rev. Dr. Price* . . . (1776), *passim.*

53. John Fletcher, *The Bible and the Sword* (1776), *passim.*

54. *An Appeal to Reason and Justice, in Behalf of the British Constitution . . .* (1778), *passim.*

55. *An Apology for the Times . . .* (1778), pp. 33–35.

56. Henry Goodricke, *Observations on Dr. Price's Theory . . .* (1776), *passim; John Lind, Three Letters to Dr. Price . . .* (1776), *passim.*

57. Ambrose Serle, *Americans against Liberty . . .* (1775), *passim.*

58. John Shebbeare, *An Answer to the Printed Speech of Edmund Burke . . .* (1775), *passim.*

59. John Moir, *Obedience the Best Charter . . .* (1776), p. 79.

60. J. L. and Barbara Hammond, *The Village Labourer: 1760–1832* (1913), p. 7.

61. Lord Hugh Cecil, *Conservatism*, pp. 39–40.

62. Allene Gregory, *The French Revolution and the English Novel* (New York, 1915), pp. 21–22.

63. Philip Brown, *The French Revolution in English History* (1923), p. 41.

64. *Cursory Remarks on Paine's Rights of Man* (1792), p. 15. See also, *Letters from Mrs. Elizabeth Carter to Mrs. Montagu . . .* (1817), III, 327–28, 335, 356–67; Thomas Gisborne, *Enquiry into the Duties of Men in the Higher and Middle Classes of Society . . .* (1794), pp. 33–34; P. White, *Rational Freedom: Being a Defence of the National Character of Britons . . . in Opposition to . . . Thomas Paine* (1792), pp. 6–8; *An Exposure of the Domestic and Foreign Attempts . . .* (1793), p. 65.

65. *The Wreath of Loyalty . . .* (1790), p. 11.

66. Lord Monboddo, *Antient Metaphysics* (1790), IV, 199–200; Richard Watson, *Miscellaneous Tracts . . .* (1815), I, 491; Fred Wendeborn, *View of England* (1791), I, 369–73; John Somers Cocks, *Short Treatise on . . . Levelling Principles . . .* (1793), p. 29; *Ten Minutes Address to Englishmen* (1793), pp. 22–23; *A Letter to Mr. Paine . . . ,* "Preface" (1792), p. ix; John Reeves, *Thoughts on the English Government* (1795), p. 17; *Brissot's Ghost . . .* (1794), p. 6.

67. Edmund Burke, "Reflections . . . ," *Works* (Boston: 1866), III, 345.

68. *An Exposure of the Domestic and Foreign Attempts . . .* (1793), p. 41.

69. Arthur Young, *An Enquiry into the State of the Public Mind . . .* (1798), p. 17; cf. *A Loyal Subject's Thoughts on an Union . . .* (1799), p. 6; "An Address to the King," *Votes of the House of Commons, in . . . the Seventeenth Parliament . . .* (1795), pp. 25–26.

70. *Plain Truth, a Political Dissertation . . .* (1792), p. 43; *Thoughts*

on the Probable Influence of the French Revolution . . . (1790), p. 13; William Miles, *Cursory Reflections . . . on the Continent* (1790), p. 14; "Arctic Lucubrations on Parliamentary Reform," *The Bee*, XVI (1793), 226–27; *The Trial of Thomas Paine . . .* (1792), p. 9; Thomas Hardy, *The Patriot* (1793), pp. 20–21; William Preston, *Democratic Rage . . .* (1793), p. 3; *Ten Minutes Address to Englishmen*, pp. 5–6; *Constitutional Letters in Answer to . . . Rights of Man* (1792), p. 3; *An Exposure of the Domestic and Foreign Attempts to Destroy the British Constitution . . .* (1793), p. 75.

71. *Letters of Mrs. Elizabeth Carter to Mrs. Montagu . . .* , III, 337–38.

72. Edmund Burke, "Reflections . . . ," *Works*, III, 312; Richard Watson, *Miscellaneous Tracts*, I, 489–90; Sir Brooke Boothby, *Observations on the Appeal . . .* (1792), pp. 275, 281–82.

73. William Knox, *Considerations on the Present State of the Nation* (1789), pp. iii–v.

74. *Thoughts upon the Origin of the British Constitution . . .* (1793), pp. 9–10; *Ten Minutes Caution from a Plain Man . . .* (1792), pp. 14–15.

75 Agnes M. Mackenzie, *Scotland in Modern Times* (1942), p. 121.

76. New York, n.d.

77. For various expressions of this and similar attitudes, see William Wilberforce, *A Practical View of the Prevailing Religious Systems of Professed Christians . . .* (Baltimore, 1833; first published 1797), p. 211; John Douglas, Bishop of Salisbury, *Sermon . . . for the Propagation of the Gospel . . .* (1793), pp. 8–9; *Dialogue between a Gentleman and a Mechanic* (1798), pp. 406, 18–19; John Bowles, *A Protest against T. Paine's "Rights of Man" . . .* (1792), pp. 4–5; *Short Hints upon Levelling* (1792), pp. 14–15.

78. Richard Watson, *Miscellaneous Tracts*, I, 487–89; *Brissot's Ghost . . .* , pp. 28–29; Bewick, *Tales for Youth . . .* (1794), pp. 5–7; *Short Hints upon Levelling*, pp. 11–12; "Old Poor Tobin, No. 131," *The Gentleman's Diary . . .* (1793), pp. 37–46; *Rights of Citizens . . .* (1791), pp. 108–11; Sir Brooke Boothby, *Observations on the Appeal . . .* , pp. 264–65.

79. William Wilberforce, *Practical View . . .* , pp. 69–77, 236; John Bowles, *Protest against T. Paine's "Rights of Man,"* p. 35; P. White, *Rational Freedom*, pp. 85–87; Lord Monboddo, *Antient Metaphysics*, IV, 189–90, 196, 177–79; Edmund Burke, "Reflections . . . ," *Works*, III, 418–19; *Brissot's Ghost . . .* , p. 10.

80. Richard Valpy, *Two Assize Sermons* (1793), p. 133.

81. For repetitions of this old epitaph in this period, see "A Word in Season to the Traders and Manufacturers," . . . *Society for Preserving Liberty and Property* . . . (1792), p. 16; Samuel T. Coleridge, *The Plot Discovered* . . . , p. 6; Bewick, *Tales for Youth* . . . , pp. 15–16. For typical views of the troubled reality of human life, see John Taylor, *Sermons on Different Subjects* (1793), pp. 275–78; *Religious Courtship* . . . , 20th ed. (1793), p. 265; *Letters to Thomas Payne . . . by a Member of the University of Cambridge* (1792), pp. 24–25; *Proceedings of the Association for Preserving Liberty and Property* . . . , Number 1 (1792), p. 2; *A Loyal Subject's Thoughts on an Union* . . . , p. 37; Richard Barton, *Farrago* (1792), I, 29; William Smyth, *Lectures on the French Revolution* (1855), II, 224–25.

82. Edmund Burke, "Reflections . . . ," *Works*, III, 312–13.

83. *Ibid.*, p. 407.

84. Richard Valpy, *Two Assize Sermons*, p. 93.

85. *Speeches in Parliament of the Right Honourable William Windham* . . . (1812), I, 193. For other typical examples of anti-intellectualism in this period, see *The Interests of Man* . . . (1793), pp. 68–71; *An Exposure of the Domestic and Foreign Attempts* . . . , pp. 39–40; Coleridge, *Conciones ad Populum* (1795), p. 39; William Preston, *Democratic Rage*, p. 17; P. White, *Rational Freedom*, pp. 105–7; Sir Brooke Boothby, *Observations on the Appeal* . . . , pp. 262–63; *An Answer to the Second Part of Rights of Man* . . . , p. 26; "Arctic Lucubrations on Parliamentary Reform," *The Bee*, XVI (1793), 229–30; *Letter to Thomas Payne* . . . (1792), p. 29.

86. *Vindication of the Rights of Woman* (1792), p. 367.

87. See *Ten Minutes Address to Englishmen*, pp. 21, 9; *Brissot's Ghost* . . . , p. 22; *Constitutional Letter in Answer to . . . Rights of Man*, pp. 28–29; Edmund Burke, "Appeal from the New to the Old Whigs," *Works*, IV, 213; Coleridge, *The Friend*, II, 21.

88. Tweed, *The Invasion* (1798), p. 10.

89. Philip Brown, *French Revolution in English History*, pp. 90–91.

90. *State Trials for High Treason*, Part III (1794), pp. 109–10.

91. *Thraliana*, ed. Katherine Balderston (1942), II, 883, entry for May 20, 1794.

92. *Ibid.*, p. 910, entry for February 1, 1795.

93. *Proceedings of the Association for Preserving Liberty and Property*, pp. 4–5, 16.

94. Francis Plowden, *Short History of the British Empire* . . . (1794), p. 171.

95. Thomas Erskine, *A View of the Causes and Consequences of the*

Present War with France (12th ed., 1797), pp. 19–20; H. N. Brailsford, *Shelley, Godwin, and Their Circle* (6th printing, 1936), pp. 40–46.

96. Henry Meikle, *Scotland and the French Revolution* (1912), *passim;* Frank W. Grinnell, "Estimates of Two 'Infamous' Judges . . . ," Reprinted from *Journal of Criminal Law and Criminology* (November–December, 1940), pp. 13–16. Stevenson says that he modeled his *Weir of Hermiston* on the character of Braxfield.

97. *The Trial of Thomas Paine* . . . , p. 8; John Young, *Essays on . . . Interesting Subjects,* (1794), p. 34; *Brissot's Ghost* . . . , p. 23; *The Antigallican* (1793), pp. 18–25; *Letter to Thomas Payne* . . . , pp. 19–20. *The Blossoms of Morality* (1796), p. 54; *Ten Minutes Address to Englishmen,* pp. 18–19; *Constitutional Letters in Answer to . . . Rights of Man,* pp. 30–31; Coleridge, *Conciones ad Populum,* p. 37.

98. Edmund Burke, "Reflections . . . ," *Works,* III, 310.

99. Coleridge, *Conciones ad Populum,* p. 28; Arthur Young, *Enquiry into the State of the Public Mind* . . . , p. 19; *Short Hints upon Levelling,* p. 5; John Bowles, *Protest Against T. Paine's "Rights of Man"* . . . , p. 5; William Paley, "*Reasons for Contentment* . . . ," *Publications . . . of the Society for Preserving Liberty and Property* . . . (1793), *passim; London Times,* (July 23, 1795), quoted in John Ashton, *Old Times* . . . (1885), pp. 144–45; *Letters of Joseph Ritson* (1833), I, 209; *The Antigallican,* pp. 42–43; John Somers Cooke, *Short Treatise on . . . Levelling Principles,* pp. 17–19.

100. W. L. Mathieson, *England in Transition: 1789–1832* (1920), p. 59n.

101. *Sermon* of January 30, 1725–26, *Prose Works,* IV, 196.

102. *An Address to Both Parties* (1765), *passim.*

103. J. Towers, "Appendix," *A Letter to Dr. Samuel Johnson* . . . (1775), p. 75; Frederick Wendeborn, *View of England* (1791), I, 53.

104. *The Speeches of Mr. Wilkes in the House of Commons* (1786), p. 2.

105. *George the Third's Letters to Lord North,* I, 91.

106. Horace Walpole, *Journal of the Reign of King George the Third* (1859), I, 40–41.

107. *Letter to . . . Edmund Burke* (1791), p. 48.

108. *Miscellaneous Works* (1796), I, 700.

109. P. White, *Rational Freedom* (1792), pp. 32–33.

110. The view of Charles I and the influence of January 30 which is taken here is based on the excellent article by Prof. Helen W. Randall, "The Rise and Fall of a Martyrology: Sermons on Charles I," *Huntington Library Quarterly,* X (1947), 135–67.

111. Lord Hugh Cecil, *Conservatism*, pp. 248–49.

112. Thomas Erskine, *View of . . . the Present War with France* (1797), p. 18.

113. G. M. Trevelyan, "The Age of Johnson," *Johnson's England* (1933), I, 7–8.

114. Edward Sayer, *Observations on Dr. Price's . . . Sermon* (1790), pp. 21–22.

115. See *Ten Minutes Address to Englishmen*, pp. 10–11; *The Bee or Literary Weekly Intelligencer* (1791), I, 159–60; *The Anti-Levelling Songster*, Part II (1793), p. 3; John Moore, *Journal During a Residence in France . . .* (1793), I, 319; "Advertisement," *The Antigallican*, pp. vi–vii; Arthur Young, *The Example of France, a Warning to Britain* (1793), *passim; Brissot's Ghost . . .* , p. 36; "The Fatal Effects of Republican Principles . . . ," *Publications . . . of the Society for Preserving Liberty and Property . . .* (1793), *passim.*

116. T. E. Kebbel, *History of Toryism; 1783–1881* (1886), pp. 59–61; William Smyth, *Lectures on the French Revolution* (1855), II, 189.

117. Richard Valpy, *Two Assize Sermons*, pp. 142–45.

118. Peter Porcupine, *Democratic Principles Illustrated . . .* , Part I (1798), p. 23.

119. Frank J. Klingberg, *The Anti-Slavery Movement in England . . .* (New Haven, Conn., 1926), pp. 94–100.

120. William Playfair, *Better Prospects to the Merchants . . .* (1793), p. v.

121. George Stead Veitch, *The Genesis of Parliamentary Reform*, pp. 113–16.

122. *Ibid.*, pp. 126–27.

123. Philip Brown, *The French Revolution in English History*, pp. 84–87. For the view that reform, even if passed in this period, would not have been really democratic, and that postponement of the issue till 1832 was a good thing, see William L. Mathieson, *England in Transition . . .* (1920), p. 90.

124. "Speeches of March, 1793," *Speeches*, II, 161–77. For other contemporary opinion that the conservatives had been overly fearful of treason from within, see *State Trials for High Treason*, III, 112–23; Frederick Wendeborn, *View of England . . .* , pp. i, 50.

125. See, for example, George Rous, *Letter to . . . Edmund Burke* (1791), p. 13*n*; William Hutton, "Narrative of the Riots in Birmingham . . ." (1701), *Life of William Hutton* (1817), pp. 280–81; Thomas Erskine, *View of . . . the Present War with France*, p. 13; *The Case of Libel, the King v. John Lambert . . .* (1794), pp. 3–8; Christopher

Wyvill, *A Defence of Dr. Price* . . . (1792), *passim;* Philip Brown, *The French Revolution in English History* . . . , pp. 59–64.

126. *State Trials for High Treason,* Part III, p. 105.

127. *The Plot Discovered* . . . (1795), p. 5; "Letter to the Editor of a Newspaper" (unpublished letter, undated, courtesy of Prof. E. L. Griggs).

128. Samuel T. Coleridge, *The Friend* (1837), II, 22.

129. *Brissot's Ghost* . . . , pp. 23–24.

130. J. L. and Barbara Hammond, *The Town Labourer* . . . , pp. 288–89; Leslie Stephen, *The English Utilitarians,* I, 128; Conyers Read, "Mercantilism . . . ," *The Constitution Reconsidered* (New York, 1938), p. 73; *A Conversation . . . between Thomas Paine, Marat . . . and Roland* (1793), pp. 5–7.

131. Sir Brooke Boothby, *Observations on the Appeal* . . . , p. 24.

132. William Hutton, "Narrative of the Riots in Birmingham, . . ." *Life of William Hutton* (1817), pp. 256–80; Joseph Priestley, *Appeal to the Public on . . . the Riots in Birmingham* (1791), *passim; Thraliana* . . . , II, 813 and note.

133. *Miscellaneous Works* (1796), I, 694.

134. W. E. Lecky, *History of England in the Eighteenth Century,* VI, 50.

135. L. Hartley, *William Cowper* . . . (Chapel Hill, N.C., 1938), pp. 113–15.

136. Fairchild, *The Romantic Quest* (1931), p. 51; Alfred Cobban, *Edmund Burke* . . . (1929), pp. 166–67.

137. Quoted in Brailsford, *Shelley, Godwin* . . . , p. 157.

IX. RELIGION AS THE SUPPORT OF GOVERNMENT

1. *Practical View* . . . (1797), p. 20.

2. See especially Lewis Hughes, *Historical View of . . . the Principles of Jacobinism* (1799), p. 44; Jonathan Boucher, *View of the Causes and Consequences of the American Revolution* (1798), p. 311n; *An Examination of the Principles of the French Revolution* (1796), pp. 56–57; Burke, *Reflections* . . . , (1790) pp. 72 and 80n; Antoine Guenee, *Letters of Certain Jews to Monsieur de Voltaire* (1777), II, 426–27n; David Scurlock, *Thoughts on the Influence of Religion in Civil Government* (1792), pp. 22–23; William Melmoth, *Letters of Sir Thomas Fitzosborne* . . . (1762), pp. 192–94; Thomas Rennell, *Descourses on Various Subjects* (1801), p. 299.

3. Richard Hooker, "Of the Laws of Ecclesiastical Polity," *Works*

(1850), II, 426–27. See also, Charles H. McIlwain, *The Political Works of James I* (Cambridge, Mass., 1918), and George J. Buckley, *Atheism in the English Renaissance* (Chicago, 1932).

4. "Persian Letters," *Complete Works*, III (1777), 349.

5. "Spirit of the Laws," *ibid.*, II, 203–4.

6. "Introduction," *Importance of Religious Opinions* (1788), pp. viii, x.

7. Burke, *Reflections* . . . (1790), pp. 72, 80.

8. Henry Sacheverell, *The Political Union* (1710), pp. 6–7.

9. J. Rotheram, *An Essay on Establishments in Religion* (1767), pp. 10–11.

10. Jonathan Boucher, *View of the Causes and Consequences of the American Revolution* (1798), p. 101.

11. *Vindication of Natural Society* (1756), p. 16.

12. R. Thomas, *The Cause of Truth* (1797), p. 326.

13. D. Scurlock, *Thoughts on the Influence of Religion* (1792), pp. 19–20.

14. Lewis Hughes, *Historical View of the Rise* . . . *of the Principles of Jacobinism* (1799), pp. 78–79.

15. Peter Roberts, *Christianity Vindicated* (1800), p. 78.

16. William Craig, *Twenty Discourses on Various Subjects* (1775), I, 49–50; William Wilberforce, *Practical View* . . . (1797), p. 236. For the contrary opinion that the government does not really need the help of religion, see Joseph Priestley, *Essay on the First Principles of Government* (1771), p. 183; William Hodgson, *Commonwealth of Reason* (1795), pp. 28–30; Benjamin Flower, *The French Constitution* (1792), p. 233.

17. Richard Bentley, "Folly of Atheism," *Works*, III (1838), 22.

18. Cf. *Ibid.*, p. 4; B. Porteus, "Charge to the Clergy . . . 1794," *Works* (1823), VI, 266; Andrew Fuller, *The Gospel Its Own Witness* (1800), pp. 24–25; William H. Reid, *Rise and Dissolution of the Infidel Societies* (1800), pp. 79–80.

19. William Warburton, *Alliance between Church and State* (1736), pp. 14–18.

20. Edward Ryan, *History of the Effects of Religion* . . . (1806), pp. 460–61.

21. Thomas Hunter, *Sketch of the Philosophical Character of* . . . *Bolingbroke* (1770), p. 102.

22. "Essays Addressed to Mr. Pope," *Works*, IV (1754), 630–31.

23. Voltaire, "Dictionnaire Philosophique: Athéisme," *Oeuvres Complètes*, ed. Moland (Paris, 1878), XVII, 475.

24. Voltaire, "Traité sur la Tolérance," *Oeuvres Complètes*, XXV, 100.

25. *The Gospel Its Own Witness* (1800), pp. 75–76. Fuller professes to be using this quotation as found in "Sullivan's Survey of Nature," *ibid.*, p. 76*n*.

26. Beilby Porteus, "Charge to the Clergy . . . 1794," *Works* (1823), VI, 278–79.

27. John Leland, *View of the Principal Deistical Writers* . . . (1807), II, 438.

28. Thomas Somerville, *The Effects of the French Revolution* (1793), p. 89.

29. J. Rotheram, *Essay on Establishments in Religion* (1767), pp. 95–96.

30. XVI, (1797), 76–77.

31. Vicesimus Knox, *Christian Philosophy* (1796), p. 203.

32. "Essays Addressed to Mr. Pope," *Works*, IV, 282; cf. *ibid.*, pp. 289, 348–49.

33. Samuel Horsley, *Sermons* (1816), III, 319–20.

34. "A Treatise on the Social Compact," in *Political Classics* (1798), III, 179.

35. Thomas Scott, "Impartial Statement of the Scripture Doctrine, in Respect to Civil Government," *Theological Works,* 1st American ed. (Philadelphia, 1810), III, 489.

36. Thomas Rennell, *Principles of French Republicanism* . . . (1793), pp. 9–10.

37. Arthur Young, *Enquiry into the State of the Public Mind* . . . (1798), p. 25.

38. *Edinburgh Quarterly Magazine,* I (1798), 130–31.

39. *Conclusion of the late Dr. Harley's Observations* . . . , ed. Joseph Priestley (1794), p. 10.

40. "Moral and Political Philosophy," *Works* (1837), II, 41–42.

41. J. Necker, *Of the Importance of Religious Opinions* (1788), pp. 67–68.

42. Voltaire, "Homélie sur l'athéisme," *Oeuvres Complètes,* XXVI, 322–23.

43. "Histoire de Jenni," *ibid.*, XXI, 574.

44. *Monthly Review,* XLI (1769), p. 129.

45. George Gleig, *Sermons Preached Occasionally* . . . (1803), p. 112.

46. Thomas Clarke, *The Benefits of Christianity Contrasted with the Pernicious Influence of Modern Philosophy* . . . (1796), p. 5.

47. Of Seditions and Troubles.

48. Jonathan Boucher, *View of the Causes and Consequences of the American Revolution* (1798), pp. 104, 202–3.

49. Henry Kett, *History the Interpreter of Prophecy* (1805), II, 161.

50. William Reid, *Rise and Dissolution of the Infidel Societies . . .* (1800), p. 8.

51. *Anti-Jacobin Review*, I (1798), 362n.

52. Beilby Porteus, "Charge to the Clergy . . . 1794," *Works* (1823), VI, 281–82.

53. John Erskine, *The Fatal Consequences and the General Sources of Anarchy* (1793), p. 36.

54. *Miscellaneous Works* (1796), I, 181.

55. John Ogilvie, *Sermons on Several Subjects* (1768), p. 39.

56. Thomas Somerville, *Effects of the French Revolution* (1793), p. 45.

57. Richard Watson, *An Address to the People of Great Britain* (1798), pp. 29–30; cf. William Playfair, *France As It Is* (1819), I, 369.

58. Robert Hall, "Preface," *Modern Infidelity Considered* (1800), pp. v–vi.

59. David Scurlock, *Thoughts on the Influence of Religious Opinions* (1792), p. 56.

60. Timothy Dwight, *Triumph of Infidelity* (1791), p. 10n.

61. *The Flapper*, I (1796), 71.

62. Henry Kett, *History the Interpreter of Prophecy* (1799), II, 218.

63. "Village Politics . . . ," *Liberty and Property Preserved against Republicans . . .* (1792), p. 2.

64. *Ibid.*, "Tracts," II, 3–4; cf. *The Universal Magazine*, XCIII (1793), 454.

65. "Tracts," p. 5.

66. Richard Watson, *Address to the People of Great Britain* (1798), pp. 28–29.

67. Thomas Rennell, *Principles of French Republicanism* (1793), pp. 12–13.

68. William Jones, "Note to Bishop Horne's 'Voltaire Dissected,' " *The Scholar Armed* (1800), II, 282.

X. EVIDENCE OF FRENCH INFIDELITY

1. *Monthly Review*, XXIX (1799), 181. *The Analytical Review*, XXVI (1797), 238, 560, also thinks that the public had long known of the deliberate plot against religion in France. See also *The Evangelical Magazine*, III (1795), 153, for the assurance that "serious and observing men" must have been aware of the efforts to undermine Christianity in the last twenty or thirty years.

2. *History the Interpreter of Prophecy* (1799), II, 116–17.

3. "Sermons on the Rebellion," *Works* (1788), V, 251.

4. Rev. John Bennett, *Strictures on Female Education* . . . (1788), pp. 51*n*, 52.

5. Nathaniel W. Wraxall, *Historical and Posthumous Memoirs* (1782–84), I, 116–17.

6. Earl of Malmesbury, *Series of Letters: 1745–1820* (1870), I, 162–63.

7. Horace Walpole, *Letters,* ed. Toynbee (1904), VI, 370.

8. Gray to Walpole, December 13, 1765, *Correspondence of Thomas Gray* (1935), II, 907.

9. Edward Gibbon, *Autobiographies* (1896), p. 204.

10. See the sketch of his life and career in the *Copper Plate Magazine,* Vol. I (1778).

11. S. Romilly, *Life* . . . *Written by Himself,* 3d ed. (1842), I, 131.

12. *Lettres critique d'un voyageur anglois* (1766), I, 6.7; cf. Malmesbury, *Series of Letters,* I, 325, where "philosophy" in France is called "absolute infidelity."

13. William Jones, *Popular Commotions Considered* . . . (1789), p. 7.

14. *Letters,* VI, 353.

15. *Letters from Mrs. Elizabeth Carter to Mrs. Montagu* . . . (1817), III, 306; Letter of December 8, 1788.

16. *Ibid.,* I, 20; Letter of January 13, 1759.

17. *A Series of Letters* . . . *Mrs. Elizabeth Carter to Mrs. Vesey,* 3d ed. (1819), III, 278; Letter of June 7, 1777. For the view that French infidelity was confined largely to the upper classes, see John Andrews, *Comparative View of the French and English Nations* . . . (1785), pp. 386–87.

18. Mr. Cumberland, "State of Society . . . in France and Spain . . . ," *The Political Magazine,* XI (1786), 11.

19. Joseph Priestley, *The Present State of Europe* . . . (1794), pp. 22–25.

20. *Letters,* VI, 352.

21. Samuel Romilly, *Life* . . . *Written by Himself* (1842), I, 131–32. See also J. H. Burton, *Life and Correspondence of David Hume* (1846), II, 220. For other English references to the atheism of various French philosophers before the revolution, see Fitzmaurice, *Life of Shelburne,* 2d ed. (1912), I, 427–28; Lord Monboddo, *Antient Metaphysics* (1779—), I, 240, 247*n*; Joseph Priestley, *Letters to a Philosophical Unbeliever,* Part I (1780), pp. 143–58, and *Additional Letters to a Philosophical Unbeliever* (1782), pp. 68–72; Horace Walpole, *Memoirs of* . . . *George the Third* (1894), II, 174–75.

22. Horace Bleackley, *Life of John Wilkes* (1917), pp. 155–56.

23. *Ibid.,* pp. 156–57.

24. John Wilkes, *Correspondence* (1885), IV, 306.

25. Frank A. Hedgcock, *David Garrick and His French Friends* (1912), pp. 214–34, 309–14.

26. David Garrick, *Private Correspondence* (1831), I, 250–51.

27. Bishop William K. Markham, *Sermon at St. Mary's . . .* (1773), pp. 10–11.

28. Joseph Addison, *The Evidences of the Christian Religion* (1763), pp. 226–27.

29. John Rawlins, *Connexion between Religion and Government . . .* (1766), p. 24.

30. N. W. Wraxall, *Historical and Posthumous Memoirs* (1772–84), I, 117.

31. Samuel Romilly, *Life . . . Written by Himself,* I, 145, 166; cf. *Lettres critiques d'un voyageur anglois* (1766), I, 59.

32. *Letters* (1932), II, 497.

33. Rev. Eugene Martin, *A Comparative View of the Advantages Resulting from Revelation . . .* (1789), "Preface," pp. ii–iii.

34. Samuel Romilly, *Life . . . Written by Himself,* (1842), I, 46, 132–33.

35. William Cole, *Journal of My Journey to Paris in the Year 1765* (1931), p. 154.

36. Mary W. Montague, *Letters and Works* (1887), II, 217.

37. *Letters from Mrs. Elizabeth Carter to Mrs. Montagu,* (1817), III, 287–88; Letter of November 22, 1787.

38. Smollett, *Works* (New York, 1901), XII, 437–38.

39. Thomas Bingham, *Triumph of Truth* (1800), pp. 115–17.

40. *A Series of Letters . . . Mrs. Elizabeth Carter to Mrs. Vesey* (1819), III, 13–14.

41. See I, 14, 15. References are here made to the third edition (1766).

42. *Miscellaneous Pieces,* pp. 56–75.

43. *P. iv.*

44. Moufflé D'Angerville, *Private Life of Louis XV* (1781), II, 350–51. For other references to the dangerous infidelity of Encyclopedists, see Chapter 3 of Sterne's *Sentimental Journey,* "Paris," and Mrs. Carter's *Letters to Mrs. Montagu,* December 11, 1775 (II, 350).

45. John Andrews, *Letters to a Young Gentleman* (1784), pp. 83–84.

46. William Cole, *Journal of My Journey . . . ,* p. 27.

47. *Ibid.,* p. 95.

48. John Andrews, *Letters to a Young Gentleman* . . . (1784), pp. 84–85.

49. John Charles Villiers, *Tour Through Part of France* . . . (1789), p. 318.

50. William Cole, *Journal of My Journey* . . . , p. 93.

51. Sir Robert Talbot, *Letters on the French Nation* . . . (1771), I, 30–35.

52. John Andrews, *Letters to a Young Gentleman* . . . (1784), pp. 68–69, and *Comparative View of the French and English Nations* . . . (1785), pp. 397–98.

53. D'Alembert, *Account of the Destruction of the Jesuits* . . . (1766), pp. 189–90, 127–39.

54. *Ibid.*, pp. 157–58.

55. XXXII (1765), 504–5.

56. *The Scots Magazine,* XXXI (1769), 120.

57. Moufflé D'Angerville, *Private Life of Louis XV* (1781), II, 333.

58. *Memoirs of the Marchioness of Pompadour* (1766), II, 86–87.

59. Moufflé D'Angerville, *Private Life of Louis XV,* II, 353. The English would have further evidence of an antireligious movement in France from the translation of such a book as Claude Helvétius', *Treatise on Man* . . . (1777), which deals fiercely with priests, religious intolerance, and the usefulness of organized religion.

60. *Monthly Review,* XXIX (1799), 181.

61. *Lettres critiques d'un voyageur anglois,* I, 58.

62. *Ibid.,* I, 141.

63. V (1762), 48.

64. *The Speech of Anthony Louis Séguier* (1781), p. 18.

65. J. Briggs, *The Nature of Religious Zeal* (1775), pp. 35–36.

66. John Ogilvie, *Inquiry into the Causes of the Infidelity* . . . (1783), pp. 320–21.

67. Walpole, *Letters,* VI, 334–35. This passage seems to have been well known after the French Revolution, and was quoted by several writers dealing with infidelity. See, for example, W. H. Reid, *Rise and Dissolution of the Infidel Societies* (1800), p. 96; Barruel, *Memoirs Illustrating the History of Jacobinism* (1797), IV, 422–23n; Henry Kett, *History the Interpreter of Prophecy* (1799), II, 192–93.

68. Joseph Benson, *Life of the Rev. John W. de la Flechere* (New York, 1840), pp. 222–23.

69. *Journal of the Rev. John Wesley* (1943), VI, 186–87.

70. Séguier, *Speech* . . . (1781), pp. 23–24.

71. *Ibid.,* p. 35.

72. *Ibid.,* p. 31.

73. Robert Bisset, *Life of Edmund Burke,* p. 159. For another report of Burke's attack on French freethinkers, see C. B. Tinker, *The Salon and English Letters* (New York, 1915), p. 68.

74. See the excellent article by Ronald S. Crane, "Diffusion of Voltaire's Writings in England," *Modern Philology,* XX (1923), 261–74, in which the wide reading of Voltaire in England is suggested from an examination of the catalogues of 218 libraries. Over three fourths of these libraries contained volumes by Voltaire with the histories predominating and the antireligious works, however, very thinly represented. My own investigations along similar lines in auction catalogues and other lists of what was contained in private libraries, suggest further the immense English interest in Voltaire's achievement. The absence of the antireligious works implies that readers were willing to take the later reputation of Voltaire as an evil influence on faith, without going so far as to own the books in which his dangerous ideas were expressed.

Material for a view of Voltaire's general English reputation before the French Revolution has accumulated in considerable abundance. I have used only enough here to suggest the outlines of the whole and to show anticipations of the later "case" against him.

75. John Andrews, *Letters to a Young Gentleman* (1784), pp. 157–58.

76. (1752), pp. 107–8.

77. Elias Braman Jun, *Letters to a Young Nobleman* (1762), pp. 191–92.

78. "Letter from the Chinese Spy," *Universal Magazine,* XXXV (1764), 292–93.

79. XLVIII (1771), 256.

80. *Free and Impartial Remarks upon the Letters Written by the . . . Earl of Chesterfield to His Son . . .* (1774), p. 35.

81. *Panegyric of M. Voltaire* (1779), pp. vii–viii, 46–49.

82. John Andrews, *Letters to a Young Gentleman . . .* (1784), p. 94; cf. *ibid.,* pp. 97, 109–10, 125.

83. John Andrews, *Comparative View of the French and English Nations . . .* (1785), p. 425. See also Lyttleton, "Dialogues of the Dead," *Works,* II, 205–9; *The Lounger* (March 15, 1785), p. 20.

84. "Advertisement" to the *Philosophical Dictionary* (1765), p. ii; "Translator's Preface" to *Jean Hennuyer . . . or the Massacre of St. Bartholomew* (1773), pp. vn, vi.

85. *Universal Magazine,* XXXVI (1765), pp. 208–10.

86. Pp. iii–viii.

87. *Treatise upon Religious Toleration* (1764).

88. P. vii. See also the 1779 edition of *A Treatise on Toleration and Other Works,* translated by the Rev. David Williams, which presents Voltaire in a most attractive light; cf. John Ogilvie, *Inquiry into the Causes of the Infidelity . . .* (1783), p. 1116n.

89. *The Candid Philosopher,* I (1778), 28–29; II, 39–42.

90. John Andrews, *Comparative View of the French and English Nations . . .* (1785), p. 56.

91. John Charles Villiers, *Tour through Part of France* (1789), pp. 318–21.

92. See note to William Warburton, "Sermons on the Rebellion," *Works,* V (1788), 250n, written about 1753.

93. *Journal of the Rev. John Wesley, April, 1756* (1943), IV, 45, 157.

94. *Letters of Mrs. Elizabeth Montagu . . .* (1813), IV, 185–86.

95. *Ibid.,* p. 197.

96. *Letters from Mrs. Elizabeth Carter . . .* (1817), I, 49.

97. "Dialogues of the Dead," *Works,* II (1776), 208–9.

98. R. Huchon, *Mrs. Montagu . . .* (1907), pp. 117–18; Emily Climenson, *Elizabeth Montagu . . .* (1906), II, 257.

99. Edward Young, *Resignation* (1762), pp. 35–38, 56–57.

100. *A Series of Letters . . . Mrs. Elizabeth Carter to Mrs. Vesey* (1819), III, 13.

101. "Advertisement," *Philosophical Dictionary* (1765), pp. i–ii.

102. *Ibid.,* p. 287n.

103. XVIII (1764), 467.

104. *Works of Tobias Smollett* (New York, 1901), XII, Part II, 6.

105. *A Series of Letters . . .* III, 226, 229.

106. *Letters to a Philosophical Unbeliever,* II (1780), 178–79.

107. *Ibid.,* "Preface," II, xii–xiii.

108. *History of the Life and Writings of . . . Voltaire . . .* (1782), pp. 6, 8, 11–12, 14, 57.

109. *Chaudon, Historical and Critical Memoir . . .* (1786), p. 265.

110. *Thraliana,* II, 615.

111. *The Political Magazine,* X (1786), 460. For other references to Voltaire's infidelity before the French Revolution, see A. Deane, *The Minor . . .* (1788), II, 97–98, where Voltaire is called the devil incarnate, the fiend, and anti-Christ; Dr. Horne, *Letters on Infidelity,* (1784), pp. 2, 300–301; W. Belsham, *Essays . . .* (1799), I, 34. These essays were probably written before 1790 though published later.

112. *Letters from Mrs. Elizabeth Carter to Mrs. Montagu* (1817), I, 44.

113. "Some Account of the Character and Writings of M. de Voltaire . . . ," *The Copper Plate Magazine,* Vol. I (1778).

114. *History of the Life and Writings of . . . Voltaire . . .* (1782), pp. 4, 5, 10–11, 31n, 54–55, and 56n.

115. Horace Walpole, "Correspondence with Rev. William Cole," *Yale Edition of Horace Walpole's Correspondence* (New Haven, Conn., 1937), II, 309.

116. Rev. John Bennett, *Strictures on Female Education . . .* (1788), pp. 59n, 60. For Frederick's irreligion, see Mrs. Carter to Mrs. Vesey, *A Series of Letters,* III, 5; Letter of June 1, 1763.

117. *The Political Magazine . . .* IX (1785), 64.

118. John Ogilvie, *An Inquiry into the Causes of the Infidelity . . .* (1783), pp. 229–32.

119. William Jones, "Preface," *Popular Commotions Considered . . .* (1789), p. vi.

XI. THE FRENCH REVOLUTION AND ITS CAUSES

1. Condorcet, *Vie de Voltaire* (1791), pp. 291–92.

2. Rabaut St. Étienne, *History of the Revolution in France* (1792), p. 224.

3. *Ibid.,* pp. 224–25.

4. *Analytical Review,* V (1790), 573.

5. Rabaut St. Étienne, *op. cit.,* p. 17.

6. E. Harwood, *Account of the Conversion of a Deist . . .* (1762), pp. 84–85.

7. Rabaut St. Étienne, *op. cit.,* p. 18.

8. *Domestic Anecdotes of the French Nation* (1794), pp. 4–5.

9. *Analytical Review,* V (1790), 569.

10. T. L. O'Beirne, "Sermon at Longford, February 28, 1794," *Sermons* (1799), p. 48.

11. *Enquiry into the Second Coming of Our Saviour,* (1796), p. x.

12. William Mavor, *Christian Politics: a Sermon . . .* (1793), pp. 15–16; *British Mercury,* II (1799), 360–61.

13. J. Courtenay, *Philosophical Reflections . . .* (1790), pp. 14–17; John Bowles, "Real Grounds of the Present War . . ." (1793) *Retrospect* (1798), p. 81; "The Englishman's Political Catechism," *Liberty and Property Preserved . . . ,* "Tracts," X (1792), 8.

14. James Mackintosh, *Vindiciae Gallicae* (1791), p. 62.

15. W. L. Brown, *Spirit of the Times . . .* (1793), p. 25.

16. Burke, *Letter to a Member of the National Assembly* (1791), p. 29.

17. S. Romilly, *Life . . . Written by Himself* (1842), I, 343. Dislike of

the French "philosophers" for their alleged wickedness, their evil influence, and their guilt in preparing for the Revolution in France was so common in England once the Bastille had fallen that it hardly seems useful or necessary to multiply quotations in further proof of it here. For other examples of these views, however, see the following: Lord Monboddo, *Antient Metaphysics*, IV (1790), 208; Linguet, *Critical Analysis and Review* . . . (1790), pp. 264–65; *Letter to a Friend on the Late Revolution* . . . (1791), p. 4; Archibald Maclaine, *Religion a Preservative* . . . (1793), pp. 8–9; Richard Valpy, *Two Assize Sermons* (1793), p. 51*n*; Sir Brooke Boothby, *Observations on the Appeal* . . . (1792), p. 266; *Considerations on the Causes and Alarming Consequences* . . . (1794), pp. 146–47; "A New Year's Gift . . . ," *Laity's Directory for the Church Service* (1795), p. 3; M. Malouet, *Interesting Letters on the French Revolution* . . . (1795), pp. 75–76; Rev. Arthur O'Leary, *Fast Day Sermon* . . . (1797), pp. 20–21.

18. XV (1790), 72.

19. Thomas Paine, *Rights of Man* (1791), p. 91.

20. William A. Miles, *Conduct of France towards Great Britain* (1793), pp. 269–70; cf. "Historic Memoir of the French Revolution," *Comparative Display of the Different Opinions* . . . (1793), I, 130–31.

21. Burke, "Reflections," *Works* (Boston, 1866), III, 517.

22. For references to these writers and their role in preparing for the French Revolution, see Richard Sulivan, *View of Nature* (1794), I, 8; V, 400; W. Belsham, *Essays* . . . (1799), pp. 196–97; John Maclaurin, "Of Religion," *Works* (1798), II, 280–81; Francis Plowden, *Short History of the British Empire* . . . (1794), p. 2; Alexander Pirie, *The French Revolution Exhibited* . . . (1795), pp. 3–4; Richard Valpy, *Two Assize Sermons* (1793), pp. 47–49; *The Age of Infidelity*, Part II (1796), pp. 108–9; *Plain Reasons for Adopting the Plan of* . . . *The Friends of the People* (1793), pp. 13–14.

23. J. Courtenay, *Philosophical Reflections* . . . (1790), pp. 17–18. In his *Rise and Dissolution of the Infidel Societies* (1800), William H. Reid quotes part of this passage. Hardly a single work referred to in this section on the "philosophers" fails to mention either Rousseau or Voltaire or both.

24. William Mile, *Conduct of France* . . . (1793), pp. 144–46.

25. Walter King, *Two Sermons* . . . (1793), p. 26.

26. Rev. William Jones of Nayland, "Popular Commotions to Precede the End of the World" (1789), *Works* (1826), III, 473.

27. J. Gifford, *Residence in France* . . . (1797), II, 20–21.

28. See, for example, *A Serious View of the Remarkable Providences of*

the Times . . . (1795), p. 21; Elhanan Winchester, *A Defence of Revelation* . . . (New York; reprinted in London, 1796), p. 77; Theophilus Lindsey, "Preface," to Joseph Priestley, *Answer to Mr. Paine's Age of Reason* . . . (1795), pp. v–vi; "Preface" *Antipolemus* . . . from the Latin of Erasmus (1795), p. xxxiii.

29. W. L. Brown, *Spirit of the Times* . . . (1793), pp. 17–18; George Gleig, "Fast Day Sermon, 1794," *Sermons Preached Occasionally* . . . (1803), pp. 118–19.

30. Jonathan Boucher, *View of the Causes and Consequences of the American Revolution* (1797), pp. 59, 150, 448.

31. John Moir, *Preventive Policy* (1796), pp. 381–82.

32. George Gleig, "Fast Day Sermon, 1794," in *Sermons Preached Occasionally* . . . (1803), p. 118.

33. Thomas Rennell, *Principles of French Republicanism* . . . (1793), p. 5.

34. Walter King, *Two Sermons* . . . (1793), pp. 24–25.

35. For such condemnation of the French Revolution and its irreligion, see "A Word in Season to the Traders and Manufacturers . . . ," *Society for Preserving Liberty and Property* . . . (1792), p. 8; *Historical Sketch of the French Revolution* . . . (1792), p. 425; *Ten Minutes Reflection on the Late Events in France* . . . (1792), pp. 20–21; W. L. Brown, *Spirit of the Times,* (1793), pp. 41–42; Rev. William Goode, *Mercies in Judgment* (1797), p. 19; *Conclusion of the Late Dr. Hartley's Observations* . . . (1794), p. 20n; *Letters from Mrs. Elizabeth Carter . . . to Mrs. Montagu,* III, 343; Letter of September 28, 1749; J. Adams, *View of Universal History* . . . (1795), III, 250; William Agutter, *Thanksgiving Day Sermon, 1797* (1798), p. 10n.

36. Walter King, *Two Sermons* . . . (1793), p. 20.

37. John Bowles, "Objections to the Continuance of the War . . . ," *Retrospect* (1798), p. 97.

38. T. Hunter, *Sermon on a Public Fast* (1794), pp. 10–11.

39. Peter Peckard, *National Crimes the Cause of National Punishments* (1795), p. 8.

40. Peter Pindar, *The Magpie and Robin Redbreast* (1791), p. 48; "Common Sense . . . ," *The Antigallican Songster,* II (1793), 12.

41. William Cobbett, *Bloody Buoy* . . . (1798), p. 209.

42. "A Sonnet on the French Atheistical Motto, 'Death Is An Eternal Sleep,'" printed with *A Ballad on the Death of Louis the Unfortunate* . . . (1793), p. 31.

43. John Gifford, *Residence in France* . . . (1797), II, 32n; this same description is referred to by Henry Fly, *Loyalty Recommended* . . .

(1798), p. 26n; William Agutter, *Thanksgiving Day Sermon, 1797* (1798), p. 9.

44. Robert Hall, *Modern Infidelity Considered* (1800), pp. 42–43.

45. J. Whitaker, *Real Origin of Government* (1795), p. 47.

46. William Playfair, *History of Jacobinism* . . . (1798), p. 419.

47. John Gifford, *Residence in France* . . . (1797), II, 32. Other expressions of amazement and dismay at the impiety of this denial of a future life may be seen in J. B. Watson, "Prologue," to the *Maid of Normandy* . . . (1794), p. 7; Count de Montgaillard, *Continuation of the State of France* (in May, 1794), translated from the French (n.d.), p. 104; Gilbert Austin, *Sermons* (1795), pp. 106–7; Rev. Arthur O'Leary, *Fast Day Sermon,* (1797), pp. 24–25; *First Fruits of the French Revolution,* p. 91 (title page missing), *Yale College Pamphlets,* CCLXII, No. 4; John Gifford, *Letter to the Hon. Thomas Erskine* (Philadelphia, 1797), p. 49n; H. R. Yorke, *Letter to the Reformers* (1798), p. 50; *Poetry of the Anti-Jacobin* (1800), p. 66.

48. Thomas Whitaker (?), *Thoughts Suitable for the Approaching Fast* (1795), p. 7.

49. John Willison, *Prophecy of the French Revolution* (1793), p. 99.

50. *The Pernicious Influence of Atheism and Irreligion on Government and State* (1793), p. 20.

51. John Locke, "Letter Concerning Toleration," *Works* (1714), II, 252.

52. *Correspondence* (1890), pp. 92–93.

53. James Mackintosh, *Vindiciae Gallicae* (1791), pp. 63–64; cf. P. A. Wadia, *The Philosophers and the French Revolution* (1904), for an interpretation of the "philosophers" as being themselves led by the revolutionary spirit and not the leaders of it.

54. "Preface," *Domestic Anecdotes of the French Nation* (1794), pp. 1–2.

55. John Bowles, *Retrospect* (1798), pp. 225, 301, 318–19.

56. J. E. Smith, *Sketch of a Tour on the Continent* . . . (1793), III, 209. This passage is reprinted in an account of Smith's tour in the *Universal Magazine,* XCIV (1794), 286.

57. I (1797), 381.

58. Burke, *Reflections* (1790), p. 120.

59. Samuel Horsley, "Appendix to Sermon of January 30, 1793," *Sermons* (1816), III, 332.

60. Beilby Porteus, "Charge to the Clergy of the Diocese of London . . . 1794," *Works* (1823), VI, 264–65.

61. T. L. O'Beirne, "Charge to the Clergy . . . 1795," *Sermons* (1799), pp. 223, 235.

62. Barruel, *History of the Clergy* . . . (1794), p. 3.

63. See, for example, *Literary and Critical Remarks on Sundry Eminent Divines* . . . (n.d.), p. 345; Daniel Turner, *Free Thoughts* . . . (1793), p. 128; *Considerations on the Present Internal and External Condition of France* (1794), p. 28n; Mme. de Staël, *Treatise on the Influence of the Passions* (1798), p. 177; Helen M. Williams, *Sketches of the State of Manners* . . . (1801), II, 87–88; Edward Ryan, *History of the Effects of Religion* . . . (1806), p. 458.

64. Burke, *Reflections* (1790), pp. 89–90.

65. *Ibid.,* p. 124.

66. Archibald Maclaine, *Religion a Preservative* . . . (1793), p. 12.

67. Burke, *Reflections,* pp. 23–24.

68. John Gifford, *Reign of Louis XVI* (1794), pp. 298–301.

69. Burke, *Reflections,* p. 90.

70. *Monthly Review,* LXXX (1789), 628–30.

71. Richard Valpy, *Two Assize Sermons* (1793), p. 47–49, 51.

72. Beilby Porteus, "Charge to the Clergy . . . 1794," *Works* (1823), VI, 265–66.

73. *Examination of the Principles of the French Revolution* (1796), p. 59.

74. "Preface," *Six Letters on Intolerance* (1791), pp. vi–vii; Charles de Coetlogon, *Hints to the People of England* . . . (1792), pp. 30–31; Richard Sulivan, *Survey of Nature* (1794), V, 397; George Gleig, "Fast Day Sermon, 1794," *Sermons Preached Occasionally* . . . (1803), p. 21.

75. T. L. O'Beirne, "Charge to the Clergy . . . 1795," *Sermons* (1799), pp. 223–24.

76. John Bowles, *Retrospect* (1798), pp. 204–5, 223.

77. *Ibid.,* p. 69; W. L. Brown, *Spirit of the Times* . . . (1793), p. 21.

78. W. L. Brown, *Spirit of the Times* . . . (1793), p. 32.

79. John Bowles, *Retrospect* (1798), pp. 84–85, 199. For similar conservative fears as to the universally destructive tendency of the French Revolution see Thomas Moore, *Address to Inhabitants of Great Britain* . . . (n.d.), pp. 25–28; *Diary of William Windham* (October 6, 1792), p. 261; *Translation of a Speech* . . . *in the National Convention, December 14, 1792, by the Citizen Dupont* (printed as a broadside); George Huntingford, *Sermon before the House of Commons* (1793), pp. 8–10; *Opinions Delivered at a Numerous* . . . *Meeting* . . . (1793), p. 2; George Butt, "Ode to the Right Honourable William Pitt," *Poems* (1793), II, 98n; *Conclusion of the Late Dr. Hartley's Observations* . . . (1794),

pp. 4–5; *Historical View of the French Revolution* . . . (1796), "Preface," I, ix; *Examination of the Principles of the French Revolution* (1796), p. 1.

XII. THE APOTHEOSIS OF VOLTAIRE

1. See, for example, *A Dialogue between an Associator and a Well-Informed Englishman* . . . (1793), p. 21; *Historical View of the French Revolution* . . . (1796), I, 17–18; *Illustrations of Prophecy* (1796), II, 681–82; J. G. Zimmerman, *Essay on National Pride* (1797), p. 181; John Maclaurin, "Of French Principles," *Works* (1798), II, 173.

2. *Illustrations of Prophecy* (1796), II, 682.

3. A. Chénier, "Epître à Voltaire," in Condorcet, *Vie de Voltaire* (Paris, 1822), p. iv.

4. William Cole, *Journal of My Journey to Paris* . . . (1931), p. 25.

5. William King, *Two Sermons* (1793), p. 22.

6. William Jones, *The Man of Sin* (1794), p. 26.

7. John Gifford, *Residence in France* . . . (1797), II, 31.

8. Antoine Guénée, "Translator to the Reader," *Letters of Certain Jews* . . . (1777), p. 5; for other mention of Voltaire and English freethinkers, see William Jones, *Popular Commotions Considered* . . . (1789), pp. 13–14; *Plain Reasons for Adopting the Plan of* . . . *The Friends of the People* . . . (1793), pp. 13–14; John Duncan, *The Libertine and Infidel Led to Reflection* . . . (1799), p. 284; G. A. Thomas, *Sermons and Charges of the Right Rev. John Thomas* (1796), I, cxl. Voltaire's indebtedness to the English deists has been thoroughly studied. See John Cairns, *Unbelief in the Eighteenth Century* (1881), pp. 125–26; Charles Abbey and John Overton, *The English Church in the Eighteenth Century* (1878), I, 241; and especially Norman L. Torrey, *Voltaire and the English Deists* (New Haven, Conn., 1930), pp. 199–206. Voltaire's dependence on Bolingbroke is emphasized in *Lettres Critiques d'un Voyageur Anglois* (Copenhagen, 1766), I, 8, but Professor Torrey thinks that Voltaire's obligation to Bolingbroke has been much exaggerated: "Bolingbroke and Voltaire: a Fictitious Influence," *PMLA* (September, 1927), pp. 788–97.

9. *History of England* . . . (1879), V, 309.

10. Leslie Stephen, *History of English Thought* . . . (1876), I, 375.

11. *Critical Review*, IX (1794), 509.

12. *The Bee or Literary Weekly Intelligencer*, X (August 15, 1792), 212.

13. *Loc. cit.*, Mme de Staël, *Treatise on Ancient and Modern Literature* (1803), II, 62–63.

14. John Gifford, *Residence in France* . . . (1797), I, 223.

15. Answer to "The Lights of Men," by "Edward," *The Oracle* (July 11, 1791).

16. Helen M. Williams, *Letters Containing a Sketch of the Politics of France* (1796), III, 58n.

17. Mallet du Pan in *The British Mercury*, (1799), II, 342–45. For other admissions that Voltaire and other "philosophers" would not have approved of the actual course of the Revolution, see *The Antigallican* (1793), p. 96; "Translator's Preface," to D'Alembert, *Select Eulogies* . . . (1799), pp. ix–x. For discussions of Voltaire's monarchism, see P. Wadia, *The Philosophers and the French Revolution* (1904), pp. 20–22; Philip G. Neserius, "The Political Ideas of Voltaire," *The American Political Science Review*, XX (1926), 35, 41–42; and especially Georges Pellissier, *Voltaire Philosophe* (Paris, 1908), pp. 237–43.

18. Mme de Staël, *Treatise on Ancient and Modern Literature* (1803), II, 62–63.

19. Mallet du Pan, *Considerations on the Nature of the French Revolution* (1793), pp. 7–8.

20. "Preface" to *An Inquiry into the Nature of the Social Contract* (1791).

21. "Postscript to *Thoughts on the Will of the People*" (1795), in *Spirit of Anti-Jacobinism* (1802), pp. 80–81. See also *Examination of the Principles of the French Revolution* (1796), p. 12; *Substance of the Speech of . . . Lord Loughborough in the House of Lords . . . December 26, 1792* (a political broadside), p. 2. For the view that Rousseau would never recognize his doctrines in the present French Constitution, however, see John Maclaurin, "Of French Principles," *Works* (1798), II, 173–74.

22. Burke, *Letter to a Member of the National Assembly* (1791), pp. 31–33.

23. Samuel Romilly, *Life* . . . *Written by Himself* (1842), I, 267.

24. William Blake, *The French Revolution: a Poem*, Book I (1791), pp. 14–15.

25. Sheridan, *Speeches* (1842), II, 155.

26. Rev. John Moir, *Preventive Policy* (1796), pp. 238–240.

27. John Gifford, *Residence in France* . . . (1797), I, 62, 169.

28. P. Wadia, *The Philosophers and the French Revolution* (1904), pp. 9–10.

29. Athanase Veau, "Hymne aux Grands Hommes," *Le Culte de la Raison* (n.d.), pp. 119–21.

30. *Historical Epochs of the French Revolution,* "Preface" (1796), p. viii. For other references to Voltaire and Rousseau together and the dangers of their works, see *A Series of Letters . . . Mrs. Elizabeth Carter to Mrs. Vesey* (August 30, 1766), III, 74n; James Prior, *Memoir of . . . Edmund Burke* (Philadelphia, 1826), p. 313; Charles de Coetlogon, *Peculiar Advantages of the English Nation . . .* (1792), p. 30n; "Appendix" to Joseph Priestley, *Appeal to the Public on . . . the Riots in Birmingham,* Part II (1792), pp. 175–76; *Queen of the Blues* (Letter from the Primate of Ireland to Mrs. Montagu, October 29, 1792.), II, 290; Charles de Coetlogon, *Hints to the People of England . . .* (1792), pp. 29–30; "Preface" to *Antipolemus; or, The Plea of Reason . . .* (1794), p. xxxix; *Letter of Condolence . . . from Antichrist to John Bull . . .* (1795), p. 6; Alex Pirie, *French Revolution Exhibited . . .* (1795), pp. 3–4; *The Age of Infidelity:* Part II (1796), pp. 108–9; Peter Porcupine, *The Bloody Buoy . . .* (1798), p. 151; Francis Plowden, *Short History of the British Empire . . .* (1794), p. 2; W. Belsham, *Essays . . .* 1799), II, 196–97.

31. June 16–18, 1791.

32. Mary Wollstonecraft, *Historical and Moral View of the French Revolution* (1794), pp. 9–10.

33. Fanny Burney, "Entry of December 19, 1785," *Diary and Letters of Madame D'Arblay . . .* (1904), II, 342.

34. Boswell, *Life of Johnson,* ed. George B. Hill (1887), II, 12.

35. "Boswell with Rousseau and Voltaire," *Private Papers of James Boswell from Malahide Castle* (1764), IV, 73–75 (privately printed, 1928).

36. James E. Smith, *Sketch of a Tour* (1793), I, 113. For other references to the comparative piety of Rousseau, see *History of the Life and Writings of . . . Voltaire . . .* (1782), pp. 2n, 9n; Daniel Turner, *Free Thoughts . . .* (1793), pp. 19–20; *Examination of the Principles of the French Revolution* (1796), pp. 63, 70–71.

37. *Boswell with Rousseau and Voltaire* (1764), pp. 19, 152.

38. "Advertisement" to *Genuine Letters between the Archbishop of Anneci and M. de Voltaire* (1770), p. 48.

39. J. Auchincloss, *Sophistry of . . . Age of Reason* (1796), p. 41.

40. For these and other typical English views against Voltaire, see the following: M. Linguet, *Critical Analysis and Review of All Mr. Voltaire's Works . . .* (1790), pp. 235–61; *The Universal Magazine and Review . . .* , VI (1791), 142; *Remarks on the Religious Sentiments of . . . Eminent Laymen* (1792), p. 155n; George Butt, "Fun," *Poems* (1793), I, 98; "Critical Remarks on Some Celebrated Authors," *The Bee . . .* , XIV (1793), 159–60; Richard Valpy, *Two Assize Sermons* (1793), pp. 39–40n;

"A Discourse by way of General Preface to the Quarto Edition of Bishop Warburton's Works . . ." (1794), in William Warburton, *Works* (1788), VIII, 123; Richard J. Sulivan, *View of Nature* (1794), V, 213–14; Alex Pirie, *French Revolution Exhibited* . . . (1795), pp. 255–56; *The Age of Infidelity:* Part II (1796), pp. 118–19; John Evans, *Sketch of the Denominations* . . . (1796), pp. 7–8; William Finch, *Objections of Infidel Historians* (1797), pp. 19–38, 150–51.

41. November 25–27, 1790.

42. VIII (1796), 506–7.

43. Beilby Porteus, "Charge to the Clergy . . . 1794," *Works* (1823), VI, 272n. This passage occurs again in *The Arminian Magazine*, XVIII (1795), 201–2.

44. William Jackson, *Observations in Answer to . . . Age of Reason* (1795), p. 64.

45. *The Oracle*, July 11, 1791. For a study of what Paine has in common with Voltaire's thought, see Harry H. Clark, "Thomas Paine's Relation to Voltaire and Rousseau," *Revue Anglo-Americaine*, IX (1931–32), 305–18, 393–405.

46. *New and General Biographical Dictionary* (1784), XII, 746–47.

47. David Williams, *Lessons to a Young Prince* . . . (1790), p. 78.

48. Isaac Disraeli, *Dissertation on Anecdotes* (1793), p. 10.

49. Alex Pirie, *French Revolution Exhibited* . . . (1795), p. 161; William Finch, *Objections of Infidel Historians* (1797), p. 39.

50. Rabaut St. Etienne, *History of the Revolution* . . . (1792), pp. 16, 196.

51. *Critical Review*, LXIX (1790), 75.

52. *An Impartial History of the French Revolution* (1795), II, 250–51.

53. *The British Critic*, I (1793), 141. For other references to Voltaire's prediction of a coming revolution, see Stephen Weston, *Letters from Paris during the Summer of 1792* . . . (1793), II, 268; "Horace Walpole's Correspondence with Mary and Agnes Berry . . . ," *Yale Edition of Horace Walpole's Correspondence* (1944), I, 28.

54. *Critical Review* (1791), II, 476.

55. This brief account of Voltaire's apotheosis is an extreme condensation of a most spectacular episode. Material which would make a substantial article is to be found in French periodicals for the month of July, 1791. Besides the *Archives parlementaires*, XXV, 661, XXVI, 610–11, XXVIII, 72, and *Le Courrier des 83 départemens* . . . , XXVI, *passim*, the following have been most useful: *Le Courier français*, Vol. XII; *Le Moniteur universel*, Vol. IV; *Le Point du jour*, Vol. XXIV; *Révolutions de Paris*, Vols. VIII–IX; *Chronique de Paris*, Vol. III. Charles

Villette, *Lettres choisies* . . . *sur les principaux événemens de la révolution* (Paris, 1792), contains a good account by an active participant in the apotheosis. In *Collection complète des tableaux historiques de la révolution française* (Paris, 1804), I, 217, is a large picture called "Triomphe de Voltaire" along with a good brief description of the ceremony. The "Translation de Voltaire à Paris . . . ," *Department of the Seine: Administration* (Paris, 1791), gives a good account of the plans before the actual ceremony took place. See also *Actes de la commune de Paris* . . . , Second Series, III; "Ordre et Marche de la Translation de Voltaire à Paris . . ." (Paris, 1791), in *Bibliothèque historique de la révolution: Fêtes funèbres;* Karl Frenzel, "Voltaire's Triumph und Tod," *Rokoko, Büsten und Bilder* (Berlin, 1895), pp. 294–351. Theodore Child, "A Museum of the History of Paris," *Harper's New Monthly Magazine,* LXVII (1888), 833–35, gives a brief account of the apotheosis in connection with several relics of that occasion. I am obliged to Dr. Clara Marburg Kirk for bringing this article to my attention. The best modern account in English is that in William Sloane, *The French Revolution and Religious Reform* (New York, 1901), pp. 173–75. The last chapter of George Brandes's *Voltaire* is entitled "Apotheosis," and describes the ceremony of 1791.

56. Apparently the apotheosis was actually seen by a considerable number of Englishmen who either were in Paris or who went there for the celebration. See "Authentic Advices from Paris," *St. James's Chronicle* (June 23–25, 1791), and *English Witnesses of the French Revolution,* ed. by J. M. Thompson (Oxford, 1938). In Paris, an enterprising man offered a room and bed to any Englishman or other person attracted to Paris by this brilliant ceremony. *Le Courrier des 83 départemens* . . . , XXVI (July 3, 1791), 43.

57. See *A Chronological Epitome of the Most Remarkable Events* . . . *during the French Revolution, from 1789 to 1795* (n.d.), p. 10.

58. *The World* (London), July 18; *The London Recorder,* or *Sunday Gazette,* July 17; *The Morning Post* and *Daily Advertiser,* July 12; *The Edinburgh Herald,* July 22; *The Reading Mercury* and *Oxford Gazette,* July 25; *The Lincoln, Portland, and Stamford Mercury,* July 22; *The Caledonian Mercury,* July 18; the *Kentish Chronicle,* July 19; *The Ipswich Journal,* July 23.

59. *The Diary or Woodfall's Register,* July 19; *St. James's Chronicle,* July 16–19; *The London Chronicle,* July 19; *The General Evening Post* (London), July 16–19; the *Dublin Chronicle,* July 21 and 23; *The Edinburgh Advertiser,* July 19–22; *The Newcastle Chronicle,* July 23; *The Kentish Gazette,* July 15 and 22; *The Star,* July 18. The account in

St. James's Chronicle seems to have been based on that given in *La Chronique de Paris,* often directly translating from the French.

60. *London Chronicle,* July 28, 1791.

61. *The Oracle,* June 30, 1791.

62. Charles Pigott, *Political Dictionary . . .* (1795), p. 96.

63. *The Oracle,* July 14, 1791.

64. *Ibid.,* July 19, 1791.

65. Sampson Perry, *Historical Sketch of the French Revolution* (1796), II, 84–85.

66. "Appendix" to Joseph Priestley, *Appeal to the Public on . . . the Riots in Birmingham,* Part II (1792), pp. 174–76.

67. Francis Wollaston, *A Country Parson's Address to His Flock* (1799), p. 27.

68. William Agutter, *Christian Politics* (1792), p. 11.

69. "Preface to the Translator," Rev. John Milner, to *Pastoral Letter . . . of the Right Reverend John Francis de la Marche . . .* (1791), pp. iv, vn.

70. Edmund Burke, *Two Letters . . . on the Proposals for Peace with the Regicide Directory* (1796), pp. 98–99.

71. Edmund Burke, "Letter of July 13, 1791," *Correspondence* (1844), III, 219–20.

72. "Village Politics . . . ," *Liberty and Property Preserved . . . Tracts: IX* (n.d.), 9. This work of Hannah More's enjoyed a wide reputation through its appeal to conservative prejudices. It was read in all parts of the kingdom, the gentry and clergy in particular seeing to its wholesale distribution. For a discussion of its popularity, see Walter Phelps Hall, *British Radicalism . . .* (New York, 1912), pp. 50–51.

73. William Cobbett, *The Bloody Buoy* (1797), p. 163.

74. *Universal Magazine,* C (1797), 272. This passage is quoted from Frederick Leopold Count Stolberg's *Travels . . . ,* translated by Thomas Holcroft (1796), I, 17–18. In a footnote Holcroft defends Voltaire and pronounces him "one of the most devoted, persevering and inestimable, friends of the human race."

75. David Scurlock, *Thoughts on the Influence of Religion . . .* (1792), pp. 31–32.

76. Francis Plowden, "Quoting a Work of His Own Dated 1791," *Short History of the British Empire . . .* (1794), pp. 11–12.

77. *History of the Clergy . . .* (1794), pp. 142–43.

78. Lord Auckland, *Some Remarks on the Apparent Circumstances of the War* (1795), p. 28.

79. Frederick Hervey, *A New Friend on an Old Subject* (1791), pp. 6–7.

80. *Evening Mail,* July 4–6, 1791.

81. James E. Smith, *Sketch of a Tour* . . . (1793), I, 76. For other remarks by English visitors to the Pantheon, see *Miss Berry's Journal,* November 7, 1802, II, 203; Rev. Henry Best, *Four Years in France,* (1826), p. 126. The Rev. John Simon in *Wesley or Voltaire* (1903?), pp. 19–20, discusses the apotheosis as a sign that the French revolutionists had gone farther in interpreting the intention of Voltaire's work than he would have personally desired.

Many rumors and alleged discoveries touching the eventual fate of Voltaire's body were later circulated. These are discussed by Joseph-Emile Bourdois, "Les Restes Mortels de Voltaire: sont-ils au Panthéon?" *Pourquoi et Comment fut tué Henry IV* (Dinard?, 19[?]).

XIII. BARRUEL'S *Memoirs Illustrating the History of Jacobinism*

1. *English Review,* XX (1792), 240.

2. Pierre de la Gorce, *Histoire Religieuse de la Révolution* . . . , pp. v, 248. See also *Universal Magazine,* C (1797), 232–33; *Critical Review,* XVI (1796), 66.

3. J. Milner, *Supplementary Memoirs of English Catholics* . . . (1820), p. 103.

4. Walter P. Hall, *British Radicalism* . . . (New York, 1912), pp. 39–40.

5. The best biographical notices of Barruel are in *L'Ami de la Religion,* XXV (1820), 401 ff. and M. Dussault, "Notice sur . . . Barruel" in Barruel's own *Les Helviennes, ou Lettres Provinciales Philosophiques* (Paris, 1830).

6. Barruel, *Memoirs Illustrating the History of Jacobinism* (1797), I, 26. Since this chapter is almost entirely taken up with this book, it seems unnecessary in the following notes to repeat the author and title. References to the *Memoirs* will be simply to volume and page.

7. I, 109–10.	15. I, 64.
8. I, 42–43.	16. I, 84.
9. I, 7.	17. I, 77–78.
10. I, 38–39.	18. I, 103–20.
11. I, 43.	19. I, 120–25.
12. I, 28.	20. I, 128–32.
13. I, 375.	21. I, 135.
14. I, 57.	22. I, 136.

23. I, 143.

24. I, 146–48.

25. I, 153.

26. I, 197.

27. I, 218.

28. I, 321.

29. I, 205–6; 220–39.

30. I, 240–83.

31. II, 7.

32. II, 163–64.

33. I, 164.

34. I, 158–59.

35. I, 284.

36. I, 171.

37. I, 353–57; a letter from M. De Luc to Barruel, corroborating this account of Voltaire's death is added to this chapter, pp. 365–69.

38. IV, 594–95.

39. II, 1.

40. I, 363–64; 400–401.

41. I, 401.

42. I, 51–52.

43. I, 50–51.

44. I, 155.

45. II, 193.

46. II, 38–40.

47. IV, 409–10.

48. IV, 566–67.

49. II, 268–69.

50. II, 283.

51. IV, 399.

52. II, 420–21.

53. II, 421.

54. For accounts of Voltaire's glorification by the masons in 1778, see *L'Espion Anglais* (Paris, 1809), II, 350–57; *Heroes, Philosophers, and Courtiers of the Time of Louis XVI* (London, 1863), I, 301–6.

55. III, 7. Barruel devotes all of volume three and part of four to exposing the aims of German Illumism. This movement does not seem to touch Voltaire directly in Barruel's eyes, although it contributed much of its ruthlessness to the revolution.

56. III, 341.

57. IV, 379–80.

58. IV, 547–48.

59. William Hunt, *The History of England: 1760–1801* (1905), p. 395; Philip Brown, *The French Revolution and English History* (1918), p 154.

60. I, 3–4.

61. I, 219.

62. II, 318–20, 280, 412–13. The complete orthodoxy of masonry, its loyal devotion to the *status quo,* its conservative character as a bulwark against revolution—all this is insisted upon in English masonic handbooks and other comments upon masonry in the eighteenth century. See Michael Smith, *Twelve Sermons* . . . (1770), pp. 167–77; *Pocket Companion for Free-Masons* (1764), pp. 19–20; *Masonry the Turnpike Road to Happiness* . . . (1768); *An Important Discovery: or Revolution in Great Britain and Ireland Impossible* (1793), pp. 16–18.

63. Barruel, "Observations Preliminaires," *Mémoirs pour servir à l'Histoire du Jacobinisme* (Hamburg, 1798), III, xiv.

64. Robert Clifford, "Advertisement," *Application of Barruel's Memoirs* . . . (1798), p. ii.

65. *Anti-Jacobin Review,* III (1799), 497.

66. "Une Erreur de Barruel," *Revue des Études Historiques,* XCII (1926), 206.

67. (1801), pp. 87–94.

68. Barruel's entire bibliographical history including these facts is found in Carlos Sommervogel, *Bibliothèque de la Compagnie de Jésus,* I (Paris, 1890), 936–37 and A. De Backer, *Bibliotheque des Ecrivains de la Compagnie de Jesus* (Liège, 1853), I, 44. The article on Barruel in the *Biographie Universelle . . . Supplement,* LVII, 217–19, also has a useful section on bibliography.

69. *The Monthly Epitome and Catalogue of New Publications,* III (1799), 32.

70. A. De Backer, *Bibliotheque des Ecrivains . . .* Vol. I, pp. 45; *Monthly Magazine,* VII (1799), 62.

71. *Analytical Review,* XXVI (1797), 559.

72. *Gentleman's Magazine,* LXVIII (1798), 38–40, 150–52. For the adventures of Barruel's work in America, see Vernon Stauffer, *New England and the Bavarian Illuminati* (New York, 1918), pp. 214–28, 300–12. Its bibliographical history on the Continent may be followed in *Nouvelle Biographie Universelle* (Paris: 1853), III, 600, and "Was will man denn endlich von der Geistlichkeit," *Eudämonia oder Deutsches Volksglück . . . ,* IV (1797), 373–94, 412–56; cf. *ibid.,* VI (1798), 425–32, for German opposition to the *Memoirs.* See also the bibliographical works of Sommervogel and De Backer already referred to. August Wolfsteig, *Bibliographie der Freimauerischen Literatur* (Leipzig, 1923), I, 324–25, offers a fine supplement to these works, showing especially the wide interest in Freemasonry and the extensive publication of the *Memoirs* in Germany. Cf. Fernand Baldensperger, *Le Mouvement des idées dans l'émigration française* (Paris, 1924), II, 20*n,* which discusses the diffusion of the *Memoirs* in several languages.

73. James Scott, *Fast Day Sermon* (1793), p. 11.

74. Rev. John Moir, "Preface," *Preventive Policy* (1796), p. xii.

75. *Analytical Review,* XXVI (1797), 238.

76. For refutation of or unfavorable comment on Barruel, see J. J. Maunier, *De L'Influence attribuée aux philosophes . . .* (Paris, 1822), 180–217; *The Monthly Magazine,* XXVI (1798), 460–61; *Monthly Review,* XXIII (1797), 529; Benjamin Kingsbury, *Answer to An Address . . .* (1798), pp. 41–45; *Critical Review,* XXVIII (1800), 543; *British Mercury,* II (1799), 354–56; *Analytical Review,* XXVI (1797), 254.

77. Bishop W. Knox, "Thanksgiving Day Sermon . . . , 1798," *Two Sermons* (n.d.), p. 17.

78. Charles Hayward, *Sermon at Clare . . .* (1799), p. 13.

79. *Jacobinism Displayed* (1798), p. 23; cf. Barmel, *Memoirs*, II, 138.

80. *Anti-Jacobin Review*, I (1798), 751–52.

81. Arthur Young, *Enquiry into the State of the Public Mind . . .* (1799), pp. 19–20.

82. Rev. William Jones, "Danger of Despising Lawful Authority," *Works* (1826), IV, 357.

83. Rev. Lewis Hughes, *Historical View of the Rise . . .* (1799), p. 3.

84. *British Mercury*, II (1799), 350.

85. Charles Buck, *Close of the Eighteenth Century Improved* (1801), p. 25.

86. George Huddesford, "Bubble and Squeak," *Poems* (1801), II, 82n. A footnote to "Eternal Slumber" quotes the inscription over public cemeteries decreed by the French Conventions: "La Mort est un Sommeil éternel."

87. T. J. Mathias, *Pursuits of Literature* (1798), p. 23n.

88. Rev. Lewis Hughes, *Historical View of the Rise . . .* (1799), pp. 129–30.

89. Henry Yorke, *Address to Reformers* (1798), pp. 74–75.

90. John Whitaker, *Real Origin of Government* (1795), pp. 46–47.

91. Thomas Scott, "Observations on the Signs and Duties . . . ," *Theological Works* (Philadelphia, 1810), II, 474.

92. Job Nott, *A Back Front View of the Five Headed Monster* (1798), p. 5 and *passim*.

93. Frederick Hervey, *A New Friend on an Old Subject* (1791), p. 12. The date of this passage suggests again how much Barruel was appealing to existing opinion.

94. Robert Hall, *Modern Infidelity Considered* (1800), p. 42.

95. Rev. Lewis Hughes, *Historical View of the Rise . . .* (1799), pp. 13–14.

96. *European Magazine*, XXXII (1797), 176.

97. *Gentleman's Magazine*, LXIX (1799), 145.

98. T. J. Mathias, *Pursuits of Literature* (1798), pp. 310–11.

99. *Lettres d'un Voyageur à l'Abbé Barruel* (1800), pp. 161–67.

100. See, for example, William Agutter, *Thanksgiving Day Sermon, 1797* (1798), p. 11; Rev. William Goode, *Mercies in Judgment* (1797), pp. 7–8; William Gregor, *A Sermon* (Truro: 1798), p. 21n; George Gleig, "Delusion Believing a Lie," *Sermons Preached Occasionally . . .* (1803), 327.

101. Bishop George P. Tomline, *A Charge . . . to the Clergy . . .* (1800), pp. 8–9. See also a review of this *Charge* in the *British Critic,* XVI (1800), 295.

102. William H. Reid, *Rise and Dissolution of the Infidel Societies* (1800), p. 92.

103. Samuel Horsley, *Charge . . . to the Clergy . . .* (1800), pp. 13, 14.

104. T. L. O'Beirne, *Sermons* (1799), pp. 160–61.

105. *European Magazine,* XXXII (1797), 105.

106. Burke's letter to Barruel is prefixed to Robert Clifford's *Application of Barruel's Memoirs . . .* (1798), p. ii.

107. *Loc. cit.*

108. Rev. R. Shepherd, *Charge to the Clergy of . . . Beford* (1801), p. 6.

109. *Anti-Jacobin Review,* IV (1799), 551.

110. XXXV (1799), 326–27. 113. CV (1799), 43–47.

111. XV (1800), 204. 114. Birmingham, 1798.

112. XXXVI (1799), 396–97. 115. XXV (1799), 93.

116. See especially II, 150–200. For other endorsements of Barruel or summaries of his main ideas, see *The Inspector; or, Select Literary Intelligence* (1799), pp. 13 ff.; John Bowdler, *Sound an Alarm* (1798), pp. 18–19; Rev. James Stillingfleet, *National Gratitude . . .* (1798), pp. 22–25. Abbé Proyart, *Louis XVI Détroné avant d'être Roi . . .* (London, 1800), practically duplicates Barruel whom the author praises but whom he had not read in time to spare him a great deal of work on freemasonry, p 128n. See also the *British Critic,* XV (1800), 563, and the *Critical Review,* XXVII (1799), 452, for views of works showing dependence on Robison and Barruel which I have not seen.

117. T. J. Mathias, *Pursuits of Literature* (1798), pp. 311–12.

118. John Adolphus, *Biographical Memoirs of the French Revolution* (1799), II, 76–80.

119. John Bowles, *Reflections on the . . . State of Society at the Close of the Eighteenth Century* (1800), pp. 125–26. Bowles comments on Voltaire's maxim also to "Strike, but conceal the hand!" *Ibid.,* 126n.

120. William Cole, *A Sermon Preached on the General Fast,* March 7, 1798, pp. 14–15.

121. T. L. O'Beirne, *Sermons* (1799), pp. 145–62.

122. Richard Watson, *Address to the People of Great Britain* (1798), pp. 27–38.

123. Samuel Horsley, *Charge . . . to the Clergy . . .* (1800), pp. 12–15.

124. *Ibid.,* pp. 6–7. For the continued ill-fame of the *Encyclopédie,* see "Introduction," *Historical Pictures . . . of the French Revolution* (Paris, 1803), p. iii. John Maclaurin "Of the Chief Promoters of Revolutions," *Works* (1798), II, 164, speaks of the authors of great talent who did all they could to prepare for the revolution. Thomas Gisborne, *A Familiar Survey of the Christian Religion* (1801), 491, hints at the plot against Christianity without any direct reference to Barruel.

Another interesting reaction to the plot theory was that the whole conspiracy only fulfilled a Biblical prophecy. See especially Henry Kett, *History the Interpreter of Prophecy* (1805), I, 115–16; Alex. Pirie, *French Revolution Exhibited . . .* (1795), pp. 52–53. For other suggestions that French irreligion and rebellion were foretold in scripture, see *Illustrations of Prophecy* (1796), II, 515 ff.; *An Historical View of the French Revolution* (1796), I, 14; *Conclusion of the Late Dr. Hartley's Observations . . .* (1794), p. vi; *Prophetic Conjectures on the French Revolution . . .* (1792), pp. 46–47; *Thraliana,* II, 853–55, 951.

125. XXI (1797), 536–37.

126. *British Mercury,* II (1799), 335.

127. *British Mercury,* II (1799), 339.

128. See notes 34–35, above.

129. X (1797), 156, 160; *ibid.,* XI (1798), 246.

130. II (1799), 561–62.   132. I (1798), 746.

131. *Ibid.,* pp. 619–21.   133. *Ibid.,* pp. 359–60.

134. *Ibid.,* "Prefatory Address," p. i.

135. John Bowles, *Reflections on . . . Society at the End of the Eighteenth Century* (1800), pp. 127–28.

136. John Bowles, "Preface," *The Retrospect* (1798), pp. 15–16.

137. J. Bowdler, *Sound an Alarm . . .* (1798), pp. 18–19.

138. *Beauties of the Anti-Jacobin* (1799), p. 103.

139. George Huddesford, "Bubble and Squeak," *Poems* (1801), II, 82–83.

140. *British Critic,* X (1797), 156–57. Other references to the universality of the French destructive scheme are to be found in Rev. E. W. Whitaker, *Family Sermons* (1801), III, 275–76; William Playfair, *History of Jacobinism . . .* (1798), p. 346.

141. For a good review of this period and its agitation in England, see Philip A. Brown, *French Revolution in English History* (1918), pp. 152–61. See also Walter P. Hall, *British Radicalism . . .* (New York: 1912), pp. 137–38, 197; W. T. Laprade, *England and the French Revolution* (Baltimore, 1909), pp. 72, 82, 153–54.

142. *The British Critic,* X (1797), 157.

143. Rev. Lewis Hughes, *Historical View of the Rise* . . . (1799), p. 85.
144. *British Critic*, XI (1798), 334–35.
145. Robert Morres, *Address of a Minister . . . to His Parishioners* (Salisbury, 1799), pp. 49–50.
146. *The Anti-Jacobin or Weekly Examiner*, I (1799), 180.
147. Job Nott, *A Back Front View of the Five Headed Monster* (1798), p. 7.
148. *Gentleman's Magazine*, LXIX (1799), 145.
149. Reprinted in *Spirit of the Public Journals*, III (1799), 40–46.
150. *Anti-Jacobin Review*, I (1798), 235.
151. Richard Watson, *Address to the People of Great Britain* (1798), pp. 27–28.
152. Charles Buck, *Close of the Eighteenth Century Improved* (1801), p. 25.
153. James Stillingfleet, *National Gratitude* (Worcester, 1798), p. 25.
154. *European Magazine*, XXXVIII (1800), 43; cf. Rev. R. P. Finch, *Scriptural Caution in a National View* (1800), p. 13.

XIV. VOLTAIRE CONVICTED

1. Rev. Lewis Hughes, *Historical View of the Rise* . . . (1799), p. 5.
2. *British Critic*, X (1797), 160.
3. *Anti-Jacobin Review*, III (1799), 500.
4. *Ibid.*, I (1798), 226–27. The Rev. Henry Kett, however, denies that England first inspired Voltaire's aim to overthrow Christianity, which dates from as early as 1720; *History the Interpreter of Prophecy* (1799), II, 117, 127–29.
5. Rev. Lewis Hughes, *Historical View of the Rise* . . . (1799), p. 5.
6. William Gregor, *A Sermon* . . . (1798), pp. 21–22.
7. *British Critic*, X (1797), 160. The English seem to have found this remark very shocking. See *Jacobinism Displayed* (1798), p. 6; Andrew Fuller, *The Gospel Its Own Witness* (1800), 244n; William Jones, "Note to Voltaire Dissected," *The Scholar Armed* (1800), II, 286.
8. *Annual Register*, XXI (1778), 6.
9. V (1790), 571. See, however, Sylvain Maréchal, *Dictionnaire des Athées anciens et moderns* (Brussels, 1833), pp. 317–19 and in the "Supplement," p. 34, where Voltaire is quoted to show atheistical leanings. Other French writers are also quoted who accuse Voltaire of atheism; but at the end of the *Dictionnaire des Athées* in the "Second Supplement," p. 85, Voltaire is not included in a "Calendrier Historique des

Athées les plus célèbres," although Condorcet, Frederick, D'Alembert, and Diderot are listed.

10. *European Magazine,* XXV (1794), 331–32.
11. *Annual Register,* XXI (1778), 6.
12. *Monthly Review,* XXIII (1797), 532. See also *English Review,* XIV (1789), 11, where Gibbon is quoted as calling Voltaire "an intolerant bigot"; William Jones, *Observations on a Journey* (1777), II, 181.
13. L. Dutens, *The Tocsin* (1798), p. 25.
14. *European Magazine,* XXV (1794), 332.
15. "Main Principles of French Philosophism . . . ," *The Inspector* (1799), pp. 23–24.
16. *Analytical Review,* III (1789), 215.
17. *The Spirit of Anti-Jacobinism* (1802), pp. 358–59.
18. William Jones, *Observations on a Journey* (1777), II, 174–75.
19. William Cobbett, *Bloody Buoy,* p. 163.
20. *History of the Rise and Progress of Revolution in France* (1802), I, 5–6.
21. *British Mercury,* II (1799), 343.
22. John Robison, *Proofs of a Conspiracy* (New York, 1798), p. 397.
23. Francis Wollaston, *A Country Parson's Address to His Flock* (1799), p. 16.
24. *Monthly Review,* XXIX (1799), 532–33.
25. William H. Reid, *Rise and Dissolution of the Infidel Societies* (1800), p. 80.
26. *Evangelical Magazine,* III (1795), 156–57.
27. *European Magazine,* XIX (1791), 95.
28. William H. Reid, *Rise and Dissolution of the Infidel Societies* (1800), p. 80.
29. *British Mercury,* II (1799), 347–49.
30. *Anti-Jacobin Review,* I (1798), 227.
31. *British Mercury,* II (1799), 356.
32. Samuel Horsley, *Charge to the Clergy* . . . (1800), pp. 4–5.
33. Rev. Lewis Hughes, *Historical View of the Rise* . . . (1799), pp. 7–8.
34. *Anti-Jacobin Review,* III (1799), 499.
35. *British Critic,* X (1798), 161.
36. *British Mercury,* II (1799), 341.
37. Rev. Lewis Hughes, *Historical View of the Rise* . . . (1799), p. 17.
38. *Ibid.,* p. 31.
39. *Jacobinism Displayed* (1798), p. 5.

40. John Bowles, *Reflections on . . . Society at the Close of the Eighteenth Century* (1800), p. 126n.

41. Francis Wollaston, *A Country Parson's Address to His Flock* (1799), 7–8. Cf. Horace Walpole's letter to Mary Berry, September 24, 1793; "Voltaire used to conclude every letter to D'Alembert with 'E. L. I.'" "Horace Walpole's Correspondence with Mary . . . Berry," *Yale Edition of Horace Walpole's Correspondence* (New Haven, Conn., 1944), II, 9.

42. LXVII (1797), Part II, 21–22.

43. *Jacobinism Displayed* (1798), pp. 24–25.

44. *Life of J. G. Zimmerman* (1797), pp. 94–95.

45. William H. Reid, *Rise and Dissolution of the Infidel Societies . . .* (1800), pp. 17–18, 25, 8.

46. *Ibid.*, p. 16. In *Jacobinism Displayed* (1798), p. 24, Voltaire's remark on strangling the last Jesuit with the last Jansenist's bowels is quoted, as well as Diderot's speech on seeing the last King strangled with the bowels of the last priest. Cf. *Solitude* (1827?), pp. xlvi–vii. See also J. N. Robertson, *Short History of Free Thought* (New York, 1906), II, 252, where Robertson shows that Diderot puts this line into the mouth of an Eleutheromene, in direct opposition to his own bias which was not against the monarchy. Voltaire uses this line again in a letter. It had originally come from the *Testament de Jean Meslier*.

47. *The Inspector* (1799), pp. 13 ff.; William Gregor, *A Sermon . . .* (1798), p. 26n.

48. *British Critic*, X (1798), 407–8; *ibid.*, XIII (1799), 389.

49. "Introduction," *Historical Pictures of . . . the French Revolution* (Paris, 1803), p. iii.

50. William H. Reid, *Rise and Dissolution of the Infidel Societies* (1800), p. 4.

51. *Anti-Jacobin Review*, I (1798), 236–37.

52. (1799), p. 56.

53. D. Whyte, *Fallacy of French Freedom . . .* (1799), pp. 1–2.

54. Thomas Rennell, *Principles of French Republicanism* (1793), p. 26.

55. *Anti-Jacobin; or, Weekly Examiner*, II (1799), p. 635.

56. Quoted from *Mercure de France* by the *Anti-Jacobin Review*, I (1798), 753.

57. Thomas Rennell, *Principles of French Republicanism* (1793), p. 11. See William Playfair, *History of Jacobinism* (1798), pp. 182–83, for the view that the writings of Voltaire and others were distorted and made to suit the revolution's purpose by untruthful interpretation.

58. William Jones, "Note to Voltaire Dissected," *The Scholar Armed* (1800), II, 286.

59. *Gentleman's Magazine*, LXVII (1797), Part II, 1010.

60. Scene iii, ll. 5–6.

61. *Ibid.*, l. 30.

62. Elizabeth Grymeston, *Miscellanea* (1606), pp. c3–c4.

63. See, for example, James Hervey, "Meditations among the Tombs" (1746), *Works* (1790), I, 70–72; Samuel Morton Savage, *Good men Dismissed in Peace* (1762); *The Great Importance of a Religious Life Considered* . . . (1780), p. 70.

64. "Preface," I (1794), 1.

65. XIX (1796), 616; XX (1797), 618.

66. *Critical Review*, XVIII (1764), 468.

67. *The Copper Plate Magazine*, Vol. I (1778).

68. Richard Tickell, *Commonplace Arguments against Administration* . . . (1780), p. 10.

69. Lines 307–10.

70. Pp. 30–31*n*.

71. LII (1782), 529.

72. *Ibid.*, LIV (1784), 423.

73. William Agutter, *On the Difference between the Deaths of the Righteous and the Wicked* . . . (Sermon preached in 1786, published London, 1800), p. 7.

74. "Advertisement," p. v.

75. Pp. 242–64, 356–57.

76. *The Repository*, II (1789), 94–103.

77. "Preface of the Translator," p. v.

78. *The Bee* (1792), p. 248.

79. Joseph Priestley, *Answer to Mr. Paine's Age of Reason* . . . (1795), p. 36.

80. P. 35.

81. Stephen Weston, *Letters from Paris* (1793), I, 108. The letters were written in 1791.

82. Richard J. Sulivan, *View of Nature* (1794), VI, 365.

83. W. L. Brown, *An Essay of the Folly of Scepticism* . . . (1796), 96*n*.

84. *Age of Infidelity:* Part II (1796), pp. 118–19.

85. Abraham Binns, *Remarks on a Publication* . . . (Stockport, 1796), pp. 3–4.

86. "A Serious Admonition to the Disciples of Thomas Paine . . . ," *ibid.*, facing title page.

87. J. Auchinclose, *Sophistry of . . . Age of Reason* . . . (1796), p. 42.

88. William Finch, *Objections of Infidel Historians* . . . (1797), p. 39.

89. LXVIII (1798), Part II, 606–7.

90. *The Contrast; or, . . . The Last Hours of a Learned Infidel and of a Learned Christian* (Religious Tract Society, n.d.), pp. 6–7.

91. *The Last Hours of a Learned Infidel, and an Humble Christian, Contrasted* (1798), pp. 7–11.

92. William Cole, *Sermon Preached on the General Fast* . . . (1798), pp. 18–19.

93. Rev. Lewis Hughes, *Historical View of the Rise* . . . (1799), p. 82.

94. *Jacobinism Displayed* (1798), pp. 17–18.

95. William Gregor, *A Sermon* . . . (1798), p. 24.

96. William Dodd, *Beauties of History* . . . (1800), pp. 237–38.

97. John Brewster, *Meditations of a Recluse* . . . (1800), pp. 45–48.

98. *Anti-Jacobin Review*, II (1799), pp. 394–95. The editors point out that the poet has depended on Barruel. The *British Critic*, XI (1798), 293, speaks of a correspondent who signed only his initials to a protest against the untrue account of Voltaire's death by Barruel. But the *Critic* decides that "we do believe M. Barruel." The letter of M. De Luc to Barruel describing Voltaire's last moments was also reprinted in *New Lights on Jacobinism* . . . (1798), pp. 46–59. Edward Ryan, *History of the Effects of Religion on Mankind* (1806), pp. 83–84, also follows the Barruel account of Voltaire's death.

99. *Spirit of Anti-Jacobinism* (1802), pp. 322–23. For further comment on the inability of "philosophy" to sustain Voltaire in his last moments, see Andrew Fuller, *The Gospel Its Own Witness* (1800), pp. 243–44.

100. It is interesting to notice that two generations before Barruel the flood of impious literature and its consequences had been anticipated by the Rev. John Leland in an appendix to his *View of the Principal Deistical Writers* (1757), II, 418–33. The undermining of religious belief, the extinction of man's fear of future sanctions, the tendency to destroy public order and to release men's passions beyond control: in short, the very core of Barruel's message was foreshadowed. This remarkable correspondence between Leland and Barruel is admitted in a note to the reprint of this appendix under the title *Reflections on the Present State of Things* . . . (1801), p. 6, where the reader is urged to "consult and compare Barruel's *Memoirs of Jacobinism*." So close is Leland to Barruel more than fifty years before the *Memoirs*, although he does not mention Voltaire and the philosophers specifically, that this work can be cited in a footnote as if Leland were actually quoting the *Memoirs*. See also the Rev. L. Dutens, *The Tocsin; or, An appeal to Good Sense*, translated by the Rev. Thomas Falconer from the French (1798), a work published in

1769, containing a long denunciation of Voltaire and corroborating much of what Barruel had later charged.

101. XXXII (1797), 105.

102. Richard Watson, *Address to the People of Great Britain* (1798), p. 39.

103. T. J. Mathias, "Introductory Letter," *Pursuits of Literature* (1798), pp. xvi–vii.

104. *Gentleman's Magazine*, LXVII (1797), Part II, 821.

105. *The Caldron, or Follies of Cambridge* (1799), p. 24.

106. *Gentleman's Magazine*, LXVIII (Part II, 718.

107. *Anti-Jacobin Review*, I (1798), 722.

108. *Gentleman's Magazine*, LXVII (1797), Part II, 1010.

INDEX